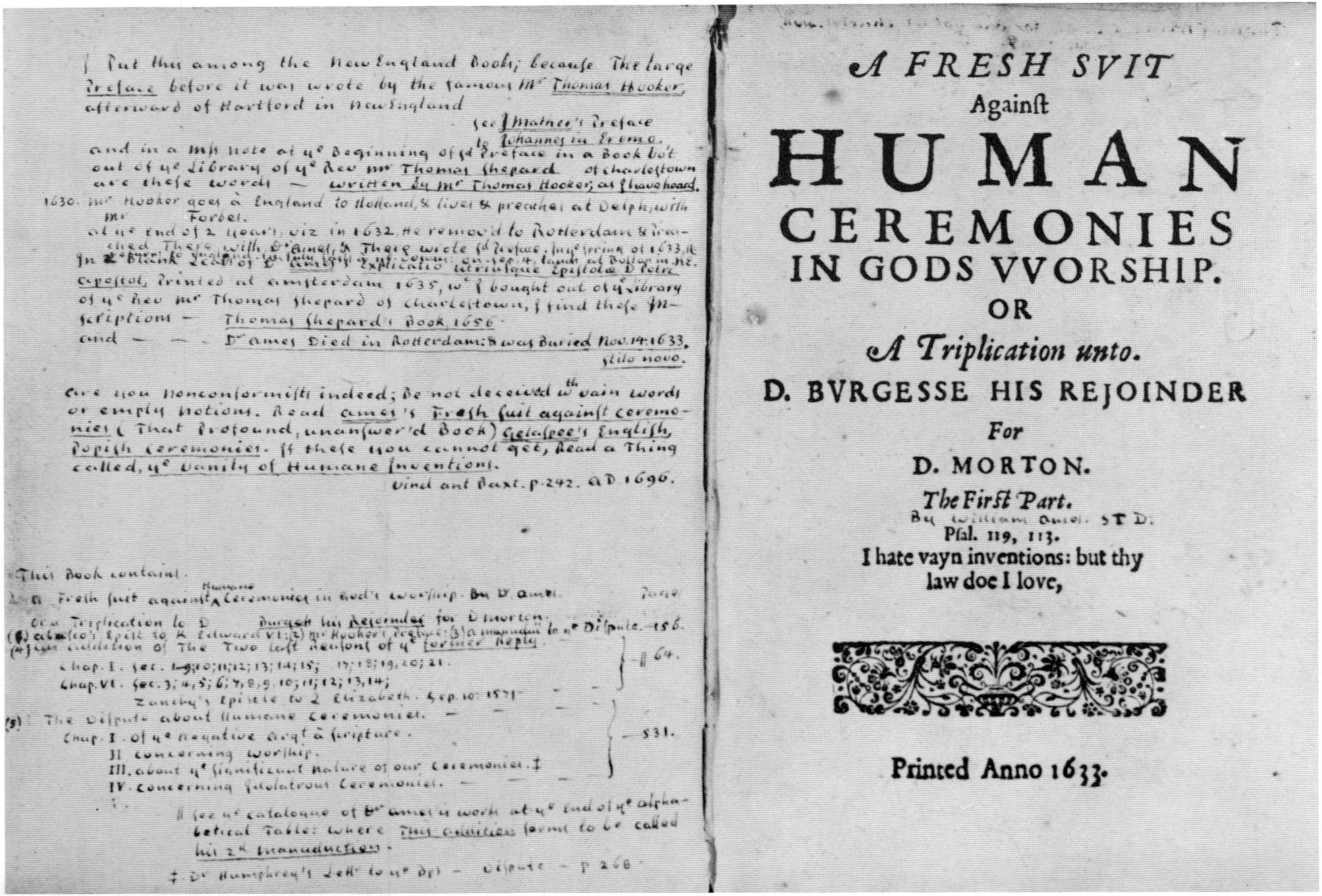

I Put this among the New England Books; because The large Preface before it was wrote by the famous Mr Thomas Hooker, afterward of Hartford in New England

see Mather's Preface to Johannes in Eremo.

And in a MS note at ye Beginning of sd Preface in a Book bot out of ye Library of ye Rev Mr Thomas Shepard of Charlestown are these words — written by Mr Thomas Hooker; as I have heard.

1630. Mr Hooker goes fr England to Holland, & lives & preaches at Delph, with Mr Forbes.

At ye end of 2 years, viz in 1632, He remov'd to Rotterdam & preached There with Dr Ames, & There wrote sd Preface. [illegible] 1633, he [illegible] to New England [illegible] on Sep. 4, landed at Boston in N.E.

In ye Blank Leaf of Dr Ames's Explicatio utriusque Epistolæ D Petri Apostoli, Printed at Amsterdam 1635, wch I bought out of ye Library of ye Rev Mr Thomas Shepard of Charlestown, I find these Inscriptions — Thomas Shepard's Book, 1656.

and — — Dr Ames Died in Rotterdam: & was Buried Nov. 14. 1633, stilo novo.

Are you Nonconformists indeed; Be not deceived wth vain words or empty notions. Read Ames's Fresh Suit against Ceremonies (That Profound, unanswer'd Book) Gelaspee's English Popish Ceremonies. If these you cannot get, Read a Thing called, ye Vanity of Humane Inventions.

Vind ant Baxt. p. 242. AD 1696.

This Book contains.

1. A Fresh Suit against Humane Ceremonies in God's worship. By Dr Ames. — Page

Or a Triplication to D Burges his Rejoinder for D Morton.

(2) [illegible] Epistle to K Edward VI; (2) Mr Hooker's Preface; (3) A manuduction to ye Dispute. — 156.

(4) The reduction of The Two last reasons of ye former Reply.

Chap. I. sec. 1–9; 10; 11; 12; 13; 14; 15; 17; 18; 19; 20; 21.

Chap. VI. Sec. 3; 4; 5; 6; 7, 8, 9. 10; 11; 12; 13, 14; — 64.

Zanchy's Epistle to Q Elizabeth. Sep. 10: 1571 —

(5) The Dispute about Humane Ceremonies. —

Chap. I. Of ye Negative Argt fr Scripture.

II Concerning Worship. — 531.

III. about ye Significant Nature of our Ceremonies. ‡

IV. Concerning Idolatrous Ceremonies. —

‖ See ye Catalogue of Dr Ames's works at ye end of ye alphabetical Table: where This Addition seems to be called his 2d Manuduction.

‡ Dr Humphrey's Lettr to ye Bps — Dispute — p 268.

A FRESH SVIT
Against
HUMAN CEREMONIES IN GODS VVORSHIP.
OR
A Triplication unto.
D. BVRGESSE HIS REJOINDER
For
D. MORTON.
The First Part.
By William Ames. S T D.
Psal. 119, 113.
I hate vayn inventions: but thy law doe I love,

Printed Anno 1633.

Thomas Hooker

Writings in England and Holland, 1626–1633

Edited with Introductory Essays

BY

GEORGE H. WILLIAMS, NORMAN PETTIT,
WINFRIED HERGET, AND SARGENT BUSH, JR.

APPENDICES

1. A Map of Hooker's Travels in England, Holland, and New England, 1618–1636, drawn by George H. Williams and redrafted for
this edition by Ethan Pettit.

2. A Photograph of the Inscription by Thomas Prince in His Copy
of *A Fresh Suit* (Boston Public Library).

Indices

Scriptural Index

Topical Index

CONTENTS

FOREWORD

Until the present edition of ten writings of Thomas Hooker, composed before his departure for the New World in July, 1633, the sources for the life and thought of this major American Puritan divine of the first generation of colonization have been accessible only in the rare book rooms of select libraries in the United States and abroad. The modern reader, in his search for Hooker, had to pore through difficult seventeenth-century imprints, filled with errata, obscure references, and the glosses of transcribers and printers. Hooker himself seldom was able to check the imprints of his sermons. Indeed, the very problem of transmitting the sermon — essentially oral literature — constitutes a barrier to ready access to one of the most notable Puritan preachers of his generation.

Of our ten documents, six are sermons, constituting a veritable anthology of the full range of Puritan style and content; among them a funeral sermon, a Guy Fawkes Day sermon, and a farewell sermon on Hooker's departure from England for Holland. The last, as here printed, approximates much better than is usually possible the original sermon as delivered, because two transcriptions of it have survived. The four other documents edited in the collection include two prefaces to the works of notable contemporaries, John Rogers and William Ames, the fragment of a letter, and a first draft of Hooker's theory of church organization in answer to questions from John Paget in Amsterdam. Therefore we now have for the first time a fully annotated edition of the first draft on polity, surviving in two transcripts, from the pen of the founder of Connecticut and the initiator of the Fundamental Laws of Connecticut.

To facilitate the reading of the ten documents, the editors prepare the way with four comprehensive essays, designed to guide the reader along. Essay 1, on the life of Hooker, *en passant* places all the documents in their historical setting. Essay 2, on the order of salvation in Hooker's thought, places his theology within the larger context of Puritan divinity. Essay 3 describes the manner in which Hooker's sermons were taken down by others and transcribed for the press; and Essay 4 provides the reader with a broad historical survey of the problems to be solved in establishing the Hooker canon. In addition to these four essays, each of the ten documents is preceded by its own introduction, in which the editors describe the circumstances under which the document was either preached, printed, or composed. Documents I through III have been edited by Winfried Herget, IV through VI by Norman Pettit, and VII through X by George H. Williams. Finally, the first complete bibliography of Thomas Hooker's works ever to be published has been compiled by Sargent Bush, Jr. and is printed at the end of the volume.

The editors have been encouraged in their task by the subvention of printing costs, which assured the publication of the documents, from the Howard Bush Foundation in Hartford through the good offices of Dr. Paul F. Battenhouse of the Center Church, Hartford, and of the Rev. James F. English, Minister emeritus of the Connecticut Conference of the United Church of Christ. Printing costs have also been very substantially sustained by the Hyder Edward Rollins Fund of the Department of English and American Literature and Language, Harvard University. The editors wish especially to thank Professor Alan Heimert, Department Chairman, and Professor Herschel Baker, Chairman of the Rollins Fund Committee, for their abiding interest and generous support. Finally, the editors wish severally to thank many friends and associates for their assistance with respect to the whole or to specific parts of this project, among many, notably: Katherine Pantzer of the Houghton Library; Thomas Harlow of the Connecticut Historical Society; the Rev. Kenneth Twinn of Dr. Williams's Library, London; John Alden, Keeper of Printed Books, Boston Public Library; Professor Bernard Bailyn of the Department of History, Harvard University; Mr. John W. Coakley, candidate for the Ph.D. in religion at Harvard; Professor Keith Sprunger of the History Department of Bethal College; Professor Stephen Foster of the History Department of Northern Illinois University; Professor Frank C. Shuffelton of the English Department of the University of Rochester; and Dr. Harry Porter of the Faculty of History, Cambridge, England.

George H. Williams
Norman Pettit

Cambridge, Massachusetts
June, 1975

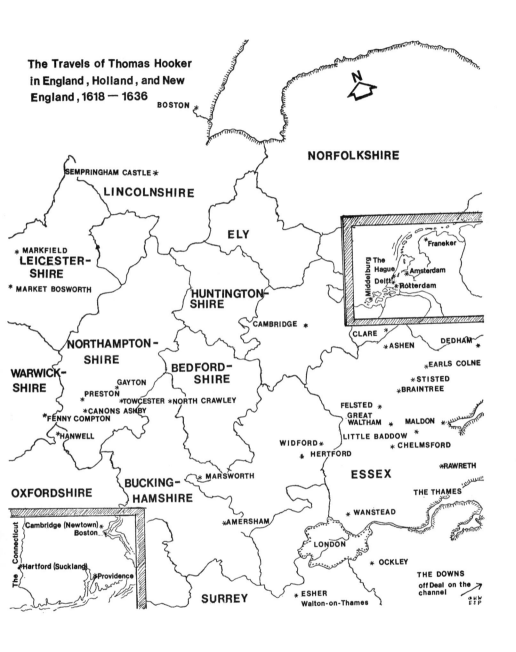

The Travels of Thomas Hooker in England, Holland, and New England, 1618 — 1636

BOSTON *

NORFOLKSHIRE

SEMPRINGHAM CASTLE *

LINCOLNSHIRE

ELY

* MARKFIELD
LEICESTER-
SHIRE

* MARKET BOSWORTH

HUNTINGTON-
SHIRE

CAMBRIDGE *

Franeker *

The Hague
Middelburg Delft * Amsterdam *
Rotterdam *

CLARE *
* ASHEN

DEDHAM *

* EARLS COLNE

* STISTED
* BRAINTREE

NORTHAMPTON-
SHIRE

BEDFORD-
SHIRE

WARWICK-
SHIRE

GAYTON
PRESTON *
* TOWCESTER * NORTH CRAWLEY
* CANONS ASHBY
* FENNY COMPTON

* HANWELL

FELSTED *
GREAT
WALTHAM
LITTLE BADDOW
WIDFORD *
* HERTFORD

MALDON *

* CHELMSFORD

* RAWRETH

* MARSWORTH

ESSEX

THE THAMES

OXFORDSHIRE

BUCKING-
HAMSHIRE

* AMERSHAM

* WANSTEAD

Cambridge (Newtown) *
Boston *

LONDON

* OCKLEY

* Hartford (Suckland)
* Providence

THE DOWNS
off Deal on the channel

The Connecticut

SURREY

* ESHER
Walton-on-Thames

ESSAY 1

The Life of Thomas Hooker
In England and Holland, 1586–1633[1]

BY GEORGE HUNTSTON WILLIAMS

WHEN Thomas Hooker stepped ashore at Boston in September, 1633,

[1] The following sketch represents a revision and enlargement of a biographical essay published in two instalments under a similar title in *Bulletin of the Congregational Library*, Boston, XIX, No. 1 (Oct. 1967), pp. 5–15 with a cover page map; No. 2 (Jan. 1968), pp. 9–13 with a cover page photograph of *The Firebrand* (see at nn. 12, 15). The second instalment, on Hooker's life in New England, has been left out of the present version.

The time approaches for a fresh study of the life and thought of Thomas Hooker to be based upon the new understanding of early Stuart nonconformity and a critical edition of Hooker's works. The only full-length critical biography is that of George Leon Walker, *Thomas Hooker: Preacher, Founder, Democrat* (New York, 1891). Williston Walker wrote a sketch under the title "Thomas Hooker and the Principle of Congregational Independency," Samuel A. Eliot *et al.*, *Pioneers of Religious Liberty in America* (Boston, 1903), pp. 83–121, and Warren Seymour Archibald did a sketch in 20 pp., *Thomas Hooker*, Publications of the Tercentenary Commission of the State of Connecticut, Pamphlet IV (New Haven, 1933). Everett H. Emerson essayed the first systematic presentation of the theology of Hooker, "Thomas Hooker: The Puritan as Theologian, *Anglican Theological Review*, XLIX (1967), pp. 190–203, a portion of his otherwise unpublished doctoral thesis at the University of Louisiana. Emerson has also published a sermon of Hooker in a facsimile edition of three Puritan sermons on redemption and a portion of another sermon in *Puritanism from John Hooper to John Milton* (Durham, N.C., 1968). Emerson has also given an "Inventory of the Materials on Thomas Hooker in the Connecticut Historical Society," and "Notes on the Thomas Hooker Canon," *American Literature*, XXVII (1956), pp. 554f.

Before these modest works and the Sabbath school *Life of Thomas Hooker* (Boston, 1849) by Edward W. Hooker, the only monographic account of the life or thought of Thomas Hooker was that of Cotton Mather, published as an appendix of his *Johannes in eremo* (Boston, 1695), and republished among the biographies of divines in *Magnalia Christi Americana* (London, 1702). There were two subsequent issues, Hartford 1820 and 1853; references henceforth are to the latter. Mather's sketch in a dozen pages was based partly on a manuscript by John Eliot, a letter of Hooker to John Cotton, John Winthrop's *Journal*, notes and other materials from William Fenner, the biography of John Angier, the observations of Henry Whitfield, and common report (possibly from the Thomas Shepard family and the widowed William Ames family in Cambridge).

1

he was forty-seven years old. Before him lay fourteen years of activity as minister of the church in Newtown (Cambridge), 1633–1636, as founder of Hartford and the Colony of Connecticut, as co-drafter of its Fundamental Orders, as extensive participant in the ecclesiastical and civil affairs of New England, and as composer of *A Survey of the Summe of Church Discipline*—the second most important formulation of the pristine polity of New England congregationalism. But his main ideas had already been formulated before he touched the New World. Of the many versions and drafts of his numerous publications, the ten Documents edited in the present volume come as close as we can to presenting the thought and disposition of Hooker as he entered upon a decisive phase of his career as an American. Assembled and critically edited and calendared for the first time are ten rather diverse Documents, ranging from sermons to a letter and a treatise, that together reflect what manner of man he was as he assumed his role as a major architect and fashioner of the developing New England Way.

Thomas Hooker, son of yeoman Thomas Hooker (d. 1635), was born at Markfield in Tilton (Leicestershire), July 7, 1586. The name of the mother is not known. There were altogether two sons and four daughters.[2] It was probably at Market Bosworth that he went to grammar school. On March 27, 1604, he matriculated at Queens' College in Cambridge but transferred to Emmanuel under the Cartwrightian head, Laurence Chaderton. He must have come into contact with both John Cotton there and with William Ames at Christ College (left c. 1610).[3] With a B.A. in 1608, an M.A. in 1611,

---

William Fenner (1600–1640) of Straffordshire and Essex was sometime chaplain to the Earl of Warwick, protector in Essex of the Hooker family. See further on Fenner and Hooker, Document VII, Introduction. Henry Whitfield (1597–1657) was of Ockley (Surrey), came to New Haven Colony (1639–1650), and died in Winchester (Hampshire). John Angier (1605–1677) was born in Dedham (Essex) and came under the influence of John Rogers there. See Oliver Heywood, *Narrative of the Holy Life of Mr. John Angier* (London, 1685), re-edited by Ernest Axon, *Remains, Historical and Literary, of Lancaster and Chester*, Chetham Society, N.S. XCVII (Manchester, 1937), where Hooker, however, is mentioned only twice and incidentally.

[2] *Magnalia*, I, p. 333, § 2. H. Clark Woolley, *Thomas Hooker Bibliography*, [Hartford] Center Church Monographs, No. 1 (Hartford, 1932), p. 8.

[3] On the close relations of Hooker with Ames, see below, at n. 82 and following, also Document X, Introduction; and with Cotton, see below at nn. 42, 78, and 91, and Document IX.

Hooker was from 1609 to 1618 a fellow on the foundation of Sir
Wolstan Dixie and catechist.[4] Emmanuel College had been founded
by Sir Walter Mildmay in the precincts of a Black Friars' monastery.
Its chapel was the only one at Cambridge not built in the customary
east-west direction and was unconsecrated. In a report on services
therein submitted to Archbishop Laud we learn:

> At surplice prayers they sing nothing but certain riming Psalms of their
> own appointment, instead of ye Hymnes between ye Lessons. And at
> Lessons they read not after ye order appointed in ye Callendar, but
> after another continued course of their own. All Service is there done
> and performed by the Minister alone. When they preach or Common-
> place they omit all service after ye first or second Lesson at ye
> furthest.[5]

At Emmanuel the groundwork for Hooker in logic came from Alexander Richardson, who wrote a commentary on Petrus Ramus.[6]

While at Cambridge Hooker went through a deep spiritual crisis,
crying out: "While I suffer thy terrors, O Lord, I am distracted!" [7]
A sizar who waited on him, Simeon Ashe, himself destined to become a chaplain to Hooker's eventual protector, the Earl of Warwick,
is recorded as having been at this time of "singular help" to Hooker
in travail. After his conversion, Hooker had an inclination to pursue
"the application of redemption" in "experimental divinity." [8] Later,
when Simeon Ashe (d. 1662) would become himself a preacher,
Hooker is recalled as having addressed him familiarly and vehe-
mently as he was about "to preach before him": "Sym, let itt bee
hot." The remark is preserved by the Rev. John Ward, vicar of
Stratford-upon-Avon.[9] (Ward adds that by "hot" "He meant zealous." There is no indication where Hooker might have been when
he was listening to his former sizar preach.) [10]

[4] J. and J. A. Venn, *Alumni Cantabrigenses* (Cambridge, 1922), II.
[5] Woolley, *op. cit.*, p. 10, without giving his source.
[6] *Magnalia*, I, p. 336, § 9. He received his M.A. at Queens' College, Cambridge,
1587.
[7] *Ibid.*, p. 333, § 3.
[8] *Ibid.*, p. 347, § 23.
[9] *Diary*, extending from 1648 to 1679, ed. by Charles Severn, M.D. (London,
1839), p. 131.
[10] Ashe was first in Strattfordshire, then in Wroxhall under the protection of
Sir John Burgoign, then under Lord Brook in Warwickshire. He died as rector

Hooker's first pastoral charge was as rector of St. George's in Esher (Surrey). It is not certain when Hooker came to Esher, but it would appear that it was in 1618, immediately on his leaving Cambridge.[11] John Dod (1549–1645), after having been successively silenced at Hanwell (Oxfordshire), Fenny Compton (Warwickshire), and Canons Ashby (Northamptonshire), had been the first minister called to help in the spiritual cure of the wife of the patron of this church in Esher, Francis Drake. Mrs. Joan Drake was involved in a protracted malady of the soul. It was Joan Drake's violent conviction that she was one of the reprobate and that she had sinned against the Holy Ghost. Every visiting minister in Esher sought to counter her powerful scriptural and theological argumentation and countervail her vagaries. She once hit Dod with a piece of her bedstead while he was praying for her. On leaving his difficult charge, Dod recommended young Thomas Hooker, who had gone through a similar spiritual agony at College; and he, moreover, "newly come from the University, had a new answering method," [12] wherewith the intellectually superior but spiritually assailed lady of the manor might be both delighted and assuaged. Hooker was invited as the bachelor rector to reside in the manor house to be as close as possible to the afflicted lady. A certain Jasper Heartwell, native of Preston Deanery and a gentleman barrister with chambers in White Friars in London, also appears to have been a solicitous spiritual advisor of Mrs. Drake. Heartwell was, far more than the magnanimous but distraught husband, responsible for the succession of Puritan divines who came to Esher to minister to Joan Drake, beginning with Dod. But it was Dod who had recommended Hooker. And Dod and Hooker, of the dozen divines calling at Esher, are credited with having accomplished the most for Joan Drake, bringing her at length to an ecstatic conversion, recorded in the pseudonymous *Trodden Down Strength* (London, 1647).

---

of St. Austin's in London. Edmund Calamy, *The Nonconformist's Memorial,* ed. Samuel Palmer (London, 1785), I, 85–87; Daniel Neal, *The History of the Puritans,* 3 vols. (London, 1837), LII, 125f.

[11] In most treatments, however, Hooker is said to have come to Esher, c. 1620, for example, Mather. Walker conjectures that Hooker stayed in Cambridge "a considerable time" as "catechist and lecturer," *op. cit.,* pp. 30; 195.

[12] *Trodden Down Strength* (1647); see below at n. 15.

While in the Drake household, Hooker fell in love with Mrs. Drake's woman-in-waiting, Susannah Garbrand. She may have been the granddaughter of the Rev. John Garbrand, who died in North Crawley (Buckinghamshire) in 1589.[13] Thomas and Susannah were married April 3, 1621, in Amersham, the birthplace of Mrs. Joan (Tothill) Drake. Their first child was named after her, and in due course, Francis Drake, grateful for Hooker's special ministry at Esher and devoted to the infant namesake of his once vexed spouse, would leave a bequest in his will for Joan Hooker, by then of Hartford,[14] Connecticut.

As death approached, Mrs. Drake desired to return to her parents' home. During ten days of beatitude, recorded by the pseudonymous author (Jasper Heartwell) of *Trodden Down Strength*, Mrs. Drake was surrounded in Amersham by her parents, husband, children, Heartwell, manorial friends, and servants, and three of the dozen or so ministers that at one time or another had been concerned with her "case": John Dod, Thomas Hooker, and Dr. John Preston (1587–1628). It is quite probable that Hooker was at the time still the rector of St. George's in Esher. Mrs. Drake died April 18, 1625, Preston preaching the funeral sermon.

With the removal of invalid but converted Mrs. Drake from Esher to Amersham, Hooker had been presumably receptive to offers of a Puritan lectureship elsewhere. But Joan Drake's protracted conversion would remain for Hooker the underlying model for his theology of preparation for grace within the strictures of predestinarian Puritanism. Hooker's success in dealing with Mrs. Drake had a permanent effect upon his theology.[15] Cotton Mather, independently of the account in either edition of *Trodden Down Strength* (1647; 2nd ed. under the title *Firebrand*, 1654), wrote in 1695:

[13] *Dictionary of National Biography* (henceforth DNB). See also Henry Johan Langden, *Northamptonshire Clergy from 1500*, V (Northampton, 1940), 163.

[14] Walker, *op. cit.*, p. 38. The will is dated March 13, 1634 to "Johana Hooker who is now in New England £30 to be paid her the day of her marriage."

[15] *Magnalia*, I, p. 334, § 4. See further my study, "Called by Thy Name, Leave Us Not: The Case of Mrs. Joan Drake, A Formative Episode in the Pastoral Career of Thomas Hooker in England," *Harvard Library Bulletin*, XVI, No. 2 (April, 1968), pp. 111–128; No. 3 (July 1968), pp. 278–303; and Norman Pettit, "Lydia's Conversion: An Issue in Hooker's Departure [for Hartford]," *Proceedings*, Cambridge Historical Society, XL (1964–66), 59–83.

Mr. Hooker being now well got through the storm of soul, which had helped him into a most experimental acquaintance with the truths of the gospel, and the way of employing and applying those truths, he was willing to serve the Church of God in the ministry, whereto he was devoted. At his first leaving the university, he sojourned in the house of Mr. Drake . . . , whose worthy consort being visited with such distresses of soul as Mr. Hooker himself had passed through, it proved an unspeakable advantage unto both of them that he had that opportunity of being serviceable; for indeed he now had no superiour, and scarce any equal, for the skill of treating a troubled soul. When he left Mr. Drake's family . . . in a little time he grew famous for his ministerial abilities, but especially for his notable faculty at the wise and fit management of wounded spirits.[16]

It is not known exactly when Hooker left Esher permanently. At some point he essayed to go to Colchester (Essex), where he might be close to his friend, the much admired preacher of Dedham (Essex), John Rogers, but he did not succeed.[17] Mather and the pseudonymous author of *Trodden Down Strength* agree in saying that Hooker's next permanent post on leaving Esher was as lecturer and curate to John Michaelson, rector of St. Mary's in Chelmsford, according to Mather "about the year 1626." [18] But archival evidence would indicate that he was settled over Chelmsford late in 1625.[19]

[16] Cotton Mather, grandson of John Cotton (who voyaged to Boston with Hooker), printed the foregoing in *Johannes in Eremo* (London, 1695) and included it in the *Magnalia* (London, 1702), Vol. I, third Book, First Part, appendix, § 4. I have characterized the account as independent; for, although Cotton Mather could have procured and read *Trodden Down Strength*, he could not have drawn from it his information about Hooker's own storm of soul. And if he had read it, he would not have been able to bypass the eleven illustrious divines besides Hooker who tried to help Mrs Drake; for in the Narrative, Hooker is only one of many attending physicians of the soul. Cotton Mather's ultimate source as to the preeminence of Hooker's role in the cure at Esher may well have been Mrs. Hooker, an intimate of both the curer and the cured.

[17] *Magnalia*, I, p. 335, § 7.

18. *Ibid.*, § 5.

[19] The will of one John Marshall refers to "Mr. Hooker, preacher at Chelmsford, 1625." This could, of course, stretch through March 24, 1626 (over against the old style which would have ended the year 1625 only at March 24). The will of John Marshall, a woollendraper of Chelmford, is preserved in the Principal Probate Registry, Somerset House, London. Reference to the will, supplying the Hooker datum, is to be found in J. C. Challenor Smith, "Some Additions to Newcourt Reportorium," Essex Archaeological Society, *Transactions,* NS. St. Mary's, Chelmsford, is now a cathedral.

Though preaching in Chelmsford, Hooker apparently abode with his growing family for a while in a rented farmhouse (still standing), known as "Cuckoos" in Little Baddow. The Parish Register of Chelmsford, recording the burial of Ann Hooker, May 23, 1626, refers to the grieving father as "of Baddow."

Possibly the oldest document from the pen or lips of Hooker is a funeral sermon. Hooker is documented as having delivered the funeral sermon for the Rev. Robert Wilmot of Clare in Suffolk, who died at about thirty years of age, June 22, 1626. Wilmot was a graduate of King's College, Cambridge. Hooker, ten years his senior, had known him there. But the sermon, *Spiritual Munition* (Document I), deals little with the deceased, except as he is said to have admirably embodied the ideal, and exercised the authority, of a minister. In the sermon Hooker holds that an "able minister" is also "a courageous general" (p. 52), that it "is wonderful to see what a good minister can do in a good war" (p. 48), that it "is a certain sign that the soul never had grace, which opposeth the ministers of grace" (p. 45), and that "he that is disloyal to the king of heaven can never be loyal to the king of earth" (p. 48).

Around November 5, 1626, Hooker, probably in Chelmsford, delivered another occasional sermon, a commemoration of Guy Fawkes Day, *The Church's Deliverances* (Document II). Hooker stresses herein four successive instances of God's deliverance of the Church and the English nation: in 1558 with the accession of Elizabeth,[20] in 1588 with the defeat of the Armada, in 1605 with the detection of the gunpowder plot, and in 1618 with the temporary, at least, sparing of "this little cottage, this little England, this span of ground" from the continental wars of religion. In this commemorative sermon Hooker oscillates between thankfulness to God for his deliverances, "above sixty years," and his preacherly distress that the means for staving off the violence of God's wrath might be on the point of being used up or neglected. In specifying five of these "means" Hooker draws attention to the precariousness of the situation.

"Means" in Hooker has a range of references from the means of grace, i.e. the sacraments: baptism, the Lord's Supper; shunning and excommunication (see Document III, nn. 12, 19, 27); through divine

---

[20] The accession of Elizabeth seems to be implied but not expressly stated.

blessings and chastisements duly recognized as such; to some, as
here in the conclusion of the commemorative sermon, five particular
means "of reformation" (p. 79) "to uphold liberty and safety of a
nation" (p. 85), to the end that God deliver it and its Church from
his wrath. In listing the five particulars in the sermon, Hooker shifts
from a concern to descry the signs of opposition to means to an
interest in cataloguing the means which, alas, may be neglected: 1)
"God's rod and blows," including famine, plague, and the prospective sword; 2) "peace and prosperity"; 3) the word of God, likened
to physic and salve; 4) mourning, fasting, and prayer on the part,
at least, of a sizeable "company of godly, gracious men" (p. 85),
and 5) the "warning shot before the cannon-shot" (p. 85).

About this time we may date another, a possibly composite sermon, printed in the form of a moral treatise, *The Carnal Hypocrite*,
c. 1626 (Document III). It might be entitled "Puritan Behavior," for
it is a remarkably complete and systematic exposition of the visi-
bility of grace, or of the forms of godliness. Although the word
"sanctification" is not used once, the treatise concerns the Puritan
ideals of holiness and the means of giving it expression. The true
church therein is in fact referred to as a "voluntary society" of presumably experiential believers (p. 113). The carnal hypocrite is not
so much the dissembler as the nominal Christian who denies the
power of grace by not expressing it in visible righteousness. Hooker's
treatise turns out to be a comprehensive scriptural defense of precisely that kind of moralism or works-righteousness once pilloried
by Martin Luther in his proclamation of justification by faith alone.
It is interesting to see how Hooker skirts by those very passages in
which Jesus himself, and both Luther and even John Calvin com-
menting on them, expressed an awareness of the common sinfulness
of man and the specific sinfulness of the would-be righteous Pharisees and scribes. Against nominal Christians, i.e., carnal hypocrites,
who regarded his position as too precisionist, against certain specific
words of Jesus, Hooker contends: "It is not the fault of gold
[grace] that it glisters [in holiness], but that it [spurious grace]
glisters and is not gold" (p. 98). Elsewhere he writes: "[I]f grace
be inwardly, it will show outwardly!" (p. 99); and he quotes
from what Luther called the "straw epistle," Jas. 2:18, to sanction

his position. He is quite insistent: "If you desire any evidence . . . that God hath wrought grace in you, then show it in your lives" p. 99). Elsewhere: "Be holy in buying, selling, traveling, trading, etc." (p. 99), for: "The power of godliness hath an universal jurisdiction and will rule in your tongue, in your course, in your apparel, in your company" (p. 105). Spiritedly he writes: "You are bound prentice to the trade of holiness. . . . let us show something we have gained, show some workmanship" (p. 100). Distinguishing himself from nominal Christians in the parish or town, he asks: "What serves grace and godliness for, but only that we should do something for the glory of God more than you [nominal Christians] can?" (p. 101). In ungodliness Hooker includes, of course, not only unredeemed behavior in the sense of imprecision in the ways of the Lord but also the grosser sins: swearing, drunkenness, loose living, adultery, usury, oppression. At the same time Hooker beholds sanctification expressed in the rigid relationships of birth, class, and station: "Masters, servants, fathers, and children, have you any goodness? Let the world see it" (p. 103). Hooker in the treatise holds that the person whose life has been transformed into visible holiness by the power of grace should shun persons visibly not gracious. At the same time Hooker cannot in any way bring himself (at least "for the present," (p. 110) to countenance withholding oneself from holy communion in the parish church, despite the two scriptural texts, Mt. 18:15 and I Cor. 5:11, which separatists were using (and correctly so far as the original intention is concerned) to justify communion separately from the "ungodly," i.e., Hooker's "carnal hypocrites" or nominal Christians. But Hooker proposes an acceptable equivalent: shunning.

A great deal of *The Carnal Hypocrite* is taken up in setting forth the modalities of social shunning, while insisting that only persons in authority in church and state, above and beyond the local congregation, have the right to excommunicate. Hooker holds that the parish communion is "common pasture" (p. 110) under "public authority," although he must "mourn" for the uncleanness of the usual parish communion (p. 110).[21] Although the strictures of social

---

[21] Dr. John Burgess, whom Hooker writes against in Document X, and who was at the most a reluctant conformist, vividly describes from the establishmen-

shunning are quite severe (in order to avoid the contamination of the saint), nevertheless Hooker acknowledges that "the bond of a man's calling" or "the bond of humanity and civility" or "the bonds of religion and natural mercy" (p. 113) will sometimes oblige the saint to have some limited intercourse with the wicked and, in any case, he should pray for the sinner and hypocrite (nominal) Christian and have compassion for him.

The first published writing of Hooker is the introductory Epistle to the Reader (Document IV), a Preface by Hooker for the second edition of *The Doctrine of Faith* (London, 1627) of his friend John Rogers (1572?–1636) of Dedham. It is of interest that Mrs. Joan Drake, whom Hooker had helped cure spiritually at Esher, had once conceived the plan of leaving her husband to dwell in the household of John Rogers, and that even no less a personage than John Dod and two others had agreed to escort her to Dedham secretly for a spiritual cure!

In the Preface Hooker briefly outlines his conception of the *ordo salutis*. Basing his distinctions in the succession of phases therein upon Rom. 8:30, Hooker descries several moments in "the saving" and "the sanctifying" work of God: "*vocation*" (both eternal predestination to election and the situational temporal calling of the believer through the promises of the gospel), "the sorrow of preparation" (contrition I), "the spawn of faith," "faith" (defined as "nothing else but the going out of the soul to God through Christ to fetch a principle of life which in Adam we lost and now need"), "sorrow of sanctification" (contrition II), "*justification*," "sanctification," and "*glorification*." The three italicized moments in the *ordo salutis* are expressly mentioned by Paul in the basic text; the

---

tarian point of view the shunning and inwardly withdrawing behavior of the Puritans: "Nay, so farre doth this conceit [precision] carry some men, that they scarce will giue a friendly countenance or salutation to any of different minde: and these doe commonly call any small company of their owne partie, *the Church*, and the *Christians* of such a Towne, as if Christ were (I say not) *divided* betwixt vs, but wholly taken away from vs to them; and what wanteth this of Schisme in the heart?" *An Ansvver Rejoyned* (London, 1631), part 1, p. 5. On this book and its place in the Hooker corpus, see Document X, Introduction. For a similar characterization of the shunning exclusivistic Puritans, see quotation in Document X at nn. 89, 138.

other moments are intercalated by Hooker, not without some ambiguity. Hooker goes on to say, for example, that glorification is not only the perfection of heaven but also "the beginning of it here in grace, sanctification and glorification differing but in degrees one from another" (p. 145). The exact location of the other moments or phases in the continuum are not spelled out unequivocally. The order would become increasingly clear to Hooker as his pastoral ministry and theological psychology evolved.[22]

On January 5, 1627, a daughter, a second Anne, was baptized in the Baddow parish church.[23] We do not know when the family moved into Chelmsford. Hooker's residence in Chelmsford is said to have been near the manor house of John Haynes, subsequently the first governor of Connecticut Colony.[24] By April 9, 1628, the Hookers had probably been for some time residing in Chelmsford; the baptism of their daughter Sarah is recorded there on that date.[25]

On an episcopal visitation of Chelmsford at an unascertained date, George Montaigne, bishop of London (enthroned, December 10, 1621, nominated bishop of Durham late in 1627), listened to Hooker preach. A contemporary report is summarized thus: "[Montaigne] heard Hooker preach learnedly and well. And so told him, and desired him, for his sake, not to meddle with the discipline of the Church—the field was large enough besides. And he [Hooker] did promise him to do so." [26] Although Hooker may have promised to heed the counsel of the ambitious high churchman, Montaigne, when the latter was nominated by Charles I to the see of Durham (and soon thereafter to York) to make way for the even higher and

[22] See Essay 2. As for contrition I and II, Hooker would both publish more (see below at n. 73) and later speak of the "repentance of preparation" ("conversion") and the "repentance in sanctification." Document VIII, query 19; cf. below at n. 63.

[23] Parish register; Walker, *op. cit.*, p. 39. The date as written is "January 5, 1626." Jesse Berridge, "Thomas Hooker and John Eliot," *Essex Review*, XLI (1932), 65–73; *idem* gives a map of Little Baddow and the location of Cuckoos, "Colan Lane, Little Baddow," *ibid.*, XXXVI (1927), 34. There are baptismal. marriage, and burial registers in Chelmsford from 1564 to 1638. F. G. Emmison, *Catalogue of Essex Parish Records, 1240–1894* (Chelmsford, rev. ed., 1966), p. 78 and for Little Baddow, baptismal and burial records, 1559–1789, *ibid.*, p. 49.

[24] Woolley, *op. cit.*, p. 11.

[25] Chelmsford, St. Mary's parish register; Walker, *op. cit.*, p. 39.

[26] Ms Plume, No. 25 in Maldon (Essex), summarized by Andrew Clark, "Dr. Plume's Pocket-Book," *Essex Review*, XIX (1905), esp. p. 67.

more ambitious churchman, William Laud, in the see of London (1628–1633), Hooker (and many another Puritan) entered a new phase of his career under thorough episcopal scrutiny.

While in Chelmsford Hooker became the spiritual leader of a large company of Essex ministers of nonconformist sympathies. Ministerial conferences with fasting and prayer were held monthly. Hooker also helped resolve difficult cases.[27] A contemporary said of him: "He was a person who, while doing his Master's work, would put a king in his pocket." [28] Mather apropos illustrates Hooker's fervor and courage by citing a sermon preached in Chelmsford on Mal. 2:11 f.: "An abomination is committed, Judah hath married the daughter of a strange god; the Lord will cut off the man that doeth this." The occasion of Hooker's prophetic sermon was the assize held in the town and at a time when there was "a fast kept throughout the nation." Hooker's bold allusion was to Queen Henrietta Maria, daughter of Henry IV of France and Catherine de Medici, to whom Charles had been married by proxy in Paris in May 1625. Mather adds: "Though the Judges turned unto the place thus quoted [also 'distinctly in the prayer'], yet Mr. Hooker came into no trouble" [29]—for the moment. One may date this sermon at the time of national consternation after the assassination of George Villiers, first Duke of Buckingham, August 23, 1628. Possibly around this time Hooker preached the recently identified *The Stay of the Faithful* (Essay 4, pp. 385 and 386).

On May 20, 1629, Samuel Collins, vicar in Braintree, informed Dr. Arthur Duck, chancellor under Bishop Laud, of the situation in Chelmsford with Hooker as the oracle and "principal library" of the younger ministers, his genius haunting the pulpits. According to Collins' report, Hooker was stirring up people near and far with his criticism of Laud as one who was suppressing good preaching and promoting popery. Collins talked directly with Hooker and, warning him, got him to consider departing "out of the diocese"

[27] *Magnalia*, I, p. 336, § 8. On the Elizabethan antecedents of the influential Essex ministers, see Patrick Collinson, *The Elizabethan Puritan Movement* (London, 1967).

[28] *Ibid.*, p. 345, § 20. The contemporary was Henry Whitfield; see above, n. 1, below, n. 76.

[29] *Magnalia*, I, p. 336.

rather than to be cited before the ecclesiastical Court of High Commission. If formally suspended from the lectureship in Chelmsford, Hooker knew (Collins went on) that his many friends and protectors would settle him locally and support his private conferences.[30] On June 3, 1629, Collins supplied Duck and, through him, Laud with further information.[31] Collins had paid another monitory call on Hooker, only to find that he had already left for Leicestershire.

It is difficult to divine Hooker's motive for going to the county of his birth. To be sure, Mather remarks that it was Hooker's practice to go thither once a year to visit his father.[32] But this might not have been sufficient motivation in a period of crisis. Moreover, his old Leicester friend Francis Higginson (1586–1630) had already set sail on the *Talbot*, April 25, 1629, for Salem,[33] while his young friend Samuel Stone (1602–1663) had not yet taken up his lectureship in the adjoining county in Towcester.[34] Nevertheless, it is possibly precisely in late May 1629 that we can date an episode in Leicester recounted by Cotton Mather. Francis Higginson from 1617 to 1626 had been lecturer in St. Nicholas', when he was suspended for nonconformity. For Higginson's conversion to consistent Puritanism (nonconformity) Mather credits both Arthur Hildersham (1563–1632) of Ashby de la Zouch (Lincolnshire) and Thomas Hooker.[35] Obliged to lay down his lectureship, Higginson had remained popular in Leicester and preached frequently on invitation from the local ministers. In March, 1628, he had offered his services as minister to the Massachusetts Bay Company. (His oldest son, John of Salem, would later be a transcriber of Hooker's American ser-

---

[30] Letter summarized in *Calendar of State Papers, Domestic, 1628–1629* (London, 1859), p. 554; given in extensive excerpt by T. W. Davids, *Annals of Evangelical Nonconformity in the County of Essex* (London, 1863), pp. 150f.

[31] *Calendar of State Papers, loc. cit.*, p. 567; Davids, *op. cit.*, pp. 151 f.

[32] *Magnalia*, I, pp. 337, § 10.

[33] Thomas Wentworth Higginson, *Life of Francis Higginson* (New York, 1891).

[34] Stone, destined to be Hooker's transatlantic companion, was born in Hertford, took his B.A. at Emmanuel College, studied theology further under Richard Blackerly in Ashen in Essex, and was vicar in Stisted in Essex from June 13, 1627, to his suspension for nonconformity on September 13, 1630. Only then was his removal to Towcester arranged by Thomas Shepard, a native of Towcester, who was at the time lecturer in Earles Colne in Essex.

[35] *Magnalia*, I, p. 356, § 3. On Hildersham, see further Document X, n. 126.

ons.) Mather, preserving the following reminiscence,[36] says that Hooker "had an invitation to preach in the great church of Leicester." Of the five parish churches of the county seat, St. Martin's seems best to qualify for "greatness." [37] One of the chief burgesses, according to Mather, was much opposed to Hooker's preaching and, when he could not prevail, "set fiddlers in the courtyard [of St. Martin's] to distract Hooker, while preaching." But Hooker was so eloquent and persuasive that the burgess found himself listening despite his fiddlers and became a convert to the Puritan position that very hour. Not called permanently to Leicester (if that had been indeed his intention), Hooker sought elsewhere for an appointment.

Collins went on in his letter of June 3 to episcopal Chancellor Duck to explain that Hooker had left word that *via* the Leicestershire detour he intended to appear before Laud in London "up on the first day of his terme." Collins remarked further that all men in Essex were taken up with speculation as to the outcome of the Hooker affair.

For Hooker's appearance in London before Laud on summons, a Mr. Nash, tenant at Much Waltham (Essex) of Robert Rich, second Earl of Warwick, had gone bond in the amount of fifty pounds.[38] Hooker appeared before Laud, possibly in June.[39] It may be that, when in London at this time, Hooker personally arranged to have printed there in 1629 *The Poor Doubting Christian Drawn unto*

---

[36] *Magnalia*, p. 337f., § 10.

[37] From another source we know that late in 1626 Thomas Sacheverell, vicar of St. Martin's and the town preacher, died. "The church is very ancient; one of the largest, and esteemed the principal church in the county." John Nichols, *History of Leicestershire*, I:2 (London, 1815), 590; James Thompson, *The History of Leicester* (Leicester/London, 1849), p. 354.

Several candidates had offered themselves for the appointment. Francis Higginson was, according to Mather, offered the position; but he declined it with appreciation, observing that "there were some degrees of conformity therein required which he could not *now* comply withal." The majority of the corporation thereupon favored a Mr. John Angel, confrater of Wigston's Hospital and himself a decided Puritan. All the ministers and schoolmasters of the town were in favor of a Puritan. It is quite possible that it was at this moment in the town's deliberations that Hooker gave a candidating, rather than merely a supply, sermon.

[38] *Magnalia*, I, p. 338, § 11; Davids, *op. cit.*, p. 152.

[39] Letter of John Browning of Rawreth, November 3, 1629. Davids, *op. cit.*, p. 152.

Christ (Document V). This is actually the seventh and final "use" of a larger and no doubt composite sermon, to be published in full and in two variants after his departure from Europe. The first segment printed is a fine example of Hooker's dramatic style, psychological insights, and pastoral compassion. In contrast to some of his earlier utterances thus far adduced, this piece is remarkable for the stress on the accessibility of salvation and may well reflect ideas once adduced when as a young minister he plyed Mrs. Drake, who believed she was counted among the reprobate, with all kinds of arguments about the lightness of the yoke of Christ.

Hooker likens the recalcitrant heart to the back of a hand and God's promise to a staff: "You know the back of a man's hand cannot take hold of the staff; but let him turn the palm of his hand to the staff, and then he can take it" (p. 169). He also likens the heart to a venal judge. The natural heart simply must be bribed by the superior joy, richness, and power of the gospel (p. 180). He likens the heart to a city besieged, which will capitulate only when deprived of all props and other means of sustenance (p. 177). In contrast to the rather exacting succession of phases in the *ordo salutis* in the Preface to Rogers (Document IV), here Hooker stresses vocation (pp. 178, 180) as the divine call to accept the promise without one's trying to pay a price or, worse still, to borrow money—good works (p. 183)—to buy the priceless treasure, which is in any case free!

Of special interest in *The Poor Doubting Christian* and possibly a *novum* in Puritan moral theology is Hooker's insistence that, in contrast to earlier Catholic and also Lutheran and Calvinist formulations, the conscience (pp. 169–170) is not primarily or exclusively an accusing conscience, but, to the contrary: "He [the doubting Christian] must labor . . . to still conscience, that it does not accuse him, but be on his side." "Therefore as we must have our judgment informed by the Word that there is some good in us, so we must get conscience persuaded of it, that conscience may speak for us" (p. 170). Hooker uses the extraordinary image in line with the medieval distinction in moral theology between the internal and the external forum (court), that once a person has been vouchsafed a saving experience he should have it, as it were, inscribed in the court of chancery to be able ever henceforth to refer to it: "[W]e should not only be content to have all our objections answered [concerning the reception of faith], but get them recorded in the court of conscience, that when sense and feeling is lost, yet we may go to the court of conscience and there find the day and year when God's love was made sure to us" (p. 171).[40] Here surely we are at the springs of the New England introspective conscience and the later revivalist's insistence on the hour and the day of a saving experience.

Although *The Poor Doubting Christian* is only a seventh of a larger collection of sermons already presumably preached by Hooker before leaving for the New World, and not printed until after his settlement there, even this segment may be of composite character or preserve strata of Hooker's thinking at an earlier date. One overhears in it, in any case, many of the arguments which he must have first presented to poor doubting Joan Drake in Esher. One can almost hear her recurrent argument repeated by him and placed in the mouth of some generalized doubting Christian: 'I am not elected, and God will not do me good, seeing I am not elected, and therefore it is vain for me to use means' (p. 165).[41] Of further interest in *The Poor Doubting Christian* is Hooker's rather Catholic usage of "graces" in the plural (p. 180) for the various stages or phases of the *ordo salutis*. In classical Protestant usage grace is an aspect of Deity rather than the expression of that divine grace or mercy in the various means and modalities of the devout life.

It is quite possible that the information picked up by Collins about Hooker's going to London *via* Leicestershire was based upon diversionary allusions to what must have been Hooker's primary concern during the summer of 1629, namely, to explore fully the possibility of going to New England under the auspices of the Massachusetts

[40] Elsewhere he writes: "[T]hough sense and feeling be sometimes gone, yet conscience remembers the day and year when he had a clear evidence of God's love" (p. 170).

[41] Among the many other reminiscences of the Joan Drake episode are such phrases as the following put in the mouth of a doubting Christian: "Do not the ministers of God affirm my state to be good?" (p. 173), where the plural suggest the many divines around Joan Drake imploring her to abandon the idea of her divine reprobation; "and you may go singing to heaven and to your graves" (p. 174); "mischief lies . . . in a proud, self-willed heart that will not yield" (p. 172).

Bay Company, which had been able on March 4, 1629, to secure a second patent from Charles I, going beyond that received from James I.

A vivid scene, in July, 1629, pregnant with the future of New England, is preserved in a passing recollection in the writings of Roger Williams.[42] On the basis of this recollection and related documentation, we know that Roger Williams joined Hooker at Chelmsford and the two rode to Boston (Lincolnshire) to confer with John Cotton. The three divines (each to be conspicuously identified with the formation of three colonies destined to become states, Massachusetts, Connecticut, and Rhode Island, rode together to Sempringham Castle (Lincolnshire, eight miles north of Bourne and eighteen southwest from Boston). Although the fourth Earl of Lincoln, Theophilus Clinton, was at the time away from his seat (commanding three hundred volunteers under Count Mansfield in the Thirty Years' War), his castle had been agreed upon as the rendezvous for the members and associates of the Bay Company in the north who met on July 25, 1629, while on the same day in the house in London of the deputy governor of the Company, Thomas Goffe, the principal stockholders (called the General Court) convened. At this London meeting Governor Matthew Cradock proposed that the government of the projected colony be transferred to the inhabitants thereof (and later, in August in Cambridge it would be agreed that even the patent should be taken over with the colonists). The governor to be of the Bay Colony, John Winthrop, left Groton (Suffolk) with his brother-in-law Emmanuel Downinge (Downey) by way of the fens of Lincolnshire and Ely to arrive muddied by travel for the Sempringham Conference. Here they discussed plans for settling, financing, and governing the projected colony, and converting the Indians.[43]

[42] *The Bloody Tenent, Yet More Bloody*, The Complete Writings of Roger Williams, IV (New York, 1963), 65; reprinted (with supplemental materials) from the Publications of the Narrangansett Club, first series, IV (Providence, 1870), 65.

[43] Letter of Dudley to the Countess of Lincoln; Winthrop's Journal; James Ernst, *Roger Williams: New England Firebrand* (New York, 1932), 54f.; Cyclone Covey, *The Gentle Radical: A Biography of Roger Williams* (New York/London, 1966), 20-23; John Garrett, *Roger Williams: Witness Beyond Christendom, 1603-1683* (New York, 1970), p. 52.

It was on the way to Sempringham from Boston that all three New England divines discussed from horseback the problem of separation and the use of the Book of Common Prayer, as Williams was to recall in his bitter controversy with Cotton over the bloody tenet of interconnecting church and state: "[Y]et possibly Master *Cotton* may call to minde, that the *discusser* [RW] (riding with himself and one other of precious memory [Master *Hooker*] to and from *Sempringham*) presented his *Arguments* from *Scripture*, why he [RW] must not joyn with them in their use of *Common Prayer—*."[44]

In Chelmsford on August 26, 1629, the Hookers' new baby daughter, Sarah, was buried.[45] On November 3, 1629, John Browning, rector, in Rawreth (Essex) complained to Laud that Hooker, despite his appearance before the bishop in London, was continuing the same practice, namely, addiction to concentration on "preaching" and "hearing the word," "as they call it," to the neglect of authorized divine worship (said Browning) and urging others to the same. It may have been about this time in 1629 that Hooker, the itinerant evangelist, preached *The Faithful Covenanter* (Document VI) at the lecture in Dedham. One of the most "awakening preachers," John Rogers, vicar in Dedham (1604–1636), was suspended from his lectureship there between 1629 and 1631,[46] an appropriate time therefore for Hooker, very insecure in Chelmsford, to give the sermon assigned in the printed version to Dedham. A third edition of Rogers' *The Doctrine of Faith* (London, 1629), appeared at this time again with the brief epistle "To the Reader" by Hooker.

In *The Faithful Covenanter* Hooker defines "evangelical obedience" to the covenant understood as a set of commandments. He acknowledges, to be sure, that the old Law could never have been obeyed fully and that only in Christ and in faith can the covenant be kept inwardly. But the whole of one's life should be directed to an approximation of plenary fulfilment of all righteousness, as set forth in the Bible. Hooker holds that one enters into the covenant at baptism, taking at that time "an oath of allegiance" (p. 203, 205). Hooker likens God to a landlord who specifically requires very high

---

[44] *Loc. cit.*, p. 65.
[45] Chelmsford, parish register; Walker, *op. cit.*, p. 39.
[46] On lectureships in general, see Paul S. Seaver, *The Puritan Lectureships: The Politics of Religious Dissent, 1560–1662* (Stanford, 1970).

rents (pp. 202, 213, 215) of Dedham parishioners because they have
had the benefit of an outstanding ministry. God is cast by Hooker
also in the role of a bailiff who will "arrest" all those who fail to
live up to the highest standards of the contract and will consign
them to the everlasting prison of hell for failing to pay their rents
(pp. 211, 213). To be sure, faith precedes righteous works, and the
fulfilment of the covenant is not that "whereby we shall obtain justification, but an evidence and sign we are justified and accepted
of God" (p. 199).

Hooker in the course of the lecture makes clear the sins he has in
mind: pride, vanity, idleness, fretfulness, stubbornness, peevishness,
lying, hypocrisy, covetousness, earth-mindedness, lukewarmness,
coldness, swearing, drunkenness, scoffing, inward lusts, secret corruptions, fornication, adultery, oppression, and "griping the poor
brethren" (pp. 204, 205, 206, 207, 208). He is perhaps less specific
about attitudes and actions on the other side: reading the Bible,
prayer, regular church attendance, longsuffering, etc. But in essence
what makes for "evangelical obedience" is not necessarily absolute
success in the moral and religious life so much as a resolution that
makes the faithful covenanter "strict in obedience to *every* commandment" (p. 200) without any *arrière-pensée*, without, as Hooker
says, having "some one back door which you mean to keep" (p.
214). With respect to the meaning of conscience, in this lecture
Hooker seems to revert to earlier usage and primarily thinks of it
here as the accusing conscience (p. 215). He stresses the great need
for honesty, not only in outward dealings but also inwardly and
especially with respect to one's heart and soul, lest it suffer from
spiritual inanition (p. 216).

John Browning of Rawreth had offered his services to Laud in
quieting the people if he removed Hooker, advancing as the principal reason for the recommended "casting out" the need to sustain all
those others in Essex who were dutifully conforming.[47] On Novem-

---

[47] *Calendar of State Papers, Domestic, 1629–1631* (London, 1860), p. 87.
Magnalia, 1, p. 338, § 11 says "about the year 1630." Browning's letter excerpted
by Davids, *op. cit.,* pp. 152f. would indicate at most an informal gathering of
conforming parsons. Browning in the same letter says that Bishop Lancelot

ber 10, 1629, sensing danger to the great preacher of Chelmsford, forty-nine beneficed clergy, many of them themselves sincere conformists, petitioned Laud for leniency, holding "Mr. Thomas Hooker to be for doctryne, orthodox, and life and conversation as honest, and for his disposition peaceable, no wayes turbulent or factious," [48] and beseeching their bishop to allow Hooker to continue as lecturer in Chelmsford. But then on November 17, 1629, another petition was addressed to Laud by forty-one rectors and vicars, among them, of course, Browning of Rawreth, which, without mentioning Hooker directly, urged again the complete enforcement of uniformity, because without a strong hand in London most men would be doing what seemed good in their own eyes without regard to episcopal authority.[49]

The Hookers resettled in Cuckoos Farm in Little Baddow. With the encouragement of the local vicar, John Newton, Hooker made of the farmhouse a school and engaged John Eliot (1604–1690) as his usher (assistant). Eliot, born in Widford (Hertfordshire), educated in Jesus College, Cambridge, taking his degree in 1622, came directly from college to the school. It is quite possible, indeed, that Hooker originally settled in Little Baddow to organize just such a school and ministerial conference center, and that, on assuming the lectureship in Chelmsford, five miles away, he had left Eliot in charge of the day-to-day operations as assistant schoolmaster. Preceding Hooker into New England, Eliot would settle in Roxbury and write the manuscript used in part by Mather for his Hooker sketch. The Cuckoos Farm was also a center of monthly conferences for the younger Essex clergy.

Because of the continuing threat to uniformity, an ecclesiastical

---

Andrewes of Winchester had wondered whether the Hooker of Chelmsford was the same as a namesake who had wrought religious havoc in his diocese.

[48] *Papers, Domestic,* p. 92; Davids, *op. cit.,* p. 153; *Magnalia,* I, p. 336, § 8. The phrase from the letter in quotation is as given by Davids; but Mather's is almost identical, indicating he had access to a copy of the letter, possibly from the Hooker papers. John Michaelson of Chelmsford and John Newton of Little Baddow were both signatories. Among the beneficed clergymen who spoke up for Hooker was Stephen Marshall (1594?–1655). See Elisa Vaughan, *Stephen Marshall: A Forgotten Essex Puritan* (London, 1907), pp. 43f.

[49] Partly quoted by Davids, *op. cit.,* pp. 158–161. Two of the signatories had already signed the petition of November 10.

court, sitting in Chelmsford, cited Hooker on July 10, 1630, to the ecclesiastical Court of High Commission in London.[50] With this dreaded prospect now a reality, Hooker resolved to flee to the country. He was contacted in London by John Humfrey and others, who presumably urged him, possibly as late as December, 1630, to consider going to Massachusetts.[51] It is to be noted that for the year 1630 we have the fewest datable incidents in all of Hooker's mature life.

We may at this juncture, for convenience' sake, mention three works probably dating from the period of the Chelmsford lectureship but which were not to be printed (1638) until Hooker was safe in New England (these three and another already noted on p. 12, all four only recently ascribed to Hooker, are described in Essay 4): *The Properties of an Honest Heart*, intended as a book and perhaps circulating in manuscript in a very limited way under the author's cautious oversight, a guide to self-examination and a manual on the means of grace, and two sermonic pieces, *Spiritual Thirst* and *The Sinner's Salvation*. It will be perhaps helpful to place some of these sermons and others and the manual in the context not only of the assembly for Hooker's lectures in St. Mary's Chelmsford, but also of the separate gatherings in homes and manor houses of the Puritan great in and around the town, as recalled by John Eliot (arrived in Boston, November 4, 1631), writing much later (1657, n. 50) about the setting of Hooker's Essex ministry:

> I have known . . . a communion of Christians who held frequent communion together, used the censure of admonition ,yea and of excommunication, with much presence of Christ, only they had not officers, nor sacraments; and, notwithstanding this their liberty together, they held public parochial communion so far as avoided offense, and interested themselves in all good means for the public good of the parish

[50] Walker, *op. cit.*, p. 58. But cf. above, n. 47. Hooker's usher Eliot left for new Boston in 1631. He would in 1657 describe Hooker's gatherings in and around Chelmsford, Letter III, partly transcribed by F. J. Powicke, "Some Unpublished Correspondence of . . . Richard Baxter and . . . Eliot," *Bulletin of the John Rylands Library*, XV, No. 2, July, 1931.

[51] Humfrey to John Winthrop, London, December 18, 1630: "Mr. [Emmanuel] Downing myselfe and some others have given mr. Hooker a call lately. Ere long wee shall see the effect of it." *Winthrop Papers*, ed., Stewart Mitchell, II, p. 336.

where they lived. . . . Now, in this way of Christians enjoying a two-fold communion, and that without offense, may not parochial communion be upheld. . . . And [yet] besides this, may not the holy Saints, who are called higher by the grace of Christ, enjoy together a more strict and select communion, unto which they may gather together from many parts of the country or city?

About April, 1631, Hooker received an invitation from the English Reformed Church in Amsterdam to become a candidate to succeed the but recently deceased assistant to the exiled John Paget, M.A., minister of the English church. The dead co-pastor (1617–1631) was Thomas Potts, M.A. The writer of the letter for the congregation, but as it turned out representative of only one faction therein (at least not in conformity with the will of Paget himself), was Stephen Offwood,[52] a former Brownist. He was an innkeeper, publisher, and purveyor of forbidden books and tracts from Holland to England. The Anglican chaplain and informer, Stephen Goffe, describes Offwood and the letter in Notes for the English Ambassador at The Hague (1632–c.1640), Sir William Boswell. The Notes were prepared in 1633:

> Stephen Oswood [Offwood], an Inn Keeper dwelling neer the old Church at Amsterdam, wrote a Letter to Mr. Hooker presently upon the death of Mr. [Thomas] Potts [c. April, 1631]. Mr. Hooker [in or about Chelmsford], upon his Invitation, promised to come, But must be Caled; he would but come first to Rotterdam, expecting the Call from hence.[53]

[52] The name is also transcribed Ostwood/Oswood. The sources here are the unedited Boswell Papers in the British Museum. The particular document on Offwood's letter to Hooker is printed in full by Raymond Phineas Stearns, *Congregationalism in the Dutch Netherlands: The Rise and Fall of the English Congregational Classis, 1621–1635* (Chicago, 1940), esp. p. 116. There are references to Hooker in Holland in Champlin Burrage, *Early English Dissenters* (Cambridge, England, 1912), esp. pp. 274–276; Alice Clare Carter, *The English Reformed Church in Amsterdam in the Seventeenth Century* (Amsterdam, 1964); p. 31 *passim;* and most fully, Keith L. Sprunger, "The Dutch Career of Thomas Hooker, *The New England Quarterly,* XLVI (1973), pp. 17–44.

[53] British Museum, *Boswell Papers* (2 vols.), Additional Manuscripts 6, 394, I, fol. 146; published in part in Champlin Burrage, *op. cit.,* I, pp. 296f.; II, pp. 270–272; Stearns, *op. cit.,* Appendix IX, esp. p. 116.

With respect to the date of the death of Thomas Potts, important for determining the time of Hooker's departure for Holland and hence for the proximate date of the Farewell Sermon (Document VII), it is to be noted that "c. April" is only an approximation. Sprunger, "The Dutch Career," p. 19 says: "Potts died in the early months of 1631, probably April."

Hooker had indeed resolved to try out the situation in the Netherlands, but to leave his family behind.

Hooker's family, numbering now perhaps five children,[54] was
taken under the protection of Robert Rich (1587–1658), second
Earl of Warwick. Born at Felsted (Essex) Rich had been at Emmanuel College at the time of Hooker's study there (admitted June
4, 1603) and was among his most attentive hearers at the lectures
in and about Chelmsford. The previous year, June 13, 1630, as presi-
dent of the New England Company, the earl had signed the second
patent to William Bradford; and two years later, March 19, 1632,
he would grant to Viscount Say and Seal (1582–1662), Baron Brooke
(1608–1643), and John Hampden what is known as "the old patent
of Connecticut." It was in the house on one of the earl's estates, Old
Park in Great Waltham, that Warwick safeguarded Hooker's family.

It is at this time that we may place Hooker's farewell sermon,
entitled *The Danger of Desertion* [55] (Document VII). It is clear
that Hooker is preaching to a familiar congregation, referring to
their return to their houses that evening. One has, indeed, the impression of a late afternoon or evening service. It is indeed possible
to date the sermon as having been preached in Chelmsford or environs or even on Warwick's estate at Great Waltham on the evening
of Maundy Thursday, April 17, 1631. That Hooker was unusually
mindful of a communion to follow upon his sermon is suggested by
the frequent references in it to "means," "ordinances," and "sacrament." There is an allusion also to worthy participation in the communion, when Hooker speaks of solemn and dutiful preparation for
the visit of Christ as King and of appropriate royal "entertainment."
It contains the daring metaphor, sustained through several paragraphs, of the divine peddler God or Christ leaving England because

[54] Cf. Edward Hooker, *The Descendants of the Rev. Thomas Hooker*
(Rochester, N.Y., 1909), p. 3, where the editor, without any but family documentation, holds that Hooker had two wives and lists only six of the children
now known to have been born to Hooker; and Charles E. Banks, *The Planters
of the Commonwealth* (Boston, 1930), who lists five children (in a different
order) as boarding the *Griffin* with their parents in 1633.

[55] When published in London in 1641, it would be identified by the printer as
the Farewell Sermon; and it has ever since been considered Hooker's farewell
to England in 1633. It appears in two printed versions, the second ascribed
posthumously to Hooker's younger friend William Fenner.

people would not pay the "price" of his gospel or holy wares nor the cost of discipleship:

> God is packing up of his gospel, because none will buy his wares nor come to his price. . . . Oh therefore, my brethren, lay hold on God, and let him not go out of your coasts. . . . [S]top him at the town's end, and let not thy God depart. O England, lay siege about him by humble and hearty closing with him. . . . Suffer him not to go far, suffer him not to say: "Farewell," or rather "Fare ill, England." [56]

In the sermon Hooker elsewhere urges his hearers to rally to the God of the covenant and to "plead" with him lest he "rather go into Turkey and say unto them, 'Thou art my people, and I will be your God.' "

Hooker barely escaped pursuivants as he sailed from shore with a fresh wind, presumably from the port of Maldon (Essex),[57] apparently in late spring, 1631. The Consistory Register of the English Reformed Church in Amsterdam records his arrival in the Netherlands(but not yet in Amsterdam) thus: "in Junij 1631 Mr. Thomas Hooker preacher came into theis countries." [58] Years later, perhaps with reference to his flight from Laud and "priests of Ahab," John Fuller thought of Hooker as "that great Elijah, that renowned man of God in his generation." [59] He got off ship at Rotterdam, visiting Hugh Peter (1598–1660),[60] recently established there (summer, 1629) in the Merchant Adventurers' Church. In Rotterdam he awaited a formal call from the church in Amsterdam.

On his arrival in the Netherlands, Hooker must have become fully aware of the unusual situation among his countrymen. There were roughly three groupings in the United Netherlands of Englishmen and Scots: English merchants organized under their own elective

---

[56] See Document VII at n. 143. When printed in 1641 the sermon was said to have been preached by Hooker "immediately before his departure out of old England." Cf. *Magnalia*, I. p. 341; Thomas Shepard, *apud* Alexander Young, *Chronicles of the First Plantation of the Colony of Massachusetts Bay, from 1623–1636* (Boston, 1846), pp. 528; 530.

[57] On the miraculous wind, *Magnalia*, I, p. 338, § 11.

[58] Amsterdam, Gemeente Archief; Consistory Register, Vol. 3 (1628–1700), fol. 13. Noted by Sprunger, "The Dutch Career," n. 5.

[59] Prefatory epistle to John Beadle, *The Journal or Diary of a Thankful Christian* (London, 1656).

[60] Raymond Phineas Stearns, *The Strenuous Puritan: Hugh Peter 1598–1660* (Urbana, 1954), p. 56.

courts with governors; English soldiers stationed in garrison towns since 1580 to help protect the Reformed states from Catholic reconquest; and religious nonconformists. Soldiers and merchants needed chaplains; the religious refugees abounded in clerics. In 1621, on the model of the classis for the Walloons and that for the Huguenots, the English and Scottish Puritans of various kinds were organized in an English classis under the synod of the province of South Holland. This was an arrangement that had seemed congenial to both King James and the Dutch authorities, civil and ecclesiastical; for in this manner all the English denizens could be under both the oversight of the English ambassador (and his clerical advisor) and the supervision of Dutch authorities, who were not always at ease with the restive English soldiers, staple merchants, and unclassifiable mixture of conformists and nonconformists in every province. Alas for the plan, not all the high church chaplains wanted to be part of an essentially Reformed classis, while some of the most outspoken nonconformists also stayed out as programmatic congregational separatists. At the same time several English congregations preferred to become members of the Dutch municipal classis where they sojourned. This was precisely the case of the congregation of John Paget in Amsterdam, with the municipality paying his salary ever since the organization of the church in 1607 in the old Begijnhof chapel. As of 1631, when Hooker arrived in the Netherlands, only the English Reformed church in Amsterdam and that in Utrecht were integrated into a local municipal classis. The rest, insofar as they were not conventicular like the Brownists, were part of the English classis, 1621–1635.

In Amsterdam it was not John Paget who would serve the church for thirty years (1607–1637), but a fully congregationalist faction (some of whom had once been Brownists) in his congregation that had taken the initiative through the aforementioned Offwood to secure the services of Hooker as an assistant to him. After some preaching in Amsterdam, Hooker, while at The Hague for medical help, received from the Begijnhof consistory an invitation, July 2, requesting him to exercise his gifts among them again and more fully. This was still not a wholly regular call from the congregation and arrangements for his municipal salary had still to be made.

Hooker's views of congregational authority, on relations with Brownist Separatists, and on the baptism of the infants of non-members, differed from Paget's. To prevent the consummation of the congregation's plan to make Hooker the new assistant, devotedly presbyterian or synodal Paget proposed Twenty Questions, which Hooker would have to answer satisfactorily before Paget would accept the newcomer as co-pastor. At the house of Hugh Peters in Rotterdam, Hooker, who had for some time been developing quite radically congregationalist ideas, was obliged to write out very carefully his *Answers to the XX Questions by John Paget* (October, 1631) (Document VIII). Paget had suspected him of outright separatism. Stephen Goffe, the high church chaplain and agent of the English ambassador, Sir William Boswell (both functionaries, of course, had no sympathy for either of the two contending Puritan divines), later characterized Hooker as having in his *Answer to the XX Questions* "shown that he thinks no church as yet knows Christ's mind, but he knows it alone." [61] Hooker was, in fact, congregationalist in that he did argue that "the first classis that ever was upon the face of the earth . . . was made by the combination of . . . several congregations, wherein it must needs follow that those particular congregations had power from Christ to call a minister." [62] In answer to Paget's query on repentance, Hooker gave out quite uncharacteristically that "There is a double repentance, the first of preparation, wrought by the Almighty; . . . the stroke of the Spirit in the very first work of conversion. . . . Secondly, there is a repentance in sanctification." [63]

It is not certain whether Hooker tarried in Amsterdam and set forth supplementary views. By October 5 the elders and deacons decided to halt their proceeding for confirming their unanimous choice of Hooker with the proposal of his name to the Amsterdam classis. They prudentially preferred a more opportune time, given

[61] Summary of Goffe's letter to Edward Misselden, April 26, 1633; *Calendar of State Papers, Domestic, 1633–1634* (London 1863), pp. 30f.

[62] Answer to Query 11.

[63] Response to Query 19. Hooker cites John Rogers in support of this view at variance with Paget. On these two repentances or contritions or sorrows, see above n. 22 and below, at n. 73.

Paget's redoubtable resistance.[64] But Paget had his answers duly Latinized and submitted to the classis, which found them on October 6 unsatisfactory and decided that Hooker was not to be permitted "now or in the future to preach." [65] Both Paget and the municipal classis were subsequently upheld (against the intrusion of Hooker) by the synod of Holland. In the meantime, the irate Hookerites pressed their congregationalist views against Paget in Consistory on October 12, carrying these arguments to the classis October 13, but all in vain. Thereafter the Hookerites defiantly on their own tried to insist on scheduling Hooker as a preacher and carried their cause well into November.[66]

By November, however, Hooker had betaken himself to Delft to become the assistant in the Prinsenhof church to John Forbes (1568?–1634). Forbes had been exiled from Aberdeenshire. Not incidentally he had briefly called upon Mrs. Joan Drake in Esher[67] and had had for a while a younger member of the Esher family, Thomas Drake, as his assistant while serving the church of the English Merchants at Middelburg (1611–1620). Hooker served as Forbes' assistant in Delft from November, 1631, to c. March, 1633. His first sermon was based on Phil. 1:29: "To you it is given not only to believe, but also to suffer." For some time Forbes tried to get at the bottom of the altercation at Amsterdam and to clear the name of his co-pastor.[68] Cotton Mather would later effusively describe the relationship of Forbes and Hooker in Delft as like that of "Basil [of Caesarea] and [Gregory] Nazianzen, . . . one soul in two bodies." [69]

Although Forbes was in origin a Scottish Presbyterian, he had come to a modified classical-congregational ecclesiology and did not in any case regard the English classis as having a final authority over his Delft congregation. During Hooker's stay in Delft, Forbes became involved in an altercation with Edward Misselden, a tractarian on economics and a deputy of the court of the English merchants there. In October, 1631, the two ministers admitted to membership

[64] Sprunger, "Dutch Career," p. 23.
[65] Ibid., pp. 23–27.
[66] Ibid., pp. 27–34.
[67] Trodden Down Strength.
[68] Sprunger, "Dutch Career," pp. 37–40.
[69] Magnalia, I, p. 339, 12.

of the Delft congregation within the English classis a number of craftsmen whose presence as voting members threatened to attenuate the control of the congregation by the merchants.[70] In the end, Forbes was outmaneuvered and briefly exiled. During most of the period of Hooker's co-ministry in Delft services without the Prayer Book became increasingly improvised under the directions of the Spirit; communion was not observed;[71] and Hooker expressly declined to baptize infants of non-church members.

In 1632 there was printed anonymously in London Hooker's *The Souls Preparation for Christ: or a Treatise of Contrition* (October, 1632).[72] (Because of its length, 242 pages, it is the only work by Hooker published before his departure for New England that is not included in our collection.) It is subtitled "How God breaks the heart and wounds the soul in the conversion of a sinner to himself"; and in a series of sermons on Acts 2:37 ("Now when they heard this, they were pricked in their heart"), Hooker urges his hearers to recognize the nature of sin and to acknowledge their own sinful condition. He persuasively outlines how the sinner can prepare for an "inward frame of heart" that will not let him despair when "wearied and burdened by sin" but will enable him to accept God's mercy. Hooker dwells especially on meditation and confession as means toward this end, and he emphasizes the duty of the minister not to preach merely in general terms but to "work upon the heart" by pointing to specific sins, and yet also to encourage and assure those that are willing to undergo the irksome process of preparation, for the minister "is the physician that God hath appointed whereby all the sickness of the soul may be eased and cured." The preacher is the man of God, who comes for hearts, stays for hearts, and will have hearts before he goes. Broken hearts are often

---

[70] Stearns, *Congregationalism*, p. 33.

[71] Sprunger: "Dutch Career," pp. 416, quotes from a notice of the summer of 1633, saying that Forbes "forbade communion before 16 or 18 months."

[72] It was entered in the *Stationer's Register* to R. Dawlman, printer, October 29, 1631. Bibliographical information, Walker. *op. cit.*, p. 185.

Hooker was once thought also to have printed, in London the same year (1632), *The Equall Wayes of God: Tending to the Rectifying of the Crooked Wayes of Man* with a prefatory address, signed "T.H." But this has been recently ascribed by Katherine Pantzer in Houghton Library to Thomas Haynes.

made by meditation—long after the penetrating sermon—on the word preached.

In distinguishing the breaking of hearts or the contrition or the "sorrow of preparation" and the subsequent and presumably recurrent "sorrow of sanctification," Hooker resorts characteristically to a helpful simile:

The difference of these two works is thus to be conceived in this similitude, as it is with the wheels of a clock that runs quite wrong. What must a man do to set this clock right again? He must first stop it that it run no longer wrong, and then turn it, and set the wheels right. Now all this while the clock is a patient, and the workman doth all. Secondly, when it is thus set right, then the workman puts the plummets and weights on it, and now the wheels can run of themselves by virtue of that poise and weight they have gotten—so that these two are plain different actions.

Just so is it with the frame of the soul, the will, and the affections, which are the wheels of this great and curious clock (the soul goes hell-way and sin-ward, and the will and the affections embrace nothing but hell and sin). Now to bring these into a holy order the Lord must stop the soul, and that is done by the discovery of sin, and by this humiliation of heart. When the soul lets a man see his sin, if thou wilt have sin, thou must have hell and all together. And then the soul saith, 'If it be so, I will meddle no more with sin. . . .'

But now when the soul is set heaven-ward, and God justifies a poor sinner, and plucks him to himself by faith, and adopts him to be a child, then he too gives him of his spirit; and this is as the weight of the soul. Then by the power of that Spirit the soul is able to run right, and hath a principle of grace in it, and the poise of the Spirit of grace which doth possess the soul, makes it able freely to mourn for sin, and to have the heart enlarged in the service of God. This is mainly the sanctifying work.[73]

---

[73] Seventh ed., London, 1658, pp. 248f. Hooker deals especially with Rom. 8:30 and the *ordo salutis, ibid.,* p. 247.

There is a sizeable selection from *The Souls Vocation* with biographical introduction, edited by Everett H. Emerson, *English Puritanism from John Hooper to John Milton* (Durham, N.C., 1968), pp. 219–235.

Nathaniel Ward (1578–1652), who played a very important literary and political role while sojourning in New England, 1634–1645, referring to Hooker in Chelmsford with specific reference to the cycle of sermons preached there but published in 1632 as *The Soul's Preparation*, once addressed Hooker thus, possibly in London, where Ward was curate of St. James's, Picadilly, 1626–28;

In mid-January, 1633, Hooker and Peter went from Delft to Amsterdam to welcome Forbes back from a brief exile.[74] There is then a notice from Edward Misselden, dated March 20/30, 1632/33, saying that Hooker had by that time left for England:

> I think I told you when I was with you that mr. Hooker went out in Norman [?]: belike to heare how the squares [affairs] goe in England & soe to give diligent advice to mr. F[orbes] & himself to resolve of his owne way, to returne hither [Delft] or haply for new England.[75]

It is possible that Hooker visited London clandestinely at this time in connection with a view to conferring with John Cotton, once of St. Botolph's of Boston, and with John Davenport (1597–1670), the destined founder of New Haven Colony (1638). The meeting of Hooker with Cotton and Davenport may well have taken place in Ockely (Surrey), where Cotton was hiding out in the house of Henry Whitfield, later founder and minister of Guilford, Connecticut.[76] From November 5, 1624, to his resignation on August 5, 1633, Davenport was the *congregationally* elected vicar of St. Stephen's, a parish in Coleman Street, London, with the uncommon privilege of local autonomy. Davenport had earlier been encouraged by Dr. John Preston (d. 1628) in the "foeffment scheme" to buy up, as one of the twelve foeffees, lay impropriations, and in this way to secure the possibility of congregational control of a network of

---

rector of Standon Massey, 1625–1633: "Mr. Hooker, you make as good Christians before men are in Christ, ever they are after; . . . would I were but as good a Christian now, as you make men while they are but preparing for Christ." This remark is preserved by Ward's son-in-law, Giles Firmin, minister in Shalford, Essex, *The Real Christian* (London, 1670), p. 19; Glasgow, 1744, p. 20.

[74] Stearns, *Congregationalism*, p. 37.

[75] Misselden to Boswell; British Museum, Boswell Papers, Additional Manuscripts, 6394, f. 114. The decipherment of what in the text is given as *Norman* remains a task. Professor Stephen Foster, who transcribed it, declares it is definitely not *Rotterdam*. Stearns, *Congregationalism*, p. 46, n. 18, incorrectly assumes without substantiation, that Hooker stayed *in Delft* till July, when he sailed for New England, *ibid.*, p. 29, n. 36.

[76] *Magnalia*, I, pp. 592–594. Whitfield, a graduate of Oxford, was rector in Ockley, when he turned nonconformist. Several divines are known to have lodged with him when in the London area. He went to New England in 1639, founded Guilford, named after Guildford, near Ockley, and became its minister. He later returned to England.

vicarages and lectureships.[77] Laud destroyed the project. Cotton, who in October, 1632, hid in Davenport's house from pursuivants of the Court of High Commission, is, along with Hooker,[78] commonly credited with having prevailed upon Davenport to espouse now the more radical Puritan congregationalism of the English in Holland. Davenport, who had already studied a copy of Hooker's *Reply to Paget's XX Questions,* was by at least November 4, 1633, known by the English authorities in Holland [79] to have received a call from the same congregationalist faction in the English church in Amsterdam that had earlier sought Hooker. (Davenport would leave London in December, 1634,[80] to become briefly another turmoiled assistant to Paget.)

Hooker was surely maintaining contact with his followers and would-be emigrants in Essex, and with Cotton, who was not yet certain whether to seek refuge in Holland or to sail to New England. A portion of Hooker's Letter from Rotterdam to Cotton (Document IX) is preserved by Mather, wherein Hooker complains of the ague and confides his discouragement and "amazement" at God's providence, "as one wave follows another." As for prospects of settlement in Holland, he dissuades Cotton: "The state of these provinces, to my weak eye, seems wonderfully ticklish and miserable. For the better part, heart religion, they [the Dutch Reformed] content themselves with very forms, though much blemished." [81]

Hooker had at some undetermined point come into contact with

[77] See Isabel M. Calder, *Activities of the Puritan Faction of the Church of England* [in London] *1625-33* (London, 1957), wherein John Davenport is prominent.
[78] Recent biographies of Cotton and Davenport allude to such a conference in London with Hooker (c. 1632) without giving a source: Isabel M. Calder, *Letters of John Davenport* (New Haven, 1937), p. 3; Larzer Ziff, *The Career of John Cotton* (Princeton, 1962), p. 69. Mather names only Cotton as converting Davenport to radical Puritan congregationalism, though he speaks vaguely of others in a conference. *Magnalia,* I, p. 323, § 5. While hiding in London or Ockley Cotton resigned his charge to Bishop Williams, May 7, 1633, and to the town council of Boston in July. Young, *Chronicles,* pp. 434; 444.
[79] A letter of Boswell so dated, cited by Stearns, *Congregationalism,* p. 64, n. 72.
[80] Calder, *op. cit.,* p. 3; Stearns, *Congregationalism,* p. 63.
[81] *Magnalia,* I, p. 340, § 13.

William Ames (1571–1633),[82] who had been professor at, and then rector of, the University of Franeker in Frisia (1622–1633). Ames once declared that "though he had been acquainted with many scholars of divers nations, yet he never met with Mr. Hooker's equal, either for preaching or disputation." [83] Such a testimony would suggest a sojourn of some duration of the two men in the same town; but it is not clear where and when this encounter took place.[84]

Ames left Franeker for Rotterdam some time after August 7, 1633,[85] to become the co-pastor there with his protegé and junior by two decades, Hugh Peter. Ames moved partly because of the ill effect of the sea air at Franeker on his asthma, partly because of "implacable controversy" with a colleague, and partly because of the prospects of heading a new English college to be established in Rotterdam.[86] In Rotterdam Ames worked on the completion of a book with a Preface (Document X) by Hooker, entitled *A Fresh Suit against Ceremonies* (Amsterdam, 1633). This book was directed against *An Answer* (1631) by his very own father-in-law, Dr. John Burgess, a sometime nonconformist, his predecessor as chaplain to the English governor and garrison in Brill, but by now a (reluctant) conformist and hence a powerful threat to English Puritanism on the issue of Laudian ceremonies.[87] William Laud, bishop of London from 1628 to 1633 (nominated for puissant Canterbury, August 6) was even attempting to extend the authority of the diocese of London over all English churchmen in the Netherlands. The publisher of *A Fresh Suit*, for which Hooker wrote the so-called Preface, was

[82] See the University of Illinois thesis by Keith L. Sprunger, *The Learned Dr. William Ames* (Urbana, 1973).

[83] This evaluation is preserved in *Magnalia*, I, p. 339, 13. Ames died before he could sail to New England; but Mrs. Ames and the children settled there and, after their house burned, Hooker and others joined to help her.

[84] The New England tradition assumes an overlap in Rotterdam. See Introduction to Document X. Apparently while Ames was still in Franeker and Hooker still in Delft, Ames asked Hooker to write a (long) *Preface* (1633) (Document X) as a foreword to what was to prove to be his last and partly posthumous book. Cf. above at n. 3.

[85] See Introduction to Document X, Introduction, n. 10, based on Sprunger, *Ames*, p. 93, n. 72.

[86] Letter of Boswell to John Coke, Secretary of State, November 18/28, 1633; State Papers, 84 ff. 174 r.

[87] What Burgess feared in extreme Puritanism is embodied in a quotation from his *Answer*, above, n. 21. See further, Introduction to Document X.

none other than the same Stephen Offwood who wrote the letter originally inviting Hooker to Amsterdam.

Hooker's "Preface" is not so much an introduction to the book of Ames which follows as it is an independent admonitory critique of Burgess for any wavering Puritan who might be tempted to read the *Answer* and acquiesce in the ceremonies, persuaded by Burgess' sometimes quite compelling exhortations to moderation and sober piety in the interest of avoiding any further dangerous polarization in the established Church. Hooker's argument in the "Preface" is that the three canonically enjoined ceremonies of the surplice, of kneeling at communion, and of the use of the cross at baptism and related "human additions" to scripturally prescribed worship should not be coercively imposed on conscientious objectors thereto (p. 365). He insists, somewhat disingenuously, that "no judicious non-conformer· is disquieted that the crowd of the formal gospellers should embrace them" (p. 361). He rejects Burgess' view that the dangerous polarization is due to those who recoil from the popish ceremonies, arguing rather that the imposed human or purely ecclesiastical ceremonies are comparable to circumcision, which, were it to be imposed by the Church, would clearly make the prelates and not the nonconformists the palpable initiators of schism. Hooker's "Preface" is a spirited specimen of his polemical style.

Sometime in the spring or early summer of 1633 Hooker left Holland for England in order to arrange his family affairs and those of his loyal company for the great voyage to America. It is almost certain (Document X, Introduction, at n.30) that throughout his Dutch sojourn (1630–1633) his wife and children had remained in Great Waltham under the protection of the Earl of Warwick, who may have helped in the meantime the Hookers to prepare for emigration. Already in August, 1632, a group from Chelmsford, Colchester, and Braintree, known in anticipation of his coming as "Mr. Hooker's company," had arrived at Mount Wollaston in the Bay.[88] The remaining Hooker company met to choose an appropriate associate minister; and their first choice, at the suggestion of Hooker, fell on

---

[88] John Winthrop, *The History of New England from 1630 to 1649*, commonly called *The Journal*, ed., James Savage (Boston, new edition, 1853), I, p. 105.

John Cotton (a year his senior), who, though purportedly pleased, declined the call. The company then turned successively[89] to John Norton (1606–1663), chaplain to Sir William Masham; to Thomas Shepard (b. 1605), lecturer or chaplain successively in Earls Colne, his native Towcester, Butter Crambe (Yorkshire), and Heddon (Northumberland), and destined to be Hooker's son-in-law and pastor of the church in new Cambridge (1635–1649); and finally to Samuel Stone, whom we have already mentioned as moving from his vicarship in Stisted (1627–September 13, 1630) to Towcester. When Stone accepted, Hooker made his way to Towcester to confer with his "designed companion and assistant" in the great adventure. Mather, without localizing the following humorous escapade, reports that on his visit Hooker found Stone "at that instant smoking of tobacco." Hooker was reproving him when pursuivants knocked at the door of the very chamber where they were conversing heatedly. Stone, "being also of a sudden and pleasant wit," with his pipe in his mouth stepped to the door and with an air of authority and "a braving sort of confidence" enhanced by puffs of smoke, told the pursuivants for Laud's Court of High Commission that he had indeed seen the Hooker "that once lived at Chelmsford" about an hour before at a certain house in the town and craftily suggested they hasten thither after him.[90]

Hooker, Stone, and Cotton arranged to sail on the three-hundred ton *Griffin*, which sailed from the Downs c. July 10, 1633, carrying about two hundred persons. Both Cotton and Hooker boarded the vessel disguised. At Yarmouth on the Isle of Wight pursuivants were in waiting, informed that the master of the ship was bound to take on provisions there and perhaps a second contingent of emigrants. Stone, the youngest of the three ministers and the least well known, was the only one to own his clerical status before the vessel was well out at sea. Thereupon a daily schedule of services of wor-

[89] *Magnalia*, I, pp. 434 f., § 3.
[90] *Ibid.*, p. 340, § 14. Mather was pleased to find in this description a parallel with the diversion that once helped Athanasius on the Nile. That the episode took place in Towcester seems more likely, given the sense of a lapse of time in the phrase "*once* of Chelmsford," which town and church Hooker left in April, 1631, while Stone was still in Stisted. Of course, Hooker left his post in Chelmsford and withdrew to Little Baddows (five miles out) earlier than this.

ship and conference was established with Cotton preaching in the morning, Hooker in the afternoon, and Stone in the evening.[91] Amidst unwonted intimacy and compactness, to the Cottons was born a first child. Called Seaborn, he was not baptized on ship because, according to Cotton, the company did not constitute a duly gathered church into the membership of which an infant might be convenantally baptized, nor were Cotton and his clerical companions considered proper ministers therein or thereof while in transit.[92]

Slight theological differences between Cotton and Hooker would have had ample time for being ventilated and perhaps overexposed during eight weeks at sea when the *Griffin* arrived in Boston on September 4, 1633.[93] In October Hooker and Stone settled in Newtown (Cambridge) and on October 11, 1633, were chosen respectively pastor and teacher of the first church.[94] Hooker's house stood on the site of the present Boylston Hall in Harvard Yard.

[91] *Ibid.*, p. 265, § 19.
[92] Winthrop, *Journal*, I, p. 131.
[93] Both September 3 and 4 are transcribed by Thomas Prince, Appendix 2.
[94] Winthrop, *Journal*, I, p. 137.

DOCUMENT I

Spiritual Munition; June 22, 1626

Introduction

Spiritual Munition is a funeral sermon which Thomas Hooker preached for the Reverend Robert Wilmot, Vicar of Clare in Suffolk, who was buried on June 22, 1626. It is the only sermon preached by Hooker in England which we can date from clear documentary evidence.[1] Skrinkfilde in Essex, mentioned as the place of burial in the Clare parish registers, is probably Springfield, a village just outside the town of Chelmsford, where Hooker had recently become a lecturer. He had come to know Wilmot while they were both at Cambridge.

Robert Wilmot attended Eton and was admitted to King's College, Cambridge, in 1612. He took the B.A. in 1615/16 and the M.A. in 1619. From 1615/16 until 1619 he was a Fellow at King's. During this time he was ordained as a deacon in London, 1617/18, and was made a priest in Lincoln on February 21, 1618/19.[2] We do not know when he came to Clare in Suffolk. He had two sons baptized there: Nathaniel in March, 1623, Eleazar on May 14, 1626, shortly before Wilmot's death. One other son, Simon, was buried in Clare on September 25, 1625.[3] Robert Wilmot was only about thirty years old when he died.

None of these biographical data appears in Hooker's sermon. Nor is there a "lean-to," as non-conformist ministers called the biographical appendices which were often attached to a funeral sermon. *Spiritual Munition* is, rather, an example of the Puritan funeral ser-

---

[1] *Proceedings of the Suffolk Institute of Archeology and Natural History*, VIII (1894), 234.

[2] John and J. A. Venn, *Alumni Cantabrigiensis, pt. 1: From the Earliest Times to 1751*, IV (Cambridge, England, 1927.), 425.

[3] *Proceedings of the Suffolk Institute of Archeology and Natural History*, VIII (1894), 233, 236.

mon of the first part of the seventeenth century, when Puritan
preachers would generally stress the exegesis and exhortation instead
of the eulogy, which they thought played too large a part in Anglican
funeral sermons. It was only when the Puritans developed their
own matyrology, and especially after 1640, that the biographical
element became more important.[4]

The Westminster Assembly, while prohibiting praying, singing,
and reading on the way to the grave, allowed the minister to put
the mourners "in remembrance of their duty." Funeral sermons were
permitted, although some ministers were opposed to them because
they saw in them "nothing but an abuse of preaching to serve the
humor of the rich people only for a reward," as Baillie put it.[5] And
in New England the practice varied. Cotton Mather expressly
pointed out that prayers or funeral sermons were not forbidden, "as
they are in the discipline of the French Churches," but that they
were omitted in some places.[6] Many funeral sermons were printed,
especially toward the end of the seventeenth and well into the
eighteenth century.[7] Moreover, funeral sermons greatly influenced
both the form and content of other pious memorials such as the
epitaph, the funeral elegy, and the spiritual biography, which were
popular literary exercises in colonial New England.[8]

Hooker begins his eulogy by noting Wilmot's "holy life," "sincere
heart" and "unspotted conversation." He then goes on to praise him
for his zeal and his love, two complimentary traits which in many
eulogies constitute the ideal Puritan character.[9] Because both traits
are exemplified by the way in which Wilmot carried out his duties
as a minister, Hooker is able to make him a "visible interpretation"

[4] On the English funeral sermon tradition, cf. Caroline F. Richardson,
English Preachers and Preaching, 1640–1670, (London, 1928), pp. 94–107. For a
discussion of non-conformist practice, cf. William Haller, *The Rise of Puritanism* (New York, 1938), pp. 101–127.

[5] Horton Davis, *The Worship of the English Puritans* (London, 1948), p. 139.

[6] Cotton Mather, *Ratio disciplinae fratrum Nov-Anglorum. A faithful account
of the discipline professed and practised in the churches of New England*
(Boston, 1728), p. 117.

[7] Cf. William D. Andrews, "The Printed Funeral Sermons of Cotton Mather,"
Early American Literature, II (1970), 24–44.

[8] The funeral elegy is discussed in this context in Robert Henson, "Form and
Content of the Puritan Funeral Elegy," *American Literature,* XXXII (1960),
11–27.

[9] For examples, cf. ibid., pp. 15–22.

of the scriptural text for the sermon, 2 Kg. 2:12, showing that he was a "father" and one of the "chariots of Israel and the horsemen thereof." But while special mention is made of Wilmot's time at Cambridge, where he had been so zealous that "he did weary himself and even consume his spirits" (p. 49), Hooker does not give any other personal details of the man's life. Except for the brief allusion to Wilmot's "days of humiliation," the stages of his salvation are not described. Hooker does not include any pious thoughts of the deceased or any specific legacy taken from his last words; nor does he recount the circumstances of his death. Any or all of these facets would be included by later eulogists, either in the funeral sermon itself, in an appendix, or in a separate spiritual biography based on the funeral sermon.

Only about one eighth of the sermon makes reference to the immediate occasion; for Hooker uses the opportunity to preach on the relationship between the ministry and the parishioners. In doing so, he stresses the authority that both ministers and magistrates are entitled to; and he claims special authority for the ministry because the minister serves as the chief intermediary between God and the community of his people. When Hooker warns against failure to submit to ministerial authority, he likens it to giving all of England's munitions to Spain, her feared enemy (p. 49). Even Wilmot's death and the resulting vacancy in the parish ministry is blamed on the sins of the parishioners (p. 52). Indeed, Hooker is concerned with the indifference of many of his auditors, who, even if benevolent, do not take the minister seriously when they subscribe to the broad generalities of the Church's teachings. In other of his sermons he often addressed himself especially to those who would not have the minister interfere with their personal lives,[10] who maintained that

---

[10] In the following document at n. 5 a parallel passage to *Spiritual Munition* (p. 44) is quoted from *The Souls Preparation* (London, 1632), pp. 74 f. In that sermon (p. 66), we also find Hooker observing with indignation: "Why a company of gentlemen, yeomen, and poor women, that are scarcely able to know their A.B.C., yet they have a minister to speak Latin, Greek, and Hebrew, and to use the Fathers, when it is certain, they know nothing at all. The reason is, because all this stings not, they may sit and sleep in their sins, and go to hell hood-wincked, never awakened, and that is the reason they will welcome such to their houses, and say, 'Oh, he is an excellent man, I would give anything I might live under his ministery!' "

the ministers' words must not be taken too literally,[11] and who tried to defeat the "aiming minister," whose purpose it is to bring about a radical commitment to reform in a strict, Puritan way.

Hooker's view that the ministry and magistracy share coordinate responsibilities, and that political and religious loyalties are interdependent, is traditional enough and could not easily be held against him by suspicious anti-Puritan forces. The civil consequences of the minister's work are outlined in a special point of the sermon: they involve men's obedience to the "governors that are set over them" (p. 48) as well as "blessings in the stations wherein God hath set them" (p. 48). But Hooker also warns the ministers not to fall prey to the interests of the rich and powerful in the parish, and he advices them instead to be first of all devoted to "the saints which excel" (p. 46). Furthermore, it can be expected that many of the ministers present at the burial shared Hooker's Puritan ideals. They would and could, of course, apply Hooker's words to the specific situation of Puritan preachers. (The open Laudian suppression of Puritan lecturers, of which Hooker, too, was to become a victim, had not yet set in.) Moreover, the scripture text, 2 Kg. 2:12, which Hooker chooses for Wilmot's funeral sermon, was very popular for the burial of ministers. Hugh Peter preached the funeral sermon for William Ames on the same text on November 14, 1633, in Rotterdam.[12] Many New England divines, among them Increase and Cotton Mather, had their funeral sermons preached on this text or on the passing of the mantle from Elijah to Elisha in the next verse, 2 Kg. 2:13.[13]

[11] Those that make excuses by supposing that the minister cannot mean all he preaches because "he must say something" are singled out by Hooker in such sermons as *The Souls Vocation or Effectual Calling to Christ* (London, 1638), p. 358, and *The Unbelievers Preparing For Christ* (London, 1638), p. 79. Cf. also Document III, p. 91.

[12] Raymond Phineas Stearns, *The Strenuous Puritan: Hugh Peter, 1598–1660* (Urbana, 1954), p. 85. Stearns quotes Stephen Goffe who reports that "to make himselfe the inheritor of his Spirit they say he preached in Dr. Ames his cloake."

[13] Increase Mather had two funeral sermons preached on the Elijah-Elisha theme: Cotton Mather's *A Father Departing* (Boston, 1723), and Benjamin Colman's *The Prophet's Death Lamented and Improved* (Boston, 1723). Thomas Prince used the Elijah-Elisha parallel in his funeral sermon for Cotton Mather: *The Departure of Elijah Lamented* (Boston, 1728). Andrews, op. cit., and H. M. Martin, "Ramus, Ames, Perkins and Colonial Rhetoric," *Western*

The structure of *Spiritual Munition* follows the conventional Puritan method. Hooker draws three doctrines from the scripture verse; two from the first part, one from the second. He mentions one possible further doctrine from the first part, but he does not treat it as such; rather, he uses it after the eulogy as the second use of the third doctrine. Typical of Hooker, the first two doctrines are not only general propositions, but also express moral obligations and practical duties.

Hooker's pastoral intent can best be observed in the uses, which take up the largest part of his sermons. *Spiritual Munition* does not gain a specific organic unity by building up from impassionate reasoning to an emotional accelerando. Aside from the fact that Hooker has to move three times from doctrine to uses, and that he has to include the eulogy, he incorporates direct appeals to the emotions and the will throughout the sermon without too much concern for the schematic exigencies of sermon theory. Hooker's rhetoric aims at his auditors' involvement at all levels. He uses the father-son analogy and the war imagery of the scriptural text for logical demonstration, and he employs their emotional potential. He reasons with his hearers. He shows a realistic appraisal of their feelings when he imagines and answers their objections, and he constantly puts words in their mouths, especially when he includes prayers and even confession-like passages. All these strategies, which are characteristic of most of Hooker's sermons, aim above all at practical application toward a change in attitudes, dispositions, and acts.

Spiritual Munition was not published until 1638, when it was included in *The Souls Possession of Christ*. It was printed from rather short notes. Our edition has corrected the scriptural references and completed quotations when necessary. We incorporate the marginal references into the text in order to make it more readable and closer to what Thomas Hooker preached at the grave of Robert Wilmot.

Speech, XXIII (Spring, 1959), 74–82, list as further examples: John Barnard's funeral sermon for Samuel Cheever: *Elijah's Mantle* (Boston, 1724), and Thomas Foxcroft's sermon for Benjamin Wadsworth: *Elisha Lamenting after the God of Elijah* (Boston, 1737).

DOCUMENT I

Spiritual Munition: A Funeral Sermon; June 22, 1626

2 Kg. 2:12   *"And Elisha saw it, and he*
cried, My father, my father,
the chariots of Israel, and
the horsemen thereof."

When the Lord had revealed that he would take away Elijah in a whirlwind, as appears in the first verse of this chapter, you shall observe that Elisha, one that lived with him and was trained up by him, did two things: first, he followed him marvelous closely while he lived, and secondly, he mourned for him at his death. The Lord sent posthaste for Elijah to heaven, and in a fiery chariot transports him thither. Now when Elisha could see him no more nor enjoy him any longer, then he crieth out: "O my father, my father." As though he had said: 'Elijah is now gone; he is past all recovery. Yet though he be a gainer, we are all losers, having lost a main prop and support unto us. Therefore I cannot but breathe and pant after him, O my father, my father.' In the verse I have read, you may observe two things: first, the affection of Elisha to his master; secondly, the commendation or description of Elijah. The words repeated imply his passion, as that of David, 2 Sam. 18:33: "O Absalom, my son, my son! Would God I had died for thee. O Absalom, my son, my son!"

First, the affection of this holy man appeareth in three things: first, his honorable esteem of him: "father"; secondly, his humble subjection to him: "My father"; thirdly, his lamentation and mourning for him: "O my father"; [wherein] the great grief and passion of his soul appears by "rending" and tearing "his clothes apieces," as you may see in the chapter.[1]

[1] i.e., the same verse.

41

I begin with the first. The word "father" is sometimes taken for a word of nature, as a natural father; sometimes it signifies a term of time discovering antiquity, as "fathers in Israel," that is, such as are aged, of long continuance and standing in the church. The point hence is this:

Doctrine: The ministers of God should be as fathers to the people. And this appears in three things. First, they should have a staidness and gravity both of spirit and life. 1 Tim. 4:12: "Let no man despise thy youth," saith Paul to Timothy, "but be an example in life and doctrine." If thou livest holily without exception, and yet men will speak against thee, thine heart tells thee[2] they lie; let them rail their fill. Secondly, in regard of the power and authority committed unto them by God. Paul had a rod as well as meek words [1 Cor. 4:21]. Ministers must be fathers, not cockerers nor flatterers of men. Thirdly, in regard of the instruction that they give unto the people, which must be according as their necessity and ability requireth. They must be, Is. 40:11 [Job 29:15], "eyes to the blind," ears to the deaf, and "feet to the lame."

Use 1: First, this should teach the Lord's watchmen to shine as burning lamps, to be examples of piety and strict obedience in their several places. Alas, what is it to have the highest place and the basest practice, the best calling and the worst kind of living?

Use 2: Secondly, it should instruct you that are hearers to deal with the ministers of God's word as with fathers. You must not despise them in a captious, censorious manner, undervaluing the Lord's worthies as many do. 1 Tim. 5:1: "Rebuke not an elder," saith St. Paul, "but intreat him as a father." It is not for a child to call the father to his tribunal. Do we see anything in the minister that is faulty, we should mourn for it, and wisely suggest it to him. [Col. 4:17]: "Say to Archippus," saith St. Paul; he doth not bid you control Archippus. But here mistake me not. It is a point of popery to believe and do in all things as the minister saith or doth. But we must search the scriptures, and try men's doctrines whether they be according to God or not. This is one passage.

[2] The imprint has *them*.

"My father"

Here is further set down the dear and respectful carriage of Elisha unto Elijah. Whence observe:

Doctrine 2: That loving subjection is that which all people ought to give unto those that are in the place of the ministry. Heb. 13:17: "Submit yourselves." What Elisha himself did, all the sons of Elisha will likewise do. Now this appears in three things.

First, they must have a reverend esteem of them and [of] the places unto which God hath called them, Gal. 4:14, 1 Th. 5:13. They must entertain them as ambassadors, as co-workers[3] with the Son for their salvation to bring the poor creature and his creator together that they may be one. Men are apt to say: 'Ministers are weak and passionate and full of failings.' Why, brethren, who is not so? It is our happiness that we have this heavenly treasure in earthen vessels.[4] Should God speak to us face to face, who were able to abide him?

Secondly, submitting and subjecting ourselves to the truths delivered. Tell not me of entertaining a minister, or bidding him to your table. Thou must subject thy soul to the Word, and labor to be under the power of divine truths revealed. Otherwise thou dost but despise the minister all the while thou slightest and disobeyest his ministry. You should say as Samuel did [1 Sam. 3:10]: "Speak Lord, thy servant heareth," and as St. Paul [Acts 9:6]: "Lord, what wilt thou have me to do?" If a command come, the soul should readily perform it; if a reproof, the soul should willingly bear it, and not repine in a fretting manner, saying: 'He aimed at me, and I care not if I never hear him more.' Brethren, this is not subjection but pride and rebellion against God and his truth. This ought not to be amongst Christians. If any man seem to quarrel and take up arms against the word of the Almighty, let that man know that his doom sleeps not, for God will certainly slay all such stubborn and stiff-necked rebels that refuse to have him rule over them. Strive therefore for a yielding, submissive spirit; get a frame of soul

---

[3] 2 Cor. 5:20; 6:1; 1 Cor. 3:9.
[4] 2 Cor. 4:7.

willing to be taught of God, to be disposed of by him in everything, to receive any impression which he shall stamp upon thee.
When thou art to hear the Word, beg a teachable mind, and say:
'Good Lord, let thy servant now hear a seasonable word. Quicken
these dead bones here before thee. Speak home to my conscience,
wound my corruptions, slay these sins that are too hard for me, let
no iniquity prevail over thy poor servant, but let Jesus Christ be all
in all to and in me. Take this heart of mine, and frame it, and alter
it, and mold it, and melt it. Work thine own will in me, fashion me
to thy kingdom of grace here that I may partake of thy kingdom
of glory hereafter.'

A good heart will not fume and vex to see his pollutions ripped
open, but lay things close to his conscience, and bless God for
this light, and say: 'Blessed be his good word and his poor servant
that met this day with my sins. I never observed that pride, I never
discovered that fraud and guile of spirit, I never took notice of such
swarms of lusts lurking in my soul as now I find. What became of
Christ I cared not, what became of his ministers I valued not, what
became of the name and honor and gospel of the Lord Jesus I regarded not. But now I see the evil of my ways, and blessed be
God for that good work which hath been communicated to my
soul by his servant.'

It is a fearful thing when men deal with their sins as David did
with Absalom. 2 Sam. 18:5: "Do not kill him, but deal kindly with
the young man for my sake." Such men's spirits are as yet very little
in subjection to God, and they may well be ranked amongst the
opposers of him and his ministers.[5]

Thirdly, this further appears by a free, willing serviceableness
unto those that are faithful in the work of the Lord for our good.
The Galatians, 4:15, would have pulled out their eyes to have done
St. Paul good, and would have parted with their dearest friends and
best commodities to be partakers of his ministry.

Thus you see: first, that Christians ought to have a due respect

---

[5] The preceding two paragraphs are similar to a passage in *The Souls Preparation* (London, 1632) pp. 74f. A comparison between the two passages affords
a good example of how the same substance can occur in different stylistic make-
ups in Hooker's sermons.

of God's messengers; secondly, they ought to submit themselves to the ambassage they deliver; thirdly, they ought to be serviceable unto them in all things.

Use 1: The use of this is for instruction, to teach us to depend and wait upon God in the use of the ministry. These are the conduit-pipes of grace. Children they go still to their father's house to be fed or clothed. So it should be with us.

Use 2: This likewise may reprove two sorts of people. First, those that instead of doing good unto a faithful minister, labor what they can to root him out, and instead of subjection to the Word by him delivered, they set up and maintain rebellion against it. If your wounds once be lanced, your corruptions discovered, and the punishment due unto them flung upon your faces, so as you can have no quiet in a sinful course, then presently all the town is in an uproar, and cry: 'Away with this fellow,[6] he shall not tarry here long.' Brethren, is he a dutiful son that would cast his father out of doors? A son? No, a slave to the devil, and a rebel against the Lord Almighty, fitter for a prison to torment him than a house to harbor him. It is a certain sign that the soul never had grace, which opposeth the ministers of grace. This is a fearful symptom of an unsound heart, and wherever it is, clearly evidences that God hath forsaken that soul. For, alas, it is not a poor weak man which they oppose, but the great God himself who shines forth in them, as they shall one day woefully find and feel with sorrow.

Secondly, this falls heavy upon all close-hearted hypocrites, "those whited walls"[7] that run with the hare and hold with the hound, who though they give way unto the minister sometimes, yet it is but to serve their own terms, to effect their own ends. They make the minister their stalking-horse to procure their own profit or credit by; and if their aims fall not out, but their expectation is crossed and their desires frustrated, then—for shame of the world they dare not persecute a good minister openly yet—they secretly revile and speak against him, saying: 'Would I had never known such a man. He is able to make one run mad.' If any man now have such a stubborn heart and distempered soul, that he will not subject

[6] Acts 22:22.
[7] Acts 23:3, Mt. 23:27.

to the word of God, he cannot have any true peace. Happily[8] he may have peace in the world, but he shall have gall enough in his conscience.

Objection: Some will say: 'I like such a man very well, and I could love and respect one minister dearly but not another.'

Answer: Hold thy tongue for shame. Is not the truth alike in all? Why then dost thou discover such gross hypocrisy as to be a respecter of persons? If he be a faithful minister, and thou canst not find in thy heart to receive him and highly esteem [of] him, it is a sign that thou hast no grace.

Objection: 'Oh, but he hath wronged me in this or that matter!'

Answer: But the word of God did never wrong you. This argueth a desperate disposition, that thou art rotten and unsound at heart. When thou respectest thine own private ends of profit, pleasure, credit, or the like, above the word of God, this plainly demonstrates that thy eye is not single[9] and that thou lovest not God for himself.

Use 3: This therefore should mind the messengers of God chiefly to respect and tender those that yield subjection to the message which they deliver. Oh, brethren, let us that are of the ministry most esteem of them, most prize them that love God and his word! The rich man, it may be, sitteth highest at the table, but they that love the Lord should be most respected by us, loved of us. It is true, happily, they have weaknesses and frailties, yet if you delight in God, affect and cleave to these. Let the rout of drunkards and all graceless miscreants encourage one another in their base courses, and extol these that work most mischief among them. Never let thy soul enter into these men's secrets, but beg of God that "the saints which excel" [10] may be the only excellent ones in thy thoughts and esteem as this blessed man here did.

"O my father, my father."

Wherein we might further observe that the loss of a faithful minister is a matter of great mourning and lamentation. But I leave

[8] i.e., haply, perhaps.
[9] Mt. 6:22, Lk. 11:34.
[10] 1 Cor. 14:12.

that, and come now to the commendation of Elijah.

"The chariots[11] of Israel and the horsemen thereof."

These words, "chariots" and "horsemen," are spoken by way of similitude, and do figuratively demonstrate the defense and protection of Israel. For in ancient times they went to war with iron chariots, and those were counted most strong that had most of these. Therefore the hearts of the children of Israel were daunted when they perceived that the Canaanites had iron chariots. Horses are warlike creatures of great strength, as both our own and former times have experienced. [Ps. 20:7]: "Some trust in chariots, and some in horsemen," saith David. The like we may read [in] Jg.4:3.

Doctrine 3: The point that I would commend from hence is that faithful ministers are the defenders of states, churches, and commonwealths. God biddeth Elijah [in] 1 Kg. 19, verse 16, to anoint Jehu king over Israel, and Elisha to be prophet in his room. And it is observable that when the sword of Jehu and his army did not hit, then the sword of Elisha prevailed; his prayers wrought a greater slaughter among the enemies than all their weapons of war could do. The reasons hereof are four.

Reason 1: Faithful ministers by their fervent prayers and supplications stop the wrath and indignation of the Lord, and so keep back judgment from us, as Moses stood in the gap, Num. 16:48. Nay, they do not only turn away God's anger and displeasure from a land or people, but are a means oftentimes of bringing it upon the adversaries of goodness, 2 Kg. 1:10. Take heed therefore of wronging a praying minister. You know David, 2 Sam. 15:31, besought the Lord that he would confound the policy of Ahithophel, and his request was granted. Prayer is of great force. It will bring punishment upon a man, and he shall not know who hurt him.

Reason 2: Again, faithful ministers reveal the sins of the people with whom they live, and labor to work them to humiliation and godly repentance, that they may turn unto the Lord, which is the ready course to turn away judgments. Oh, brethren, we fear the sword! We may justly do so; but let me tell you: it is not the weakness of our land, nor the power of the enemy, that can so much

[11] Hooker, in the original text, uses *charrets*, the older word for *chariots* that had been used both in the Geneva Version and the Authorized Version of 1611.

hurt us as our treacherous hearts at home. These swarms of unruly lusts and corruptions which we carry about in our breasts and harbor in our bosoms daily, do us more hurt than all the world besides. Our sins are they which lay us open to God's judgments more than anything else. Now, a faithful minister endeavors to turn away sin, and so by consequence the wrath of God incensed thereby, from a place. It is a great deal of good that a Samuel may do, 1 Sam. 7:3.

Reason 3: By this the hearts of men are made willing to yield obedience to the governors that are set over them. It makes men studious of God's honor, faithful to their religion and country, industrious in doing good in their places, and strict with their God in all conditions and relations whatsoever. This brings men to be blessings in the stations wherein God hath set them, to live desired, and die lamented, 2 Chr. 20:20. Whilst Jehoiada lived, we read how all things prospered. The gospel flourished and piety was advanced throughout the kingdom. But when he died, his son[12] fell quickly to abominable and wicked courses, and the Lord soon overthrew him, his kingdom and all. So that that which makes men loyal and true-hearted, and hinders the overflowing scourge from seizing upon a nation, that must needs be the defense of that nation; for it is a certain truth: he that is disloyal to the king of heaven can never be loyal to the king of earth.

Reason 4: This putteth courage into the hearts of people. Sinful and base courses fill a man with continual fears and discouragements. 2 Chr. 15:2: "The Lord is with us whilst we cleave to him, but if we forsake him, he will forsake us." It is wonderful to see what a good minister can do in a good war, how he can fight against [Eph. 6:12] "principalities, and powers, and spiritual wickedness in high places," not fearing the face of man. The clear knowledge of this, that the battle he fights is the Lord's, assures him that the Lord will fight for him. Any coward will fight when he is assured of victory beforehand. A good cause will make men spend their dearest blood. When a man hath God to go before him, and the Word to warrant

---

[12] i.e., King Jehoash. Hooker calls him Jehoiada's son because of the special relationship between the priest and the king. Jehoiada brought Jehoash to the throne and had a beneficial influence on his reign. After he died Jehoash is said to have fallen into idolatry (2 Chr. 24:2; 24:15–18).

him in what he doth, he goes through thick and thin. We see with what joy and cheerfulness the martyrs sacrificed their lives to the flames.

Use 1: This shows that those which are the enemies to God's faithful ministers are the greatest adversaries that the Church or State hath; for they spoil the munition of the land. If a man should take away all the munition of England, and transport it into Spain,[13] every man will say he is a traitor. So if thou hast set thyself to oppose and secretly undermine any that is a true faithful minister of Jesus Christ, know, thou art a traitor to thy King and country, because thou persecutest him who labors in his place to keep back wrath from seizing upon the land. Be humbled therefore, take notice of this crying sin, and let it not be once named amongst you, as becometh Christians.

So much for the text. Now a word or two of the occasion.

If I should say no more, nay if I had said nothing at all, the example here present would be a visible interpretation of this text. The very carcass standing before you makes good the truth that I have now delivered. He is dead; we shall be so. Let us live as he did, that we may enjoy the end of our hope, as no doubt he fully doth. Brethren, while he lived here, he was a father in our Israel, not for years but for grace. It is not continuance of time but ripeness of parts that makes a man ancient; and though he be departed, yet that dead trunk speaketh unto us, and the dead body saith, though the inhabitant be gone, it once carried about it a holy life, a sincere heart, an unspotted conversation.

Nay, I may add further: he was a "chariot and horseman of Israel." He was in the forefront of the battle, a main defender of the faith of Christ. Witness, brethren, the heart-breaking sighs and earnest prayers that he put up to the Lord in the days of his humiliation. If any sins were stirring, or any iniquity abounding, he labored by fasting and prayer to oppose the same. I knew him sometimes in Cambridge in his younger days, at which time the Lord had wonderfully enriched him with spiritual gifts in the exercise whereof he was so industrious that he did weary himself and even consume his

---

[13] On Spain as the perpetual enemy of England, see the introduction to Document II, pp. 54f.

spirits by reason of his constancy in holy duties. He was so taken with love of the Lord Jesus and his blessed truths, that he was fain to be checked and by many good friends to be hindered in his pious service and endeavors.

How oft hath he stood in the gap and labored by fervent prayers to avert God's wrath and remove his heavy judgements! Witness his strong cries and intercessions to the Almighty in the time of common calamity when the pestilence raged so violently amongst us.[14] Witness also those painful employments that he took up [2 Tim. 4:2] "in season and out of season, exhorting, rebuking with all long-suffering and patience"; sometimes alluring the heart with sweet promises, otherwhile denouncing[15] vengeance and threatening judgment against obstinate sinners; preaching ordinarily every Lord's day, and extraordinarily upon the week, as occasion was offered, for the good of his people. Witness also—and I pray, brethren, think of that—the many sweet comforts and heavenly consolations wherewith he refreshed and supported many a fainting soul. Thus this blessed saint weakened his body and wasted his spirits out of love to Christ's little flock, which now he enjoys the fruit and comfort of; for though our grief cannot be expressed, having sustained so great a loss, yet it cheereth my heart, methinks, how now he resteth from all his labors. Oh, the sweet repose that he enjoys! Now his eyes that were full of tears, and his tongue that did almost cleave to the roof of his mouth, for the good of the Church, do all cease and lie still. We leave his precious soul in the hands of his Maker, and his body to be laid in the dust, there to sleep in a bed of down until the trump shall awake both him and us all at the great day of appearing.

Use 2: Again, are faithful ministers the help and fortress of a nation? Then the loss of an able true-hearted minister is to be greatly mourned for. "O my father, my father!" saith good Elisha. So though we must leave this our dear brother, yet let us look after him as he did. He looked wishly[16] on him, had his eye fixed constantly toward him. And when he could see him no more, he crieth out: "O my father, my father!"

[14] Hooker is referring to the plague of 1625, one of the worst in English history.
[15] i.e., announcing.
[16] i.e., full of longing.

Why should not we bewail this great loss of ours in like manner? Methinks every one of us should take up this sorrowful complaint. Methinks your spirits should relent and mourn at such an object. Yea, I am persuaded, many here present do so. Methinks I hear one say: ' "O my father" by whom I was converted!'; and another: ' "O my father" by whom I was directed!'; a third: ' "O my father" by whom my soul was comforted!' and the little children that are left fatherless; they cry: ' "O my father" by whom I was begotten, maintained, and nourished in spiritual things!'

Brethren, let us look after him, though we must now part with him, yet let us call to mind all his prayers, and humiliation, and fasting, and supplications to the throne of grace. All his tears are now dried up, all his complaints are now finished, all his pains and labors are now accomplished, and he to receive a plentiful reward of them. Let us mourn for our neglect of the means of salvation whiles he lived amongst us. Oh, his labor and tears and painful studying are now all gone!; they are now in heaven whither he himself is gone before us. The Lord give us to follow his steps that, we finishing our course as he did, our latter end may be like unto his.

Use 3: To conclude briefly. Is one of "the horsemen of Israel" gone? Are the "chariots of Israel" taken away? What must we then do? Certainly we should double our forces now and make a new press, because a general is slain. The Lord hath brought us hither at this time. O let us lay this doleful spectacle to heart and be affected therewith as we ought! I should speak as if I were never to speak more. You should hear as if you were never to hear more.

Men, fathers, and brethren, what hath befallen this saint before you may be any of our portions ere long. We know not how soon death may knock at our doors. Our times are in God's hand, who can take us to himself when he pleaseth. Happily this day may be thy last day, and this very season the last opportunity that ever thou mayest have to meet God in his ordinances. O therefore be encouraged to add one prayer more! Go home, I beseech you, and consider with the departure of this our dear friend how many prayers and tears are departed with him; how did he importune the Lord for the good of the whole land in general, and for the country and place wherein he lived in particular. Think you all his earnest striving with God was in vain? Or seemeth it a small thing in your eyes to lose so many fervent, effectual supplications? I beseech you, lay it to heart, and every man in his place put to his helping hand for repairing of so great a loss. Now make a press of prayers, raise up armies of petitions; go your ways home, be humbled, pray one prayer more, that the army may be increased still.

You that were of his parish and enjoyed the work of his ministry, oh, you have lost a good pastor, a faithful laborer in God's harvest, one that had a longing desire after your salvation! But know this: however your provocations are increased, yet the Lord—who for your sins hath made this breach among you—hath further blessings in store, if you seek to him. He can supply your place again with a faithful, able minister, and with a courageous general.

Therefore, brethren, if ever you pray, pray now; if ever you fast, now fast; if ever you humble yourselves, now be humbled in dust and ashes before the Lord. Never more need, never greater want. By this means the land will be strengthened, and our peace and safety continued. What though our enemies are many and our sins great, fervent prayer hath to do with a God stronger and mightier than they all. This will undermine the most subtile underminers of God's truth. And, children, therefore set yourselves seriously upon the work; however the flesh is awkward, yet stir up and provoke your spirits hereunto. It will never repent you upon your deathbeds of your prayers and tears put up unto God. It will be a great refreshment to your drooping soul at that day, if you can say in truth as Hezekiah did [2 Kg. 20:3]: "Good Lord, remember how I have walked uprightly before thee." This is that which will continue a man's comfort and support his soul in the greatest extremity. An unpraying heart is a dismal thing. Therefore be encouraged to the duty: pray, pray, pray!

DOCUMENT II

The Church's Deliverances; November 5, 1626

Introduction

The yearly observance of November 5, the day of the gunpowder plot of 1605, was instituted as a day of public thanksgiving by an act of Parliament in January, 1606; and when Thomas Hooker preached *The Church's Deliverances* as a thanksgiving sermon some twenty years later, he had already a set of conventions and an official historiography on which he could draw. The events leading to November 5, 1605, and the discovery of the Catholic conspirators, were well publicized at the trials, the proceedings of which were printed soon afterwards.[1] But Hooker does not recount the sequence of events. Rather, he makes use of some of the well-known facts to illustrate how great the danger was from which the Lord had to deliver England, and briefly alludes to the cellar under Parliament where the conspirators were able to ship the barrels of powder across the Thames from their house in Lambeth on the other side of the river (p. 68). He describes more fully the malice of the plot against the established order, echoing the wording of the formal indictment by Sir Edward Phillips, his Majesty's Sergeant-at-Law, at the trial[2] (p. 69 f). As a third point he specifically mentions the holy communion taken by each conspirator after the oath of conspiracy (p. 70).

As other preachers had done before him, Hooker calls the plot hellish and attributes it to Satan. He does not, however, dramatize the connection any further. He does not, as was frequently done,

[1] *A true and perfect relation of the whole proceedings against the late most barbarous traitors* (London, 1606). The work was included in *The Gunpowder Treason: with a discourse of its discovery; and a perfect relation of the proceedings against the conspirators; wherein is contained their trials and condemnations, also the confessions of Guido Fawkes and Thomas Winter: Likewise King James's Speech to Both Houses of Parliament* . . . 1609, and reprinted in 1679.
[2] Ibid., (London, 1850), p. 91. Cf. also the Document at nn. 13 and 15.

picture Satan as the first conspirator, or imply that the use of gunpowder under Parliament was a part of Satan's effort to create a
miniature hell.[3] Nor does Hooker demonize the gunpowder, which
in Book VI of *Paradise Lost* is to be Satan's supreme weapon against
God. This sermon does not identify it as the infernal fire, the hellish
perversion of God's heavenly thunderbolt.[4] But Hooker is very
much within the gunpowder tradition when he depicts God spiting
his enemies, anticipating their machinations before they even conceive them, and knowing the unsuccessful outcome beforehand.
While the conspirators go about their hellish plotting instigated by
the devil himself, God "sits in heaven and sees all, and laughs at
them" (p. 64). These words of the Psalmists (Ps. 2:4) inspired many
preachers (as well as Milton in his brief *In Quintum Novembris*)
to mock the pretentious futility of the gunpowder conspiracy.[5]

Hooker's sermon is a powerful reminder that the God of Israel
is acting in history, and that he has done so on the side of the
Protestants in general and of England in particular. For Englishmen
of the early seventeenth century there was a remarkable continuity
in the history of defeats which Protestant England had dealt to the
Spaniards abroad and to the Catholics at home. Hooker, like his
countrymen, sees the discovery of the gunpowder plot as an act of
God in line with the accession of Elizabeth in 1558 and the defeat
of the Spanish Armada in 1588 (p. 67 f). The same national senti-
ment is graphically represented in the frontispiece of a thanksgiving
sermon of the time,[6] which shows Queen Elizabeth and King James
holding banners depicting the Armada and the gunpowder plot,
both standing behind *Ecclesia Vera*, a symbolic figure of the Church
of England, who is crowned with Canterbury Cathedral and is tram-
pling on the Pope, a cardinal, and the devil.

In *The Church's Deliverances* Hooker makes an emotional appeal
to his auditors to show themselves worthy of God's past mercies,

---

[3] Stella P. Revard, "Milton's Gunpowder Poems and Satan's Conspiracy,"
Milton Studies IV (1972), 64.
[4] Ibid., p. 66.
[5] Ibid., p. 63.
[6] The frontispiece of G. Carleton's *A Thankfull Rememberance of Gods
Mercie* (1624) is reproduced in Hugh Ross Williamson, *The Gunpowder Plot*
(London, 1951), facing p. 156. The description is given on p. 14.

and to be thankful and confident. Both thankfulness and confidence were deemed necessary in view of the current political situation and very recent experiences, such as the plague of 1625, which make themselves felt throughout the sermon. In the mid-1620's, Spain, the perpetual enemy of England, appeared stronger than ever. The Thirty Years' War was raging on the continent, and the Protestant cause was in jeopardy. That there had as yet been no military action on British soil seemed further proof of God's special mercy for England. As Hooker expresses it in the sermon: "the Lord hath had an eye unto me above all the rest, when the fire of God's fury hath flamed and consumed all the country round about us, Bohemia and the Palatinate, and Denmark; when the fire hath thus burnt up all; yet this little cottage, this little England, this span of ground, that this should not be searched?" (p. 67). Indeed, Bohemia and the Palatinate[7] exemplified the fate that would befall Protestant England if God despite all past deliverances made true his threat to "deliver no more," as the scripture text of *The Church's Deliverances* warns. Hooker goes to great lengths in pointing to the many symptoms which to him indicate that England is about to lose her special role as the Lord's "mirror of mercies" [8] because her people have proved unworthy. He singles out the commonness and openness of sin, the neglect or abuse of the means of reformation, especially of preaching, and the contempt for the few righteous—all of which he finds observable in the England of his time; and he predicts God's wrath unless the preacher's passionate call for a radical reformation is

[7] Cf. also Hooker's Farewell Sermon, *The Danger of Desertion* (Document VII), p. 232. About the same time that Hooker preached *The Church's Deliverances*, Hugh Peter, another leading Puritan, in London on November 7, 1626, concludes his sermon from Rom. 6:23 imploringly: "Shall we after all thy mercys be damned? God forbid. How hath God wept over England. Com lord knock one more & enter; give us holy consideration to thinke for what we drudge, & finding hell our end, let us abhorre ourselves. Hast thou dealt so with Bohemia & the Palatinate? Bow & buckle our harts at last." The notes taken by one of Peter's auditors were published in "Letters and Documents by or relating to Hugh Peter," ed. with notes by Raymond P. Stearns, *Essex Institute Historical Collections* LXXI:4 (October 1935), 306–309. The quotation is from p. 308 f.

[8] *The Danger of Desertion* (Document VIII), p. 232. The whole concept has been treated in Arthur Marvin Breslow, *A Mirror of England. English Puritan Views of Foreign Nations, 1618–1640* (Cambridge, 1970).

heeded.[9] The plague of 1625 had apparently failed to bring about this reformation,[10] and Hooker has only to remind his hearers of Lev. 26[11] (pp. 80 f.), where the sword is said to follow the plague, to give his exhortations a special urgency in view of the prevailing fear of an imminent Spanish invasion (p. 81).

Hooker does not hesitate to burden each individual with a spiritual responsibility for the course of history. It is the sinfulness or the power of godliness of each individual which will decide the outcome of the temporal struggle between nations. Whether the covenant which God made with England is broken or continued is also the corporate responsibility which first of all rests with the magistracy and the ministry. In Hooker's thought both coordinately share the duty to prevail upon the people to make use of the means of grace which God has provided for them, and to further the reformation.[12] In this and in other of his sermons,[13] Hooker points to "foretelling signs" which demonstrate that God is losing patience with England but is still waiting for his people to change their sinful ways. It is indeed this hope of yet another chance which gives the rhetoric of the sermon its greatest momentum. By 1630 Hooker seems to have become convinced that England's days as God's special people were over; the radical reformation that he had called for during the many years of his preaching could not be wrought. When he left England for Holland he preached his farewell sermon once again on "the

[9] For another example of the many warnings given out by Puritan preachers, cf. also Thomas Brightman's insistence that God's favor will depart from England "unless we meet him speedily with fruits worthy of true repentance, and of his glorious Gospell." (Quoted in William M. Lamont, *Godly Rule: Politics And Religion, 1603-60* (London and New York, 1969).

[10] Hugh Peter, op. cit., p. 308 also complains that many promises and sick vows were made during the plague but few were kept.

[11] To see Lev. 26 applied to the current situation must have been quite familiar to congregations in 1626. For a sermon which employs much the same rhetorical strategies as Hooker see William Hampton, *A Proclamation of Warre From the Lord of Hosts or Englands warning by Israels ruine: Shewing the miseries like to ensue upon us by reason of Sinne and Securitie. Delivered in a Sermon at Pauls Crosse July the 23, 1626* (London, 1627). Hampton also sees the plague of 1625 and the expected Spanish invasion as certain signs that England, which has been "the eye of Europe . . . *terra frugifera*, a fruitfull land, fitly resembling the land of Canaan" (p. 11) is ripe for God's judgment.

[12] Cf. also Document I and Document VII, p. 234.

[13] Cf. Document IV and VII.

signs of God forsaking a people," and this time he came closer than ever to forecasting England's destruction (cf. Document VII).

In dating *The Church's Deliverances* one encounters difficulties that are typical of almost all Hooker's sermons in England. The date of delivery is not given; the date of publication is misleading. This sermon was not published until 1638, when it was included in the *Four Learned and Godly Treatises.* Its scripture text was entered in the Stationers' Register April 8, 1637, together with Hooker sermons from others texts which later appeared as *The Souls Exaltation* and *The Unbelievers Preparing for Christ.* The dating must therefore be based on internal evidence. When Hooker alludes to God's special concern for England "above sixty years" (p. 66), he must be referring to the accession of Elizabeth in 1558; and this would mean that the sermon must have been preached after 1618 and probably before 1628. The allusions to the Thirty Years' War and to Denmark (pp. 66–67) suggest a date after the entry of Christian IV of Denmark (and Norway) into the war. The Danish war began when Tilly crossed the Weser into Lower Saxony in July, 1625. But it was not until November 29/December 9, 1625, that by the Treaty of The Hague Christian IV formally agreed to support Elector Frederick V of the Palatinate against the Catholic forces with the promised help of English and Dutch subsidies. Christian was decisively defeated at the battle of Lutter-am-Barenberge in August, 1626. In 1627 Hutland was invaded and plundered by the imperial forces. A date as late as November 5, 1627, might be considered for the sermon if Hooker's mention of Denmark as being "burnt up" (p. 67) is taken to refer to Jutland; but he may also have been thinking of the Lower Saxon *Kreis* of the Empire, which he calls "Denmark," because Christian IV was its elected director.

The fear of an imminent Spanish invasion which is reflected throughout *The Church's Deliverances* makes 1626 a more likely year of composition than 1625 or 1627. It is true that there was some expectation of a Spanish landing in 1625; Robert Rich, Earl of Warwick, who was to become Hooker's protector by the end of the decade, was appointed land-lieutenant of Essex and was active in making defense preparations.[14] It is equally true that there was

[14] *Cal. St. Papers. Dom., 1625–1626,* p. 102 (September 10).

some fear of an invasion in 1627; in August there were reports of a Spanish landing on the Shetland Islands and the threat of an attack by the Spanish fleet coming from the North.[15] But anticipation of an imminent Spanish invasion was strongest in 1626. The King and his war council as well as both houses of Parliament deliberated measures of defense, especially devising ways to strengthen British naval power and to fortify towns.[16] Reports reaching England seemed to indicate that the Spaniards were about to set sail for the British Isles.[17] Sailors interrogated as to their observations supported these reports.[18] Rumors that the enemy fleet had been sighted near Land's End[19] added to a general feeling of insecurity among the population. People living not far from the coast felt particularly unprotected.[20] On July 10, 1626, the King deemed it necessary to issue a proclamation "commanding all Inhabitants on the Sea-Coastes, or in any Ports or Sea-Townes, to make their speedy repaire unto, and continue at their Habitations there . . . in these times, when an Invasion is threatened." [21] Moreover, had *The Church's Deliverances* been preached in 1625 or 1627 one could expect that Hooker would allude to two other historical events which must have been uppermost in many people's minds. In November, 1625, the ill-fated expedition against Cadiz was under way (the news of its failure reached England in December). November 5, 1627, came only a few days after the British debacle at the Isle of Rhé, when Buckingham to save himself from defeat had to break the siege and return home discomfited; he arrived at Plymouth on November 11 amidst rumors that he had incurred terrible losses.[22] Hooker never mentions Cadiz; nor does he once refer to the hopes

[15] Op. cit., 1627–1628, pp. 312 (August 25), 319 (August 28), 322 (August 29), 327 (August).

[16] Op. cit., 1625–1626, pp. 348 (June 6), 353 (June 14), 356 (June 17), 369 (July 7).

[17] Ibid., pp. 207 (March 31), 313 (April 17), 359 (June 19), 368 (July 6).

[18] Ibid., p. 304 (April 5), 401 (August 11), 408 (August 20), 446 (October 3), 487 (December 4).

[19] Ibid., p. 374 (July 12).

[20] Ibid., pp. 363 (June), 371 (July 8).

[21] Broadside copy at Houghton Library, Harvard University.

[22] Cf. Samuel R. Gardiner, *The Thirty Years' War, 1618–1648* (New York, 1903), p. 114. Samuel R. Gardiner, *History of England from the Accession of James I to the Outbreak of the Civil War, 1603–1642*, VI (London, 1886), 198 ff.

and fears which his parishioners must have felt for the Protestants of Rochelle in the summer and fall of 1627. Therefore it is possible to conclude that the gunpowder plot thanksgiving sermon was preached on November 5, 1626. Hooker was then a lecturer in Chelmsford, which can readily be pictured as "the town" mentioned thrice in his sermon (pp. 76, 77, 77). What is more, November 5, 1626, was a Sunday;[23] and it is likely that Hooker continued the thanksgiving sermon proper (perhaps pp. 68–75) at the Lecture on the following Tuesday (pp. 68 ff.), and that both sermons on Judges 10:13 make up *The Church's Deliverances*, exhibiting Hooker's two sides as a preacher: assuring, and inspiring confidence in God's mercy in one sermon; threatening, and evoking fear of God's wrath in the next.

[23] Christopher Cheney, *Handbook of Dates* (London, 1945), p. 121.

DOCUMENT II

The Church's Deliverances

Jg. 10:13:   *"Wherefore I will deliver you no more."*

These words are the speech of the Lord to the people of Israel. From the sixth verse of the chapter to the end of the seventh we have the condition of the people of Israel in great distress discovered, together with the dealing of God toward them and their behavior toward him.

In the chapter three things are especially considerable. First, we have the children of Israel apostatizing and declining from the Lord and the sincerity of his worship. In the first part of the verse, "Ye have forsaken me, and served other gods," here was the declining of the people of Israel. They forsook the true God and served false gods, and as their sins were, so were their plagues. The Lord pursued them with heavy judgments and fierce indignation. Heinous sins are commonly accompanied with great plagues and punishments, and that appeareth in the ninth verse: "Israel was sore distressed."

Secondly, we have the people of Israel crying and complaining to the Lord in the time of their trouble. They that forsake the Lord in the time of prosperity were fain to fly to him in time of adversity for succor. And therefore we shall see how earnestly they cry unto the Lord in the tenth verse. Heavy afflictions breed hearty prayers and earnest supplications. Their punishment was not so grievous but their prayers were as hot and vehement. "They cried to the Lord," saith the text.

Then lastly, we have the answer of God in the twelfth, thirteenth, and fourteenth verses, where the Lord doth relate his good dealings with them and their unkind dealings toward him: 'I have delivered you,' saith the Lord, 'out of the hand of such and such enemies.' He reckons up his former mercies, but now he doth deny to show

60

any more favor toward them, because they had abused his former mercies, and that is, in the words of the text [verse 13], "Wherefore I will deliver you no more." As who should say: 'Go now to the gods of Sidon; let those idols save you now; let those images deliver you now. But my kindness was not regarded, my mercy was not respected, and for my part I will deliver you no more. Expect no succor from me at all.'

In the general, before we come to the main, see here the denial of the Lord to the people of Israel, though they fought him and cried unto him. The point is this:

Doctrine: Those that come unto God in prayer in their sins, they shall be sure to have a denial of their prayers. Ps. 66:18: "If I regard iniquity in my heart, God will not hear my prayer." So it was here. Though they sought God marvelous earnestly and cried in the vehemency of their spirits, yet the Lord stopped his ears and listened not unto them. He gives no answer unto their cry. He professeth plainly he will not deliver them, he will not succor them.

Use: The use of this point in general is this: first, of instruction, we may here see the reason why we call and God answers not, why we seek the Lord and he is not found of us in mercy and compassion, why we pray unto him and yet he rejects our persons and flings out our petitions and is angry with the prayers of his servants. The cause is, we bring our sins with us before God, and therefore we cannot receive mercy from God. The abominations of our hearts spoil the petitions we pour forth before the Lord, that he neither accepts them nor showeth any favor unto us. When we come before the Lord and bring our sins with us, our pride and our malice and our covetousness, it is not praying but lying and dissembling, and mocking and abusing the great God of heaven. As though we should come before the Lord to ask him leave to sin, and entreat favor of him that we might commit our sins without any disquiet, that he would give us a privy seal to sin. These drunken prayers, these idle, proud, profane prayers and lying prayers, the God of heaven will not hear them when they come from a lying, dissembling, filthy, drunken heart. Thou that bringest such prayers, the Lord will not hear, the Lord will not accept, the Lord will not regard such prayers.

This is the thing I would have wicked men take notice of, that think to heal all in the time of distress with a few large desires and idle wishes. They will be proud and loose and opposers of God and his gospel, and yet you think God cannot but grant you what you desire, if you have but half an hour's warning to ask pardon. No, you that live in your sins, and pray to God in your sins, you bring judgment upon yourselves, and plague upon your souls, but mercy you shall have none, answer you shall not receive in this kind. Pr. 28:9: "The prayer of the wicked [shall be abomination]."

Use 2: The second use is a ground of exhortation. Would you so come to God that you may find acceptance with him? Would you so call that the Lord may hear you when you call? Then wash your hands in innocency and so compass his altar. This is the counsel God gave, Is. 1:16, 17: "Cease to do evil; learn to do well." 'And then whatsoever your abominations be, they shall be pardoned, whatsoever your miseries be, I will ease you.' Ps. 10:17, 18: the Lord prepares the hearts of his people to call upon him, a heart mourning for sin, and a heart loosened from sin. When you leave sin behind you and send up a prayer from an humble heart and a broken soul, then God will hear you, and you shall receive an answer from the God of heaven, as he seeth you have most need to carry you on in a Christian course.

In the [textual] verse there are three things observable. He saith [Jg. 10:13]: 'I will not deliver you; go to your gods; let them comfort you! For my part, I have no comfort, no mercy for such as you are. Those gods you served in prosperity; go to them now for succor in the time of trouble.' In the verse itself take notice of three further things. First, that God doth deliver his church, for that is presumed: "I will deliver you no more"—as who should say—'I have preserved you and protected you, and the like.' God takes this for granted, and they found this by experience. Secondly, God sometimes denieth succor to his people: 'I have done so, but now I will deliver you no more. I have no more mercy for you to succor you in the day of trouble.' Thirdly, we have the cause of this: "Wherefore"—that is, 'because you have served other gods and departed away from my worship, because you will not reform your wicked ways'—"I will deliver you no more."

First, for the former. God doth deliver his Church. The doctrine is this:

Doctrine: The Lord is the deliverer of his Church and people in the time of trouble. The Church is in great misery, it is confessed, and the Church hath been delivered, it cannot be denied. Now I must add the third, namely, that God is the author of the deliverance of his servants.

The Scriptures are marvelous pregnant in the proof of this. Two or three witnesses will cast the cause. [In] Ps. 3:8 the prophet David attributeth this as a matter of propriety to the Lord: "Salvation belongs unto the Lord." It is not to be understood of spiritual redemption only but also of temporal deliverance in the time of trouble. It is that observable [in] Jer. 14:8. It is, as I may so say, one of God's names whereby he is known to his Church, and whereby he shows himself: "O thou the hope of Israel, and the savior thereof in the time of trouble." It is not meant in regard of spiritual redemption still,[1] but in regard of temporal deliverance from those troubles that do betide, and those grievances that lie upon, and those heavy burdens that press down the Church of God. And therefore however it is true, there are many means used and many helps appointed by God for his people's good. Yet it is not men, it is not the policy of the wise, it is not the power of the mighty, it is not the fence of the walls nor the strength of the castles, it is not the number of the soldiers nor the skill of the army, but it is the Lord that is the deliverer of his people. As we may see, Ps. 44:4: "Command thou deliverances unto Jacob." The Lord hath deliverance at command. The Lord can bring, keep, and succor as he sees fit. Nay, it is that which God takes and challengeth to himself as that [which] he will not have any other to share in. He will not have any other part stakes[2] with him in the performance of goodness and mercy to his children. Dt. 32:39: it is that the Lord takes unto himself, "Salvation is mine; preservation is mine." The issues of life and death are only in the hand of the Lord.

The point then is plain enough. We will open the ground of it, the which the cause now requires, being a remembrance of that

---

[1] i.e., yet: "It is not *yet* meant in regard . . ."
[2] i.e., to share.

miraculous deliverance from the gunpowder treason. The grounds of the point are four.

[Reason 1]: The first is this: God is infinitely wise and only knows how to deliver his people. Men are driven to their wits' end many times. They see no means offered, no means appointed. They can find no cause how to succor themselves in the time of distress. But he is an experienced deliverer. 2 Pet. 2:9: God knows how to deliver his. When enemies are practicing beneath and digging deep in their devices, the Lord sits in heaven and sees all, and laughs at them.[3] All their practices, he observes them. Nay, the Lord knows all the purposes, policies, and engines which the wicked purposes to contrive, before they contrive them. As when David was in Keilah, he asked the Lord: 'Will Saul come?' 'Aye,' saith God. 'And will they deliver me into his hands?' 'They will deliver thee,' saith God. The Lord knew what the men of Keilah intended before they showed their malice; therefore he makes way for the escape of David.[4]

[Reason 2]: Secondly, as God only knows, all the engines and policies and practices of the wicked when they are devised in the depth of the earth, as the Psalmist speaketh: 'Let them do what they will, and endeavor what they can ever so cunningly and secretly, the Lord knows them.' But secondly, the Lord is only able and sufficient to deliver his in want of means, above means, nay, against means, 2 Chr. 14:11. When Asa was in great extremity, when there was five hundred thousand came against him, the greatest army we read of in holy scriptures and not many more in profane stories, the text saith: "He cried unto the Lord, and said, thou canst deliver by many or by few." God could save Asa and his nobles though he had no army at all. For observe it, this all-sufficiency and ability of God in delivering his children in time of troubles will discover itself in three branches; and they are the particulars of this second general [reason].

First, the Lord provides means before any means can be. Ps. 47:9:

[3] Ps. 2:4, Ps. 37:13, Ps. 59:8. Cf. also the introduction to the Document, p. 54.
[4] Hooker does not quote directly but rather seems to paraphrase the theme of Ps. 37.

"All the shields of the earth are the Lord's." All the shields in Spain, Germany and Denmark, and England, they are all the Lord's. All means before they are, have their being from the Lord. And [in] Is. 54:16 the text saith there was no smith before God created him, nor no coals before God made them; so that there are no means but they are from God.

Secondly, God works with all means before they can work. As there is no means unless God provide them, so the means that are can do nothing unless God work with them. [In] Ps. 18:34, 39 we shall observe it: God doth not only give David arms but he teacheth his arms to war; he doth not only give David hands but he teaches his hands to fight; he doth not only give him strength but he girdeth him with strength to the battle; so that all means in the world, further than God is pleased to, go out with them. They are like the withered hand of Jeroboam [1 Kg. 13:4]. When the prophet cried against the altar, Jeroboam stretched out his hand, and he would plague the prophet and would imprison him. But, alas, his hand withered. So all the armies, all the plots and policies are like withered hands unless the Lord come with them.

Thirdly, it is the Lord that gives success to all the means when they are improved for the deliverance of his Church. So that as there is no means unless the Lord provide them, as those means can do nothing unless the Lord work with them, so these means can obtain no issue unless the Lord be pleased graciously to breathe upon them and give success unto them. Therefore when the Midianites thought to have carried all before them and quite to overthrow the people of Israel because they had a mighty army, yet the Lord defeated their purpose and turned their swords into their own bowels [Jg. 7].

Thus we see the ability and sufficiency of the Lord in delivering his people. It is he that gives all means; it is he that works with all means; it is he that gives success to all means.

[Reason 3]: In the third place, the Lord is marvelous gracious and merciful and tender over his people. As he is every way sufficient for to do them good, so he is marvelous careful of their good. Is. 63:9: "In all their afflictions he was afflicted." Many a man hath power and wisdom and all; he knows how to help another; yet he wants a heart, he wants pity and compassion whereby he may lend succor to those that stand in need thereof. But it is not so with God; but in all the afflictions of his people he is afflicted with them. In all troubles he is with them. In all banishment he is in banishment with them.

[Reason 4]: Fourthly, as the Lord is merciful and loving and free and tender-hearted toward his people, as ready to help them as they are ready to call upon him, so, lastly, the Lord is marvelous watchful to do that which he is able and willing to do. We know what the text saith, Ps. 121:4: "He that keepeth Israel neither slumbers nor sleeps." Nay, he is exceeding zealous for Israel. That is the phrase of the prophet Jl. 2:18].

Let us sum up the point then and see the issue of all, and the case will be marvelous clear. If it be so that God only knows how to deliver his people, if he be able to do what he knows, if he be merciful to do what he is able, and if he be watchful to do what he is willing, then God must needs be the deliverer of his Church.

We come now to the use of the point, and so we will proceed to the next. It is great pity that we should so behave ourselves that this God should not succor us but say he will deliver us no more. But let us make use of the point in hand. And the use we are to make is this:

Use [1]: Is it so, that the Lord is the author of all the deliverance and succor of his servants? First, then, it must teach us a point of wisdom, namely, to whom we must give the praise of all our marvelous deliverance and preservation we have enjoyed, to whom it is we ought to render all the glory of our protection and safety that hath been continued for the space of above sixty years to this kingdom[5] Do as the prophet David doth. The Lord is the author of all, let the Lord have the honor of all. [Ps. 29:2]: "Give unto the Lord the honor due unto his name." The prophet David doth distrain, as it were; he is violent with the hearts of men, and he labors to wrest praise and honor from men: "Give unto the Lord the honor and the glory due unto his name." The truth is, we must not sacri-

---

[5] Hooker must be referring to the accession of Elizabeth in 1558. Cf. also the introduction to the Document, pp. 54 f.

fice to our own nets;[6] that is, we must not praise our own power and say it is our power that hath accomplished it, and our wisdom that hath effected it. No, it is not our shipping, it is not our power or courage or means that have done it. Therefore let us do as the prophet David doth in the forty-fourth Psalm [6f.]: "It was not my bow that did succor me, it was the Lord that hath delivered me and relieved me, and his be the praise forever." And if all people should do this, and ought to do this, then I had almost said, 'Nay, why may I not say so, why should we not do it more than all the world besides, for whence comes it, whence is it, that the Lord hath had an eye unto me above all the rest, when the fire of God's fury hath flamed and consumed all the country round about us; Bohemia, and the Palatinate, and Denmark;[7] when the fire hath thus burnt up all; yet this little cottage, this little England, this span of ground, that this should not be searched?' Nay, when the sword hath ruinated and overcome all the other parts of Christendom where the name of the Lord Jesus is professed, we sit under our vines and fig trees, there is no complaining in our streets, our wives are not husbandless, our children are not fatherless. Mark the reason and ground of all is nothing else but God's mercy toward us. And above all, here is seen the abundant goodness of the Lord: notwithstanding our unthankfulness and carelessness, we yet continue to be a nation.

There is no other reason to be given of this but God's love will have it so. When as in other countries here one is banished from his house, another from his country, that we are here this day to call upon the name of the Lord, this is evidence enough that it is the Lord that delivers England. And shall the Lord do this, and shall not we acknowledge it, shall not we observe it and remember it forever, shall not we score up the kindness of the Lord, and set up pillars of his preservation and records of his mercy to our souls forever? And above all other deliverances that in '88 was a great deliverance,[8]

---

[6] Hab. 1:16: "Therefore they sacrifice unto their nets, and burn incense unto their drag."

[7] In his Farewell Sermon, *The Danger of Desertion* (Document VII, p. 232), Hooker again uses the example of these countries to contrast the devastation and misery that the Thirty Years' War has brought upon them with the peace that has been enjoyed in England.

[8] The defeat of the Spanish Armada.

but we specially record that upon the fifth of November.[9] This we record unto all posterity. And let us but cast our thoughts upon the malice of our enemies, and then it cannot but be confessed that the Lord hath delivered us. It is the Lord's own work. And this shall appear, if we compare the practice of the wicked and the deliverance of the Lord together agreeably. Three things in the former may be observed, three things in the latter may be considered. And [it] doth show that God only delivered, if we look to the enemies of God's grace and gospel. Three things will make it appear that none but the devil could devise that plot. And if, on the other side, we consider the succor and deliverance the Lord did lend, it will appear that none but the Lord could deliver us and succor and relieve us.

Let us consider three things in the gunpowder plot. First, observe their policy; secondly, their malice; thirdly, their stoutness, whereby it will appear that they intended the whole ruin, not only of us but of the gospel. They thought to have carried out the matter so cunningly that it should never have been spied, nay, so fiercely that it should never have been recovered.[10]

First, for the former, behold in the forefront the depth of their policy: the place, that is marvelous fit, the conveyance marvelous easy, the pretense marvelous unsuspected; for they have a cellar;[11] it is in the earth and hard by the water[12] that they may convey things thither. And what can be alleged better than barrels of beer for a cellar? And therefore no man questioned or imagined that there was any matter of treason intended against the State.

Secondly, as their policy was great, so the rage of these sinful persons was beyond measure hellish; for murder is so unnatural that

[9] The day the gunpowder plot was discovered. Its remembrance is the immediate occasion of the sermon.

[10] i.e., discovered.

[11] On November 17, 1605, Guy Fawkes said that they had heard a noise above their heads one day when they were trying to dig a mine from under the house which they had leased next door to the Parliament House, but they had found it increasingly difficult to penetrate the thick walls. The conspirators discovered a coal cellar directly below the House of Lords, which they were able to lease because its owner was moving away.

[12] The conspirators were easily able to ship the gunpowder across the Thames to Parliament Steps and into the cellar, because one of them had a house in Lambeth on the other river bank.

the earth groans under it, and the sun blushes to behold a murderer. But to slay a magistrate, the law of nations and civility loathes it; but to lay hands upon the anointed of the Lord,[13] reason and religion and the law of all nations condemns it to the pit of hell. It was not the blood of a subject they did intend to spill, nor of a magistrate that they did desire to take, nor yet the blood of the King, but when the best of the commonality[14] and gentry of the land were assembled, the choicest of the nobles and the council, the King himself, the highest of all degrees and the choicest of all estates, when King, Queen, and nobles were there assembled for the glory of God and to enact good laws for this commonwealth. Now these in that place in one hour, in one instant should all have been miserably blown up and torn in pieces, so that they should not have been found, or being found, should not have been known that they might be buried according to their degree.[15] This is that matchless villany and that unconceivable treachery which the Papists had contrived; and had not God delivered us—blessed be his name, he did so—but had he not delivered us, we may easily conceive what the success would have been. Oh, the lamentable confusion that would have been in every corner of the land when a man's goods should have been taken from him, and no law to help him, nay, his liberty should have been deprived of [16] and his blood should have been shed, and no man to relieve him! Therefore since this might have been, and since the Lord hath preserved us that it is not

---

[13] James I. The indictment of the conspirators pronounced by Sir Edward Philips, his Majesty's Sergeant-at-Law, is similarly worded. It also speaks of the horror and monstrous nature of the plot, which it says is greater than "the malice of hellish or earthy devil ever practised." The indictment goes on to say: "For if it be abominable to murder the least; if to touch God's anointed be to oppose themselves against God; if (by blood) to subvert princes, states, and kingdoms, be hateful to God and man, as all true Christians must acknowledge; then how much more than too monstrous shall all Christian hearts judge the horror of this treason." *The Gunpowder Treason: with a discourse of the manner of its discovery; and a perfect relation of the proceedings against the conspirators* (London 1609), p. 91.

[14] The Commons as an estate of the realm. The imprint has *cominalty*.

[15] At the arraignment of Henry Garnet, S.J., Sir Edward Coke, the Attorney-General, expressed it similarly: "at one blow traitorously and devilishly to destroy them all, and piecemeal to tear them asunder, without respect of majesty, dignity, degree, age, or place" (op. cit., p. 143).

[16] i.e., he should have been deprived of his liberty.

so, score up his goodness and think of this kindness of the Lord. This is the fruit of Popery and the practice of the Papists. Oh, that you would loath such savage cruelty worse than hell itself!

Add hereunto the third thing we must take notice of. If anything more may be conceived to manifest the heinousness of the fact, the actors of the work took the sacrament upon it that they might not go back from the performance hereof.[17] What cursed wretches were these, not only to commit sin but to make the Lord the author of it, nay, to make the sacrament the seal of the desolation of the Church! Could the devil do more? I think he could scarce endeavor to do worse. This was their policy, and it should have been our misery, if the Lord had not delivered us.

Thus we see the policy, their malice, and resolution. That we are defended from this malice of theirs and succored from this policy of theirs, there is no other reason can be rendered but the Lord is the defender of his people. It was by his power that we were delivered. And that we are a nation this day, it was the Lord's work; and to him we ought to return all the praise. So much for the first use of the point.

Use 2: The second use is this. If God be the deliverer of his people, then it is a great ground of confidence to bear up the hearts of poor souls in affliction. If God will deliver, who can destroy? If God will keep, who can hurt? Think of this in the day of trial and in the time of extremity. Think of this that God never leaves nor forsakes his servants. He will say to the south [Is. 43:6],[18] "Give up," and to the north, "Bring back my servants from far and my daughters from the end of the earth." We that are assembled here, if it[19] had taken place, many of us had been scattered, and the children that have been born since had not now been here. Therefore, if the Lord

[17] Holy communion was administered to the conspirators after the oath of secrecy, which the first conspirators took as early as May, 1604, at the house of Father John Gerard, a Jesuit priest. The oath makes specific reference to the Sacrament: "You shall swear by the blessed Trinity, and by the Sacrament you now propose to receive, never to disclose directly or indirectly, by word or circumstance, the matter that shall be proposed to you to keep secret, nor desist from the execution thereof until the rest shall give you leave."
[18] In Is. 43:6 it is, however, the north that will be asked to give up, while the south must bring back the sons and daughters.
[19] i.e., if the gunpowder plot had been successful.

shall send desolation upon the land and we be scattered one from another, yet uphold your hearts and sustain your souls. The Lord will say to the south, "Give up," and to the north, "Keep not back, but bring my servants from far and my daughters from the end of the earth." He will restore those little ones again, and they shall live to praise his name and magnify the greatness of his power. He can deliver against all means, against all hopes and expectations. Think this against the time of trouble. The enemy is very strong, and we are weak. If you expect any strange extremity intended against us, think of this against that time. Though the policy, malice, and power of the enemy be great, and we are weak and feeble, yet the Lord is still the deliverer of his servants; and behold the salvation of the Lord. The Lord hath power enough still and can overpower the power of the enemy. The Lord hath wisdom still and can defeat the policy of thy enemy. Think of this and hear for aftertimes.

Use 3: The last use is an use of exhortation. Hath the Lord done all for you? Then you will save me a labor. What will you then do for God again? Methinks you that are here this day should all come and resolve to consecrate yourselves, your souls and bodies, to give up all to the Lord. It is he that hath delivered you, let him have obedience from you. It is he that hath maintained you, therefore give up liberally all that he hath bestowed upon you. [In] Lk. 1:74, 75, see the collection there made: "He hath delivered us from the fear of our enemies, that we should serve him in righteousness and holiness all the days of our lives." God hath redeemed us from the jaws of hell and the bond of the devil. To what purpose? That being redeemed from the devil and from our temporal enemies, we should live in baseness and looseness, and dishonor him as he hath delivered us? No, but to serve him "in holiness and righteousness"; not in holiness only, in regard of the first table,[20] but in righteousness also, in regard of the second table; and "before him," that is, in sincerity; and "all the days of our life," that is, in the days of grace and prosperity as also in the days of affliction.

Therefore say: 'The Lord hath delivered us in '88 and in the

[20] i.e., the first table of the Law (commandments 1–4) dealing with the divine.

gunpowder treason.' To what purpose? Therefore call upon one another and say: 'Our lives, our substance, and all we have is the Lord's. Therefore let us serve him and glorify him.' [In] I Sam. 1:27, 28 when Hannah asked [for] a child, and the Lord heard her, when she had the child, she returns, and mark how she pleads: "I prayed for the child, and the Lord heard me. Therefore I will give him again unto the Lord." You fathers of Israel and daughters of Sarah, men and brethren, think of it. Nay, I go further, you little ones that are preserved this day that you live, you may thank the Lord. If '88 or the gunpowder treason had taken place, where had you and your fathers been? But if children will not or cannot, yet you mothers teach them, and fathers instruct them. Think of it and join in the same resolution. Do as Hannah did. Present all you have before the Lord, and say: 'These children are thine. We begged them in '88 and in the gunpowder treason. They are thine by creation, they are thine by preservation. It is the Lord that hath delivered us from the jaws of the lion, from the power of malicious enemies.' Therefore now join hands and hearts together, and say: 'Lord, bless goods and children. All we have is thine, we consecrate all to thy majesty. Had the Papists prevailed, had the powder plot taken ground, we had been defeated. But thy power resisted them, and thy wisdom defeated them. Therefore all is thine, and we render all unto thee.' Thus I charge you, give up all unto the Lord. He gave all at first; he hath preserved all hitherto. Therefore give up all to the Lord, as you have received all from him.

The second part of the exhortation is this. As we must consecrate all to God that hath given all, so secondly, here is a point of wisdom: labor to be in league with this God. Oh, that I could persuade you to tender your own comfort! If you heard the enemies were landed, you would run in a hurry and say: 'How shall we be saved and delivered? What course shall we take, and whither[21] shall we go?' Now learn a point of wisdom, and labor now to be in league with that God that is the deliverer in time of trouble. Make God on your side, and then all will go well with you. Deliverance is not in men, it is not in power, it is not in policy, it is not in shipping, it is only of the Lord, in whom you may have it and from whom you

[21] The imprint has *whether*.

may receive it. Persuade your hearts therefore to be in league with this God and to join sides with the Lord, that in the time of trouble he may pluck you out of the paw of the lion, that he may turn the heart of the enemy toward you, if he should come—God grant he may never come. But in the meantime we shall do well to provide against the day of trial and misery which is like to approach unto us.

I say no more but conclude this point with that, Jos. 9, as the Gibeonites dealt with Joshua, so deal with God. At the [ninth, tenth], eleventh, and twelfth verses, when the Gibeonites heard what Joshua had done, that he had subdued all enemies, and slain all kings that came against him, and gotten a great victory, what course took they? They labored to make peace with Joshua. They saw he was coming against them, and that the Lord had given him exceeding strange victories. Now the Gibeonites come to Joshua in Gilgal and tell him [Jos. 9f.]: "We are men of a far country, and we have heard all that the Lord hath done for you in Egypt, and what he hath done to Sihon, King of Heshbon, and Og, King of Bashan. Wherefore our elders said, go and meet them, and say, we are thy servants, make a league with us." They heard how God had destroyed Pharaoh and his host that came against his children, and how he delivered diverse kings into their hands. Therefore now they seek to get favor with Joshua: "We are thy servants, now therefore make a league with us." Let this be your course. Have you not heard of the greatness of God who succored you in '88? And who was it that made good his promises unto us in all extremities? It was the God of Israel; the Lord did all this. Do as the Gibeonites did. Therefore humble your souls and seek to him, and say: 'We are thy servants, only make a league with us, make peace with us; a league defensive, and a league offensive,' that the Lord may deliver us and stand by us, that the Lord may be at peace with us, that in the day of trouble we may receive comfort and grace from him. So much for that point. But this is that which cuts our hearts, and damps a man's endeavors, and makes his heart break almost: 'Aye, but what if God will not deliver and make a league with us?' A shame it is and a sorrow it should be, that ever we should so behave ourselves toward this God, that he that hath delivered us should give us a flat denial, and say: 'Go to your cups, you that are drunkards, and to your whores, you that are adulterers. Those are your gods, let them now deliver you; I will deliver you and save you no more. Remember, the time was I have heard you and delivered you, but you turned my grace into wantonness. Therefore I will deliver you no more.' This will be a heavy doom, if God thus answer us. I come therefore to the second point.

Doctrine 2: The estate of God's Church may be such that he may lend no further succor and deliverance unto it. It is that which God doth here profess peremptorily: 'I will deliver you no more. You have not acknowledged what I have done heretofore nor walked worthy of it. Therefore I will now stay my hand and deliver you no more.' The point is clear: the estate of God's Church may be such that he will send them no further succor and relief. [In] Lk. 21:22 it is observable, when the day of Jerusalem came on and when desolation should come upon it, the Lord calls them "the days of vengeance," as who should say: 'The Lord hath a fit season appointed wherein he will punish his Church and people, and when the time is come, those are the set and determinate days of vengeance, and the seasons of plagues and punishments, which the Lord which is the God of all seasons will observe.' The Wise Man saith [Ec. 3:1-2]: "There is a season for everything; a time to plant, and a time to pluck up; a season to do good to a nation, and a season to overthrow a nation." [And we can read in] Rev. 14:15: "There is a harvest of vengeance; when a people is ripe to ruin, put in thy sickle for the harvest is ripe." The harvest is nothing else but the desolation of a people, and the sickle is nothing else but the ruin of a people, so that there is a kind of ripeness and fitness for desoluation wherein the Lord will execute judgment upon his people. Hence it is that the Lord saith [Is. 1:14] he is weary with bearing. Nay, the patience of God is even put to a stand. Jer. 5:7: "How shall I spare thee for this?" As who should say: 'God was put to a stay.' As I may speak with reverence, he was put to plea with himself. He knew not how to preserve his own honor, and save them. As who should say: 'My long-suffering will endure it, but my faithfulness will not endure it. My anger burns out against you. I have spared you often. I will spare you no more.' [In] Is. 1:24, there the ministers of his patience are at an end: "I will ease me of my adversaries, and avenge me of mine enemy." As if I had said: 'I have born with you so long that I have been pressed as a cart is pressed under sheaves, at last I will turn you off.' "I will ease me of my adversaries, and avenge me of my enemies."

Therefore [in] Ezek. 14:14 there are three passages to be observed when the Lord seeth the time of destruction coming on and determined. The text saith: "If Daniel, Noah, and Job were among them, they should deliver none but their own souls." You know, if anything will prevail with the Lord, it is prayer, the prayer of the faithful. Noah, Daniel, and Job were eminent in their prayer. Yet the prayers of the best deliver not sometimes. Nay, if they should join all together, for that is observable, if they were in it as in a draught, when a cart is at a plunge, one or two horses cannot pull it out, but if there come two or three horses more stout and strong, they will pluck it out or tear all in pieces. But if these three should join all together their prayers and desires for a people, the Lord saith [Ezek. 14:16], "as I live I will not save them." The Lord takes an oath of it. Now whatsoever the Lord swears to, it is undoubtedly accomplished. That shows immutability of the decree. Other threatenings may be dispensed withal, but "as I live," saith the Lord, "though they all pray and join together, yet they shall not deliver this nation from punishment."

So then the case is clear. You see there is a day of vengeance, a ripeness of a people unto ruin. The Lord will bear no longer, nay, he will ease himself, and all the means under heaven cannot prevail with him, they continuing in their estate. But now the main thing comes on. When is this time, what is this estate when the Lord will not deliver any more? How shall we know it? When may we fear it? How shall we judge of this condition of a people when it is thus with them? Give me leave first to discover it in general, and then descend to particulars.

The case in the general is marvelous; the time when, and what the condition is, when the Lord will not deliver. [In] Gen. 15:16 this is evidently set forth. The text saith of Abraham that the fourth generation that should come of Abraham should come into the land of Canaan. But why should they not come now? "Because," saith the text, "the sins of the Amorites are not yet full and perfectly ripe."

This is the reason why Abraham and his posterity shall not take possession of the land of Canaan for the present, intimating that if the sin of the Amorites had been now full, the Lord would have brought his people into Canaan and destroyed the Amorites. They should not have continued; but because they were not yet ripe, therefore the Lord doth still bear with them. So then when the sin of a nation comes to full ripeness and perfection, then the truth is, the Lord will save and deliver no more. Now the ripeness of an estate and condition will appear in two things, as it is in other things, in fruit and in the body of man. We say a child is come to full growth when two things befall him: when he hath attained his full bigness, and when he is come to be full of strength. We say then, he is as good a man as ever he will be. So it is in the nature of sin. When sin is come to the full bigness and strength and power, it is the deadly symptom of desolation and confusion of a nation where such kind of sins are. Therefore mark it, this is the cause generally to be observed and concluded.

Now I come to the particulars, and here I must stay a little, because the point lieth here, and I must show two things: first, when sin is come to the full bigness, and when it is come to the full strength and ripeness. And when these two are proved, the case will be clear. When a destruction of a people is determined of God and will be effected by God, these things belong to every soul of you, if you have not hearts of Christians about you but even of humanity. As you are men that belong to the same country and live in the same nation, these things belong unto you; therefore attend thereunto. And first, I will open the first thing and show you when the sin is come to the full bigness, and that it may be discovered by two things. The first is this: when sin is grown universal and common and general, so that corruption is, as it were, crept into every corner and coast of the nation, nay, it accompanieth every sort and condition of men, in every place, in every village and town. I must confess that amongst a world of people, some there will be that will keep their garments unspotted and themselves undefiled from the courses of the wicked, but this is not the meaning of the point. But sin is said to be general when the face of a church and a commonwealth is overspread with base abominations, though some particulars be preserved and some few keep themselves unspotted therewith. What is that to the main, what is a handful to the multitude, what is one family to a town, or one in a family, or one street in a city, when sin overwhelms the whole face and course of the Church, when for the general almost all sorts and conditions of men depart from the Lord? [In] Gen. 6:13 this we shall observe is the very note that hastens desolation and discovers the bigness of sin: all flesh had corrupted their ways, and God saw that the earth was full of violence; behold, here is universal injustice, profaneness, and contempt of God and his ordinances. All flesh had corrupted their ways, all kind of men, great ones, poor ones, honorable ones, base ones, all in all places and conditions; they all run in the stream of ungodliness. Therefore mark in the sixth verse the text saith: "It grieved the Lord at the heart that he had made man." God was inwardly vexed with his people, and then he begins to make an end. A deluge of sin, and a deluge of destruction; a flood of wickedness overflowed the old world, therefore the waters drowned the old world. Look as it is with a garden. If all the good fruit and herbs be spoiled, only here and there a root of an herb but all the rest is like a wilderness, then it is time to dig up the ground. So when wickedness in a land is grown like a wilderness, drunkenness and swearing like a wilderness, here and there is a saint of God and a poor soul that walks in sincerity; but for the common, the general sort deny the power of godliness. When it is come to this pass, this is the time for desolation and ruin. [Jer. 5:1]: "Go to and fro through the streets of Jerusalem, and see if there be any that doth righteousness." It was a strange desolation of righteousness. As if the Lord had said: 'Go from town to town, and see if there be any magistrate abiding or any churchwardens abiding.' And mark, he goeth to the poor, and they know not the judgments of the Lord. Then he goeth to the rich, and they know it, but they break all bonds. Now mark what the Lord answereth [Jer. 5:6]: "Therefore a lion out of the forest shall slay them, and a wolf of the evenings shall devour them because rich and poor and all were backsliders." The Lord beset them with plagues, with lions and bears and wolves; that is, ravenous enemies shall rend and tear them in pieces and none shall deliver [them].

As it is in a man, if all the blood and spirits be infected, if the substantial parts, the head, the heart, and the liver be consuming and rotting, there must follow a total ruin of the whole man because there is an universal kind of corruption. Look as it is in the building of an house; when the main pillars begin to rot, and the supporters of the house molder away, there is no supporting of it, but it must be made new, or else it will fall down. As it is in the body natural, so also in the body politic as in the house, so in the estate. When there is a kind of rottenness in the body and estates, when the head is sick and the heart heavy, "when the children gather sticks, and the father kindles a fire, and the mother bakes cakes to the Queen of heaven" [Jer. 7:18], this is when young and old and all conspire together in wickedness; the Lord sendeth fire from heaven and none shall quench it. [In] Jer. 7:18 they all were busy to perform idolatrous worship: father and mother, children and all; and saith the Lord [Jer. 7:19]: "Do they provoke me to anger, and not themselves to the confusion of their own faces?" So it is, when the husband and the wife and children and all swear, when the father and mother hates holiness, the Lord will send fire from heaven, and none shall quench it; iniquity swells and groweth big in such a case.

Secondly, the bigness of sin is discovered when with the commonness of sin there is openness joined, when sin grows open and shameless, when the practicers thereof become bold and base in their abominable practices. Look as it is with a graft: when it is little, it cannot be perceived, the hedge or pale may hide it; but when it is grown, it overtops the pale and wall, and every man may perceive it. For when sin is committed only by a few, when it is confined into a cottage or into an house, then it is not so open to the view; but when all sorts are given to it, the sin comes to have a whore's forehead and a brazen face. Sinners are more bold to oppose governors that are in place to punish it than they are to execute the law upon them. Drunkenness was wont to be a rare thing, as one spoke, drunkenness was for beggars; but now it is for gentlemen and knights. This shows that now sin is open and shameless, and therefore that it is come to its full bigness, and therefore we may justly expect desolation. But in the next place you will say: 'How shall we know when sin is come to the full strength?' I answer: look as it is [in] grace, so it is in sin, when a man can undergo all trials and bear up himself against all temptations and doubtings, when he can either recover himself being fallen, or else keep himself, this is an undoubted sign of a perfect and strong Christian. So it is in the nature of sin, in the body of sin, in this old man of corruption, when a sinner is come to this pass that he is able by the power of his corruptions to withstand all the means of reclaiming and reformation, when he is not bettered by them, nor cannot be wrought upon by the power of them, then he is a strong wicked man; he is one of the elf[22] sons of Satan; he is one of the generals of the field in the camp of the devil, when [in spite of] all the helps that God hath appointed, and all the means that God hath ordained for the subduing of base corruptions. Yet if the sins that are in a family or town or nation, if the stream and tide of them bear down all before them, the work of the magistracy and ministry[23] and means appointed, then it is a sign that sin is come to the full strength, and that ruin and desolation shall befall that person or family or town or nation.

When sin is come to that perfection as it is in the body of a man when a gangrene is spread so far that nothing can stop it, no physic can remove it, it presageth the certain ruin of that man; that member must be cut off or else the body will perish. So when sin is grown so remediless that all the means which God hath ordained for the purging out of the same will not prevail, then it is a sign that sin is come to the full strength, and that such a nation or person is fit for ruin. But you will say: 'Wherein doth this strength of sin appear in the opposing the means of reformation?' I answer: it appears in five particulars.

The first is this: when a nation or people doth not profit by all the corrections that God lays upon them, when the rod and blows wherewith God hath exercised them have not proper and powerful effects in the hearts of those that have been beaten mightily by the hand of God, when the corrections of the Lord humble not a people and reform not a nation, purge not the corruptions and subdue not their distempers, nor make them come home to him that smote

[22] i.e., malignant, mischievous.
[23] The linkage of magistracy and ministry is typical for Hooker. Cf. the introduction to the Document, p. 56; also Document I.

them, this argues the strength of corruption. When the fiercest indignation of the Lord is not able to crush a proud drunkard howsoever the Lord hath sent many plagues into this country and into this town—here one is dying and there another is taken away by the destroying angel of the Lord, yet is not his drunkenness any whit abated—that man will be as drunk and proud, and as scorning and as contemning of God and his ordinances as ever. Think of it: the God of heaven will require it one day at your hands. When men will not be bettered by God's corrections, he will break them in pieces. This is the course that God takes with them, Lev. 26:24.

The famine hath been threatened, the plague inflicted, and the sword is coming. When your husbands went to rack, then you were howling and crying; if the sword come to pluck away the child out of the mother's arms, then there will be howling and taking notice of the abomination that harbors among you. If all the former judgments do it not, he will send the sword, and there are seven plagues in a sword. He hath a quarrel against all profane persons that hate godliness. God will be revenged upon the heads and hearts of them in that day when he sendeth to visit them.

Look as it is with a goldsmith: if he have a vessel or any piece in that nature that is all battered or broken together, or if there be a crack in it that all the scouring and hammering of it will not bring it out, then he will melt it. So when the cancer of a base heart, this cancer of pride and covetousness, when these eat into the hearts of a company of sinful creatures, he hammers them, he sends plagues and sicknesses; but if all this will not do it, then he will melt them and destroy their cursed generation, and raise a new building that will walk with more care and conscience, and be subject with more uprightness to take his yoke upon them. And if the Lord should not proceed after this manner, God could not maintain his own glory and justice. If a company of wretches might scoff at the corrections of the Lord and count them as matters of nothing, they will brave the Almighty: 'Let God do what he can, we will be profane and carnal and unjust; let God plague us, we will be more vicious than God can be angry with us and execute plagues upon us.' When it is thus with wicked men, the Lord will make them feel his fingers, and they that will not be amended, the Lord will knock them to

pieces and consume them. And when we shall see the streets run
with the blood of drunkards and loose persons, then you will say:
'Had the hand of the Lord wrought upon us, it would not now have
been thus with us.' [In] Is. 9:13 the Lord smote the people and
they returned not. Therefore what saith the Lord? He will plague
and make an utter ruin of them, because they would not humble
themselves before the Lord, nor seek to him, nor make their peace
with him. The Lord hath seven plagues more, and he will welter you
in your blood and pluck your cursed abominations from your bosoms.
Then you will say: 'God is just and terrible, and had we been reformed by former punishments, we had not been under this fierce rod
which we now feel.'

The second sign of the strength of sin is this: when the Lord
sends peace and plenty and prosperity, and these blessings of God
do not persuade men to love him so much the more and use them
so much the better, but they fall in love with the gift and forsake
the giver. You make your honor and ease and pleasure, you make
them gods and depart from the Lord which is the giver of all. Then
it is just with the Lord to pluck away that ease and honor and preferment that you dote upon and are addicted to, that in the want of
these you may learn to prize the gospel and learn to esteem of the
Lord Christ and his grace above all these contents the world can
afford. Now unless the Lord should be accessory to the dishonor
of his own name, what would you have the Lord to do? Would you
have him give you peace and prosperity to neglect the peace of a
good conscience? By this means God should be, as it were, the
author of his own dishonor. No, no, think of it! I fear it will be
true, if the Lord should take away our ease and liberty that we
have made idols of, then you shall say: 'If you had prized God
and gospel more than ease and liberty, you might have had these
and God and gospel too.'

Dt. 28:48: ["Therefore shalt thou serve thine enemies which the
Lord shall send against thee."] This is that which will one day stick
heavy upon your hearts. For your souls' sake think of it and remember it. If the Lord should send the enemy upon us and lay
hardness over us, and we should be made vassals unto the tyranny
of wicked men, this will stick to your hearts. 'Had I served the Lord

in plenty and such a time when I enjoyed the means of salvation, then it had been well with me; but I was loose and profaned the Lord's day, and therefore it is just now I serve the enemy upon the Lord's day. I am made a drudge and a vassal and a slave to the malice of the wicked.' It is just with God and righteous with the Lord; you would not serve God when time was, you would not hear the word when time was. God will provide a course for you: you shall have service enough and God will hold you to it; you shall serve cruel and bloodthirsty enemies to the shame of your faces here and to the ruin of you and yours hereafter forever.

2 Chr. 36:21: "Then shall the land rest one sabbath," saith the text. Mark this: among the Jews the Lord appointed every seventh year to be a sabbath that the saints should rest. There should be no plowing nor sowing and all creatures should rest. Now they were so covetous that they would pluck commonly out of the earth the seventh year. 'Well,' saith the Lord, 'you will not let the land rest; you shall be led captive, and then the land shall rest on her sabbath.' It is just that God should pluck away these benefits to the confusion of our faces forever when we abuse them. Look as it is with a wife: if she should have a servant in the house which she loves more than her husband, what course must be taken? He must fling him out of the house and away with him. So when we should love God and prize his glory and truth. Aye,[24] yet we will love the world and profit and ease and quiet and peace and liberty, and we will do nothing that may hazard these. It is righteous with the Lord to cashier those commodities and pluck away the adulterous lover of wealth and honor and ease, that he may make a way himself in our souls, that he may rule in you and take possession of you.

The third means is this: when corrections reform not and the blessings of God persuade not men, then the Lord vouchsafeth to send his Word among the people, and that should supply the want of all other means and should be more powerful than any other in the world besides, so that howsoever the covetous carl [25] dotes upon his wealth, the Word should loosen his mind from it and reveal the vanity of it. However corrections humble not, yet the Word is able

[24] The imprint has I.
[25] i.e., churl.

to break the soul and work the soul to an humble subjection. The Word is the power of God to salvation, which is able to crush all corruptions and subdue all sins; but [when] sin is come to this height that the Word is unfruitful and unprofitable, then sin is desperately strong, and we are then come to the last and worst estate that can be. It is more than we are aware of, and more than commonly we consider of; we know not what we do when our hearts continue in resisting the word of the Lord.

2 Chr. 36:16. It is a deadly sign of desolation of any people. When the liberty of Jerusalem was at the last gasp, giving up the ghost, and there was but an inch between them and desolation, mark what the text saith: "They mocked his prophets and despised his messengers till the wrath of the Lord arose and there was no remedy." Here was the ground, this was the main thing, that the sin eats the estate in sunder and pulled down the pillars of the commonwealth of Judah. You would think: 'Was it so much to despise the word of a minister?' "Ah," saith the text, "the wrath of the Lord arose and there was no remedy"; as if he had said: 'The Lord is able to bear much at the hands of ungodly man'; and methinks the Lord saith: 'I could have endured your drunkenness and endured your profaneness; had you but submitted to my Word, those corruptions might have been subdued.' But not only to practice ungodliness, but to refuse the Word that should subdue those corruptions, when the Lord saw this, his wrath arose, and there was no remedy. God can endure much though a man have many corruptions in him, though many sins have been committed by him, if the soul be yet content to hear and tremble at God's ordinances; but when a man is not content to commit sin only, but he will oppose God's word, then the Lord like the lion of the tribe of Judah can help no longer, then "the wrath of the Lord arose, and there was no remedy," but he would lay waste the land.

When we spill the physic that should cure us and cast away the salve that should heal us, how can we be helped and cured? This is the ground and reason of those many phrases we have in scripture. Why? The Lord is said to extend his providence over a people in vouchsafing the gospel, Mt. 23, the latter end. It is a well-known place; we will open it a little and apply it to our purpose because it is pregnant. The text saith [Mt. 23:37]: "O Jerusalem, Jerusalem, how often would I have gathered thee under my wings!" By the preaching of the Gospel and revealing of their sins, he would have gathered their hearts unto him and would have cast the wing of his providence over a people as they are willing to submit to the Gospel. But Jerusalem would not. He sent his prophets to reveal his will. They stoned them. Therefore saith the text [Mt. 23:38]: "Your habitation is left unto you desolate." That is the issue: they would not have the Word reform them, therefore they shall have the sword to plague them. [In] Lk. 19:44 the case is evident. The Lord discovers the besieging and the sacking of Jerusalem: "There shall not a stone be left upon a stone, because thou knowest not the time of thy visitation"; as who should say: 'The Lord came to visit Jerusalem with mercy to comfort her, with pardon to cheer her, to show her her sins and humble her soul; but she regarded not this kindness of the Lord, therefore there is a siege about her, and that is very heavy.' And take notice of it. The Lord is specially angry with a nation for the breach of his covenant and neglect of his worship. The Lord doth hate it and is carried with great violence toward those people that worship God falsely. [In] I Kg. 13, the two last verses, the text saith [33, 34]: "He made of the lowest of the people priests"; as who should say: 'He made a company of drunkards and belly-gods ministers.' And is that such a great matter? Yes, that one sin turned to the utter ruin of the house of Jeroboam, to root him out.

Fourthly, if this will not do the deed, but men will resist the means that God puts into their hands, then fourthly, this is another evidence that sin groweth strong, when there wants a competent number of mourners in a land which might uphold it and join sides against sin and Satan. and maintain the good of a kingdom in despite of the wicked in a kingdom. This is one of the last succors of supplies a kingdom hath. How ever wicked men will not be persuaded and humbled, yet if there be a competent number, if there be so many as will make an army of fasting and prayer to grapple with God, they may prevail with God for mercy for a kingdom. There is hope, though the most be naught, yet the better side will prevail. But when the floods of iniquity flow in amain so that the best of God's people are taken aside with the stream of corruption and begin to grow careless and not to oppose the sins of the times, this is a sore argument that there is almost no remedy for such a nation, no means to beat back the indignation of the Lord. [In] Gen. 19, when Sodom could not save itself, ten righteous persons would have saved it. Though they would have pulled God's indignation upon them, yet a competent number of ten men would have stayed the indignation and gone between the living and the dead. So were there a proportionable number of mourners in a land, though there be a company of mock-gods that would pull down the indignation of God upon them, yet a company of godly, gracious men might strive with the Lord and uphold their liberty. But when corruptions are grown so strong that good men are defiled and their hearts tainted and their mouths stopped, woe to that kingdom and people. Look as it is with the sea-coast: when the banks are such that they can bear out the waves, be the sea never so boisterous, there is hope of safety; but if the sea break all before it, there is no hope to stop it. So it is in this case: the banks that bear out the indignation of the Lord are righteous, holy men. They stay the hand of God and stop the flood of God's vengeance that they do not break in and overflow all; but if the bank be gone, if a convenient company of godly men be taken away, then there is no hope of mercy, but the sea of God's indignation will flow in amain upon that place.

The fifth and last means to uphold liberty and safety of a nation is this: when men begin to be sensible of misery, when they have eyes to see the plague, and hearts affected with the sins committed and with the judgments deserved, when they observe what will befall, they will use some means that it may not befall; but when a people grow senseless and benumbed, and secure in a base practice and ungodly course, that they observe not the evils committed nor take notice of the judgments of God deserved, but lie in a careless, secure condition, there is no expectation in reason how such a nation should prevent the wrath of the Almighty, when they see not what shall befall, have no care to prevent what may befall. [In] 1 Th. 5:3 there is a warning-shot before the cannon-shot, there is a watch-word before destruction cometh: "When they cry peace, then cometh destruction." When they quiet themselves in their own courses, when they are not only wicked but secure in their wickedness, then comes sudden destruction.

I conclude with that: Mt. 24:39. As it was in the days of Noah — there the Lord, as it were, smites men with plagues answerable to their sins; they were careless and secure in the days of Noah, and then came sudden destruction — so it will be now. As in the days of Noah, when Noah was knocking the Ark, every nail he drove was a sermon: 'Repent you carnal and unjust oppressors, the flood is coming and desolation approaching.' But they knew nothing, that is, they feared no such matter: 'Let Noah say what he will. What, a flood come and destroy all the world? It will not be, it cannot be!' They knew nothing before the flood came.

So then the issue is this: when sin is grown universal, when men are shameless in the commission thereof, and outbid all means of reformation, the corrections of the Lord humble not; the mercies of the Lord persuade not; the word reforms not; nay, when the righteous are perished from the earth and the banks are broken down, when there is not a competent number of mourners to withstand the wrath of the Lord, nay, when men are senseless and secure (all men commit sin and fear not the wrath of God for sin), then sin comes to be of a giant-like strength and bigness.

Use 1: We will now make use of the point. The case is clear: when sin outbids all means of reformation, then men are ripe for desolation. We will first raise a ground of instruction and then make way for an use of examination. And learn this point of instruction: that this of all plagues under heaven is one of the heaviest of all judgments; it is the sorest that a wicked man should prosper and thrive in his ungodly courses, that he should be able to break through the net and come off clearly. Whatsoever comes to the contrary, he hath what he will and doth what he please, and no word reforms him, no means hinder him. Think of this when the Lord pulls up the stake and gives him the rein, and lets him go posthaste and hurry headlong down to destruction, that is the only way to pull the soul of a sinner into the bottomless pit.

It is said, Hos. 2, that when the Lord doth please to bring any of his people home, this is God's special care. In the sixth verse, the

Lord pricks his fingers and stops him, and makes a hedge about a covetous deceitful wretch, that he cannot break through, but he hath now a knock of conscience, now a judgment of God, now a terror of the Almighty. This is the only way to bring a soul home to God. Then she will say [Hos. 2:7]: "I will return unto my first husband." But this is one of the heaviest judgments and sorest plagues that can befall a sinful creature, that the Lord should pull down the hedge and break open the wall, and let them run riot: 'Take thy course and follow thy vanities, I will hinder thee no more till I have thee in hell, and then thou shalt be plagued for all together!' [In] Jer. 12:3 it is a fine phrase. When Jeremiah was perplexed with the prosperity of the wicked, he was marvelously troubled because of the excellency of ungodly men. At last he quits himself with this: "They were as sheep fatted for the slaughter."

What will become of you that have all means of reformation? The Lord's mercies and ministers and judgments have striven with you. What will become of you when such a creature comes to hell? The devil will make bonfires of him, but they shall make holy day in hell; their plagues shall be nothing to theirs that have had all means, and resisted all means, of grace and salvation. The devils will rejoice to meet a drunkard in hell, and say: 'What, art thou come to hell after all means vouchsafed and all helps bestowed?' The devils will make bonfires and stand on tiptoes and crow over such persons: 'What, you that enjoyed the means of grace and salvation, what, you come to hell, too?' All the whole rout of them will outbrave such an opposer of God and his ordinances. He shall be a head block in hell.

I will conclude the point and say no more. If there be any such here present (as there is too many) that can brag of their loose courses and glory of their villany, 'I drunk him under the table,' no counsel shall prevail with him, no means shall take place in him. Dost boast of thy villany in this kind? Dost glory because thou thrivest in thy wickedness? Woe, woe to thy soul! Thou art ready for the slaughter, and the Lord shall bring thee down into everlasting destruction. Know it. God hath said [Jl. 3:13] when the harvest is ripe he will put in the sickle, and thou that art ripe shalt be sure of desolation.

Look as it is with a sick man: when meat cannot nourish him, when physic works not and physicians are at a stand and all leave him, then we say he is but a dead man, the physicians have left him. Think of it, the Lord of heaven comes to visit thee. Thy sick soul is like the sick man; many mercies he poureth into thy soul to humble thee, many judgments to eat out thy proud flesh. He comes to lance thee on one side and bind thee upon the other side, but if all these will do thee no good, it is a fearful symptom. Nay, it is certain: there was never any man so sure to die when all means left him, as thy soul shall be damned when all means prevail not.

Use 2: The second use is a use of examination. Is this true then: when sin grows ripe, then the Lord will not succor and relieve any more, then we may have a shrewd guess and gather a sure argument of the ruin and desolation of any person, town, or country. When a nation is, as it were, giving up the ghost and drawing on to everlasting destruction, the former doctrine will be a marvelous help and great succor unto us for direction in this case. The physicians, one part of their skill is this: they call it a foretelling sign whereby they have a sure guess when the body is dying and nature growing onto dissolution. When they see such and such signs in a man, they say he is dying. Why, the truth saith, the text saith, and the scriptures profess it: wherever there is a full increase, a full strength of sin, an universal kind of incorrigibleness in a sinful course, it is a deadly sign that that state, kingdom, or person is breathing out his last and drawing to desolation as near as may be.

DOCUMENT III

The Carnal Hypocrite; c. 1626

Introduction

There is rarely a sermon by Thomas Hooker in which he does not deal with some type of hypocrite. In his terminology a hypocrite is anyone who thinks he can escape the radical Puritan alternative of "being either a saint or a devil," who attempts to by-pass Puritan zeal by adhering to some *via media,* or who hopes that "a man may be saved though he be not so exact and precise," as it is put in *The Carnal Hypocrite* (p. 104). At the start, Hooker devotes a few short remarks to hypocrisy, in which he describes it in the conventional sense as saintly outward appearance without inner substance; and he illustrates his point with the traditional simile of the stage-player (p. 93). But he then goes on to be more concerned with the conflict between "bad lives" and "good hearts," and to insist that his parishioners cannot be good Christians unless they conform to Puritan standards. He argues that the "power of godliness" has to "show and discover itself" in the performance of "good duties," and that the heart must be judged by outward conduct, or by "life and conversation" (p. 94). Hooker makes it clear that the way is not an easy one to follow in a society where "riches, honors, and pleasures" are highly valued; and he is especially critical of parishes where the majority is not willing to undergo the radical process which would make them "new creatures," but prefers to look upon the "strict and precise" as monsters.

Hooker, in keeping with Puritan practice, encourages his listeners to profess their godliness openly and "to show what grace can do" (p. 98). But he strongly argues against separation, and he confirms the power of the public authorities in church and state in all disciplinary matters. He realizes that the requirements of daily living, as well as of civil obligations, make communication necessary with those that still deny "the power of godliness." It is only in private relations, therefore, that the scriptural text "from such turn away" applies. Hooker insists, however mournfully, on the mixed communion in the parish churches. Instead of excommunication, which is not within the competence of the local parish and should be used only as a last resort, he advises social shunning as a substitute which "God hath appointed as a special means . . . to withdraw a wicked man from his wicked course and work sound repentance in his soul" (p. 118).

The Carnal Hypocrite consists of more than one sermon. It may have been a series of sermons, but it may also represent a composite of several sermons on the same theme, delivered at separate times. We do not know precisely under what conditions the sermons were preached. Allusions to "those dangers that are threatened against us" (p. 92) or to the plague (p. 118) point to a historical situation similar to that which Documents I and II referred to more clearly. Without great certainty, we place *The Carnal Hypocrite* c. 1626. It was not published until 1638, when it was included in the *Four Learned and Godly Treatises*.

DOCUMENT III

The Carnal Hypocrite; c. 1626

2 Tim. 3:5   *"Having a form of godliness,*
but denying the power
thereof: from such turn
away."

If you cast your eyes into the first words of the chapter, in the first verse you shall find the holy Apostle, writing to Timothy, his son and scholar, doth by way of prophecy and direction from God discover the manifold dangers that would come to pass in the last days, and also annexeth the great danger in the third, fourth, [and] fifth verses. He makes up, as it were, a catalogue of those corruptions that should harbor in their hearts and discover themselves in the lives of wicked men in the last age of the world, which is the age wherein we now live. In the first verse, "perilous days shall come," the reason of the trouble and the ground of the misery that the Spirit hath foretold shall befall and be brought upon the world, it shall not be in regard of the punishment inflicted but in regard of the sin committed.

Among which sins he reckons up the cursed dissimulation that men should carry a fair show outwardly when they had a great deal of wretchedness and vileness in their hearts inwardly. That is one of the last, though not one of the least sins here reckoned up. Thus far the Apostle doth exhort Timothy to turn away from them.

Before we come to particulars, take up the point in general from these words as they stand in reference to the former.

Doctrine 1: The multitude of sins bring the dangerest times. When there are the greatest abominations committed, there is the greatest danger to be expected; for the danger of times lieth not in regard of outward troubles but in regard of the manifold corruptions that are in us and the many evils committed by us. When men

91

are most wicked, then the time is most dangerous; for it is not the power of Satan nor his wicked instruments that can bring misery to the people of God, but the root of all ruin lieth within ourselves. Jer. 2:19: "Here is the evil, here is the venom of all afflictions and the gall of all troubles, that we have forsaken the Lord, that his fear is not within our hearts." 2 Chr. 15:5: They were without blessings, because without God.

Use: [For] instruction: to teach us how to procure comfort to our own souls and to recover our country and times out of those dangers that are threatened against us. It's not means nor men nor policy nor strength that can do it till our evils be reformed. Let every man look to his own ways and reform his own corruptions and turn from his evil courses, and then all dangers and inconveniences will turn away, and God will be a God to us. [Jer. 22:15]: "When they did eat and drink and did righteously, was it not well with them?" I say no more, but remember it is God's only wish that it should be thus with us. Is. 48:18: "O that thou hadst hearkened to my commandments!" What then? What would we have got by it? Mark then what followeth: "Thy righteousness had been as a river." Oh, why might it not be our wish, too, that we that enjoy peace and plenty under our sovereign may have the same still continued to us? Still hearken to God and all things shall hearken to us. Hos. 2:21: If we could call and obey him, he would hear. Mt. 11:23: This was the ground of the desolation of Sodom and Gomorrah; so that to humble and to reform our sins is the best means to maintain the safety of a kingdom or nation.

In the verse observe two things: first, what carnal hypocrites and cursed dissemblers will do; they have a form but deny the power; secondly, what the carriage of the saints should be toward these; they should turn away, because they turn away from God and the power of godliness.

First, the hypocrite: what he doth. He is only the picture of godliness. As Machiavel,[1] that cursed politician, speaks, he would have a man to take up the name of virtue because there is no trouble in it, no disquiet which comes by it, but he would not have him

---

[1] Hooker undoubtedly refers to chapter 18, "Concerning the way in which the Princes should keep faith," of Machiavelli's *The Prince*.

take up the practice of it. So it is with an hypocrite: it is easy to have a show and appearance, but when it comes to the virtue, power, and strength of it, he cannot endure it.

Here is two things to be discovered before we come to the doctrine: first, what is meant by "godliness"; secondly, what is meant by a "form."

First, this word "godliness" implieth two things: first, the doctrine of religion which by the apostles is called the doctrine according to godliness; secondly, that implieth that gracious frame of spirit whereby the heart is disposed and the soul of a Christian is fitted to express some gracious work outwardly. For what the oil is to the wheels of a clock, it makes them run glibber, so godliness to the soul; when the soul is oiled and anointed therewith, it is fitted to perform any good duty.

Secondly, what is meant by the "form of godliness." I answer, the word "form" or "fashion"; it is taken by way of resemblance and similitude from outward things. It is nothing else but that outward appearance that any thing hath, discovering the nature and being of it. We use to say that he hath the guise of his behavior and the proportion of such a one's carriage, though he hath not the like disposition of mind. So in this case a carnal hypocrite may have the guise and portraiture or the outward profession of a child of God; that what a holy heart doth express outwardly, he may express outwardly.

Look as it is among stage-players. The stage-player puts on brave apparel and comes on to the stage, and resembles the person of a king and acts the part of a monarch; but if you pull him off the stage and pluck his robes from his back, he appears in his own likeness. So it is here. A carnal hypocrite, a cursed dissembler, is like a stage-player. He takes upon him the person and profession of a godly, humble, lowly man, and he acts the part marvelous curiously, and he speaks big words against his corruptions and he humbles himself before God, and he hears and prays and reads; but when God plucks him off the stage of the world and his body drops into the grave, and his soul goes to hell, then it appears that he had not the power of godliness; he was only a stage-player, a stage professor. When Saul [1 Sam. 28:7f] went to the witch to raise him up Samuel, the devil took upon him the guise of Samuel; but he was the devil. So many hypocrites, though they have the guise of holiness and the form of godliness, yet there is no soundness, there is nothing but dissimulation within. Hence note this:

Doctrine 2: That godliness hath a form; or more clearly thus: sound godliness always shows and discovers itself where it is in the life and conversation of him that hath it. For it is not a mere fancy as some think. And they think when we talk of godliness and inward moving, etc., — 'What,' say they, 'will you have us saints and angels?' — as if godliness were some secret thing that never saw the sun. The Aspostle doth professedly oppose these, and says they are real things, and it is really in your hearts that have it, and it doth not keep close, but appears and discovers itself in a holy conversation outwardly.

[In] Ps. 45:13 the text saith: "The king's daughter [is all glorious within]," and that is not all, but "her clothing is of gold." The king's daughter is the church of God. The saints that God hath soundly humbled and powerfully converted, they are the daughters of God; they are sanctified and purged, and the image of God is stamped upon them. And what is their raiment outwardly? It is of gold. They have golden speeches, golden conversations, not dirty, filthy conversation as the wicked have. [In] Acts 4:20 see how prevalent grace is where it is. It was also the resolution of the Apostle, 2 Cor. 4:13. It is also said of David [Ps. 116:10]: he believed inwardly and therefore spoke outwardly. So must we, for if we rest upon God we will express the power of his grace in the course of our lives.

Look as it is with a clock: if the wheels run right, the clock cannot but strike. So it is with the trees of the field: if there be sap in the root, it will discover itself in the branches by the fruit and greenness of them; though it be hidden in the winter, yet it will appear in the spring and in the summer. So it is in the souls of God's servants. The frame of a man's heart, that is like the wheels of a clock. If a man have an humble heart, he will have a holy life; it will make the hand work, the eye see, the foot walk, and the actions be proportionable unto the disposition of the heart. So if there be the sap of godliness and holiness and meekness and patience in a man's spirit, it will appear in the blossom and fruits, in good speeches, actions, and an holy conversation. If there be sound grace in the heart and godliness within, we must not think godliness will make a monster, but it will make a comely, decent, proportionable Christian that is four square in all good duties, at all good duties, at all times, in all places, upon every occasion.

I conclude with John the Baptist, Lk. 3:8: ["Bring forth therefore fruits worthy of repentence"]. "Worthy," the word in the original, is fine. Let your fruit be worthy, that is, answerable. Let them hold weight for weight with an amendment of life. If there be obedience in the heart, it will answer such obediences outwardly. Lay obedience in one balance, and then repentance will poise that obedience in the other scale.

Objection: But you will say: 'How comes this to pass? May not a man have a gracious good heart, may not a man have a soul truly humbled and converted, and yet be a retired Christian, and not express it outwardly?'

Answer: I answer no. If there be holiness in the heart, it will show itself without.

Reason 1: From the power of grace, wherever it is imprinted upon any soul, it will break through and make way for itself, whatever maketh opposition against it. [In] Mt. 6:22 ["The light of the body is the eye"] the meaning is: the eye is the conscience; the sincere eye is the sincere conscience. Now if a man have a good conscience inwardly, his whole conversation will be proportionable to the same. [In] Mt. 13:33 the grace of God is compared to leaven. It will never leave leavening till it hath leavened all the whole lump. If the heart be leavened with grace and godliness, never think to keep godliness in a corner and contrive it into a narrow compass. No, no, it will never leave leavening till the eye looks holily and the hand works mercifully!

Nay, observe this in particular: first, let corruptions be never so strong in a gracious heart, the power of godliness will overpower all and work out itself and get ground in conclusion. Look as it is with the mole: put her into the ground and stop her up, she will work herself out one way or other. So it is with a gracious frame of spirit. Though there be a great deal of earthly corruption, yet a gracious heart will work under ground and work itself out of all these. It is observed by natural philosophy: when a ship is cast away, the sea vomits on the shore the dead persons, and the sea will not fetch them in again. So there is a sea of grace in the souls of God's servants. There is but a beginning of grace indeed, but there is abundance of life and virtue and power in the graces of God's children, so that though there be many corruptions, much deadness and untowardness, yet if this gracious work be there, it will vomit out all; it will fling out those dead bodies, but never take them in again.

[In] Jer. 20:9 observe when Jeremiah out of a kind of discouragement and pride of spirit — because he could not find that success, and some despised it, and some scoffed — "I will preach no more," saith he. But even then the word of the Lord was as burning fire. This was the power of this gracious frame of heart we speak of. Mt. 12:35: "Bring forth good things." The word in the original is "All cast out good things," and it implies a kind of compulsion, so that a holy man out of the treasure of holiness casts out holy things; that is, however many corruptions hang about him and would hinder him from doing what he should, yet a good heart will cast out all and break through all.

Look as it is with fire: let it be raked up never so close, yet there will be fire; it will heat and burn and consume all into itself. So it is with the fire of grace in a man's heart. Though there be many clogging corruptions, yet if this grace be there, though a man have a great deal of filthy, noisome humors of vanity and choler and anger and carelessness, yet this fire will heat and burn and make way and kindle and turn all into a flame at conclusion.

Secondly, it will not only break through all corruptions but through all outward occasions that comes against it. [In] Ps. 39:3 the good man was among a company of mock-gods that were flouting and jibing, and now saith he: "I burned and spake with my tongue"; as who should say, the grace of God was so powerful that he could hold no longer, he could bear no more, but spake with his tongue.

Look as it is with the husbandman: he casts his seed into the ground and covers is over with earth, yet that little seed will break the earth and rend the ground and come out. So it is with a godly and holy heart wherein the immortal seed of God's word is sown. Though there be clogs and occasions of oppositions this way and that way and another way, yet a gracious heart will break through, and the good work of the Lord that is implanted in the soul will appear in the life and conversation.

Reason 2: Consider the end why God gives grace, which cannot be attained unto unless we express the power of this grace outwardly as well as to have it inwardly. For mark, the ends why God gives grace are principally these two: first, to glorify the Lord, Eph. 1:6. There was such a proud heart humbled, such a carnal wretch purified, 1 Pet. 2:12. I would have God's children carry themselves so holily that the wicked may admire at them and glorify God.

The second end why God gives grace: that we may be a means to draw others on in the same way wherein God hath enabled us to walk. [In] 2 Kg. 7:9 there they say: "We do not well; this day is a day of glad tidings; come therefore, let us tell it to the King's household." So it is with a merciful, gracious, loving heart. If God ever opens his eyes and shows mercy to his soul and pardons his sins, then he thinks: 'Sure I do not well that I do not tell it to my fellow servants, that they may love grace and embrace it and be blessed by it.' This thou must do and ought to do, and this you cannot do if you keep your grace secret within your hearts. Therefore tell your fellow servants: 'Of a truth, I had as stony, as careless a heart as you, but it hath pleased the Lord to break it. It hath cost me many a sob and salt tear, but now the Lord hath pardoned me. Did you but know the peace of a conscience, you would never live as you do.' This is the frame of a gracious heart.

Use 1: [For] instruction: that it is not a fault for any man to show himself forward in a holy course and holy conversation. Know, it is no fault to express that grace which God hath bestowed upon thee. I speak this the rather by reason of the cavils of a company of carnal persons that cast reproaches upon this course. 'Ah,' say they, 'they can make a show, but they are all hypocrites. If a man knew their hearts, they are as bad as the worst.' I answer: how dost thou know their hearts to be bad? We judge the tree by the fruit, and we may judge the heart by the life and conversation. But be his heart naught, yet there is not a fault in that he makes a show.

To make a show and to express holiness is good; but that is a fault, that the heart is naught. Let that therefore which is good be commended and that which is naught be avoided. It is not the fault of gold that it glisters, but that it glisters and is not gold. But what heart is thine in the meantime, that cannot endure so much as the show of godliness? It shows a heart marvelous violent against God, a heart marvelous satanical. He that loves his father will love the picture of his father. So if thou lovest holiness thou wilt love the picture of holiness.

Objection: But you will say: 'We do not discommend holiness, but it is this hypocrisy that we disallow. God forbid that we should speak against holiness.'

Answer: Give me leave to reply two things: first, that which thou seest them want, labor thou for, and that which is good in them, labor thou to take up. Thou that sayest, 'Those are sermon-hunters, yet they will cozen and lie and the like,' dost thou speak against hearing the Word and praying in families? 'No, oh, but this cozening, dissembling!' Why then, take thou that which is good, sanctify thou the Lord's day, and pray thou in thy family, show thy holiness outwardly and be thou also inwardly sincere. But thou that hatest the form of godliness, it is a sign thou hatest the power of godliness.

Secondly, if thou hatest them for hypocrisy, then thou hatest them because they are sinful; and if thou dost, thou wilt hate those more that are greater sinners: as a man that hates a toad, the greater the toad is, the more he loathes it. So if thou hatest hypocrisy because it is sinful, then thou wilt hate that man which hath more sin. But thy conscience testifieth that thou canst love drunkards and harlots, adulterers, and speak well of blasphemers. Those thou art content with and wilt not reproach them. This is a great sign thou hatest holiness and sincerity because thou hatest the show thereof.

Use 2: For reproof: it condemns the opinions of a great company of carnal professors that brag of their good heart, when in the meantime they have base lives. Take any carnal wretch that hath neither the form nor show, he will, though he make not such a show as many do, but he hath as good a heart to Godward. [Gal. 6:7]: "Be not deceived, God is not mocked." This is an idle conceit of thine own carving and coining, a thing that the saints of God never found, a thing that the Scriptures never revealed. No, no, if grace be inwardly, it will show it outwardly!

You would think a man were beside himself that should tell you of a sun that did never shine or of a fire that did never heat. This would be a strange sun and a strange fire. So it is a strange kind of imagination thou hast. Thou thinkest thou hast a good heart and yet never express it outwardly in thy conversation. It is well sometimes there may be a show without substance, but this is impossible — that there should be a substance without some appearance.

Should thou see a body lie on the bed, and neither sense in it nor action proceeding from it, you would say it is dead, it lives not. So in this case. If faith work not, it is a fancy, it is an idle, foolish, carnal presumption. Why, faith purifies the heart and works by love; faith is mighty and powerful, and faith is operative and effectual. Therefore thou that thinkest thou hast a holy heart and never showest it in thy course, it is a foolish delusion of thy heart. Therefore know this for an everlasting rule, that the worst is always within. [Mt. 12:34]: "Out of the abundance of the heart [the mouth speaketh"]. If thy eye, thy tongue, and thy life be naught, what a vile heart hast thou then! There is the puddle of all abomination and profaneness from within, for the heart moves the eye and the tongue and the foot to wickedness. If the streams be impure, the fountain is much more filthy. Therefore away those carnal pleas and foolish delusions.

Use 3: [For] exhortation: we hear the duty God hath revealed and the task God hath set us; therefore take up the task. If you desire any evidence to your souls or testimony to your hearts that God hath wrought grace in you, then show it in your lives. Express the virtues of him that hath called you from death to life. As [with] the Apostle, do not only have virtues [such] as patience, meekness, etc., but show forth these virtues that others may be bettered by them. Therefore the Lord saith [1 Pet. 1:16]: "Be ye holy as I am holy"; not in affliction only, but [1 Pet. 1:15] "in all manner of conversation." Mark, he doth not say, 'Have good minds only and honest hearts,' but "in all manner of conversation." Be holy in buying, selling, traveling, trading, etc. God's saints should be so holy in their lives, as men should say: 'Surely there is a holy God; see how his servants are holy. There is a righteous God; see how righteous his servants are.' Away therefore with those idle, sottish policies[2] of a company of carnal persons in the world that are directly opposite to the power of godliness.

There is a generation of politicians in the world that count it a point of great wisdom for a man to conceal his religion to himself. And the phrase is among men, 'Keep your holiness and your hearts to yourselves'; and they confine godliness within a man's closet or study. But if any holiness appear in his life or any exactness in his courses, there is an outcry made presently: 'Oh, discretion would do well; if men were but wise, much might be done!' Wisdom I dare not style it, but that the Scripture speaketh of a wisdom that is not from above, that is carnal, sensual, and devilish wisdom which the Word requires not. These men may imagine the holy apostles wanted wisdom. [In] Phil. 4:5 he [Paul] exhorts you to "let your patience be made known to others, and let all know it, for the Lord is at hand." This takes away a cavil. Some may say if a man doth show and express godliness outwardly, then contempt and persecution will be at hand presently. 'Why,' saith the Apostle, 'the Lord is at hand to comfort you, to deliver you.' Nay, in these men's conceits Christ should have wanted wisdom when he commanded peremptorily, Mt. 5:16, "Let your light [so shine before men that they may see your good works"]. He doth not say, 'Hide your light in your souls and keep your hearts to yourselves.' No, no, but 'Let it shine forth!'

You that are tradesmen; you are not content only to have your sons put to prentice, but you would have them to learn their trade also. You are bound prentice to the trade of holiness; you profess yourselves to be scholars in the school of the Lord Jesus Christ. Therefore let us express something we have learned; let us show something we have gained, show some workmanship, as the Apostle calls it. Eph. 2:10: "I would have every Christian man express the workmanship of the Lord"; that is, I would have him express such holy graces in his course and conversation that all the world should find no flaw; that when the wicked shall say, 'What have you done

[2] i.e., practices.

with your grace?' [or] 'Are you a professor, and pray, read and hear sermons?' — now let a Christian put the word to silence: 'I am more able to suffer persecution than thou art to think of it; I am more able to bear trouble than thou to hear of troubles,' Heb. 10:34. But some may say, 'I wonder you can endure such indignities to be laid upon you.' Fie, you may wonder indeed, but now godliness showeth itself. What serves grace and godliness for, but only that we should do something for the glory of God more than you can?

Objection: 'Aye,' but you will say, 'to me this is the only way for to make a company of proud professors in the world. This is the only way to blow up a haughty heart, to make it show itself to the world; which is nothing else but pride.'

Answer: I answer: the saints may show forth godliness and yet not themselves, however [much] a carnal heart is ready to abuse the best duties sometimes. As the corrupt stomach doth turn the best cordials into choler, so a corrupt heart may set forth his own vainglory; but yet the duty itself is good, though the abuse is to be avoided.

Objection: But you will say: 'How shall a man so order himself that he may be neither cowardly in hiding his grace, nor vainglorious in expressing his grace?'

Answer: I answer: there are four rules to be observed.

Rule 1: First, labor to lay down all carnal excellency of thy parts and abilities, and of all outward respects that are in thee and God hath bestowed upon thee. Lay down all those in all thy service, that only the power of the Lord Jesus may be discovered to the view of the world. Let grace be above all; make that known and lift that up above all other things whatsoever. Mark how careful Paul is to knock off his own fingers, 1 Cor. 15:10: "But not I," saith he (he shrinks in and will take nothing to himself), "it was not I but the grace of God which was the author and the cause of it." And therefore [in] Phil. 1:20 Paul did set up God on the pinnacle so that nothing appeared but Christ and his grace. He lay in the dust that the Lord only might tread upon him, that he only might be magnified, admired, and extolled.

I would have a Christian deal in Christianity as men do when one lifts another over the wall. He that is lifted up is only discovered, but the other is not seen; all men may view him, but the other not descried. So I would have the soul lie down low in the dust and at the foot of the Lord and lay down all excellency of gifts, that Christ and his grace might only appear. I would have a Christian heart in reading, praying, and professing to show forth Christ; only lie thou hid and bear up the Lord and his grace, that he only may be presented to the view of the world.

Rule 2: Secondly, labor that others may acknowledge that work of excellency, and that the excellency of that grace might be seen of others but not of ourselves. [See] Mt. 5:16. Oh, that Christians would so walk and converse that the whole world might see what grace can do!, that men may say: 'Such a one by nature is marvelous choleric, but see what grace can do; he is very calm and meek. Such a man is very coward naturally, but see what grace can do; he is courageous for the cause of grace.'

Observe the difference between a proud and a meek spirit. [In] 2 Kg. 10:16 Jehu [saith]: "Come and see [my zeal for the Lord"]. This is the pattern of a proud spirit, for always a vainglorious man either begins or ends with something of his own; and if for shame he cannot commend himself, yet he will so express himself that he will leave some praise of himself behind him. If he talks with some great man, he will flatter and fawn and praise the man he speaks to, so that when he is gone they may say he is a wise, discreet man. And [he] fits every man's humor that it may appear what parts are in him. This is the temper of a proud man.

But now take an example of an humble heart, Acts 3:12-13. That was a fair booty to take a great deal of glory to himself, [but Peter saith:] "Be it known, not I but the name of Jesus hath made this man whole"; [and in] Jn. 1:20: "I am not that great prophet."

Rule 3: Labor that others may be in love with thee, and labor to be partakers of it. This we ought to labor at in all our performances, for we are but [Jn. 3:29] "friends to the bridegroom," and all that we have to do is to woo and win the hearts of people, not to us but to the Lord Jesus. [See] 1 Pet. 3:1. I tell you, a holy wife that hath the work of grace in her heart, she may so behave herself to her husband that he may say: 'What, doth the grace of God work this? Then sure I will love that word and that grace.'

The servant that stands at the stall asks the chapman: 'What will you buy?' He doth not sell for himself; it is his master's commodity. So it is in this case. A Christian should not set out anything, either parts or gifts, to make men buy, but that they might buy grace and love grace, esteem of grace and rejoice in the power of grace.

Rule 4: This should be our aim and care in showing forth the power of godliness: that others may glorify God with us and bless God. Men glorified God in Paul [Gal. 1:24], and said [Gal. 1:23]: "Oh, the admirable power of God that can thus prevail! He that hath been an opposer [is] now a preacher of Christ." Men here wondered at the grace of God. So then labor to express thy grace outwardly when time shall serve.

Art thou a holy wife? Show thyself meek to a churlish Nabal [1 Sam. 25]. Are you holy servants, and yet do you think you may be wayward and proud and take one end of the staff and think your master nor mistress may reprove you? This is not a show of godliness but of sauciness. If you have grace inwardly, show it outwardly and let all the world know what it is to have a gracious heart; let them that have no grace be proud, etc., but be thou meek, obedient, and lay thy hand on thy mouth and say nothing. Oh, what a glory would come to the name of Christ hereby!

Carry home the point in hand. Masters, servants, fathers, and children, have you any goodness? Let the world see it; let thy father see it if thou beest a child; let thy master perceive it if thou beest a servant, that the wicked of the world may not say: 'What are your professors that you talk so much of? They are as proud and as peevish as others; they are as unjust as others.' For shame, let it never be said so of you. But if you think you have any godliness, express it then. Why, show it then. The fire cannot be without light, the sun without heat. So if grace be in your hearts it will appear in your lives.

Now the second thing is the behavior of the wicked to this power of godliness. They deny it; that is they submit not; they close not therewith. As a servant that denies such a man to be his master, and the master deny such a one to be his servant, when the one will not own the other, so hypocrites deal with the virtue of grace and power of holiness. They will by no means bear the authority of it.

Look as it was with Peter in another case. He denied Christ,[3] as who should say: 'I would not own him; I do not belong to him; I owe no subjection to him; he hath no authority over me.' So many go under the name of Christians, but when it cometh to the power of godliness, then you say: 'Godliness hath nothing to do with me.' You will do what seems good in your own eyes; you fling off the power of godliness and the authority of grace which should rule you. Hence observe:

Doctrine 3: That hypocrites take up the profession of godliness, but deny the power thereof to close with it or to take possession of it. For the opening of it two things are to be discovered: first, wherein consists the denial of the power of godliness; secondly, the reasons why they that outwardly profess it yet will not stoop to the power of it. First, your carnal hypocrites deny the power of godliness three ways.

First, partly in their judgment; when they will not assent to the authority of the truth and acknowledge the necessity of godliness; when they say: 'I hope a man may be saved though he be not so exact and precise. What, though he swear now and then, and hath none but that, such a man I hope may be an honest man and go to heaven. I see no necessity put upon a man that a man must thus conform his life to the rule of righteousness with the strictures that ministers call for and require.' This is to deny it in your judgments.

Secondly, in your wills and hearts; when the will and affections will not submit themselves to be framed and ordered and disposed by the power of godliness. You will be proud and peevish, etc., and will walk in your own ways, let God say what he will and the Word command what it please, though we are damned and go down to hell for it. This is a professed opposition of the truth and of the power of godliness.

Thirdly, when we deny it in our practice, in our actions; for if a man's actions be naught, this is certain, his heart is naught. This rule will never deceive you.

Now we come to show the cause why a company of hypocrites

[3] Mt. 26:69 ff., Mk. 14:66 ff., Lk. 22:56 ff., Jn. 18:25 ff.

can swallow down profession; but [because] these will only compliment with [take up the show of] godliness but away with [deny] the power of it.

Reason 1: Because godliness and the power of it, where it comes, is of a powerful nature, of a commanding authority, it will subdue all those beloved corruptions, those prevailing lusts which wicked men so highly prize and are not content to part withal. Therefore they cannot away with the power of it. Take an usurer or covetous man and tell him he must make satisfaction or else perish. This goeth to the heart. And I knew some of these extortioners that could be content to pay some small sums, but when it comes to forty or a hundred pounds, then they flew off and, for aught I know, lived and died in their sins. The adulterer saith he must have his queens, the power of godliness saith he shall not; the drunkard his companions, the power of godliness saith he must not have them unless hell with them. Now here is the quarrel; therefore they take up the show and deny the power thereof.

Reason 2: The power of godliness is accompanied with a great deal of straightness and painfulness in a Christian course. Now a carnal man would fain have some elbowroom and go a broad way; but the way of godliness is thus, and the hypocrite is not able to be pinched. Hence he is not able to bear the power of godliness. Take notice of this. The power of godliness requires a conformity of the whole man in speech, practice, course, and behavior. The power of godliness hath an universal jurisdiction and will rule in your tongue, in your course, in your apparel, in your company; nay, it requires, besides, the heart and sincerity thereof; and this is straight and difficult. Therefore they deny it.

Reason 3: The power of godliness is severe and sharp and keen and cuts to the quick. It ransacks men's consciences, troubles men's souls, and will not let them alone. Therefore it cannot be endured. When the power of godliness comes, it will make a man see upon what ground he goeth and with what evidence of life and salvation. Gal. 6:3: ["For if a man think himself to be something, when he is nothing, he deceiveth himself."] As who should say: 'Many men think themselves somebody in the world, but they are nothing

when they come to the trial.' Rom. 7:9, 21: Before God opened his
eyes, he [Paul] thought he was in a good course, but afterwards it
was otherwise, etc.

Outward hypocrites can lie, cheat, swear and be drunk for company, and go away and never be troubled. They say they will repent
and hope God will pardon them, etc. But the power saith: 'Oh,
those cursed distempers of heart are enough to sink your souls into
hell forever!' This now vexeth them, and then away goes godliness.

These deniers and opposers of godliness may be referred to three
sorts or ranks. Such as openly and customarily continue in the commission of any sin in any kind, after their conscience hath been
convicted and after their judgment hath been informed, and also the
nature of the sin and the condemnation due unto it out of the Word
hath been discovered, these do undoubtedly discover unto the world
that as yet they have no work of true grace wrought in their souls.
I do not say they that commit only heinous sins and continue in
them, as drunkards, etc., but those that lie in and ordinarily take up
the practice of any evil which is known, these have not the work
of grace in their hearts. I know God's saints oftentimes trip and are
taken aside, but ordinarily to take up the practice of any evil [one]
cannot have true grace. As for example a common and ordinary
swearer, a common profaner of the Lord's day — a man may pass
this conclusion upon such persons to be graceless. This is seen [in]
1 Jn. 3:7, [8], as if he had said: 'Many will bear you in hand that
are honest and holy.' But "let no man deceive you," 'tis not saying
but "he that doth righteously is righteous, he that committeth sin
is of the devil." But you will say: 'Doth not every one commit
sin?' No, he that is said to fall into sin is not said to commit sin, but
he that takes up a trade in sin, it is his occupation. They are "workers
of iniquity," Ps. 14:4.

The lawyer goes up to London in term-time, but he hath his
vacation-time too. So sinners have their vacation-time; the drunkard,
usurer, adulterer have their vacation-times. But so soon as the term-
time comes, so soon as the occasion is afforded and the opportunity
offered, they fall to their old trade. Now if you see [one of] these
men, you may know him. He is one of the limbs of Satan; he is
one of the imps of the devil, and in truth a child of the devil so

long as he remains in that estate. He doth not say he falls now and then into an evil way; he is now and then taken aside; but the road wherein all travels is a naughty way. The gamester sets himself to gaming, etc. That same setting of the bias of the soul in an evil way and the expressing of the same in a man's practice, [make it] certain yet he is in the gall of bitterness. These persons are called the "children of Belial," 1 Kg. 21[:13]. This word signifies 'such as will bear no yoke.' It is their ordinary course to shake off the commandments of God. As drunkards, etc., are children of Belial; their hearts are base and their lives as bad as their hearts. But you will say: 'Their hearts may be good for all this.' Nay, I say, they cannot. 'How prove you this?' I answer, thou toldest me so, that is, thy life and conversation doth testify it. The drunkard saith: 'I am a notorious drunkard.' Bear witness, men and angels and friends and neighbors, they proclaim it to mad men and children.

Jas. 2:18: "Show me thy faith by thy works." Hence I conclude, faith inwardly may be seen by works outwardly; then I conclude also that he may [show] his infidelity too by his works. If grace be expressed by precious works, then a man's base heart may be descried by base practices. No physician sees the heart when he trieth whether his disease be in the heart, but he feeleth his pulse. But if that be vehement and violent, he saith his heart is very much distempered. Happily[4] I do not see the wheels of a clock; but when it strikes I know it moves. So it is herein. Do not think that you may have good hearts and yet wicked lives. No, no, I can feel your hearts by your pulse! If your conversation be naught, your hearts are worser. Ec. 10:3: "The fool proclaims himself a fool"; so doth the drunkard.

Objection: 'Aye,' but you will say, 'is it not possible for man's heart to be good all this while? Such a man will be tipsy now and then, and such a one will lie, cozen, and dissemble now and then; but cannot a man have a good heart for all this?'

Answer: I will not tell you so, but the Word tells it, Mt. 7:18: "A good tree cannot bring forth evil fruit." He doth not say: 'A good tree may now and then bring forth evil fruit, but commonly

---

[4] i.e., haply, perhaps.

it brings forth good.' No further! It is impossible! Why, judge you, can grapes grow upon thorns? Or do men gather figs on thistles? Can this be? You will presently say: 'This is impossible, it is against nature and reason.'

He whose judgment is informed and his conscience convinced what duty it is he should take up, which godliness requires and also enables him to take up, and yet will not set upon it, this man denieth also the power of godliness in his practice. I do not say thus, that he that cannot perform good duties after such a manner or in such a measure, that he denies the power of godliness. I say not neither that he [doth so] which is surprised either by temptations or corruptions, if he omit good duties now and then, and recovers himself and useth greater speed and care afterwards, because he hath been negligent. As it is with a horse that stumbles, as soon as he recovers himself he goeth the faster. So if his stumbling and neglecting works this effect, he doth not this power of grace deny. But they that know this only and will not take it up, he only denies it. Grace wherever it comes, it makes not a man a monster but a new creature; so that it hath a heart but no foot, a foot but no tongue, a hand but no head, a head but no heart. Some will do something but know nothing; some will know something and affect nothing. Grace will not do thus. No, no, grace makes a man a new creature! Whatever a Christian should do, grace enables a man to do. 2 Tim. 2:21: ["If a man therefore purge himself from these he shall be] a vessel of honor, not only fit for some good work but for every wholy duty." And a good Christian dare not but at the first submit, Col. 4:12. Drunkards now submit; usurers now submit; oppressors now submit: make restitution, or else thy heart cannot be sound.

Objection: 'Aye,' but you will say, 'it is but a duty I omit. I perform all the rest; let the world spare me in this.'

Answer: I say: he that will not set upon the performance of every duty that God requires, and endeavors not to do it as well as he can, he that will not perform every duty, he never had the power of grace to perform any. Hence it comes to pass that if any man will paddle[5] with the Lord and take up services by halves and will have his reservations and excuses — 'I have oppressed and can-

---

[5] i.e., to deal in a petty, trifling way.

not make restitution (anything but that!); I am loath to pray in my family' — that is seditious, etc. Now if you are convinced of any duty and set not upon it, you are professed opposers of the power of godliness.

He that is wilfully ignorant and will not search nor seek out those truths whereof he ought to be informed, nay, he will not receive directions from those that are able to teach and guide him in the way of salvation; he that purposely flies off because he may have some plea and pretense for himself to take up the course he would walk in, he is a denier of the power of godliness. As for example['s] sake, a man will often hold this as a shield and a buckler: 'Knew I it, or were I persuaded of it, then would I do it.' Thus men, as it were, withdraw themselves from the jurisdiction of the truth, and they will not know that [which] they should know, that so they may have color to excuse them in the not doing of that [which] they would neglect. Now these men, though they be not informed, yet they, because they are wilfully ignorant and because they withdraw themselves from under the power of the means that should inform them, these are professed opposers; for godliness hath that power which is able for to make a man perform any duty, 1 Cor. 2:5, 1 Jn. 2:27.

Now we come to the carriage of the saints: what their behavior should be to such dissemblers. The text saith [2 Tim. 3:5]: "Turn away from them, because they turn away from godliness." As they are estranged from God, so should we be estranged from them.

First, for the meaning of the words. This phrase "turn" [ἀποτρέπω] is not to be found in all the Scripture but in this place, and it is a borrowed speech from things that are contrary one to another. And therefore [2 Th. 3:6]: "Withdraw yourselves one from another, and set yourselves one against another." These are implied in the phrase: first, the heart is estranged from another; secondly, the life and conversation is in some measure withdrawn from another.

Secondly, we come to show the nature of this communion we ought to have with these, and how far we may go. First, we will discover it in general; secondly, we will lay forth the rules in particular.

Communion therefore is twofold: public [and] private. Public concerns the public congregation; and it is an open meeting of many together by virtue of public authority to partake of holy duties. Three things observe in the description. First, there must be an open meeting, because it is in the congregation. The congregation is like to common pastures that are common for every man's cattle; so the ordinances of God are common pastures for everyone. Secondly, it is by virtue of public authority, for that is observed of Hezekiah [2 Chr. 29:3], that he opened the temple doors; so that public authority gives warrant to public meetings. Thirdly, [it] is the sharing of men together in the holy ordinances of God.

Now the question groweth on: how far is it lawful for the saints of God to converse with those that are common swearers and drunkards and adulterers and the like for the present? What are these rules?

The rules are two. First, those that have public authority in their hands, they to whom God hath committed authority over others, such as are either scandalously naught or openly profane should by them be excommunicated, as we may see by the example of Paul, 1 Cor. 5:5, [7], [and in] Mt. 18:15.[6] The second rule. Suppose they that are in authority will not separate them, the second rule then is this: yet the saints of God should not abstain from the congregation. It is pitiful indeed, and the thing is troublesome and tedious to a gracious heart (and we must mourn for it), but being [so], it is not in my power; I must not abstain. I know there are many objections and cavils of the Anabaptists against this, and they thus reply:

Objection: 'This ought to be done, that such persons should be excommunicated; therefore why should I enjoy communion with the body of Christ?'

Answer: I answer: it is true; we must mourn for it; and as King James said of the abuse of excommunication,[7] it is a shame in the church; but that part is yours to whom authority belongs.

---

[6] Hooker here develops a scriptural basis for social shunning. He does not develop here or elsewhere in the treatise a scriptural basis for solicitous warning of a sinful member, leading to his excommunication (Mt. 18:15), by the congregation.

[7] James I, on coming to the throne in 1603, asserted the independence of the state against the "Hildebrandism" of Rome and Geneva alike.

Objection: But they cast this as a reproach upon our church: 'Common drunkards,' they say, and 'swearers.' 'If they do but pay twopence for their offering at Easter, [they] may receive the Supper of the Lord.'

Answer: We confess this fault; let it lie where it is; we cannot reform it. We can only mourn for it, and that God will accept.

Objection: [In] 1 Cor. 5:11, there they bring scripture for it: "If there be any adulterer or unclean person," saith the text, among you, "let him not eat," that is, communicate with him, say they.

Answer: I say "to eat" there is not referred to the communion in eating the body of Christ, but 'eat not with him,' that is, 'be not familiar with such a person'; and it includes the word 'familiarity,' not communion at the Lord's table.[8] [This is seen in] Ps. 41:9. There "eating" implieth a common inward familiarity: "My own familiar friend [in whom I trusted, which did eat of my bread."]

Objection: But yet they reply again from the greater to the less: 'If we may not eat with them privately, then much less publicly may we communicate with them.'

Answer: It is no good reason, because I have more authority to refuse the company of a man in my own house than I have to refuse him in the open congregation. I can keep a man out of my house, but I cannot fling him out of the open congregation; that belongs only to those that are in place and authority.[9]

Constant communion is that, when there lieth such a bond upon a bondman that he cannot break this communion. Such is the communion between the husband and the wife. So, having hired a servant [the master cannot go from the servant] nor the servant from the master when he please, until the covenants be fulfilled. This is constant communion.

The question now is, how far a man may turn unto the wicked, such as are openly wicked. The rules of the questions are three.

Rule 1: First, for a faithful man, when he hath his liberty, then to enter into communion with the wicked is unlawful, as for a free

[8] Hooker is wrong about the original intention of the text. With the help of Ps. 41:9 he turns I Cor. 5:11 into a sanction for social shunning of those with whom one has shared communion!

[9] i.e., by those in public authority in church and state.

servant to make choice of an ungracious master, and so for a holy
master to make choice of a wicked servant, so for a good woman
being single to make choice of a wicked man, or for a holy man
to choose a wicked wife.

Rule 2: If a servant be entered into covenant with an unrighteous
master, or a wife to a wicked husband, they are bound as long as
those bounds last, submissively and humbly to subject themselves
to all services that are required of persons in their place and condition.

Rule 3: As God affords liberty and opportunity in a good way
and a good conscience, every man is bound to sever himself from
such as are wicked and scandalously naught. Now for a servant,
thy year being out, fly the house. Thou that art a prentice, when thy
years are expired, loose thyself and deliver thy heart from this communion.

Now we come to mutable or voluntary private communion. Voluntary communion is a closure with such in common company and
inward familiarity, so as when occasion serves they may all alter
and change again. In the mutable communion observe these three
things:

First, it is a closing and fastening together, a meeting and con-
curring of men together, so far as occasion drives them one to another, or else as affection draws them one to another; and therefore
[in] Ps. 119:63 the word translated 'a friend' signifieth a companion.[10] That is the first passage.

Secondly, we have the propriety or quality of this communion in
the next words. It is a closure in common company and familiarity
when they close one with another in common conversation, Pr. 28:7;
so wicked company [close] one with another in drinking, swearing,
etc. They are joined together in inward familiarity when there is
a closure and combining one with another, when the souls of sundry
men are cabins to keep the counsels and secrets one of another. [In]
Job 19:14, the word there translated 'a familiar' is 'a man of secrets';
so we may see it in the example of Jonathan and David: the text

[10] Both the Geneva Version and the Authorized Version translate "companion."

saith [1 Sam. 18:1] that "the soul of Jonathan was knit to the soul of David."

Lastly, they so close in common company and inward familiarity that yet, notwithstanding, it is in a man's power as occasion serves to change either this company or familiarity. Therefore we call it mutable communion, because there is no bond nor tie lieth upon a man to engage himself to his company, but as occasion is offered a man may turn the back to a base fellow that hath cozened him. This I take to be the communion mainly to be intended, though the other[s] are included; but this voluntary society, I think, is that [which] the Apostle here [1 Cor. 5:11] specially aims at. Hence it is the duty of all the saints of God not to close in communion and unnecessary company and inward familiarity with those that are the deniers of the power of godliness.

I say, meetly observe: the saints must not close in common and unnecessary communion with the wicked. I call it unnecessary, because a man may be forced sometimes to keep company with profane men, as for example these three bonds force him:

Bond 1: Sometimes the bond of a man's calling will force him to keep company with the wicked. As the magistrate must be ordinarily in the company of the wicked to reform them, the physician among his patients, the minister among his people, the lawyer among clients; so innkeepers: the law will force them to entertain a stranger and to give him that which is reasonable.

Bond 2: The bond of humanity and civility that binds a man sometimes to keep company with the wicked, as the bond of neighborhood, for example; people that live in the same place or town, they are forced to consult about the affairs of the town and other occasions one with another.

Bond 3: The bonds of religion and natural mercy binds sometimes to keep company with such, for the souls of all men should labor to do good unto all so far as necessity requires and opportunity is offered thereunto; for we are bound to preserve the honor, life, goods, good name of any man whatever he be. Be the company never so wicked, yet the duty is good and holy.

Therefore I say we must not close with men in unnecessary communion. So far we must turn away from them, 1 Cor. 5:11, 2 Th. 3:6: "Withdraw yourselves from them." It is a comparison taken from full sails. When the sails of a ship are drawn and it hath full sail, it goeth very swiftly. So saith the Apostle: 'Do not strike sail. Do not freely express yourself in familiarity with him, but withdraw yourselves.' Ps. 56:8: Shut the door against them. So you see the point is clear.

For our better direction, observe these three particulars: first, something by way of explication (how far the limits of turning from the wicked doth go); secondly, the reasons why we must turn away; thirdly, the use and application.

Where may we set the bounds and compass of our familiarity with the wicked? For this we must remember these two passages: some that deny godliness make it their trade and practice; secondly, others only deny it upon occasion, and though they have grace, yet from both these we must turn away.

Objection: But first touching the former that are known to be wicked men, such as are openly naught: how far shall we carry ourselves familiar toward these?

Answer: In these particulars: first, partly in regard of the disposition of the heart; secondly, of the outward behavior of our lives. In both these particulars we must turn away.

First, how far must the heart of a good man be restrained from the company and familiarity of those that are scandalously wicked? I answer, the rules are two.

Rule 1: The saints of God are bound to have a vile esteem and a base account of those that are such vile and base persons. Let the word of God rule us in this and let us be commanded by it. [In] Ps. 15:4 observe two passages: first, every wicked man is a vile man; secondly, they should despise and contemn them. It is a badge of a Christian, the note of a holy heart in whose eyes a wicked man is vile, a vile drunkard, a vile adulterer, etc. It is not a matter of liberty but of necessity, as [can be seen in] Is. 5:20 ["We unto them that call evil good, and good evil"]. It is marvelous lying so to do. The Scripture styles wicked men dogs, hogs, and fools. What the Scripture saith, we ought to give ear unto: a drunken man a fool, a covetous man a fool, etc. If we judge not so, we judge otherwise than the Scriptures.

Where wicked men think it a pride and audacity for God's saints to esteem basely of them, it is no such matter. Be you better and they will judge better of you. Should a man judge that to be gold which is dross, that to be silver which is lead? Should we judge you to have the love of God when you have none?

Rule 2: The soul of a gracious man is marvelous secretly jealous lest it should be infected with such wicked persons. This will follow from the former by clear and evident and sound ground. That which the soul abhors and that which the heart is carried with abomination against, there cannot [be] but [that] a separation will follow, and he must needs be marvelous jealous of being tainted thereby.

Now we come to the second thing, which was the outward behavior and carriage; and this also may show a dislike. How far must our outward carriage be turned away from a wicked man?

Objection: How should a man carry himself toward the wicked of the world? Must he express no point of love unto them?

Answer: I answer: you must bear a great deal of love toward them, and you ought to maintain a great deal of affection to them and do a great many services for them; and they are three especially.

You must labor to have a spirit of compassion and to mourn inwardly and be grieved thoroughly for the sins that are in them and for the manifest miseries they pluck upon themselves. This was the behavior of our savior Christ [Mt. 23:37]: "O Jerusalem, Jerusalem, how often would I have gathered thee under my wings!" If ever you have had any relish of mercy and compassion from the Lord Jesus, oh, then pity those that want this pity! When you see a company of drunkards staggering, and a company of blasphemers stabbing the Almighty and drowning their souls in the pit of destruction forever, if you have any mercy, any bowels of compassion within you, let your eyes drop down tears in secret and mourn and lament for the misery and desolation of such poor creatures: happily enemies to God, happily enemies to thee. But what of that? We ourselves were once haters and hated of God and ran the broad way to hell and everlasting destruction. Therefore show pity and compassion to such poor souls. Jer. 13:17: ["My soul shall weep in secret places . . . mine eye shall weep sore, and run down with tears."] Oh, pity them, poor creatures [Lk. 23:34], "they know not what they do!" If you howl and mourn in secret inwardly for the confusion that is like to fall upon their poor souls, and think with yourselves, 'What, must all those cursed drunkards and wretched adulterers and wicked blasphemers live here sinfully and perish everlastingly and go down to hell and grave, there in everlasting torments never to be comforted, never to be refreshed?' — if you have any bowels of compassion, you cannot but mourn for them.

Pray for them in secret. When thou art praying to God and seeking to the Lord for mercy for thyself, put into the same prayer all those that are in the gall of bitterness and in the bond of iniquity. Put up a petition for the drunkard; put up a petition for the adulterer. As thou desirest God to save thy soul, so entreat the Lord to turn the heart of the drunkard, etc. Remember what Abraham did for Ishmael [Gen. 17:18]: "Oh, let Ishmael live in thy sight, Lord!" So pray you: 'Oh, that such a drunkard might have his life amended! Oh, that such a profane heart may live in thy sight, Lord! You must use all means to reclaim them. You must reprove them sharply, counsel them compassionately, and strive with them mightily, that so you may bring them home to know [Lk. 19:42] "the things belonging to their peace" here and everlasting happiness hereafter.

Now we are to inquire whether we must not turn from such as heretofore have not been noted to be wicked persons, but such as hath received mercy and favor from the Lord. It may be in these two cases that follow, that [it] is not only left to a man's liberty, but a duty of necessity which God hath laid upon us, to turn away from such.

Case 1: Those that have professed Christianity and approved themselves outwardly to the Church of Christ, yet not withstanding — if by reason of inward corruptions or temptations or occasions pressing in upon them — they fall foully and scandalously into some notorious offense, then we should turn away from having any inward society with them for the while, till they have — upon sufficient proof by their humiliation and reformation, and, if it be possible —

they have given satisfaction publicly to the Church of God, 1 Cor. 5:9 ["I wrote unto you in an epistle not to company with fornicators"].

The reason of this is pregnant, for the truth is, such falls give a good ground of suspicion that there was never yet any sound grace wrought in their hearts. I do not say a ground of conclusion, but of suspicion that the work was not sound nor this grace sincere in the heart, because he hath sinned so foully and fallen so fearfully. For however the saints fall so foully, yet this is ever observable: it is not ordinary, as few be drunk, few commit adultery after their conversion. They have their infirmities and weaknesses, and though they may fall extraordinarily, yet ever observe: as that their fall is foul, so their repentance is great, as in David [Ps. 38:8]: "He roared [by reason of the disquietness of his heart"]. And mark it: after the saints of God have repented of their falls, who ever read that they fell into the same sins again?

Case 2: A man that hath lived in the bosom of the Church and hath been conceived and judged in the course of reason and charity to be in the state of grace, yet, notwithstanding, if he come to this pass that he is obstinately incorrigible, though the fault be but small and not known of many, if yet he will not yield when all arguments are answered and all pleas removed, then shake hands with him and have no familiarity with him for the time. This I take to be the scope of the text, Mt. 18:15. It skills not [11] what the matter of the fault, but what the incorrigibleness of the parties. [In] 2 Th. 3:14 ["And if any man obey not our word . . . note that man and have no company with him, that he may be ashamed"] observe it: it is very reasonable a man should do so; for he that will not receive good by the society of the members of Christ, it is fit he should be cast out from having any communion with the members of Christ. For what is the end of communion but that men might be informed? Now if a man will not hear nor be convinced, it is fit he should be deprived of the comfort of the society of the saints. I reason thus: he that may be excommunicated publicly may be separated privately from the company and intimate society of the saints;

[11] i.e., it makes no difference.

but he that is obstinately incorrigible may be excommunicated publicly; therefore he may be separated from the society of the saints.

Reason 1: Because it [shunning] is the practice of much love, nay, of the greatest mercy that a man can show to a wicked, profane wretch. I presume you will hardly think it so. You will say: 'This is love indeed, when a man cannot look upon another but he must disdain him! Doth a man show mercy to another when he will not keep his company? If this be your love, God bless me from such a love.' Take heed what thou sayest. God bless thee from folly and not from this love. And you shall plainly see it so, because this course and behavior is that which God hath appointed as a special means. It is that which is marvelous helpful and useful and profitable to withdraw a wicked man from his wicked course and work sound repentence in his soul. Therefore it must needs be an argument of great affection, 2 Th. 3:14: "Note him." Why? "That he may be ashamed." Now he that is ashamed of his course is in some way and readiness to forsake and abandon his course; for shame implieth these three things:

First, he that is ashamed of a thing seeth the vileness of a thing; secondly, he seeth himself vile and base, and that discredit is like to befall him by reason of the vileness of the thing; thirdly, he labors to keep himself, that dishonor and discredit may not fall upon him, and he labors to keep himself from such occasions and practices which may bring this discredit upon him. So this is the next way for thee: to make him ashamed, etc. How justly may such a one reason with himself when he seeth the saints of God are weary of his company and loathe to converse with him: 'How vile is my course! How base is my sin and ungodly practices! What reason have I to loath my sin! Therefore let me forever abhor these base courses that make me to be abominated of the saints and servants of the Lord.'

Reason 2: This reason concerns ourselves, that we may not be defiled, that we may not be infected with their wicked courses and polluted with their society. It is in this case with sin as it is with the plague of the body. He that will be clear of it, the old rule is: fly far enough, fly soon enough; he that is with those that are infected, likely he shall be infected. So it is with sin, which is the plague of the soul. He that hath a plague sore blossoming, he that hath a tongue belching forth his venom against the Lord of host, he that hath a plague sore of drunkenness, a plague sore of adultery, if ever you would be preserved, then go far enough, fly soon enough. The alehouse is the pest-house where the plague is; the drunkards are the persons infected. If thou wouldst be clear, come not near them. Joseph learned to swear when he was in Pharaoh's court [Gen. 42:7], and Barnabas [Gal. 2:13] ["was carried away] with dissembling" when he saw Peter halt before him. So it is said [Jg. 2] the Israelites mingled themselves among the Canaanites and learned their works. As they say, one rotten apple spoils all the rest, and one scabbed sheep infects the whole flock; with the froward we shall learn frowardness, etc. It hath been the bane and ruin of many a man, and he hath carried this company-keeping to his grave, nay, happily to hell, etc.

This is the cause why the Lord is constrained: when all reasons prevail not, when all arguments persuade not, the Lord is fain to bring him out by an almighty hand. Unless the Lord let in the fire of hell on the conscience of the drunkard and tire him out of his base company, there is little hope that the means of grace will work upon him for his good. Therefore fly far enough, Pr. 22:24 ["Make no friendship with an angry man"]. [In] I Cor. 5:6 sin is there compared to leaven. Now leaven doth not [leaven] that which is only next it, but the whole lump. So mark the Apostle's argument. A wicked man comparably doth not only leaven himself, but he leavens all his company, all that converse with him and all that maintain familiarity with him. With the swearer thou wilt swear; with the dissembler [dissemble], with the liar [lie], etc.

Reason 3: Because it [shunning] is a special means to fit us and so to furnish our hearts to be much more ready and cheerfully enlarged in a constant and holy performance of all good duties that God requires of us, and to discharge all those holy duties which ought to be performed by us, Ps. 119:115 ["Depart from me, ye evil-doers; for I will keep the commandments of my God"]. As if he had said: 'Until you be gone there is no doing for me.' The presence of the wicked and God's sincere service cannot stand together. He that will keep the company of the wicked cannot keep the commandments of God. He that will not depart from them, God will depart from him. Therefore away with these. Observe the manner of the phrase. David [Ps. 119:115] presumes this: that ill company is not so much the breach of one commandment as the breach of all God's commandments. As who should say: 'I shall keep the first table, not the second, etc.' He saith not, 'I cannot keep the sabbath, or pray, etc.,' but, 'I cannot keep the commandments.'

The company and society of the wicked doth hinder a man in keeping God's commandments in three particulars.

Particular 1: First, it takes off the fitness and disposition of the soul to the performance of any service, that when the heart is some-time teachable and pliable coming to God, when there are some good desires after God — when wicked company meet it, [it] plucks all these up by the roots. And if his conscience will not suffer him to do as they do, oh, then there is cause enough of jibing and taunting and scoffing extremely! 'Your conscience,' saith the drunkard, 'will not suffer you to be drunk?' 'Your conscience,' saith the swearer, 'will not suffer you to swear? Oh, you are a tender-conscienced man!' Thus, if there be any desire or disposition of doing good, wicked company blast it even in the bud. This is the cause that many young men curse their companions, or else, when they are going the way of all flesh, this strikes him to the heart: 'The time was, I may say, that God gave me some inclinations after goodness, and my heart was wandering after heaven and mine eyes were opened and my mind enlightened and I had a resolution to take up good courses and perform duties, but oh, this ill company spoiled all! This was the man that cut me off from my course and that took away my disposition of spirit from me and made me twice as bad as himself, though he be as bad as the devil.'

Particular 2: Cursed loose company; it deprives the soul of the benefit of all the means and hinders the success of all the ordinances of God, that they can never work upon the heart. Wonder not, then, though they cause a man to break all the commandments of God, since the word of God works not, nor cannot, for these three causes:

First, it keeps a man from coming under the means, and therefore [he] shall never receive good thereby. Loose company load all holy courses with such scandalous reproaches that they scare poor sinful creatures from undergoing of them.

Secondly, nay further, it is the policy of all loose persons: they will appoint their meetings when they may hinder men most from the means that may do them good. And this is the reason: that of all the days in the week they choose the Lord's day, and of all the hours in the day the sermon or prayer-time is the hour wherein they meet. And if he be resolved to attend upon the means, they then forestall the market and make him have a slight account of preaching: 'What need we all this preaching? Let him preach till his heart ache! Who is the better for his preaching?' So then, if the poor soul doth come, the soul hears and cares not. If he cares, he attends not; if he attends, he regards not; if anything touch him, he casts it off as if it did not concern him.

Thirdly, loose persons; if it be so that anything do remain upon the heart, if the Lord comes home and affrights his soul and discover his sin and writes bitter things against him, and the soul promiseth, resolves to turn unto the Lord and to leave all, never to return — oh, then what ado is there with this cursed rabble to peck out the good seed of the Word which is sown in the heart! They will never leave plucking and haling[12] of the poor soul till they have made him cast away the blessed truth. It is with cursed ones in this case as it is with the ravenous bird, Mt. 13: [4].

Hence it is that if they see one hang the wing a little and go aside, they think the minister hath wounded him, and they imagine he will withdraw himself from their company. Therefore they make after the soul overcome, and thus they set upon him: 'Why is it? How comes it? What is the reason? What is the cause that thou art thus disquieted? What, art a mad man to be troubled thus at the words of a minister? I would never do it while I lived. What would I care what all the ministers in the world should say! They must say something. Now let not this trouble thee.' And thus they pluck the soul from under the power of the means. And haply the seed of the Word that the Lord then sowed, [he] will never sow it again.

---

[12] i.e., dragging, hauling.

Maybe it was the last time of asking. Had he then withdrawn himself from the society, that seed might have taken root and he might have been blessed forever. But the ravenous companions stole it away. Thus then we see wicked companions keeps a man from coming to the Word. If he doth come, they forestall the power of the Word. If the Word doth prevail, they pluck the seed of the Word out of the soul, that it can do their souls no good that keep company with the wicked.

Particular 3: Your cursed companions will never leave a poor sinner till they mold him even according to their own mind, until they bring him to their own bent and frame. Therefore note thou that keepest company with wicked, ungodly persons; they will leaven thee according to their own frame, and they will leave thee the very same lusts and corruptions. This is the cause of a final and total destruction of a world of people. There is this kind of privilege in ungodly company-keepers, that there is a kind of army of corruptions. They are the devil's army and they fight the devil's battles; therefore the soul is beset round with them. Were a man to fight against another man, there were some hope of resistance. Or if there were two against one, there were some hope of escape; if he could not oppose them, yet he might fly from them. But if he be among an army there is no way to escape. So it is with those that keep wicked company. Thou art beset with an army, perhaps profaneness hit thee not; [then] their hypocrisy, haply hypocrisy doth not; [then] their looseness, haply their looseness doth not; then envy or some other distemper. Imagine you see a man in the midst of an army of archers. Haply, though one hit him not, yet one of twenty [may]; if one of twenty hit him not, one of a hundred may; if one of a hundred may not, one of a thousand may; one or the other will hit him, he cannot avoid it. All ungodly courses, all wicked speeches, counsels, persuasions are but like so many arrows, and thou that art in the midst of wicked persons, thou art in the midst of an army. One or [the] other will hit thee, thy conscience will be wounded, thy soul ruinated by this means.

This I observe by my experience: wicked men will never leave till others be worse than themselves. They are like the foggy air in the fens. If a man live in the place, it will be sure to arrest him.

It is called the "fen bailiff." [13] And [it] will never leave till it hath turned the humor of his body into the same nature with itself. And then he may live there and have his health well enough. So it is with a company of filthy, foggy drunkards and adulterers and company-keepers. They will never leave thee till they arrest thee with base courses, till they have molded thee with their frame. Then thou mayest enjoy their society here with them and go down to hell hereafter, Mt. 23:15. So it is generally in this case. He that before company-keeping was somewhat tender and shamefast, he would blush to be seen in an alehouse and in base courses; but after he hath been a while with them, they make him twofold the child of the devil. Now he hath a whore's forehead and his brow is of brass and his neck of iron sinews, and [he] dares be drunk at noonday, etc. The reason is: he is perfectly new molded.

Use 1: [For] instruction to the wicked themselves: you must not be displeased with the saints of God in that they judge meanly of you and estrange themselves from you.

Objection: But you will say: 'What care I what the saints of God say and do! Do you think I care for their company? Let them keep what company they will; I can keep as good as they!'

Answer: Oh, take heed of this! If the saints of God say, 'Depart from me, ye wicked!,' what will then the God of all saints? If the gracious saints will not abide thee here, will the God of all grace abide thee in heaven hereafter? No, no, the fearful sentence will pass upon you at the great day of account! [Mt. 25:41]: "Depart from me, ye cursed!" Therefore labor to be sensible of this and so to be humbled and abased for this, and labor for to be better, and then the saints of God will love and delight in your society.

---

[13] A fen-reave was a deputy of the sheriff in charge of fen lands. A fen bailiff was apparently a nickname for the mania that caught hold of anyone exposed long to fen conditions.

ESSAY 2

The Order of Salvation in Thomas Hooker's Thought

BY NORMAN PETTIT

Thomas Hooker, more than any other Puritan divine, looked to the order of salvation, or the *ordo salutis*, as the central concern in Christian life; and he applied himself to the needs of troubled souls with extraordinary vigor. It was at Chelmsford, in 1626, that he first began to preach in a "popular way" on preparation for, and assurance of, salvation — subjects that his Essex followers would ask him to resume in New England; and it was at Chelmsford that he first began to describe in detail the workings of the Spirit on the unregenerate heart. No other Puritan pastor so concerned himself with matters of doubt, hope, and despair: none has so thoroughly described the interior life. Of the leading Puritan divines who sailed to New England between 1629 and 1635, Hooker had the most to say about the process of redemption — a topic on which he preached with unusual knowledge and skill. He had, moreover, the ability to define each phase of the process with extraordinary care, so that if sinners could not discern the moment of saving grace, they would certainly know the manner in which it had been achieved. He was, above all, a preacher of the covenant bond, and he linked that bond to the notion of regenerative growth with great originality of mind. The covenant with Abraham, renewed in Christ, promised the salvation that the process of redemption described.

Hooker knew, as did most Puritan preachers of his time, that if sinners were to be exhorted to the religious life, self-involvement had somehow to be made a part of that life; and he knew as well that all men could not agree on the nature of conversion. The first Reformers, notably Ulrich Zwingli, had asserted that faith comes only as an effectual call, or that repentance is synonymous with assurance of saving faith. And the earliest English churchmen, following Zwingli, had described conversion as sudden and unexpected

— as Paul knew it on the road to Damascus (Acts 9:3-9). But in time certain English divines began to express the idea that man, although utterly depraved, might nevertheless take part in his own salvation. As early as 1570 these preachers of "practical divinity" had begun to ask whether or not there might be something man could do, so to "draw near in full assurance of faith" as Scripture demanded. Such Elizabethan Puritan pastors as Richard Rogers and William Perkins had begun to think of regeneration as a process, rather than as a moment in time, with the result that conversion no longer implied immediate assurance of salvation. Man had now to search for evidence of grace. Perhaps, in time, he might gain some inkling of sainthood, but rarely could he claim election without the agony of doubt. And it was to this doubt that Hooker addressed himself in his earliest published remarks. The process of redemption — from the soul's preparation and effectual calling to the final ingrafting into Christ — had fully to be described; for it gave the doubting Christian an indispensable guide to the spiritual life.

In Documents IV, V, and VI — the Preface to John Rogers' *The Doctrine of Faith* (1627), *The Poor Doubting Christian Drawn Unto Christ* (1629), and *The Faithful Covenanter* (c. 1629) — Hooker turns his attention first to the spectrum of redemption, then to the problem of assurance, and finally to the covenant relationship, all concerns that are inseparably linked in his mind; and he attempts throughout to describe these concerns as they are linked to the process of conversion. How sudden, gradual, or imperceptible a change is involved from the beginnings of regeneration to final assurance of saving grace? Can effectual faith be weak as well as strong? and if strong at first can it eventually fade? The writer of Hebrews had said, "Let us draw near with a true heart in full assurance of faith" (Heb. 10:22); but William Perkins, the most eminent pastor of his day, had maintained that a weak faith, or the endeavor to apprehend, the will to believe with an honest heart, was as much as most Christians could hope for — that assurance of salvation need not depend upon the strength of faith, as even a "seed" of grace could save ("If ye have faith, as even a grain of mustard seed . . . nothing shall be impossible unto you," Mt. 17:20). Hooker had therefore to define, for his own pastoral ends, what saving grace implied; and he had also to define the "hindrances" to faith that stood in men's way. What, he asked, keeps the soul from coming to Christ? Why, within the covenant of grace, do men resist the first motions of the Spirit? For help he turned not only to Rogers, Perkins, and other great Elizabethan lights, but also to the master of the pulpit in his own day, Richard Sibbes; and he turned as well to those biblical and scholastic texts that best helped him to describe the workings of the Spirit on the unregenerate heart.

Thomas Aquinas had said that the first movement of the soul is "not indeed of coercion, but of infallibility," and that if God intends the one "whose heart He moves" should attain to grace, he will "infallibly attain to it." [1] But preachers of Puritan bent, although willing to give way on coercion, were never without doubts about infallibility. In the *Seven Treatises*, considered to be the first complete expression of the spiritual life in Puritan thought, Richard Rogers declared conversions to be so variable that the greatest difficulty is knowing whether or not an alteration has taken place at all. "That which most troubleth the weak about this matter," said Rogers, "is that this change of the heart, and renewing thereof, is so hardly seen and so meanly felt within them, that they cannot satisfy themselves . . . Now idle motions and vain thoughts and fantasies much trouble them . . . they cannot be rid of them; now they fear that they are not renewed and changed at all." [2] As opposed to the accepted Pauline corpus of the time, which acknowledged the "weak in faith" (Rom. 14:1), but which stressed "full assurance of hope unto the end" (Heb. 6:11), Rogers turned time and again to lack of assurance, which he said could be attributed to the subtle, almost indiscernible motions of the Holy Spirit. Man, in the process of conversion, said Rogers, is "secretly drawn, he cannot tell how, by the unspeakable work of the Spirit." Therefore, though he "longeth and almost fainteth for God's mercy," he cannot be entirely assured of it. Through weakness and want of experience, he cannot "call God Father"; nor can he "suffer the contrary thought to have any place in himself." [3]

[1] Thomas Aquinas, *Summa Theologica*, Quest. 112, Art. 3.
[2] Richard Rogers, *Seven Treatises* (London, 1610), pp. 95, 103.
[3] Ibid., pp. 10–26.

Rogers proclaimed, and Hooker later concurred, that assurance of salvation need not come at the start, and that lack of assurance need not imply a lack of saving work in the soul. But what sets Hooker off from Rogers (and to a lesser degree from Perkins and Sibbes), is a special concern with man's resistance to the work of the Spirit. "Thou art the cause why thy heart is not softened," he cries; and "this distemper of thy heart hinders the working of the word, and dispensation of God's providence, and the tenure of the covenant of grace." [4] Hooker, unlike those noted "physicians of the soul" who pondered man's failure to respond to the Spirit, points first to the offenders, to those who actively resist, to those who set up their own barriers to grace, and so shows a novel concern for what can only be called the "psychology" of conversion. He was the first of the Jacobean Puritan divines fully to explore the resistance of the soul to the "motions" of the Spirit, a topic on which he and John Cotton later disagreed in Massachusetts Bay; and he remains to this day the master of the so-called "steps" in the process of conversion, pointing up as he does not only the need for preparation, but also the dangers to be encountered along the way — dangers of pride, overintrospection, and of excessive reliance on "feeling" and "sense."

In *The Poor Doubting Christian Drawn Unto Christ*, first published as a part of Sibbes' *The Saints Cordials* (1629), and printed here from that text, Hooker turns first to the "lets and impediments" that stand in men's way. It is "not properly our unworthiness," he says, but "our pride and haughtiness" that keep us from coming to Christ; and this pride he attributes to all activities of soul that in any way diminish our dependence upon the promises. Sibbes, early in his preaching career, had said that grace may be more readily discerned if conceived in terms of feeling and sense experience: if we "beg . . . a heart able to discern spiritual favors, to taste and relish them," he had declared, that will allow us to "relish spiritual things." [5] But Hooker, although willing to admit that man's sensory response to the "sweetness" of the Spirit might at times fit him to

[4] Thomas Hooker, *The Poor Doubting Christian Drawn Unto Christ* (London, 1629) p. 350.
[5] Richard Sibbes, *Works*, ed. Alexander Grosart (7 vols. Edinburgh, 1862–74) 3, 23, 248; 7, 60; 4, 195; 2, 218.

receive God's love, and that this sense of taste might even make way "for the promise to come and meet with the soul," nevertheless warns against the practice. Men may have faith, he insists, without "sense and feeling." "[A] man may have a good faith," he argues, "and yet want the relish and sweetness which he desires." Far more important than sensation and taste, which may detract from the strength of the Word, is the covenant promise of eternal life. "A man's faith may be somewhat strong when his feeling is nothing at all," Hooker declares. "Therefore away with your sense and feeling, and go to the promise" (pp. 160–161).[6]

If a man relies on sensory assurance alone, Hooker points out, he may not only neglect the Word, but exaggerate his failings as well: he may, in his quest for the sweetness he desires, "look too long" or "pore too much" upon his own corruptions, and so be "disheartened." He may, indeed, "open the stream and floodgate of corruption," which in the end will overwhelm him; for self-accusation, if extreme, can pull down the soul to the point of despair. Over-introspection in the quest for assurance can "stop the stream of God's practice" and "let down the sluice against it," so that the promise cannot come into the soul (pp. 161–162); and if a poor creature thinks that his sins are unpardonable, "he shall never get assurance of God's love" (p. 166). He must therefore distrust that part of his mind which, without the evidence of God's word in the promise, turns in upon itself. "All sense and feeling of carnal reason," Hooker warns, "are like fogs and mists which make a man that he cannot see the way." And because each man is inclined to see the worst in himself, his vision is further clouded; he must learn at the start to take the soul "at the best" (p. 168). If he sees only those failings that "accuse" him, and cannot value the "uprightness" in his soul, his case is lost,

---

[6] Hooker, *The Souls Implantation* (London, 1637) p. 233. Hooker's warnings against excessive reliance on "sense and feeling" may stem from his personal observations of the protracted conversion of Joan Drake, whose spiritual adviser he became while serving as rector of St. George's, Esher, in 1620. Because she looked to her inmost feelings rather than to the biblical promises of salvation, she endured in her quest for faith a prolonged agony of soul that left her in torment and despair. See George Huntson Williams, "Called by Thy Name, Leave Us Not: The Case of Mrs. Joan Drake, A Formative Episode in the Pastoral Career of Thomas Hooker in England." *Harvard Library Bulletin*, XVI, Nos. 2 and 3, 1968, pp. 111–128, 278–300.

for he will think himself unworthy of the promises, and so turn the "backside" of his heart to God. "We must have our judgment informed by the Word that there is some good in us," Hooker tells the poor doubting Christian; and the main worker in assurance must be conscience, which if settled and established in biblical truth will not disquiet the heart.

Conscience alone, Hooker insists, remembers a "clear evidence of God's love" when "sense and feeling be sometimes gone" (p. 170). And because he suspects that men tend always to demand more immediate evidence of faith than they need, and then to place the burden of proof on self-evaluation alone, he warns against rejecting "the evidence which God makes known and passeth upon thy soul for everlasting good." If you think yourself worthy of the promises, Hooker asserts, and so turn the "right side" of your heart to God, you can then take up the covenant bond, and so prepare yourself for effectual conversion. If you "lean on the promise," your heart will then be "ready to go unto Christ" (p. 178). Above all, "thou must not first have faith and then go to the promise," he insists, "but thou must first go to the promise and from thence receive power to make thee able to believe the promise" (p. 182). Preparation for grace, which breaks the soul's resistance, means the turning of the heart toward the promise of salvation before the moment of conversion takes place; and for Hooker there can be no salvation without such preparation. There must, he declares, be "the voice of Christ" to the soul before there can be "an echo again" of the soul to Christ: "we must hear the voice of God in the promise before we can return an echo again to the Lord" (pp. 182–183). Preparation for grace is the plucking away of "carnal props" to make way for the promise to come; it is a willingness to "behold" Christ in order that we might then reflect his love for us back to him again; for "We all with open face beholding as in a glass the glory of the Lord, are changed into the same image from glory to glory" (2 Cor. 3:18) (p. 185).

For Hooker, as *The Poor Doubting Christian* clearly shows, there are few theological abstractions seriously to be taken into account. The document itself, in tone and intent, is personal and biblical throughout. Man can enter the covenant relationship, says Hooker, only through personal acknowledgement of the bond, which in turn must lead to sound contrition and "brokenness of heart." Such preparatory humility, he maintained, had been demanded by God through Isaiah: "I dwell in the high and holy places with him also that is of a contrite and humble spirit, to revive the spirit of the humble, and to give life to them that are of a contrite heart" (Is. 57:15). Furthermore, the degree to which conversion resembles a forceful seizure, or conversely, a turning toward God, may depend upon one's very awareness of this covenant obligation. And here it should be observed that Hooker's own conversion provides a vivid illustration of the principle involved.

According to Cotton Mather, Hooker was converted some time between 1611 and 1618, while serving as catechist and lecturer at Emmanuel. At first, we are told, "It pleased the Spirit of God very powerfully to break into the soul of this person with such a sense of his being exposed unto the just wrath of Heaven, as filled him with most unusual degrees of horror and anguish, which broke not only his rest, but his heart also, and caused him to cry out, 'While I suffer thy terrors, O Lord, I am distracted!'" In the "time of his agonies," Mather goes on, "he could reason himself to the rule, that there was no way but submission to God"; yet "when he came to apply this rule unto himself in his own condition, his reasoning would fail him, he was able to do nothing." Tormented by the "spirit of bondage" to no avail, he began to consider his "interest in the new covenant." It became his manner, "at his lying down for sleep," to "single out some certain promise of God, which he would repeat and ponder, and keep his heart close unto it"; and afterwards he counseled others "to take the same course," telling them that "the promise was the boat which was to carry a perishing sinner over unto the Lord Jesus Christ." [7]

In Mather's account, the agonies of divine constraint are clearly moderated by the covenant promises, for "horror and anguish" cease with open acknowledgement of the "promise of God." Hooker, to be sure, was violently constrained at first, but his willingness to enter the covenant voluntarily was also of the utmost importance. He therefore did not insist, as John Cotton later would do, that

---

[7] Cotton Mather, *Magnalia Christi Americana*, I (Hartford, 1855), III, 333–34.

conversion be violent or sudden: he allowed, as Mather tells us, for a clear alternative to seizure. The promises of "largest extent" in Scripture, said Hooker, belong to those who "take up their own hearts." If a man be a "scandalous liver," God "lays a heavy blow upon the heart . . . as he broke Paul's heart." But the Word "saith not" that it must be done in an "extraordinary and fearful manner." [8] Legal terrors, to be sure, have still a significant rôle to play in the *ordo salutis:* fear of punishment, for one, awakens the conscience to the need of covenant grace; the spirit of bondage in preparation fits the soul for the spirit of love in vocation. Nevertheless, the degree of constraint depends to a large extent upon man's willingness to enter the bond; and though the Spirit constrains, it also awakens the desire for saving grace.

The full implications of covenant theology are not, however, in *The Poor Doubting Christian* thoroughly worked out; nor is the preparatory stage thoroughly discussed. It is not until we turn to *The Faithful Covenanter,* preached at the lecture in Dedham (probably in 1629) that the meaning of the promises within the larger framework of the covenant is fully explained, and preparation entirely thought out. In this document, which represents his earliest views on covenant theology (but which remained unpublished until 1644), Hooker speaks not to the Christian who doubts, but to those who misuse the covenant — to those who must endure threats of punishment if ever they are to come to Christ.

Although delivered to a Dedham congregation, this sermon is addressed to all of England, which for Hooker has forsaken the covenant bond. "What meaneth this fierce wrath of the Lord?" he asks. "What was this goodly England, the only nation of all the earth, and yet now all laid waste in this fearful manner?" (p. 191). England, like ancient Israel, has sinned; she has professed outwardly to follow her God, but inwardly has turned away from him; and so the punishment of Israel (Dt. 28, 29) serves as a "type" for England's. Indeed, if God could bring wrath upon the Jews, his chosen people, then England is surely in trouble: only fear of punishment and terror of conscience can correct her ways. "All you that hear this word

---

[8] Hooker, *The Souls Preparation for Christ* (London, 1632) pp. 172–180.

this day, whose conscience accuse you, that you are enemies to God and goodness," Hooker warns, "hear and fear and tremble forever" (p. 193); otherwise God will destroy each house and church in the Land. "Would it not make our hearts ache, brethren," he asks, "to pass by these places and see the houses of God burnt down to the ground?" (p. 192) And here his thoughts may have turned toward his coming exile abroad as he went on to describe what the covenant bond implies, and what it means to "walk" in covenant with the Lord.

Man in covenant cannot gain eternal life by deeds, but by the gift of grace alone, for which he must eternally give thanks. It is God's goodness alone that cements the bond, and "The goodness of the Lord endures . . . Upon those that keep his commandments" (p. 132). The covenant with Adam had been given to man "in his innocency"; but now, because of the Fall, that covenant is annulled; now "No man doth or can perform the law out of his own holiness and goodness exactly, to obtain life thereby." Therefore "legal" performance has been replaced by "evangelical" performance, or "obedience to the law of God according to moderation and the mitigation of the gospel" (p. 199). And it is only by obedience in the way of thankfulness that we can fulfill our covenant obligations; the covenant itself is "but an evidence and sign we are justified and accepted of God" (Rom. 8:3, 4). But once man is justified and made acceptable, the Lord then requires that he "express the covenant and walk answerable unto it"; so that his "walking in covenant" is the way that he demonstrates his faith in practice (p. 200). It is, furthermore, his best evidence of assurance. "[T]he frame of an evangelical heart," says Hooker, is "to the covenant," which is "the spring of a man's practice, the first mover" (p. 200).

Such assurance, however, depends to a large extent on what Hooker in this document calls "the bias of the soul," or that which determines the direction of the heart in the covenant relationship. The bias of the soul, he maintains, determines whether the nominal Christian stands inwardly or outwardly in the covenant, whether the "inward disposition and frame of heart" is good or merely conforms to the good. Moreover, it allows the soul in a justified state to walk in "new obedience" and "thankfulness." But it plays, in the unregenerate state, an even more significant role: it helps the would-be saint to knock down the many hindrances to faith that stand in his way. If the bias is right, Hooker tells his Dedham listeners, you will begin with a cry of the heart, a cry that represents "godly sorrow and grief of heart for thy failings" (p. 209). Without such grief, he assures them, there can be no closing with Christ; for contrite sorrow alone can entirely offset a "dead heart." Contrition, he explains, loosens a man from his sins and makes him see the need to be a new creature. Humiliation then loosens a man from himself and makes him see how ineffectual his graceless acts may be. Contrition, which is the work of the Law, brings the soul to sight of sin and sound sorrow; humiliation is an emptying of the soul from that which makes it "swell." The sinner must, however, in all of this guard against discontent. There is a great difference, Hooker warns once again, between a truly humbled and a discouraged heart. True humiliation should leave the soul calm, whereas the discouraged soul is unable to bear adversity. It is one thing for a man to be discontented with his corruptions, and another to be discouraged with his condition. If he looks to his corruptions with the bias of the soul properly inclined, he shall move with greater courage toward the covenant bond with God.

This concern with the contrite state, a concern that pervades not only *The Faithful Covenanter*, but also all of Hooker's early remarks on the regenerative process, sets the tone as well for his Preface to the 1627 second edition of John Rogers' *The Doctrine of Faith*. Although brief, the Preface is nonetheless important; for it was the first of Hooker's texts to be set in type. Moreover, it contains both his earliest published statement on the complete *ordo salutis* and the earliest public declaration of his firm belief that without contrition there can be no saving faith. "The way which the author of this treatise hath followed in making a saving contrition to go before faith," writes Hooker of Rogers in the Preface, "will be found to be beyond exception by such as are not forstalled with prejudice" (p. 144). And what is of interest here is that Hooker, for the first time in print, states a principle that he later carried to America, a principle which became, in spite of Cotton's opposing stand, the orthodox position in New England. What is more, Hooker seems in the Preface almost to predict a dispute that took place seven years after the document was printed, and that put his theology to the test. Although he asks of the reader that "this may serve by way of preface, not proposing to enter the lists of dispute" (p. 145), what he says can be more readily understood if considered in the light of John Cotton's stand; for it was Cotton, speaking on behalf of an earlier tradition in Reformed thought, who alone amongst the founding New England divines challenged the doctrine that the Preface defends. It was Cotton, moreover, who might almost be said to have caused the founding of Connecticut; for in the midst of crisis Hooker left the Bay, taking thirty-six families on the Indian paths to the West.

To Cotton's mind, the doctrine Hooker preached could be criticized from two sides: it both lowered and raised the standards of grace at the same time. It lowered the standards in that preparatory "evidences" of grace put sanctification too far down the scale in the *ordo salutis*. It raised the standards in that preparatory anxiety put off assurance, so that man could never really know whether or not he was saved. For Cotton, however, the greater danger was that of bringing the standards down. Although the Prophet exhorts Israel to "return unto the Lord" (Hos. 14:1), Israel cannot return, said Cotton, "unless the Lord take away their iniquity"; for "this is the way of the covenant of grace; whatsoever duties the Lord requireth to be done on our part, let us look unto him." There can be no condition before effectual conversion, said Cotton, as "Christ is offered in a promise of free grace without any previous gracious qualification mentioned"; and the sinner who looks to the conditional promises "hath built upon an unsafe foundation . . . hay and stubble," or a doctrine of "works." [9] "If the Lord means to save you," Cotton declared, "he will rend, as it were, the caul from the heart . . . as a man would rend the entrails of a beast from him." Until then we have no "gifts" of the Spirit to provide us with choice; for "Christ is one thing, the soul is another," and "the spirit of God that uniteth them is different from both." Before complete

---

[9] John Cotton, *A Treatise of the Covenant of Grace* (London, 1632) pp. 121–23; Cotton, *The Way of Life* (London, 1641) pp. 133–34.

reconciliation with God, we are "utterly unable to help ourselves." [10]

In keeping with Zwingli, Peter Martyr Vermigli, and other Reformed theologians of the strictest school, Cotton held that conversion is synonymous with assurance of salvation. He therefore reduced the experience itself to a preordained "sign" of election, with the result that the efficacy of the external call is clearly excluded from the *ordo salutis*. Unlike Hooker, who allowed for a contrite, preparative sorrow, that is "saving" but not "sanctifying," Cotton carried his doctrine to such an extreme that he could not allow for any "saving preparations" before effectual conversion; he would not concede that it is possible, in vocation and calling, to receive the saving work of the Spirit. "Reserving due honor to such gracious and precious saints as may be otherwise minded," he remarked, "I confess I do not discern that the Lord worketh and giveth any saving preparations in the heart till he give union with Christ. For if the Lord do give any saving qualifications before Christ, then the soul may be in the state of salvation before Christ; and that seemeth to be prejudicial unto the grace and truth of Jesus Christ . . . It seemeth to be that whatsoever saving work there be in the soul, it is not there before Christ be there." [11] Hooker, however, continued to distinguish between what is "wrought upon us" when we are "patients of the work of the Spirit bringing of us into Christ," and what is "wrought by us" through the Spirit "given to us and dwelling in us when we have received Christ" (p. 145). "Though . . . we must have faith before we can be in Christ," he declared in the Preface, "and the soul must be contrite before it can have faith," this "saving work may be, and yet this no work of sanctification" (p. 145).

It is not hard to see, then, why the Preface to *The Doctrine of Faith* so clearly foreshadows a dispute. Nor must we look far for evidence of rising contention, which in the early years of settlement gradually developed into public controversy and strife. In a letter received at the Colonial Office, London, dated January 3, 1637, from a Mr. Law, minister in Barbados Island, certain "grievances of the clergy" are submitted for consideration by church authorities; and

---

[10] Cotton, *A Treatise of Faith*, no date, pp. 14, 6.
[11] Cotton, *A Treatise of the Covenant of Grace*, p. 35.

the writer asks "whether there be any saving preparation in a Christian soul before his union with Christ." This, says Law, is "Hooker's opinion," whereas Cotton is "against him and his party in all." [12] And in a second letter, dated April 17, 1637, the Reverend Robert Stansby of Suffolk, England, wrote to John Wilson, pastor of the Boston Church, that he had heard "There is great division of judgment in matters of religion amongst good ministers and people which moved Mr. Hooker to remove." [13] Indeed, there can be little doubt that from 1633, when Hooker and Cotton preached their first sermons in New England, the differences between their doctrines became increasingly apparent; for Cotton was ever careful to remind his congregation that nothing done on their part could bring them closer to Christ. But what Cotton did not foresee was that the preaching of a state of depravity from which man may be saved only by immediate assurance of salvation could lead (and often had in the sixteenth and seventeenth centuries) to antinomian opinions, or to an inner assurance of being brought into a right relation with God by direct revelation of his Spirit. Therefore when certain of Cotton's followers, led by Anne Hutchinson, began to claim "individual revealings" from God, Cotton found himself at odds not only with Hooker, but also with Thomas Shepard, Peter Bulkeley, and other leading divines, all of whom declared such notions to be false; for delusion and enthusiasm were held to be the perils of the doctrine. Hooker, in 1637, served as co-moderator of the Synod at which the Antinomians were tried and banished. Cotton, it is clear, would certainly have shared their fate had he not altered his stand. But he realized in time that an extreme emphasis on the freeness of grace posed hazards that could not under all conditions be controlled. His followers had denied preparation on grounds that were clearly an offshoot from his own views, although outright Antinomianism was significantly different and more extreme.

[12] Great Britain, *Public Record Office, Colonial Record*, Class 1, Vol. 9, No. 72, Library of Congress Microfilm Ac. 10, 741, Reel 4.
[13] *Massachusetts Historical Society Collections*, Series IV, V (Cambridge, 1865), 10–11. For a more extended examination of the theological differences with Cotton that caused Hooker to leave Massachusetts, see Pettit, "Lydia's Conversion: An Issue in Hooker's Departure," *Cambridge Historical Society, Proceedings 1964–1966*, Vol. 40, pp. 59–83.

Hooker's dispute with Cotton, however, had not so much to do with the doctrine of preparation as with the doctrine of assurance; for Cotton refused to concede the main point that Hooker sets out to make in his Preface to *The Doctrine of Faith*, namely that men should descend into themselves in order to gain assurance of saving grace. Such activity, Cotton believed, left out the true object of faith, which is Christ. Sinners who embark on a search for signs of faith, he maintained, lose sight of its object, which is Christ; and Hooker, so far as Cotton was concerned, offered assurance only as a final reward for prolonged self-scrutiny and doubt. This meant, to Cotton's mind, that his opponent not only had dismissed Christ, but also was willing to substitute assurance of salvation for salvation *per se*, and the conditions of the covenant for Christ. Covenant theology, as Hooker described it, set aside for Cotton the experience of grace as participation in Christ. Because Hooker suggested that assurance could be found in "signs" of sanctification as conditions of the covenant, he and those "forstalled with prejudice" could not agree. Indeed, for Cotton the process of searching out assurance from covenant conditions forced one's attention on emotional experiences that diminished the centrality of Christ. And this insistance on Christ as the exclusive concern in Christian life inevitably led to his challenge of Hooker's stand, which by then had become the prevailing orthodoxy of the day.[14]

What these documents represent, then, is a development in Puritan theology of considerable importance, namely a movement away from the Pauline concern with participation in Christ, toward a profound interest in the spiritual value of experiences; for to gain assurance from the conditions of the covenant is ultimately to be involved with such experiences. Although Hooker wants always to judge a Christian by the rules of charity, he is still afraid lest effectual faith seem too easy; and so he holds to the absolute necessity of preparatory steps, with the result that each becomes a point of elaborate introspection along the way. In one sense, he relies upon a clear expectation of grace to encourage the doubting Christian in the quest for salvation. In another, he deliberately fosters an attitude of

[14] John S. Coolidge, *The Pauline Renaissance in England* (Oxford, 1970).

doubt, so that no man can claim to be regenerate without embarking on a process that is harsh, tedious, and long. The question to be answered, then, is how these two sides of the preparatory experience can be reconciled. Is it enough to say that the contrite heart (while helpless against God's truth) can be supreme over its own corruptions, and therefore will not despair? Or can such a heart, humbled in fear, be torn by agony and doubt?

Hooker, as these texts clearly show, is aware of the dangers that would be involved were emotions allowed to hold sway. He therefore warns against excessive emotional stress, and declares himself against "sense" and "feeling" as a final test of faith. The covenant conditions, he maintains, are intended not so much to evoke emotional response as to lead a man toward a sound and "good faith" that can be judged as genuine and true; and the figure of Christ should not grow dim if the interior life is enriched. For Hooker, the centrality of Christ lies in the "motions" of the Spirit on the life of the soul: man can still have Christ at his side though his conversion be painfully slow. In spite of the Christophany of Paul, Hooker will not describe conversion as an isolated flash detached from ordinary experience. He will not, as these documents make clear, allow the abstract principle of sovereign, mediating grace, to diminish the variety of man's response.

In *The Application of Redemption*, written at Hartford, Connecticut, toward the end of his life, Hooker held that truly regenerate souls should judge themselves not by external criteria, but "upon experience, that which they have found and felt in their own hearts." There is a "secret hope," he maintained, by which the Lord supports "such as be soundly contrite"; so that if preparative contrition never guarantees saving grace, this hope upholds the heart against doubt, agony, and despair.[15] We must prepare, Hooker had declared in his earliest English works, not merely out of fear, but in true anticipation of divine love; and in this respect he not only set the tone for New England theology, but also established a position that rivaled Cotton's from the start. Cotton, because he clung more strictly to the mystical Christ of Paul, could not encourage sinners to strain

---

[15] Hooker, *The Application of Redemption* (London, 1659) pp. 557, 596.

every fiber of their souls for the sake of "sound contrition" and "brokenness of heart"; and in this respect he stands for an earlier phase in the development of Puritan thought — one more closely linked to the great Reformers of the sixteenth century. Hooker, however, made it clear that while contrition and humiliation must precede saving grace, the Spirit at the same time "lets in some intimation of God's love into the soul . . . and conveys some relish of the love of God into the heart." Divine love, which first must settle upon the heart, "breeds a love to God again." Indeed, "the greatness of the freeness of this mercy of God, being settled upon the heart, enflames it; this sweetness warms the heart, this freeness kindles the fire; and when the greatness of this freeness comes to be valued, this sets the heart all upon a fire." [16] Like Sibbes, Hooker is ultimately concerned not with metaphors denoting coercion, but with that which "warms the heart" and "kindles the fire." Like Sibbes, he stresses the spark of love, or the need to "value" grace before effectual conversion. In spite of rigorous and demanding introspection, he is essentially concerned with hopeful anticipation. If a man can give "a reason of his hope toward God," said Hooker, "this casts the cause, with judicious charity, to hope and believe there is something of God in the soul." [17] Throughout his career, he refused, as he said, to search into "the heart of another," which "no man can know"; and his respect for the sanctity of the heart allowed him to judge with charity. He insisted, to be sure, that all prepare for grace; but for those who came forth with a "hope toward God," he assumed that the work had been done.

[16] Hooker, *The Souls Implantation* (London, 1637) pp. 171–78.
[17] Hooker, *A Survey of the Sum of Church Discipline* (London, 1648) III, I, 5; I, VI, 61.

DOCUMENT IV

Epistle to the Reader
Of John Rogers' *The Doctrine of Faith;* 1627

Introduction

John Rogers' *The Doctrine of Faith* was entered in the Stationers' Register to Nathaniel Newbery and William Sheffard on February 19, 1626, the year that Hooker first went to Chelmsford.[1] The first edition, published in 1627 and prefaced only with Rogers' "Epistle to the Reader," was followed in the same year by a second edition, "newly corrected and enlarged by the author," which contained Hooker's Preface as well. Later a third edition was printed for Newbery and Henry Overton in 1629, Sheffard having died the year before. When on May 13, 1630, Overton entered for "all the copies . . . of Master Sheffard whose widow the said Henry Overton lately married," including "One half of *The Doctrine of Faith* by Thomas [sic] Rogers," [2] the third edition had been off the press for some time. Indeed, it sold so well that a fourth edition appeared in 1632, a fifth in 1633, a sixth in 1634, a seventh in 1638, and an eighth in 1640. All were printed for Newbery and Overton, and all contained Hooker's Preface, which represents the first Hooker document ever to be published, and which throughout the decade was greatly admired for its brevity, directness, and undisguised affection for the author of the text. "For the author," Hooker declared, "though my love could say much, yet I will say nothing, but let his works praise him" (p. 146). It was a model Preface that clearly did much to increase the sales of the book.

Hooker had gone to Chelmsford in 1626 mainly to be near John Rogers, who by then had earned a wide reputation as "one of the most awakening preachers of the age." [3] A close relative of Richard

---

[1] *A Transcript of the Registers of the Stationers' Company,* IV (London, 1872), 113.
[2] Ibid., p. 201.
[3] *Dictionary of National Biography* (London, 1897), Vol. 49, p. 130.

Rogers, who provided for his education at Cambridge, John had begun in 1605 to preach at Dedham, where on lecture days his church overflowed. At an earlier time he had been vicar at Honingham, Norfolk, where he first took up a living in 1592; and after 1630 he had briefly served as vicar of Haverhill, Suffolk. His career, however, had not been without tarnish. As an undergraduate he had twice sold his books and wasted the proceeds. His kinsman, then at work on the famous *Seven Treatises*, threatened to discard him, but the boy reformed and took his degree with credit. Thereafter he was pledged to make up for his youthful sins, and he did so with increasing Puritan zeal. His Dedham lecture was surpressed on grounds of nonconformity in 1629, with the result that Hooker came from Chelmsford to deliver the sermon later published as *The Faithful Covenanter, A Sermon Preached at the Lecture in Dedham in Essex*. In 1631 the lecture was restored, but Rogers' subsequent compliance was not strict. Giles Firmin, one of his converts, reported that he never saw him wear a surplice. Only on occasion did he use the Prayer Book, and then he repeated passages from memory. He died October 18, 1636, five months after Hooker had settled in Hartford; and he was buried in the churchyard at Dedham, where his tombstone still stands. He published also during his lifetime *A Treatise of Love*, printed for Nathaniel Newbery in 1629 (followed by a second edition in 1632, and a third in 1637). Two posthumous works have since been attributed to him: *A Godly and Fruitful Exposition upon the First Epistle of Peter* (1650), and (without date) *Sixty Memorials of a Godly Life*.[4]

According to Cotton Mather, it was said of Rogers that he could "do more with his wild notes than we . . . with our set music";[5] and Hooker's Preface to *The Doctrine of Faith* is clearly a tribute to Rogers' brightest tones. "Briefly," said Hooker, "that word which God hath blessed, that way which God hath laid open to bring so many to life by, behold, Christian reader, that word and way is here chalked out before thee" (p. 146). But Rogers, in his own preface to the text, remarked that "Sundry of my friends, some by letters, some by word of mouth, have told me that the uses of the points

---

[4] Ibid., p. 131.
[5] Cotton Mather, *Magnalia*, p. 376.

are very short and weak in comparison of that they were in preaching." And he went on to say: "I easily confess it, and know not how to mend it, unless I had preached them over again, or had more leisure to enlarge them than I can attain to." The point that he wished to make, which was a familiar one to Hooker, had simply to do with the disparity between the forcefulness of the spoken word and that which is written down. "Neither find I it possible to me in cold blood and so long after," Rogers sadly declared, "to call to mind or write those stirring passages that God brought to hand in the heat of preaching." [6] The function of Hooker's Preface, then, was not only to clarify and defend the main points of doctrine, but also to ask that the reader re-create in his own mind the "heat" of the word. "See it, go in it . . . for thy soul's good" (p. 146), Hooker begged, and with these words gave his full support to the literary strength of the text.

[6] John Rogers, *The Doctrine of Faith* (London, 1629), "To the Reader."

DOCUMENT IV

The Doctrine of Faith

To the Reader

The good of the soul and the supreme happiness of a sinner, being a reasonable creature, is to be united to an all-sufficient, even to him who is goodness and happiness itself, God blessed forevermore, the fullness of the infiniteness of all perfections which are in the Lord being able to fill up all the empty chinks, void places, the unsatisfied gaspings and yawnings of the spirit of a man. All truth is in God, and thereby the understanding is satisfied; it can know no more. All perfections of excellency [being] in him, and thereby the will is contented; it can have no more. And all this our first father Adam being made for God, had he been united to him by the obedience of love, he had been possessor of him and of all this good in him. But our first parents playing the apostates, through the abuse of their own liberty and Satan's delusion, plucked away themselves (as I may so speak) from under that spiritual and especial guidance and government of the blessed God, and so became to fall off from the possession of so great a good and to topple down from the height of all that happiness into the depth of all misery, Rom. 5:15;[1] for as the good was from which they departed, such was the evil into which they plunged themselves. They departed from the God of all power into weakness, from all wisdom down to folly, from the God of all holiness, glory, and consolation, unto all baseness, desolation, and misery, which cannot be conceived. They being thus departed from the Lord, recovered again they cannot be into the state of spiritual life and goodness unless they be brought again to him who is the fountain of life and good to all that shall have it,

---

[1] Rom. 5:15: "But not as the offence, so also is the free gift. For if through the offence of one many be dead, much more the grace of God, and the gift by grace, which is by one man, Jesus Christ, hath abounded unto many."

namely, to the living God. And brought they will never be but by faith; for man being bound to live the spiritual life of grace, and to please God, he must either live by himself or by another. By himself he cannot, being dead in sins and trespasses; therefore he must live by another. Therefore go to that other, that is, God, rest upon him and believe in him, faith being nothing else but the going out of the soul to God through Christ to fetch a principle of life which in Adam we lost and now need. And hence it is that there is such an extraordinary worth in this precious grace, Eph. 1:19,[2] and such an extraordinary virtue, even the mighty working of the exceeding great power of the outstretched arm of the Lord put forth to bring the soul to himself by believing.

The work being so extraordinary wonderful, no marvel though it be more than ordinarily secret. Jn. 3:8: "The Spirit, as the wind blows where it lists, thou knowest not whence it came nor whither it goes, and so is every man that is born of God." And if the framing of the body be fearfully and wonderfully wrought beneath in the earth, as the Psalmist speaks [Ps. 139:14, 15], why should we not imagine that the fashioning of the soul to a dependence of [on] God through the depth of his counsel should be much more difficult to dive into.

The way which the author of this treatise hath followed in making a saving contrition to go before faith in the second main point of the treatise, discoursing about the author and means of faith, if it may find a judicious and fair construction it will be found to be beyond exception by such as are not forestalled with prejudice. Let not that deceive thee, good reader, which is a common conceit, but a common error, to wit, that every saving work upon the heart is a sanctifying work, which in strictness of speech (as the terms must here be conceived) cannot stand by the verdict of Scripture. For Rom. 8:30 the Spirit speaks plainly: "Whom God called, them he justified; whom he justified, them he glorified." Here is the order of God's own work, of purpose described by his own Spirit; and by those last words, "and them he glorified," by the best interpreters is meant not only the perfection of it in heaven, but the

---

[2] Eph. 1:19: "And what is the exceeding greatness of his power to usward who believe, according to the working of his mighty power."

beginning of it here in grace, sanctification and glorification differing but in degrees one from another. Whence the conclusion is thus undeniably collected: vocation is not a sanctifying work because they [sanctification and glorification] are there distinguished one from another, set in order of nature one before another; but vocation is a saving work. Therefore every saving work is not a sanctifying work. Though therefore we must have faith before we can be in Christ, and the soul must be contrite before it can have faith, this saving work may be and yet this no work of sanctification.

If then thou shalt hear or read of sorrow, hatred, detestation against sin in a contrite person, which cannot be in a reprobate, and observe also the like spoken elsewhere as a fruit of faith, thou must not boggle or start at the terms as implying a contradiction one to another, when all will easily be reconciled thus: the one is a sorrow of preparation, the other a sorrow of sanctification, and yet both [are] saving. The one [is] wrought upon us, wherein we are patients of the work of the Spirit bringing of us unto Christ; the other is wrought by us through the Spirit given to us and dwelling in us when we have received Christ.

Much more may be said in this particular, and shall be when occasion shall require; only for the while this may serve by way of preface, not purposing to enter the lists of dispute. And let me speak ingenuously without either pride or prejudice. Somewhat I have heard by conference of the point from sundry men, a little I have read and thought much according to my meanness and the measure of light received, and I could never yet apprehend anything which should shake this truth rightly understood.

Touching the coming in of faith, if any doubt arise, those words, page 175,[3] should wisely be weighted; and they seem fully to deter-

---

[3] The page of the text to which Hooker refers reads as follows:

"It is hard to say at what instant faith is wrought, whether not till a man apprehends Christ and the promise, or even in his earnest desires, hungering and thirsting; for even these are pronounced blessed.

"Some having got hold, hold it faster than some by much, yet none but with doubtings sometimes; yet some are much priviledged this way, especially they that came hardliest by it.

"Some ever and anon let it go, and are full of doubtings, and to seek of that sometimes they had; some upon one occasion, some upon

mine the controversy, namely, that in the hungerings and thirstings of the soul there is, as it were, the spawn of faith not yet brought to full perfection. The soul is coming toward God, but not yet come to him to rest so fully and wholly on him as hereafter it will.

And this is all I have to advertise thee, good reader, touching the matter. For the author, though my love could say much, yet I will say nothing, but let his works praise him. I know he envies not the parts nor desires the praises of others. That which is to be commended of a man is his goodness. And in my silence the souls in heaven now blessed, and many hundreds of the saints brought to God by the power of his ministry, are as large letters, and the best of his commendation, as Paul speaks [2 Cor. 3:1],[4] read of all and known of all. And that which is a crown and comfort to himself, I see not but it may be a credit to him from all such who are content that God should be glorified by others as well as by themselves. Briefly, that word which God hath blessed, that way which God hath laid open to bring so many to life by, behold, Christian reader, that word and way is here chalked out before thee. See it, go in it, and the God of heaven go with thee and give a rich blessing to thee and to this work for thy soul's good, which he wisheth who rests

thine in the Lord Jesus,
Thomas Hooker.

---

another, some upon no occasion. But even God that gave them power to believe, withdrawing his hand but a little, they are much troubled that hereby they may know whence their strength is."

[4] 2 Cor. 3:1: "Do we begin again to commend ourselves? or need we, as some others, epistles of commendation to you, or letters of commendation from you?"

DOCUMENT V

The Poor Doubting Christian Drawn Unto Christ; 1629

Introduction

The Poor Doubting Christian Drawn Unto Christ, Hooker's earliest published sermonic text, is not "one sermon," as the title page proclaims, but part of a longer sermon that was not published in its complete form until 1637. The text reproduced here, which Robert Dawlman published in 1629 as one of the anonymous selections of *The Saints Cordials*, is actually the seventh and final "use" of a series of sermons on Jn. 6:45 printed eight years later for Andrew Crooke in *The Souls Effectual Calling to Christ* (pp. 538-611). We shall never know, however, under what circumstances the 1629 Dawlman text was compiled. Nor shall we know precisely how it was composed; for Dawlman used a copy-text significantly different in style from that later used by Crooke. Thomas Goodwin and Philip Nye, editors of Hookers' American sermonic works, claimed that the sermons he delivered in England before his "recess into those remoter parts of the world" had been "taken by an unskulful hand" and published without his consent, so that all these texts were "utterly deformed and misrepresented in multitudes of passages." [1] But the original Dawlman text of *The Poor Doubting Christian*, entered in the Stationers' Register April 2, 1629, under the title of *The Saints Cordials*, might well have been published with Hooker's consent; for it was entered more than a year before he was cited by the Court of High Commission and went into hiding.[2] We know that he went up to London in 1629, and he may at that time have given Dawlman permission to print the text.

[1] Thomas Hooker, *The Application of Redemption* (London, 1659), "To the Reader," p. 18.
[2] *The Souls Preparation for Christ*, published for Dawlman in 1632, was not entered in the Stationers' Register until October 29, 1631, by which time Hooker had settled at Delft.

What cannot be known for certain is the nature of the link between the Dawlman and Crooke texts. There is no way of knowing how Crooke came to possess the whole sermon (compiled by a different hand), which Dawlman apparently did not own. All we know is that Crooke set up in business March 26, 1629, precisely one week before Dawlman entered *The Saints Cordials* in the Stationers' Register.[3] We know also that by April 21, 1637, when Crooke entered his version of the text, Dawlman (who in 1635 had formed a partnership with Luke Fawne) had already published two separately bound anonymous editions of *The Poor Doubting Christian:* a "second" edition was published in 1635, followed by a "third" in 1636. But Dawlman, perhaps because he feared that the licensers would not approve the work of such a well-known Puritan divine, had entered neither edition in the Stationers' Register; and because he had entered his original text under the title of *The Saints Cordials* he had no legal claim to the text as a separate title.

It was not until May 6, 1637, fifteen days after Crooke had "Entred for his Copie under the hands of Master Weekes and Master Downes warden Certaine sermons upon John the 6th, verse the 45th, by T.H.," that Dawlman and Fawne entered under the same licensers "for their Copie . . . a Booke called *The poore doubting Christian drawn to CHRIST.* etc. upon John the 6th, the 45th by Master Hooker." [4] Therefore it is clear that Crooke, by declaring a legitimate claim to the manuscript, had forced Dawlman not only to declare his right to the printed book, but also to disclose the name of the author. Nevertheless, when the Dawlman and Fawne "fourth" edition appeared in 1637, followed by a "fifth" in 1638, both remained anonymous; while the Crooke text, published in 1637, displayed "T.H." on the title page. Crooke, it would seem, was willing to take advantage of his author's reputation, which by 1637 was wide; for by then people knew who the author of *The Poor Doubting Christian* had been.

The Dawlman and Fawne editions of the 1630's had not, however,

[3] Henry R. Plomer, *A Dictionary of Booksellers and Printers* (London, 1907), p. 56.
[4] Edward Arber, ed., *A Transcription of the Registers of the Stationers of London: 1554–1640,* IV (London, 1875–1895), 229, 355, 357, 372.

reproduced the original text of 1629. The "second" edition of 1635, printed several years after Hooker had left England, contained additions to the text amounting to some two thousand words; and though the added passages are similar in style to the original text, it cannot be said for sure that they are Hooker's own.[5] Hooker, by 1635, had been in Holland three years and in New England two; it is doubtful, therefore, that at this time in his life he actually composed a revised edition of *The Poor Doubting Christian*. Perhaps the editors, hoping for increased sales, were tempted to expand the text with notes from another source. Whatever the case, the revised "second" edition, which does not resemble the Crooke text, was in 1635 set entirely from new plates. It was then reset for the "third" edition of 1636, the "fourth" of 1637, and the "fifth" of 1638. Another "fourth" edition was published in 1637 "for the benefit of the English Nation," by the Richt Right Press, Amsterdam; and a "sixth" edition was printed in 1641 for Luke Fawne, Dawlman having that year "assigned over unto him . . . all the estate, right, title, and interest which the said Mr. Dawlman hath in these . . . copies." [6] Both these editions contained the revised text.

Fawne at this time then took it upon himself to publish what can only be called a "compiled" edition; for by 1646 he had produced a text significantly different from earlier copies of the work. Because Fawne knew that the Dawlman text was not "one sermon," as the 1629 title page had claimed, he allowed his editor to add and interject those sections from the Crooke text that he thought appropriate. He combined the Dawlman and Fawne revised text of *The Poor Doubting Christian* with *The Souls Effectual Calling*, and in the process slightly changed both versions, condensing certain passages and altering others, with the inevitable result that style is not consistent throughout.[7] Fawne, it would appear, believed that a fuller

[5] Sargent Bush, Jr., in "The Growth of Thomas Hooker's *The Poor Doubting Christian*," *Early American Literature*, VIII (1973), 3–20, has drawn attention to five major additions in the 1635 text. He argues on the grounds of style that these additions are Hooker's own, and that Dawlman in 1635 had simply restored the text to an earlier form. The issue is open to debate.

[6] *A Transcript of the Registers of the Stationers' Company: 1640–1708*, I (London, 1913), 32.

[7] For a detailed description of the Fawne text, see Bush, "The Growth of Thomas Hooker's *The Poor Doubting Christian*."

edition would expand the reputation of the book, and perhaps he was right; for all editions published after 1646 followed his revisions of the text. In 1652 and 1659 he again produced copies for the press, and his format was followed by Nathaniel Ranew and Jonathan Robinson in their editions of 1667, 1674, and 1684. A so-called "twelfth" edition of the same text was printed in 1700 for Robinson, Churchill, Taylor, and Wyat.

Finally, in 1743, Thomas Prince, minister of the Old South Church at Boston, brought to press the first American edition of *The Poor Doubting Christian;* and he relied for his copy upon the Ranew and Robinson 1667 edition of Fawne's "compiled" text.[8] Prince, in making up his own version, thought it proper to correct the "divers mistakes committed by transcribers and printers"; but he assumed that the edition from which he worked contained only the preacher's original words, "delivered to a popular auditory" and "taken in short hand by one of his hearers in England." [9] Prince did not realize what Fawne had done with the combined versions of the work.

Published for Daniel Henchman at Cornhill, this 1743 edition was widely sold in New England. Because Prince strongly supported the religious revivals of the time, he praised Hooker's appeal as an "awakening" preacher; [10] and the edition remained throughout the century the standard American text. More than one hundred years later, in 1845, it was set in type again, and then for the last time. Published privately at Hartford by Robins and Smith, with an introduction by the Reverend Edward William Hooker, this reprint of the Prince edition was thought to represent the "original design" of the author's work. Therefore the Fawne text, out of reverence for Hooker's style, was left untouched. "There is nothing in the fact that a man has been gone to his grave," declared the editor, "to justify taking liberties with his book, which we should not dare to

[8] Frank Shuffelton in "Thomas Prince and his Edition of Thomas Hooker's *Poor Doubting Christian*," *Early American Literature*, V (1971), 68–75, wrongly assumed that Prince had put together the first bastard edition. Prince's copy of the 1667 Fawne text is now held in the American Antiquarian Society. See Bush, "The Growth of Thomas Hooker's *The Poor Doubting Christian*."
[9] Thomas Hooker, *The Poor Doubting Christian Drawn to Christ* (Boston, 1743), "The Preface," p. 13.
[10] *Ibid.*, "The Preface," pp. 1, 3.

take were he living; and in which he may be made to speak unlike himself, either as to his style, or the character of his thoughts." Except for "changes in the orthography," the Prince text was faithfully reproduced, "leaving the author to speak in the style of his time." [11] It is only in the following pages that the first of Hooker's published sermons has come from an American press in its original form.

[11] Thomas Hooker, *The Poor Doubting Christian Drawn to Christ* (Hartford, 1845), "Introduction," p. 8.

DOCUMENT V

The Poor Doubting Christian Drawn Unto Christ

Jn. 6:45   *"Every man therefore that hath heard, and learned of the Father, cometh unto me."*

There are divers lets and impediments which hinder poor Christians from coming unto Christ, all which I desire to reduce to these following heads:

First, such hindrances as really keep men from coming to take hold of Christ at all, which are these four briefly:

1. Blind carelessness, or presumptuous security, whereby men content themselves in their present condition, presuming all is well with them, when there is no such matter.

2. Being convinced of this thing, bethink how to save themselves by their own strength, and thereupon set upon a reformation of life, thinking to make God amends by reforming some sins which they hear themselves reproved of by the ministers.

3. The sinner being convinced of this also, now he gets up a stair higher and sees all his performances, and prayers, and duties, are of no power in themselves, but he must leave all and cleave only unto Christ by faith; he thinks he can do that well enough, and so thrusts himself upon Christ and thinks all the work is done and there is no more to do.

4. If he sees this fails him too, then he goes yet further and confesses he cannot come to Christ except Christ give him his hand and help him up: now he will attend upon the ordinances, thinking that if he do labor and bestir himself hard he shall hammer out a faith of his own making, and here he rests, and so hangs upon the outside of the Ark, as it were, so long till at last the waves and winds are so fierce and violent, that he is beaten off from his hold, and

so sinks forever. These we have formerly set forth at large, and the remedies and cures of them.[1]

Now in the second place we are come to those kinds of hindrances which do not indeed deprive a man of title from Christ, but makes the way more tedious, that he cannot come to Christ so readily; and the ground of this hindrance is this, when men out of carnal reason contrive another way to come unto Christ than ever he ordained or revealed, when we set up a standard by God's standard, and out of our own imagination we make another condition of believing than ever Christ required or ordained. Thus we make bars in the way, and manacle our hands, and fetter our feet, and then we complain we cannot go: thus it is with you poor Christians, and the fault is your own. Now amongst many there be three hindrances which are chiefly to be observed, by which many gracious hearts are marvelously hindered from coming to, and from receiving that comfort from Christ, which they might, and he is willing to bestow.

First, the distressed soul being happily truly humbled, takes notice of the beauty of holiness and the image of God stamped upon the hearts of his children, and of all those precious promises which God hath made to all that are his; now the soul seeing these, begins thus to reason with himself, and saith, 'Surely if I were so holy and so gracious, then I might have hope to receive the pardon of my sins; for were my heart so enlarged to duties, and could my heart be so carried with power against corruptions to master them, then there were some hope; but when I have no power against corruption, nor any heart to seek so importunately for a Christ, how dare I think that any mercy belongs to me, when I see so many wants?' Thus they dare not come to the promise, and they will not venture upon it, because they have not that enlargement to duties and that power against corruption which sometimes the Saints of God have. This doth not hinder. We make it a hindrance, but it doth not hinder in truth; for observe it: we must not think to bring enlargement and hope to the promise, but we must go to the promise for them. Hope must be stirred, and desire quickened, and love and joy kindled. Nay, who made this a condition of the covenant, that a man must

[1] Hooker refers at this point to the earlier part of the sermon, later published in *The Souls Effectual Calling to Christ* (1637).

have this enlargement before he come to the promise? Our service requires no portion but mere poverty and emptiness: if thou hast nothing he will have thee, provided that thou wilt have him. Lk. 1:53: "The rich he sends empty away," but the poor is satisfied, and the thirsty refreshed: so there is nothing required on our side but only to receive him as a husband. Is. 55:1: "Buy without money," saith the text; you must not think to come and buy a husband; the Lord looks for no power or sufficiency of ourselves, nor power against corruption, nor enlargement to duties. If you will be content that Christ shall take all from you, and dispose of you, then, in truth, take a Savior and have him.

Question: But the poor soul saith, 'If I go thus hoodwinked, how shall I know that I do not presume, and how shall I know that I have title to the promise?'

Answer: I answer, there is no better argument in the world that thou hast an interest in Christ than this: thy taking of the Lord Christ as a Savior wholly, and as a husband. Jn. 1:12: "But as many as received him, to them he gave power to be the sons of God, even to them that believe on his name." He doth not say, 'to as many as had such enlargement in duties and such power against corruptions'; but if thou wilt take Christ upon those terms which he offers himself, there is no better argument under heaven that thou hast a title to the promise. Every ditch must be filled, as in Lk. [3:5]. This is a desperate despair that sometimes seizeth upon the hearts of distressed sinners.

Therefore in the second place, as the sinner looks upon the excellency of Christ, and grace, and his own insufficiency, and so will not venture upon the promise, so he looks upon his own sinfulness and worthlessness, and therefore dares not venture upon mercy. He views the number of his sins so many and vile, and the continuance of them so long, and he seeth the floods of abominations coming in amain upon his soul, and Satan helps him forwards hereto; for this is the policy of the devil, that, if he can, he will make a man that he shall never see his sin, but say, 'There is mercy enough in a Savior, and therefore I may live as I list.' But when the sinner will needs see his sin, then he will let him see nothing but sin; the one that he may presume, and the other that he may despair. Now the poor sinner stays here; tell him of the mercy of God, and of the plentious redemption in Christ, and of the riches of the freeness of God's grace. 'What,' saith he, 'should I think that there is any mercy for me, and that I have any interest in Christ, that were strange?' And thus the soul is here pouring, and fastened, and settled upon his corruption, and is ever stirring the wound and never goes to the physician; for a man is as well kept from looking to Christ by despair as by presumption. Before he sees his sin he thinks his condition is good, and he hath a sufficiency of his own and needs not go to Christ; and when he sees his sin, then he sees so much vileness in himself that he dares not go to Christ, lest when he goes before him, he send him down to the pit. But herein the devil is very subtle, but this doth not hinder our title to Christ, that we should not, neither ought it to discourage our hearts from coming to Christ. For first (observe it): for whom did Christ come into the world, and for whom did he die when he was come? It was not for the righteous, that needed him not, but for the poor sinner that condemns himself, and knows he cannot save himself. Paul saith, I Tim. 1:15, "Christ Jesus came into the world to have sinners, of whom I am the chief." And Zech. 13:1: "There is a fountain opened for sin and for uncleanness"; that is, for all sorts of sins, and for all sinners. Be their sins never so great and never so vile, there is a fountain set open, come who will. There was never any saved but a rebel, and never any man received to mercy but he that opposed the mercy of God and his grace in Christ. The fiery serpents sting the people in the wilderness, but there was a brazen serpent to heal them [Num. 21:8, 9].

Again, observe the folly of this plea: what Scripture ever said that the greatness of man's sins hinders the greatness of God's mercy? No Scripture reveals this; nay, David prayeth the contrary, Ps. 25:11: "Have mercy upon me, O Lord, and pardon my sins, for they are great." Nay, God himself doth the quite contrary, Is. 43:24, 25: "Thou hast made me serve with thy sins, and wearied me with thine iniquities, yet I am he that blotteth out thy transgressions, for my name's sake." When the Jews did tire God with their distempers, and burthened him with their sins, then the Lord for his own name's sake would not so much as remember their iniquities against them.

Again, observe that sins though they be never so heinous of themselves, yet if the soul can see them and the heart be burdened with them, they are so far from hindering the work of faith, and from making thee incapable of mercy, that they fit thee to go to Christ: but the truth is (which I pray you take notice of), it is not properly our unworthiness, but our pride and haughtiness that hinders us from coming to Christ; for we would have something in ourselves, and not have all from Christ. Take the distressed soul that sees the vileness of his sins; were thy sins fewer, then thou mightest go to Christ. Nevertheless even then thou goest not, [not] because thou art persuaded of the freeness of his grace, but because thou hast something in thy self, and wouldst bring something to Christ, and not receive all from him. So it is thy pride and thy self-conceitedness that hinders thee, and thou must have thus much, and Christ must not justify the ungodly, but the godly man. I tell thee, then, he will never justify a man while the world stands.

Objection: But the soul repines again, 'My sins are worse, not only because they are many, but because of the grace and salvation that I have rejected, which hath been offered me from day to day.'

Answer: This hinders not, provided that thou canst see those evils of thine. Though thou hast cast away the kindness of the Lord, yet the Lord will not cast away thee, if thou wilt come and seek again for his mercy, Is. 57:17: "For the iniquity of his covetousness I was wroth," saith God, "and I smote him; I hid myself and was wroth, and he went on frowardly in the way of his own heart." If this could have hindered, Judah should never have received mercy, but the text saith, Is. 57:18, "I have seen his ways, and will heal him." Jer. 3:1: "Thou hast played the harlot with many lovers, yet turn again to me, saith the Lord." There is no time past if a man have but a heart to return; there is no limitation of the riches of God's free grace, except the sin against the Holy Ghost. Rev. 3:20: "I stand at the door and knock"; though he cry till he be hoarse, and stand till he be weary, yet he stands still: if any adulterous wretch will open, the Lord will come in, and bring comfort, and sup with him.

Objection: 'Oh, that is true,' saith the poor soul, 'had I but a heart to mourn for my baseness! See my sins I do, but this is my misery, I cannot be burdened with them, I have a heart that cannot break and mourn for the dishonors of God.'

Answer: This hinders not neither, provided that thy heart is weary of itself, that it cannot be weary of sin. Mic. 7:18: "The Lord shows mercy because he will show mercy." It is not because thou canst please him, but because mercy pleaseth him. When did the Lord show mercy to Paul? Even then, when Paul did express most malice against him. [Acts 9:4]: "Saul, Saul, why persecutest thou me?" He persecutes Christ, and yet Christ pities him and shows him mercy; and so the churlish jailer, when he was most opposite against the means of grace, the Lord then showed most compassion upon him; he that resists the means of grace is now brought home by those means [Acts 16:25ff].

Objection: 'But woe,' saith the poor soul, 'you are now come to the quick. This very word is like a millstone about my neck, to sink my soul forever; for this is the depth of that baseness that lies on me, that all the means do not better me. Why, though Paul and the jailer were bad enough, yet they were made better by the means; but this is my hopeless condition, that the means of grace prevail not. Is there such a heart in hell? How ill am I, when all the means in the world will do me no good? But, methinks, I feel my heart more hard and stubborn under all God's ordinances, and therefore my condition is hopeless, when the means that should soften me do but harden me and make me worse.'

Answer: This is the last plea whereby the devil holds down the heart of a poor sinner; but let me answer thee, this hinders not neither, but that at least thou mayest have hope of mercy. Therefore observe three passages by way of answer:

First, the word and means do work good if it make thee more sensible of thy hardness and deadness, though happily it work not that good, and after the same manner that thou desirest; yet if it make thee see thy baseness, and hardness of heart, and dullness, in regard of that body of death which hangs upon thee, then the word works in the best manner, because it is after God's manner, howsoever not after thine. That physic works most kindly that makes the party sick before it works; so it is with the Word. Thou hast a proud heart, and liftest up thyself in thine own abilities, and trustest in thine own strength, and thinkest that thy care and improvement of the means would work wonders; but now the Word works sweetly, when it makes thee apprehensive that a wounded soul is the gift of God, not of man, nor of the means. And therefore the Word makes thee look to God for it, and to prize it when thou hast it; and the Word makes thee look to God to continue it, to feel deadness is life, and to feel hardness is softness. Only here remember one caution — except there be some lust or distemper that thy heart hankers after; for then the Word will harden thee, because thou hardenest thyself.

Secondly (mark this I beseech you), thou art the cause why thy heart is not softened, and why the Word works not upon thy soul. This distemper of thy heart hinders the working of the Word, and dispensation of God's providence, and the tenure of the covenant of grace. Thou must not think to limit the holy one of Israel; for it is the covenant of grace. The Lord will not stand bent to thy bow and give thee grace when thou wilt; it is not for us to know the times and seasons. What if the Lord will not give thee grace this year, nor the next, nor all thy life, if at the last gasp he will drop in a little favor? It is more than he owes thee. Therefore hear today, and wait tomorrow, and continue so doing, because thou knowest not when God may bless his own ordinances. And complain not of delays, but wait, for God hath waited for you long; and therefore if he make you wait for peace of conscience and assurance of his love, the Lord deals equally and lovingly with you, and as shall be best for you. God gives what, and when, and how he will; therefore wait for it.

Thirdly, know and consider that thou hast rested upon thine own duties and indeavors, and thou dost not go to God, that blesseth both the means and endeavors. The fault is thine own, I say, because thou restest in thine own performances, and in the power of the means that thou apprehendest, and dost not go to God, that would have wrought more than all these. For did a man depend upon God's power and mercy in his ordinances, he should always find some proportionable succor, as well when he finds no success as when he finds any; for God sometimes gives and sometimes delays, but God's love is as constant when he gives not as when he gives. Therefore labor to get out from all carnal confidence in holy duties, and rest not in thy performances, but look beyond all duties to God, and desire him to give thee success above them.

Objection: 'Oh, but,' saith a poor sinner, 'I would go out of myself, and I see I rest upon my duties, but I cannot get out of myself!'

Answer: I answer, it is Satan's subtlety to keep us in ourselves hereto, by endeavoring to make us go out of ourselves by our own strength; and this is a marvelous depth of malice and cunning in the devil, when he makes us believe (and we out of ignorance are deluded) that we have power in our own hands to go out of ourselves. No, it is a supernatural work, and the same hand must bring us out of ourselves that must bring us to Christ. But this in truth is self-denial, when the soul knoweth it hath nothing, and therefore is overpowered with the mighty hand of God, the work of God's Spirit, that the poor sinner doth not so much as expect any power or ability in himself or from the creature. In the doing of any duty he knows he is dead, and therefore cannot help himself; and when he is brought to deny himself, he looks not to the creature nor to himself. Now (observe it) whilst that I thus think with myself that I have ability to go out of myself, I do not then say that I have a principle within me to deny myself, which is quite contrary; for to deny a man's self is to know that he hath no power in himself to do any spiritual duty. Therefore we must look only to the voice of Christ, and know, he that calls us from the ways of darkness, and from ourselves, must also bring us to Christ. And expect power from Christ to pluck thee out of thyself, and to make thee believe; for the same hand doth work both.

Therefore I would not have a poor creature think thus with himself: 'If this means and these ordinances will do me no good, and will not work upon my heart, I shall never have it;' but speak thus unto God and say, 'In truth, Lord, I expect no power from myself, nor from the means, but my resolution is to look up (as in Isaiah) to him that hath hid his face from Jacob. I will not look inward here for power to receive it from within, nor to the minister, nor to the means, but I will wait upon thee Lord, and look up to this power to work by the means. Is. 50:10: "Who is amongst you that feareth the Lord, and obeyeth the voice of his servants, that walketh in darkness, and that hath no light of comfort, let him trust in the name of the Lord, and stay himself upon his God." When all other things in the world fail, let the soul then look up to the Lord, and look out from itself; this is the fittest time of all to meet with God. I would have a Christian choose this time above all times to meet the Lord, and this is the only time to disappoint Satan; for, as I said before, it is the last refuge that the devil hath, and if he miss this opportunity he is conquered. Now the sinner partly seeing the beauty of grace, will not, and partly seeing the baseness of his own heart, dares not, come to Christ.

Objection: Then in the next place it is want of sense and feeling, which he would have and cannot find; therefore the distressed soul saith, 'Alas, I never knew what it was to have the assurance of God's love. I never received any evidence of God's favor; and shall I think that I have faith? They that believe have their hearts filled with joy unspeakable and glorious. The Word reveals this. But I am a stranger to that joy. How can I then think that I have any work of faith to come to Christ?'

Answer: I answer, this doth not hinder either that thou hast not faith, or that thou mayest not come to God by believing; therefore remember these three particulars:

First, thou must not think to have joy and refreshing before thou go to the promise, but thou must look for it when thou dost chew and feed upon the promise: thou wouldst have the Lord to give thee all the bargain before thou make the match. This joy is a fruit that proceeds from faith after much wrestling; it doth not follow from faith at the first. First believe, and then joy; for the heart is not filled with joy before believing, but afterwards. When thou hast had the sweet dew of the comfort of the promise many a day, then look for this joy.

Secondly, know that these joys and this sense and feeling may be absent from faith: a man may have a good faith and yet want the relish and sweetness which he desires; man may want his desirings and yet want neither life nor heat. A tree may want leaves and fruit and yet want neither sap nor moisture. A man's faith may be somewhat strong when his feeling is nothing at all. David was justified and sanctified, and yet wanted this joy; and so Job rested upon

God when he had but little feeling, as when he saith, Job 13:15, "Thou makest me a butt to shoot at; yet I will trust in thee though thou kill me." [2] Therefore away with your sense and feeling, and go to the promise.

Thirdly, the saints of God many times are deprived of comfort, not because God withholds it, but because they put it from them and will not have it, though he offer it, as David, Ps. 77:2, "My soul refused comfort," like a sullen child that will not eat his milk because he hath it not in the golden dish. So because God doth not for you what you would, you will have nothing at all. These are the main hindrances, and I might add many more; for carnal reason is very fruitful this way. But we through our folly and the devil's subtlety abuse these things and make them hindrances, and yet none of all these do hinder our right and title to Christ. Now I come to the cures of these hindrances; for if we had the wisdom and care we should have, we might break through them all and come to Christ. The means are four whereby we may be fortified against these, and at last be able to leap over all.

The first cure and help is this: we must not look too long, nor pore too much or unwarrantably upon our own corruptions, so far as to be feared or disheartened from coming to the riches of God's grace; for this is an everlasting truth, that whatsoever sight of sin unfits a man for mercy, when he may take it, and it is offered to him, that sight of sin is ever sinful, though it have never so fair a pretence of sorrow and deep humiliation. As we think many times, 'Had I a soul so throughly humbled!' and so forth. Thus the devil keeps us in sin, by poring upon our sin, when we think hereby to be carried from our sins. That course, I say, is sinful. Tell not me of sorrow and repentance and humiliation; all that sorrow and humiliation is nought that keeps a man from receiving mercy, when it is offered. See this in Abraham. He had this promise, that he should have a son in his old age, Rom. 4:19, 20: "He being not weak in faith regarded not his old age or deadness, nor the barrenness of

[2] Here Hooker gives a free interpretation of Job 13:15, which in the 1583 Geneva Version reads: "Lo, though he slay me, yet will I trust in him." The word "butt" is used here to designate a mound or other backdrop for catching arrows shot at a target.

Sarah's womb, but he believed in him who had promised it," and there he rests and stays. He saw his body was dead, yet there was a living promise; and what though Sarah's womb was barren, yet the promise was fruitful: he knew his deadness and her barrenness, but he considered them not. So we must see our sins and consider our own weakness, but never so settle ourselves with, or consider of them so as to be hindered from coming to God for mercy, which God offers us and we want; for while the soul of a man is daily plodding upon his own misery and distempers, these two things follow: first, we stop the stream of God's promise and let down the sluice against it, so that the promise cannot come into our souls; and secondly, we set open the stream and floodgate of corruption, and make it to run most violently in upon us, and in the end to overwhelm us. And the inconvenience arising hereby will slay the best Christian in the world; for what can a man get out of his corruption? He can have no more thereof than is there to be had.

It is vain to look for comfort where it is not to be had; it may dishearten us, but never encourage us. See the humility and wisdom of the woman of Canaan. She follows Christ, but he listens not to her, but gives her the repulse, and calls her "dog," and saith, Mt. 15:26, "You Gentiles are dogs, and the gospel of grace and salvation is the children's bread." Now if she had only considered the words of Christ, and only looked into her own baseness, she had never come to receive mercy and comfort; but she saith, Mt. 15:27, "Truth Lord, I am a dog, yet the dogs eat of the crumbs that fall from their master's table." There are two things here which do express the frame of this heart that is truly wise to attend to its own baseness: there is her humility and wisdom, as if she had said, 'Thou sayest I am a Gentile and a dog, I confess it; yet though I am a dog I will not go out of the doors but lie under the table for mercy.' So we must and ought. When our corruptions come in upon us and we see ourselves damned creatures, let us then say, 'In truth, Lord, I am as bad as thy word can speak.' Yet let us not fly away from mercy, but lie at the feet of our Savior. It is fit and we ought to see our sins, but stay not too long here; see thy sins thou must, but not be settled there to be kept from Christ. That sight of sin which doth not drive a man to Christ for mercy is ever sinful. See thy sins thus:

First, see thy sins till thou see them odious and loathsome.

Secondly, till thou see an utter insufficiency in thyself to help thee.

Thirdly, till thou hast seen an utter and absolute necessity of Christ to succor thee, and then away to the throne of grace, and dwell no longer on thy sins; for there is pardon enough to remove the guilt that sin hath brought upon thy soul; there is power enough to make thee master thy corruptions. Indeed, every soul should say thus: 'It is true Lord, my sins are many and great, for I have departed from thee Lord. And shall I go from God and persist in evil? God forbid.' All this while I speak to brokenhearted Christians. You profane ones, you have your portion already, and shall have more afterwards; but stand you by, and let the children come to their share.

Now the second means of cure is this: take heed of judging thy estate by carnal reasons without the rule, as thus it is the fashion of poor distressed spirits to pass fearful sentence upon themselves upon groundless arguments, as to say, 'I never found it, and I feel it not, and I fear it is not so.' Thus we hear those carnal pleas which Satan helps us to invent, and we judge ourselves by them. Now, I say, take heed of this and make conscience of this same, as of any other sin of swearing, stealing, whoring, or murder; for this is as truly a sin as those, though not so great. Nay, this is a greater sin than you imagine. Consider this, you humble-hearted Christians, for to you I speak; for when upon these grounds thou concludest thy case and estate is naught, see against how many commandments thou sinnest. First, thou dishonorest God and the work of his grace; and thou breakest the third commandment in denying that which God hath done for thee, and speakest unreverently against God; and thou art a murderer, and woundest thy soul, and hast sinned against that commandment; and thou robbest thyself of comfort, and art a thief; and thou bearest false witness, to speak against thyself, against Christ, and his Spirit, and this work of his grace, and joinest with the devil against the Lord Christ. But thou wilt say, 'I speak as I think.' That hinders not but that thou bearest false witness. As we see, if a man affirm such a one is a drunkard, and knows it not, this man bears false witness, because though the man be a drunkard, yet he knows it not: so thou sayest thou hast nothing, when as thou dost only fear it, and suspect it, and the like. I speak this the rather, because of the sinful distemper that creeps in upon the hearts of many broken-hearted Christians, that out of a self-willed rod of carnal reason, and a wild haunt that they have got, their hearts are persuaded that they do well to do so, and they are never well except they do thus.

But know that you have sinned fearfully all this while; and such as these, mark it, when reason is plain, and the Scriptures are evidently against them, they do not so much attend what the minister saith, but they stand and invent how they may answer the minister, and so put away their own comforts. Let the fear of God fall upon every soul that hears this, and know that howsoever you have taken leave to yourselves, and have taken up pleas against the truth, yet now go your ways, and mourn for it, and wonder that the Lord hath not taken away all the comfort of his grace, and all the motions of his Spirit from you. The prophet David prays the Lord to turn away his eyes from beholding vanity. Now if God must do that, then much more must he turn away our hearts from attending to vanities. I must attend to God, and the voice of his Spirit, but to listen to those carnal pleas which I have no warrant to do, I sin deeply, and hurt my own soul dangerously thereby. No man would deal with a cheater. Carnal reason is a cheater; therefore let us not attend thereto, unless we resolve to be cozened. And if the danger of the sin cannot make us do this, then let the sorrow that will come by it constrain us. Is. 50:11: "Behold all you that kindle a fire, and that compass yourselves about with the sparkles that ye have kindled. This shall you have at my hand; ye shall lie down in sorrow."

I will show what is meant by sparkles and by fire. In the old Law, you know, there was heavenly fire continually in the sanctuary, that shadowed out to us the will and wisdom of God in his Word. But there was also strange fire, that is, there were divers sparkles of their own imaginations; and there were conceits. Every poor creature carries his tinderbox about him, and he is ever kindling of it; the Lord doth not allow of this. In that text are two things: first, that the heart of man will naturally invent carnal reasons and pleas against itself, and be settled upon them; secondly, then mark what follows thereupon: "This shall ye have of mine hand; you shall lie down in your own sorrow." When the Scriptures are clear, and reasons are evident, you will have your own devices. Thus much I tell you; you shall lie down in your own sorrow. You may thank yourselves for it. Away with your tinderboxes, therefore, and lie down before the Lord, and be wise to salvation.

Thirdly, let us be marvelously wary and watchful that we enter not into the lists of dispute with Satan, upon those points which are beyond the reach of man; as thus to say, 'I am not elected, and God will not do me good, seeing I am not elected, and therefore it is vain for me to use the means'; and 'Oh, the time is gone, oh, the day of grace that I have seen!; the Lord knocked sweetly, and was pleased to reveal my sins at such a time, but then hard-hearted wretch that I was, I shut the door of my heart against the Lord Jesus Christ; and now it is gone and past; and now there is no hope forever of receiving mercy again.' If the devil get thee here, all thy comfort is gone, for upon this ground a man shall never receive rest to his heart; for if no man can ever know the thing, how shall I be able to give, or any man to take comfort? Look as it is with a poor traveling man that lighteth among thieves, who come and promise to carry him a nearer way, and at last they bring him into a wood where no passengers come, and there they do what they will with him: so it is with a poor soul, when the devil gets him into these secret disputes of God's eternal counsel, there are no passengers come this way, and therefore thou art void of succor. Therefore for your direction in this case observe three rules:

First, let the soul in this case stay itself upon the all-mightiness of the power of God, Gen. 17:1: "I am God all-sufficient." If thou art persuaded of the all-sufficiency of God, this will help thee: thou canst not know God's power, and yet God can do more than thou canst think; and therefore God is able, and will do thee good, though thou know it not. And therefore observe thus much: the soul never doubts of God's will, but it doubts of his power also in some measure.

Secondly, check thine own heart for meddling with God's secrets; let no man go beyond his bounds. Check thy heart, I say, for prying into God's secrets, and know that it doth not belong to thee. Dt.

29:29: "Secret things belong to God, but revealed things belong to us." And, 1 Cor. 2:16: "Who hath known the mind of God?," saith Paul. Mark this, you that will be going up into the skies to know what God's secret mind is: keep your stations wisely, for the devil and all the devils in hell never knew the mind of the Lord. When Jonah cried against Niniveh, saying, Jon. 3:4, "Within forty days all your drunkards and adulterers shall be destroyed," mark there how the King stays himself, saying, Jon. 4:9, "Who can tell if the Lord will repent and stay his fierce wrath that we perish not." When the devil tells thee thus, and saith, 'God hath appointed a way to salvation, and you have had the means and did not profit by them, therefore God will never show you mercy, nor give you grace,' how can the devil tell that? Nay, all the devils in hell cannot tell. Let me walk in that course which God hath appointed and commanded, and do that which I ought, and let me say, 'Who knows but God may break the heart of a proud rebellious sinner; none but God knows it.'

Thirdly, measure not the riches of God's love and the sweetness of his grace according to your own conceits, and do not think that because you cannot conceive it, therefore God will not do it. Is. 55:7, 8, 9: "Let the wicked forsake his ways, and the unrighteous man his thoughts." As if he had said, 'All you wicked ones, and you that have lived lewdly, return from your wicked ways and from your vain imaginations, for he will abundantly pardon.' [3]

Objection: 'But will the Lord pardon all my sins?,' saith the soul. 'I cannot think it. If I were a God I should never pass by such intolerable things.'

Answer: And because you cannot, you think God cannot. 'Yes,' saith the Lord, 'I can abundantly pardon, for my thoughts are not your thoughts, nor my ways as your ways,' saith the Lord. A poor creature thinks his sins are unpardonable, and he shall never get assurance of God's love. 'You are men,' saith the Lord, 'and have finite thoughts; but I am God and have mercy infinitely when you think I have no mercy.'

Objection: 'But there were never any such received to mercy,' saith the soul, 'and therefore why should I be the man?'

---

[3] Throughout this imagined dialogue, and in the objection and answer following, Hooker paraphrases Is. 55:7,8,9.

Answer: When Christ had wrought many strange miracles, the people said there were never such things done in Israel. And therefore it is plain; God can do things that never were done. Job 9:10: "Which dost great things past finding out, and wondrous without number." Therefore judge not God's power and love by what thou canst conceive.

The fourth cure is this, and it is specially to be observed above all: in thy proceeding with thyself in judgment, that is, pass no judgment against thy soul but according to the evidence of the Word. If thou art to be approved, let the word of God approve thee; and let the Word examine thee, if thou art to be examined. If the Word speak for thee, it is no matter though all men and angels speak against thee; and if the Word condemn thee, it is no matter who speaks for thee. What though some wrangling railer step in, and will be determining the causes before the judge comes, yet a wise man will stay till the judge comes, and wait his leisure. Deal thou so with thine own soul; put not the case to be tried by a company of peevish, carnal reasons, but stay till the Word come and judge thyself by that, and hold to that forever. Eph. 5:13: "The light is that which manifesteth all things." The meaning is this: the light is the light of the Word, and the evidences of God's truth manifested to the souls of God's people. All sense and feeling of carnal reasoning are like fogs and mists which make a man that he cannot see the way; but bring him to the light, and then his state and condition will be manifested what it is. Mt. 11:29: "Learn of me," saith our Savior "and you shall find rest." And the Psalmist saith [Ps. 27:4], "I will inquire what the Lord will say." So say thou, 'I will not hearken what carnal reason will say, but what the Lord will say.' The want of this is the reason why we want rest, and are still in doubtings, because he that teacheth us is a deluder.

Objection: For the poor soul saith, 'What shall I have gained? Shall I have title to the promises? Nay, this belongs to those that are brokenhearted. Indeed, if I had such power against corruption, and this and that, there were some hopes; but I am so full of weakness, and many times led captive by my rebellious heart. Nay, I never had grace; nay, I never shall have it.'

Answer: But who told you so, and where learned you this religion? I am sure you never learned it of Christ. Who, or what word tells you, 'If I have such corruptions I shall never have grace'? Not the word of Christ, I am sure. Wherefore I charge you hold to the truth of the Word. Learn of me, saith Christ, and put not your cause to be decided by carnal reason, nor hearken what it telleth you; for if you take that course you shall never come to Christ whilst the world standeth. Learn of the Lord Christ, for his word is faithful and his promise sure; and there you shall find rest as strong as Mount Zion. It is that word whereby thou shalt be judged at the great day, when sense and feeling shall be cast out for wranglers and never come into court. Thus much of the four cures. I will now propound four rules how a man may order himself aright in this course, so that he may repair to the Word at all times, as he ought to do, and gain evidence by the Word of truth.

[Four] Rules to Direct a Christian How to Use the Word of God for the Evidence of His Assurance

First, that we may so use the word of God as we ought. As thou must in all conditions that concern thy soul repair to the world, so thou must consider thine own uprightness, and what work of grace is in thy soul, that will answer the Word and testify that the work of grace is true. Be sure to take thy soul at the best. Do not always consider what is the worst part in thee, nor thy failings that may accuse thee, but if there be any uprightness that may speak for thee, hear that too. It is injustice for any court to hear one side and not another. The Lord doth not lie at catch [4] with his children, but he takes them at the best, as Rom. 4:22, it is said that "Abraham believed the promise, and it was imputed to him for righteousness." Yet in the 12 of Genesis we see he had some doubtings, but we see God took him at the best, and so records this of his faith. So we see that Sarah is spoken of as a gracious woman and a pattern for women in calling her husband "Lord," Gen. 18:12, I Pet. 3:6, which was a sign of an humble heart; but yet we read she derided the message

---

[4] To "lie at catch," or "upon the catch," is a seventeenth-century expression meaning to set onself to entrap a person. James A. H. Murray, ed., *A New English Dictionary*, VI (Oxford, 1908), 253.

of the Lord by the angel, notwithstanding the Lord buries that and only mentions the other in the commendations of her.

Now as the Lord deals with his servants, so must we deal with ourselves. Whatsoever is found sincere and upright, observe that as well as the other, nay, rather than the other. If a man should have his cause handled in any court after this fashion, and they should only observe the failings in his cause, the best cause may happily go against a man. Therefore the court will hear all read; as if any bond or bill come in, or any matter of agreement, they hear all; but if a man have an indenture, and the lawyer only hears and reads the failings in it, and that which seems to make against that party, if the judge only hear that, it must needs go against him, and therefore the man saith, 'Good my Lord, hear all.' And when they find it written that such a debt is paid and the party satisfied, then the cause goes well; whereas if they had heard only the first part and not the second, he had lost all. So, many bring in great indictments against themselves, and say, 'Oh, what pride and stubbornness is in my heart! Oh, how weak am I, and dull, and dead, and backward to holy duties!' It is true; but is not thy heart troubled with these, and is it not the greatest grief of thy soul that lies upon thee? 'Yea,' saith the poor soul, 'I confess my heart is weary of these, and I could be content to be anything, that I could not be thus.' Now take thy soul on this side and hear the best part. As it is with a man's hand and the staff, I compare the promise to a staff. You know the back of a man's hand cannot take hold of the staff; but let him turn the palm of his hand to the staff, and then he can take it. So turn thou the right side of thy soul to the promise, and then thou mayest take it. But we turn the backside of our hearts to the promise, when the soul saith, 'Oh, my stubbornness is great, and mine inabilities and corruptions are many!' This is the wrong side of thine heart, and this will ever hinder thee from taking hold of the promise. But thy soul hates these and is weary of them. This is the right side of the heart; turn that to the promise.

Secondly, labor to have thy conscience settled and established in that truth which now out of the Word thou hast gotten, to bear witness of the work of grace in thee; for if there be any want of the assurance of God's love, and if the evidence of the work of grace cannot pour fully in upon thy heart, but there is some guilt of sin still remaining, then conscience will breed new broils[5] and continually nip and disquiet the heart. Therefore as we must have our judgment informed by the Word that there is some good in us, so we must get conscience persuaded of it, that conscience may speak for us. As the debtor, if he be indebted to many creditors he must agree with all (for if he agree with all save one, that one may imprison him as well as all the rest), so it is with the poor distressed soul that lies at the mercy of the Lord, and is so deep in arrearages that he cannot help himself. He must labor therefore to still conscience, that it does not accuse him, but be on his side. The want of this is the cause why new suits and new bills are daily put up against us, only because conscience is not pacified. Take a poor sinner that hath all his doubts and objections answered, come to him, and say, 'Are these all your doubts and objections?' 'Yes.' 'And are they all answered?' 'Yes.' 'And have you now anything to say against that which hath been made known unto you?' 'No, not now.' Say to him again, 'Did your conscience say to you, it is a sin to say you have no grace?' Now here he demurs and stays, and saith, 'No, I dare not say so, but I rather say the contrary.' Mark this: all the books are crossed [6] and all objections answered, and yet conscience puts in a new plea because it was not satisfied. Now come to him again and say, 'You are sometimes captived by sin, but are you willing to be at God's disposing, and that he should pluck away all those corruptions?' 'Oh,' saith the poor sinner, 'I must needs yield to that!' Then this is a work of grace. Now let conscience be fully satisfied, and cancel all occasional accusations, and it will clear the heart and cast out all cavils that come in against us. I Jn. 3:21: "For if our consciences condemn us not, then we have boldness toward God." We must make conscience, and be convinced, that it is a sin to say, 'God hath not wrought this work of grace in our hearts'; for though sense and feeling be sometimes gone, yet conscience remembers the day and year when he had a clear evidence of God's love, and saith, 'Lord thou knowest it, and thou didst say out of thy word that my heart was upright and sincere in thy fight.'

[5] Trouble, disorder.
[6] "Crossed" is used here in the sense of having got the debt-book crossed.

It should be with a poor sinner as it is with a wise man when he would make his lands sure unto him and his posterity by evidences and writings: he is not content only to have his evidences in his own keeping, but will have them enrolled in Chancery such a year and such a day that if he should lose his deeds he may be sure to find them again there. So it should be with a distressed soul: we should not only be content to have all our objections answered, but get them recorded in the court of conscience, that when sense and feeling is lost, yet wit may go to the court of conscience and there find the day and year when God's love was made sure to us.

Thirdly, we should strive mightily to have our hearts overpowered with the evidence which reason and conscience makes good to us, that so we may quietly receive it and calmly welcome it, and yield and subject our hearts to that truth. But here we all stick, for there are three things in the soul of a man which maintain these quarrels and oppositions against the evidence of the Word: 1. reason objects; 2. conscience accuseth; 3. the will of man will not submit. And we find it in experience that when a man hath stilled conscience, and answered all reasons, yet the stubbornness of the heart maintains a gainsaying against the truth, and keeps the old quarrel that hath been answered long ago, and that a man would think had been buried long since. It is in this case with a poor sinner as it is with a man that hath a contentious adversary; happily the cause that they two have in hand hath been tried in all the courts of England and at last comes to Chancery, and there it is concluded against a man, so that all things are settled and ended, as a man would think, and an honest man would sit down and be quiet. But the other, a quarrelsome fellow, will not yield yet, but to the old law he will again, and he will sell all he hath but he will have his will; till at last the judge comes to take notice of this man, and casts out the cause and puts him in prison, and saith, 'These things were all answered, and the cause ended long ago.' Just so for all the world is it with the heart of a gracious man that is humbled in some measure and could be content to yield to the credit of God's word and to the witness of his conscience, and saith, 'My condition is better than I thought it was.' But there is an old proud, self-willed heart that will not be quiet, but still be quarrelsome and maintain the old quarrel, though reasons are all confuted and conscience bears witness against him, and every minister casts out the cause. Yet observe it, a poor distressed sinner will keep the old objections; and though they were answered the night before, yet he will have them fresh the next morning, and the next month, even when a man would think he should not dare to come in court. And the mischief lies even here, in a proud, self-willed heart that will not yield. Therefore labor to get thy heart so far overpowered with the authority of the truth whatsoever it is that God reveals to thee for thy good, and do no reject the evidence which God makes known and passeth upon thy soul for thy ever-lasting good. Do not, I say, reject it. And because thou hast not that comfort that thou wouldst, therefore thou wilt have none at all. It is not properly because thou canst not, but because thou wilt not receive the promise. This is it which breeds the quarrel. And hence it is that when reason is satisfied, and conscience convinced, ask the soul this question, and say, 'Are you persuaded that the Lord hath done you good and will show mercy unto you?' 'No,' saith he, 'all the world shall not persuade me of that. Ministers are merciful, and Christians are charitable, and are loathe to discourage me as I should do to them; but did they know me indeed they would never think of it, and I would never find it so. What I, grace? All the world shall never persuade me to it.' But I say it is thy pride and self-willedness that will not receive that good that God is willing to give thee, and it is hellish and devilish pride.

Objection: But will some say, 'How is it pride? They are ever complaining and condemning themselves; this is not pride.'

Answer: Yes, I say it is devilish pride, and that I will show you these two ways. First, for a man to follow his own conceits and self-willedness against the truth and the force of reason and the witness of the servants of God and his own conscience, is not this pride? Secondly, thy pride appears in this: namely, because thou hast not what thou wouldst, and in that manner and measure thou desirest, and hast not that sweetness of grace that thou wouldst have, therefore thou flingest away all God's kindness. This is infinite pride. That measure of mercy which God hath already showed thy soul is incomprehensible, and yet because you cannot have what you would, you will have nothing at all. As a man that hath the law on his side, and his estate settled on him, yet because his evidences are not written in great huge letters, and in large paper, he throws them all away; so you have no grace because you have not so much as you would have; you have no humility because you have not so much humility. Oh, pride, and devilish pride too! Labor therefore to bring thy heart to this blessed subjection to the truth of God, and make it thy duty as well to receive comfort when God offers it upon good grounds, as to do a duty commanded; and know that it is a sin to reject mercy when God offers it, as to kill a man, which God hath forbidden. And therefore you saints of God that have been pestered thus, and have been enemies to yourselves, when your hearts begin to slide away thus, take your hearts and reason thus with your souls, and say, 'Good Lord, this is the proud stubborn distemper of this vile heart of mine! What would I have? Is not God's word clear, and my conscience satisfied? Do not the ministers of God affirm my state to be good? And shall I thus dishonor God?'

Objection: But what saith the poor soul again? 'Must I eat mine own words and say I have grace when before I said I had none?'

Answer: Yes, and be thankful to God that thou mayest say so too. It is better for you to cross your own humors than cross God's Spirit. Take notice of it, and fear forever, lest that proud and stubborn soul of thine (which now refuseth consolation when God offers it) be forced to eat thy flesh and come upon thy knees and never get comfort; and though God save thee in the end, yet thou shall be, as it were, in hell upon earth.

One would have thought it had been humility in Peter to refuse to let Christ wash his feet, but it was nothing but pride, and therefore Christ takes him up for it sharply, and it is the only way to cure this distemper. Jn. 13:8: "If I wash thee not thou hast no part in me." If you will needs have your own humors, and will not be persuaded, you may get you down to hell with them. But when his stomach came down, then, Jn. 13:9, "Lord, not only my feet, but my hands and heart and all." It is humility of heart to take what God offers. Most Christians think they are humble-hearted, but they are proud so far as they give leave to this distemper. Therefore labor to over-master this gainsaying heart of thine with the authority of the word of God; and learn to receive mercy when God offers it, lest he take away the comfort of his Spirit from you, and make you go howling and roaring to your graves.

Though he bring you to heaven in the end, yet you may have a hell before you come thither.

The last rule is this: maintain the good word which thy heart hath submitted to, and keep it as the best treasure under heaven; and when thou hast this evidence, hear nothing against it, but stick fast to it, which is good in law. Hear nothing but out of the word of God against that comfort and evidence of the Word which thou hast been persuaded of by the Word. If Satan or carnal reason have anything to say against thee, let them bring Scripture, and then yield to it; but without the Word hear nothing.

Look as it is with a man that is at law for lands; if he have his adversary on the hip, and have gotten some advantage against him, he will keep him there and hold him to the point. If a man will follow every wrangling lawyer at every impertinent out-straying, he will never have any good success; for it is the fashion of many attorneys rather to breed quarrels than to end them. And therefore hold to the main point. So deal with Satan. It is the cunning of the enemy to lead you out, and he will have many vagaries; but be sure to hold to that truth which you have received from the evidence of the Word and the witness of conscience. When a man hath gotten some comfort, then the devil begins to play the lawyer, and saith, 'Dost thou not see how weak and poor thou art?'

How the Soul being Tempted may Answer Satan's Accusations

'It is true,' saith the soul, 'yet it is as true that he that confesseth and forsaketh his sin shall have mercy.'

'But,' saith the devil, 'dost thou not see that thou art full of pride and weakness, and secretly unwilling to come to duties?'

'It is true,' saith the soul, 'I am so; yet I hate and forsake and shall find mercy. The Word saith so.'

'But,' saith the devil, 'are you of God's counsel? Secret things belong to God.'

'Oh, but,' saith the soul, 'I know not what God's secret will is; yet this I know: that the Word saith he that confesseth and forsaketh his sin shall find mercy.'

'But,' saith the devil, 'many cozen themselves, mercy is a great thing, and few obtain it; and why not you be cozened as well as others?'

'But,' saith the soul, 'the Lord will not cozen me, and the Lord knows my heart, and the Word knows what the Lord knows.'

'But,' saith the devil, 'may not you be deceived in the Word? The Word is true indeed, but how know you that you rightly apply it, and that the Word and your heart doth suit together?

'Why,' saith the soul, 'I know my heart by the Word, and to the Word I repair. And the Lord knows that I hate all sin inwardly and reform it outwardly; and therefore I know I shall find mercy. Show me a place of Scripture that saith I do not rightly apply the Word, and I will believe it; but I will not believe thee, for thou are a deluder and a liar.'

Thus hold to the Word, and the devil will be tired and go away. Keep you here, for if he catch you a wandering after sense and feeling, you are gone. Ps. 119:98: "Thou through thy commandments hast made me wiser than mine enemies," saith David, "for they are ever with me." Satan is wise, and the flesh and carnal reason and the world are wise; but blessed be our God that makes every poor ignorant servant wiser than all these. But how? The Word must be ever with them; you must keep the Word with you daily, and that will make you not know only what was amiss, but get ground against whatsoever is amiss.

Satan deals in this with the soul, as the enemy deals in war. As Joshua 8:19, when he defeated the men of Ai, he got them out of the city, and then they that lay in ambush went and took it in and burnt it with fire, so the devil doth. Our castle or city is the promises, and the word, and ordinances of God. Now if the devil can but get you out of this castle, he hath you where he would; if you will look after every bird that flies, and listen after every carnal reason and temptation, you are gone. If he once get you from the promise, he will entangle you in his snare and overcome you.

I Jn. 2:28: "Little Children, if ye abide in God's Commandments, ye abide in God." As if he has said, 'Children, your enemies are many, and great, and cunning; therefore keep home, keep home, come not abroad, and then you shall be safe, whatsoever troubles arise.'

It is the fashion of parents, if their children run abroad and catch a knock, they tell them that they are well enough served: 'You might have kept home then when you had warning.' The issue of this point is this: judge thy soul by the Word, and look upon thy sacred part, and let that bear witness for thee; and what the word of God doth evidence to thee, that maintain and hear nothing against it. This is the way to receive constant comfort and go on merrily in our Christian course: let quarrels, troubles, and temptations come, yet keep you within doors and rest yourselves upon the riches of God's free grace in Jesus Christ; and be forever comforted, and you may go singing to heaven and to your graves though you meet with never so many temptations and oppositions.

Means to Obtain Grace and Faith

Now I will show you some means whereby a man may so improve his time that at last he may obtain this blessed grace, which are four. But before I do begin with them, you must be advertised of thus much: that we may use the means, but there is no means under heaven will do it. Yet you must wait upon God in the use of the means, for it is not the means that will do it, that will work faith, but the Spirit of God in the use of the means; and therefore the text saith [Phil. 1:29], "To you it is given to believe," for faith is the free gift of God. It is God that must do it, and yet he will not do it without us, because we are reasonable men and women, and God affords us means; and therefore we are to wait upon the Lord in the use of the means, and let the Lord do what he will, and let us do what we should. We must not think when we have the means then we can get faith, for as Paul saith, Eph. 1:19, 20, "The same power that raised up Jesus from the dead must make us able to believe," or else all the angels in heaven, and all the ministers on earth, and all the help that men and means can do thee, will do thee go good. The means are divers, as hearing and prayer, which are the conduits whereby God communicates faith; but I let those pass and only fasten upon those which are needful for feeble Christians to bring them into this blessed grace, and those are these:

First, we must, as much as in us lies, labor to pluck away all those props that the soul leans upon, and all those outward succors, and whatsoever outward contentment it is which a poor sinner doth repair and betake himself to for succor and relief, that when all these are taken from us we may be forced to go for succor there where it is to be had. It is that which remains in the nature of man, and that which is natural to us even from our first parents, that we would have the staff in our own hands, and support our own souls, and supply all those necessities that lie upon us.

Now the way to make the soul lean upon Christ is to pluck away all other props; for the last thing that we come to is the promise, and if we could find good anywhere else we would never go to Christ. God hears last of us, and therefore we should do with ourselves as the enemy doth with a city besieged: when he would make them yield, the only way is to famish them, cut off all provision, and stop all passages that none may come to relieve them; and then they will be forced to yield themselves to the mercy of the enemy. So it is with our nature: we would trust to our own strength and rely upon something of our own. And therefore famish thy heart and cut off all the means and comfort whereby thy heart may be succored and thy conscience quieted; and when thy heart is famished, it will then seek to a savior and lie there, because there is no other thing to support it.

The poor woman in the gospel, Mk. 5:26, 27, had spent all her goods upon the physician, and if she had had but a little means left, yea, but one farthing token for anything, I know she would never have gone to Christ; but when all these failed, then she was forced to seek to Christ, that was ready and willing to do anything for her distressed nature. So our souls must have something to support themselves upon, for they cannot live without some support. Now therefore when all our carnal hopes are taken away, we must needs stay upon the promise, because we have nothing else. It is not required that a man should cast away those outward comforts that God affords him, but only this: that though you have all, yet labor to get

your heart to see and acknowledge the emptiness of all these, and
let not the heart seek too much content in them, for these are all
but lying vanities and broken staves, which will not only cozen a
man, but pierce him to. Now when the soul seeth all this cannot
succor him, but lay him in the dust, when he seeth this, then he
will be content to have his heart severed from these. It is with the
soul as it was with Noah's dove: when the Ark began to rest upon
the mountain of Ararat, Noah sent out the dove. [Gen. 8:9]: "But
the dove found no rest for the sole of her foot." No question there
were many dead carcasses, but the dove found no rest till she came to
the ark again; so when a man finds no rest in all these, and can get no
footing for the soul to stay itself upon them, then it betakes itself
to Christ and goes home to the promise and rests there, and expects
from thence what is needful. As in the art of swimming, he that
will swim must pluck his feet from the bottom and commit himself
to the stream to bear him up, so we must pluck our hearts from these
things, and them from us; and though we have honor and preferments, yet we must not put any confidence in them, but learn by
our believing to commit ourselves to the power of the promise, and
receive comfort from thence.

Let not the gods of this world, honor, and profit, and pleasure
deceive thee. Did the pride of Pharoah's heart deliver him? Did the
riches of Dives[7] save him? Did Herod's applause that he had deliver
him? Did these gods deliver them? Nay, have they not left them in
the lurch? Therefore let us take our hearts off from these things
and have a base esteem of them, and see a vanity and emptiness and
insufficiency in them, that we may be forced to seek to Christ and
say as David said [Ps. 12:1, 2], "Help, Lord, for vain is the help of
man." Labor therefore to see the privy pranks of thine own heart,
and hunt out all these mazes; for it is wonderful to see how the soul
is ready to hang her comforts upon every hedge, and shift and shirk
in every by-corner for comfort. Now when thou seest thy heart
thus seeking to settle itself, pluck away that prop and see the emptiness of it, and then thy heart will be fit and ready to go unto Christ.

---

[7] "Dives," the Latin word for "rich (man)," occurs in the Vulgate, Lk. 16, and
was therefore commonly taken as the proper name of the rich man in that
parable. *A New English Dictionary*, III (Oxford, 1897), 551.

Now when this is done there is a little way made that the promise may come to the soul; therefore labor in the second place to have your hearts possessed thoroughly and persuaded effectually of the fulness of that good which is in the promise, and of that satisfactory mercy and freeness of the grace of God in Christ, that so the soul may be established with that full content which is to be had in the riches of the promise. But mark what I say, persuade your heart of it, and content not yourselves that you are able to dispute somewhat fully of the excellency of the promise and of the riches of God's free grace. What is this to the purpose that the heart knows this, and yet is forestalled that it comes not [to] the promise? Therefore leave not thy heart till it come to make that account of the promise that the Word saith it is worth. I say, leave not thy heart till thou see the promise of grace most beautiful in thy eye, and that thy heart may gain some earnest touching the goodness of God, and the riches of his grace toward thee, and bring thy heart to know and see that the promise is better than all the riches and honors that thou canst have, or the world can bestow. Ps. 9:10: "They that know thee will trust in thee, for thou, Lord, hast never failed them that seek thee." This kind of knowledge ever breeds confidence and resolution, and persuades the heart. We dare trust a friend whose faithfulness we have tried, and to rest upon that which it knoweth. The promises are of a tried truth: seek from one end of the heavens to the other, and see if ever any man leaned on the promise, and the Lord did not perform that which he had promised to do for the good of his soul. Ps. 119:92: "Except the Lord had been my delight, I should have perished in my troubles," saith David; and, Ps. 73:26, "My flesh faileth and my heart also, but thou art the strength of my heart and my portion forever." Here lies a great weight, and it is a work of marvelous difficulty and great necessity; and therefore that thy heart may sit down satisfied in the sufficiency of the promise, I will propound three rules that you may improve the promise for your uttermost benefit.

First, observe and labor daily to present a greater good in the promise than the soul can see anywhere else. It is a man's skill, and it should be his endeavor daily, to dog his heart and to look what it is that the heart desires most, and present a greater good to thy soul than all things thou canst have elsewhere. We should deal with our hearts as a man would do with a corrupt Justice; when he would have him to be on his side, the only way is to bribe him. Though that is sinful, yet it is good to bribe the corrupt heart with the goodness of the promise, that the heart may go with it. Do honors, or riches, or the applause of men, or any earthly pleasures offer thee content and satisfaction? Then persuade thy heart there is a greater worth and excellency in the promise than can be had in all the world. Here is an exceeding weight of glory: he that hath this promise shall be made a king, and shall have glory that will never vanish. Doth thy heart hanker after earthly joy and mirth? Thou shalt find a greater mirth in the promise than in the cracking of these thorns (and so I may say of anything else). Doth thy heart hanker after riches? Then tell thy heart that there are unsearchable riches in Christ, and through him we have title to all the promises of this life and a better.

Thus we should observe the goings out of our hearts, and what offers itself to give it content, and present it with a greater good in the promise than in all things else. We know he that offers most for the bargain hath it. I would have the soul outbid the world. Therefore labor to have access to the promise with thy soul, and speak a good word for it, and say, 'Stand by profits and pleasures, and preferments: room for the Lord Jesus Christ.' And put a wonderful price upon the promise. This is an everlasting rule: whatsoever the soul doth account as best, that it will choose and leave all others for it.

To conclude: labor to outshoot the devil in his own bow. And those things which the devil casts in thy way for hindering thy soul from coming to the promise, let those things be as means to usher in the promise. As thus, when thou seest thy heart look after friends, let those friends usher the way to think on the infinite love and favor of God in Christ; and when thy heart would fain hunt after wealth, let this usher a way to the promise, and say, 'If the heart find such content in riches, what would it find in the riches of God's grace in Christ?' Thus present a greater good in the promise than in anything else.

The second rule is this: labor to convince thy heart with this; that all the things in the world without the promise are not good. And hadst thou all that the earth can afford without a promise, they were rather a curse to thee than a blessing. Heb. 11:1: "Faith is the substance of things hoped for"; it gives a kind of being and substance to all. There is no substance in honor and riches. If they be not in faith they are clogs and snares to a man, except faith give a title thereunto and a blessing therewith; and all our prayers have no substance in them, but they are poor and empty words without faith in the promise to have what we pray for. The poorest and meanest prayer, when a poor creature can scarce utter four words with any sense, yet if there be but faith, it is a very powerful prayer. And the substance of all your hearing and my preaching lies in faith; otherwise they are but lost labor; for faith is it that gives a kind of being to whatsoever we speak or do.

The third rule in this second means is this: labor to acquaint thy heart with the goodness of the promise before carnal reason comes and possess thy heart, that the promise is most sure and will come when it is most seasonable, when it is best, when God sees it most fit we shall have it. Heb. 4:16: "Let us therefore come boldly to the throne of grace, that we may receive comfort and mercy in time of need," not when I see it fit, but when God sees it fit. This is it which carries away many poor sinful hearts from resting upon the promise of God: sometimes the heart is a little affected with the excellency of the riches of God's grace, and seeth what great things the Lord hath done for his soul, and saith, 'Oh, that I were such a one!,' and 'Let me die the death of the righteous!' But when it comes to pass that he hath not present ease and comfort, then he casts away the good promise of the Lord, and the devil prevails wonderfully with these poor creatures. Hab. 3:17, 18: "When the fig tree shall not blossom, neither shall the fruit be on the vines; when the labor of the olive shall fail and yield no fruit, then will I rejoice in the Lord, and joy in the God of my salvation." Now comfort from the promise and from the Lord Jesus Christ is seasonable. When I have most need and may receive most good thereby, then shall I be sure to have the promise so to surprise my heart, that it may be possessed with the all-sufficiency of it. Now when thou hast seen the goodness of the promise, and thy heart is fully persuaded of the good that is in the promise . . .[8]

Then in the third place see that thou expectest all the good which thou needest and canst desire from that sufficiency of the promise; do not think to bring any good with thee to the promise, but go to the promise for all good. There are all the cords of mercy that must draw thee, and there is the all-sufficiency that can supply all thy wants. Look for all from thence, and expect power from the promise to enable thee to do whatsoever thou wouldst, and to make thee able to believe the promise.

Objection: It is a weak plea for a man to say, 'I dare not look to the promise; I cannot believe; if I could then I might expect some good.'

Answer: Thou shall never believe upon these terms; thou must not first have faith and then go to the promise, but thou must first go to the promise and from thence receive power to make thee able to believe the promise. Ps. 119:49: "O Lord, remember thy word to thy servant, wherein thou hast caused me to trust." When men are enlarged in love to a man, and made fair promises, this persuades the heart to trust to them and to rely upon them for good; therefore a man doth use to say, 'I durst not have thought it, nor expected, if you had not promised it.' So the promise of God made to the soul makes the soul to rest upon it. To expect faith without a promise is alone as if a man should expect a crop without seed; for the promise is the immortal seed of God's word whereby the Spirit breeds this faith in the hearts of all that are his. Jn. 5:25: "The hour is coming, and now is, when the dead shall hear the voice of the Son of God; and they that hear it shall live." It is spoken of raising of a dead man from the grave of sin. First, there is the voice of Christ to the

---

[8] The final sentence of this paragraph, with its missing part, was eliminated from all later Dawlman editions. In the Ranew and Robinson edition of 1684, the following remarks were put in its place: "But we go not so far. This is for the second rule" (p. 115). And Thomas Prince repeated these remarks in his 1743 edition. In the complete sermon, as published in *The Souls Effectual Calling to Christ* (1637), the paragraph ends: "And therefore persuade thy heart the good of the promise will come when it is most seasonable; let riches satisfy when death comes, then call for your cordial. I tell you the promise will help when all fails" (pp. 606–607).

soul before there can be an echo again of the soul to Christ; so the power of the promise must come to the soul, and we must hear the voice of God in the promise before we can return an echo again to the Lord. The Lord saith, 'Come to me,' and the soul saith, 'I come, Lord.' When thou seest much deadness and unfitness of heart, do not thou go away and look off from the promise and say, 'Thus I am, and so it is with me'; but rather go to the promise and say, 'Whatsoever frailties I find in myself, yet I will look to the Lord and to his promise; for if I want faith, the promise must settle me more and more therein. I must not bring faith to the promise, but receive faith from thence, and therefore I will wait till the Lord please to work it.'

Lastly, labor to yield to the equal condition of the promise and make no more conditions than God makes. The promise will beget faith and make men come to it. Now the promise requires no more of a man but that he should come to take it. Therefore do thou require no more than God in the promise requires; there is enough in the promise to do thee good. And expect all good from it, and be content to go to the promise and take of God whatsoever he hath therein offered. Is. 55:12: "Buy without money." This is the condition that God offers mercy upon. Buy wine and milk; that is, grace and salvation without money; that is, without sufficiency of your own. If a man should go running up and down to borrow money before he come to buy, he may famish before he come; so the Lord offers Christ's mercy and salvation, and saith, 'Come take it without money.' And we run up and down to borrow money of prayer and duties and power against corruption; but you may be starved before you buy, if you go this way to work.

Therefore make God's commodities no dearer than God himself makes them; for this is the cause why many a poor soul is kept from coming to the promise. 'Oh,' saith one, 'if I were able to master my sins and distempers as such a one can do, then I would believe!' This is to bring money. But art thou content to have Christ, and that Christ may have thee and rule thee and supply thy wants, and reveal thy sins and heal thy corruptions? Then go to the promise, and the Lord thereby will supply thy wants and master all thy sins and corruptions. But that must come afterwards. Ezek. 16:8, 9, 10:

"When I passed by thee, and saw thee in thy blood," saith the Lord, "and behold the time was as the time of love; and I spread my skirt over thee, and covered thy nakedness; yea, I entered into a covenant with thee, and thou became mine" (that is, you were content that God should marry you in all your rags). "And I washed thee with water; yea, I thoroughly washed away thy blood from thee, and anointed thee with oil. I clothed thee also with broidered work." First, he marries the church to himself, and then he gives grace and passeth over his estate to his spouse. Were it not a wonderful great folly if some great king should make love to a poor milkmaid, and she should put it off and refuse the match till she were a queen; whereas, if she will match with the king, he will make her a queen afterwards. So we must not look for sanctification till we come to the Lord in vocation; for this is all the Lord requires of thee: to see thy sins and be weary of them, and be content that the Lord Jesus shall reveal what is amiss and take it away, and that the Lord should give thee grace. Then the Lord will bring thee to himself, and thou shalt receive mercy from him, and then all thy corruptions shall fall to the ground. To sum up the point briefly thus:

First, when we have plucked away all carnal props, there is way made for the promise to come to us.

Secondly, when our hearts are possessed thoroughly of the sufficiency of God's promise and grace, then the promise draws near to the soul.

Thirdly, when we expect all from the promise, even power to come to the promise, then the promise lays hold upon us.

Fourthly, when we are content to yield to the equal conditions of the promise, then the promise carries us quite away.

Thus we have seen the hindrances removed and the means propounded; and now that we may be moved and persuaded importunately to seek after this blessed grace of God, let us consider thus much: if you once get this grace you get all other graces with it; it is a ground of comfort to set a man a work when in the doing of one work he may do another, nay, all works. So it is in the work of faith; it should encourage us to labor for faith, because if we get this we get all. Men that are wise to provide for themselves and to lay out their money in a purchase for the best advantage, if they see it well wooded and watered, especially if there be some golden mines,[9] all their mind will be upon that, because if they have that they have all with it. So it is here. Get grace and get all. Strengthen this and all is strong. Want this and want all. Once get this and you need not seek for wisdom; for faith will make you wise to salvation. And you need not labor for patience; for faith will make you patient and faith will bring holiness with it to purge you; for faith brings all grace. Now the saints of God endeavor with much pains to get grace and to subdue their corruptions, but yet they are feeble and weak therein because they take not the right way.

Many a poor soul mourns and cries to heaven for mercy, and prays against a stubborn hard heart; and he is weary of his life because his wild heart remains, and yet happily never gets little or any redress. And the main wound lies here. Alas, you go the wrong way; for if you would have grace you must first of all get faith, and that will bring all the rest. Buy the field and the pearl is yours. You must not stand struggling and striving with your own hearts and think to master a proud heart. That will not do it. But let faith go to Christ, and there is meekness, patience, humility, and wisdom; and faith will fetch all these to the soul. Brethren, if you set such a price upon any of these graces, then labor for faith. Get that and you shall have all. The Apostle saith, 2 Cor. 3:18, "We all with open face beholding as in a glass the glory of the Lord, are changed into the same image from glory to glory." The Lord Christ is the glass, and the glorious grace of God in Christ is compared to the glory of the Lord. Therefore first we must behold the grace in Christ by faith before we can receive grace. First see humility in Christ, and then fetch it there. First see strength and courage to enable thy weak heart, and then fetch it. Would not you be content to have a meek, gracious, and humble heart? I dare undertake for many of you that you had rather have it than anything under heaven, and you would think it the best bargain that ever you made; and you say, 'Oh, that I could once see that day that this proud heart of mine might be humbled, and see the blood of my sins, I should think myself happy and desire to live no longer!' Then get faith, and so buy the whole; for they go all

[9] Mines containing gold.

together. You must not think to have patience and meekness without faith, but buy faith and you shall have all together. Would you have the glory of God and be more heavenly minded? Then look to it, get it by the eye of faith, and look up to the glory of God in the face of Jesus Christ; and then you shall see it. But hold you there then, and this will increase all your graces to your everlasting peace and comfort. When men use to make a purchase, they will reckon up all and say, 'There is so much wood, worth so much, and so much stock, worth so much; and then they offer for the whole, answerable to all the parcels. So there is item for an heavenly mind, that is worth thousands, and item for an humble heart, that is worth millions. And are these graces worth so much? What is faith worth then? Oh, precious faith! It will bring all graces with it, one degree of grace after another; grace here and happiness forever hereafter. If we have any hearts of men (I do not say of Christians), methinks this should provoke us to labor for this blessed grace of God.

DOCUMENT VI

The Faithful Covenanter; c. 1629

Introduction

What Christopher Meredith published in 1644 as *The Faithful Covenanter* had been entered in the Stationers' Register, November 16, 1643, simply as "a sermon preached by Mr. Hooker upon Deuteronomy the 29th, the 24th and 25th verses."[1] The elaborate title page proclaiming *A sermon preached at the Lecture in Dedham in Essex by that excellent servant of Jesus Christ in the work of the Gospel, Mr. Thomas Hooker, late of Chelmsford, now in New England* was later devised. But the form Meredith gave it may accurately reflect the circumstances under which the Dedham sermon was published.

Meredith, who dealt chiefly in theological works, had set up his business in 1624, at a time when licensing laws were severe. Later he may have suffered from the Star Chamber Decree of 1637, which gave to the Stationers' Company increased powers to muzzle the press. But by November of 1643, when he entered the Dedham sermon "under the hand of Master Cranford,"[2] the Decree had long since been discarded, having been abolished by Parliament in 1640.[3] Therefore the times were right for such a bold declaration of authorship on the title page. The prevailing party in the Stationers' Company now were Roundheads, and Hooker — then a leading figure in New England — was at the height of his career. Indeed, the demand for his works, both in England and America, was great.[4]

---

[1] *A Transcript of Registers of the Stationers' Company: 1640–1708* (London, 1913), I, p. 84.

[2] James Cranford (1592?–1657), B. A. Oxon. 1621, M.A. 1624. Rector of Brockhall, Northamptonshire, 1627-43, and of St. Christopher, London, 1643 until his death. Licenser for the press under the Commonwealth, he prefixed many epistles to the books which he allowed to go to the press. [*Dictionary of National Biography* (London, 1888), Vol. XIII, p. 16.] His name appears under "Imprimatur" on the final page of *The Faithful Covenanter.*

[3] Polmer, *A Dictionary of Booksellers and Printers: 1641–1667*, pp. xi–xiv.

[4] *Ibid.*, p. 127.

187

Robert Dawlman, Andrew Crooke, and Robert Young had published most of Hooker's works before 1640, but as many as ten separate booksellers competed for Hooker texts in the decade that followed. It is impossible to say, therefore, how long Meredith had owned the manuscript before he published it, or why a full fifteen years elapsed between the date the sermon was delivered and the date of publication. Did Meredith hold back the text in the years before the Star Chamber Decree was abolished? Or did he not come upon the manuscript until after 1640? Because this sermon, like *Spiritual Munition* and *The Danger of Desertion*, is an occasional sermon, one is curious to know why it was not more quickly brought to press.

The Faithful Covenanter, as the text clearly shows, is occasional not in the sense that it was preached to celebrate a particular event, but in the sense that it was designed to be used as the occasion demanded. Hooker had been asked to Dedham not merely to expound the principles of federal theology, but to stress, as he said, "the main point which I intend to stand upon, as thinking it in my thoughts most fit for this congregation"; and that point he described as "a cooling card for the wicked." [5] As the text reveals, the sermon was delivered in response to a special request to preach at the Dedham lecture, and in few of Hooker's sermons are we made so vividly aware not only of the circumstances involved, but also of his personal relationship to the congregation addressed. We sense, above all, an urgent need on his part to reach a congregation that he does not know, but which he must — for special reasons — instruct.

When John Rogers, vicar of Dedham, had his lecture suppressed in 1629, Hooker had been at Chelmsford three years.[6] Two years before, in 1627, he had written his Preface to the second edition of Rogers' *The Doctrine of Faith.* It is safe to assume, therefore, that the two were in close association, and that Rogers had asked Hooker to come to Dedham. It can also be assumed that the Dedham congregation, to whom Rogers had ministered since 1605, was slipping into lax practices; for Hooker felt obliged at the start to single out the sinners in the crowd. "Though I do not know you, brethren," he

[5] *The Faithful Covenanter,* p. 193.
[6] D.N.B. Vol. XLIX, pp. 129–130.

remarked at first, "I doubt not but you can point at such here in this congregation and say, 'That is such a man, and that is such a man!' " As the sermon progressed, Hooker became even more direct. "Brethren, you may think I deal something harshly with you," he declared along the way, "but I deal for the best for you." And finally, as he drew to a close, he was able to strike at the heart of the matter. "A Dedham drunkard, or hypocrite, careless carnal gospeller, or covetous one," he proclaimed, "the devils will rejoice for him when he comes to hell." Hooker seems, throughout the sermon, to have known about conditions within the church that required change. It might be assumed, therefore, that Rogers — silenced by Laud — had need of the support that the preacher from Chelmsford could provide. "Husbands, call upon your wives; and parents, call upon your children, when you see them break the covenant," Hooker implored; and be especially concerned, he warned, when "you begin to be careless of the Sabbath, and cold, and luke-warm, and dull." [7] Although we cannot know for certain, these words appear to describe the conditions that he faced at the time. Because Hooker in his sermons rarely preached on ethics, but more usually on the nature of piety alone, we may have here a document that records not only his earliest theory of the covenant, but also the state of the Dedham church in 1629.

[7] *The Faithful Covenanter,* pp. 210, 213, 217, 204.

DOCUMENT VI

The Faithful Covenanter
A Sermon Preached
At The Lecture In Dedham in Essex

Dt. 29: 24, 25. "Even all nations shall say, wherefore hath the Lord done thus unto this land? What meaneth the heat of this great anger? Then men shall say, because they have forsaken the covenant of the Lord God of their fathers, which he made with them when he brought them forth out of the land of Egypt."

[That] the holy prophet Moses, having in the foregoing chapters (the 28th especially) discovered unto the people as his last words almost which he spake unto them, the marvelous mercies of the Lord to those which walked with him and were obedient unto his commandments which he had set before them, and the heavy judgments he had prepared for and would execute on them that walked stubbornly against him and were disobedient and rebelious, notwithstanding all means he used to reclaim them, and all the blessings that he bestowed upon them, as the commandments – you may see in the foregoing chapter [Dt. 28:1-5]: "If you will observe and do all that I command you this day," verse 1, then, verse 3, "Blessed shalt thou be in the city, and blessed shalt thou be in the field"; verse 4: "Blessed shall be the fruit of thy body, and the fruit of thy ground"; verse 5: "Blessed shall be thy basket and thy store," etc.

But if not; but [if] they will be disobedient and rebel against him, he sends fire after them presently, and says [Dt. 28], verse 16: "Cursed shalt thou be in the city, and cursed shalt thou be in the field"; verse 17: "Cursed shalt thou be in thy basket and in thy store," etc. Now having dealt with them both ways, he winds up all and deals with them by way of prophecy, and tells them what Israel would do and what the Lord would do if their hearts turned away from him and from his statutes, which he had set before them to walk in. He tells them that the people after his death will go a

190

whoring. [Dt. 28:14]: "O that this might not be," says Moses; "but yet if it be, the Lord will root you out of this good land, and will bring upon you [Dt. 29:20] all these curses that are written in this book, to plague you here, and will cause everlasting vengeance to seize upon you hereafter."

Now after he had dealt with them by mercies and judgments, these not prevailing, the Lord sends an enemy upon them that sweeps them away as unprofitable dung off the face of the earth. Now the prophet brings in the nations here, justifying the Lord's dealing with them, and saying [Dt. 29], verse 24, "Wherefore hath the Lord done thus unto this land? What meaneth this fierce wrath of the Lord?" As if a man should say, 'What was this goodly England, the only nation of all the earth, and yet now all laid waste in this fearful manner? Whence came this heavy displeasure, and what doth mean this fierce wrath of the Lord?' Now mark what follows [Dt. 29:25]: "All men shall say," [1] that is, even the wicked themselves. All standers by shall give sentence on the Lord's side, and justify his doings, and say, 'Alas, can you blame the Lord for dealing thus fiercely against such a stubborn, rebellious people? What, would you have had the Lord done more? He gave them a law, and mercies, and judgments, but they would not serve the Lord, but brake the bands asunder, and, Ps. 2:3, "cast the cords behind their backs." '

Therefore now they shall serve enemies. God is not to be blamed. What could he have done, or what would you have had him do more than he did for them? Threatenings from Mount Ebal and blessings from Mount Gerizim flew about from this side and on that side, and yet nothing would do them good. Why should they live any longer then? What should the Lord do? They profited by nothing, neither by his mercies nor his judgments. And what was the cause, brethren? Here was the cause: they were false hearted; they would not walk sincerely with the Lord; and therefore the anger of the Lord was kindled against them, and he rooted them out of their land in his wrath and in great indignation. Oh, the fearful wrath of the Lord that came upon them!

---

[1] The full text of the passage reads: "Then men shall say, because they have forsaken the covenant of the Lord God of their fathers, which he made with them when he brought them forth out of the land of Egypt."

In the words take notice of three particulars. First, the judgment of the Lord denounced, threatened, and executed against them. It was very sharp. The nations were aghast that stood by and beheld it, and wondered and said, 'Why, who would have thought it, that the adversary and the enemy should have entered into the gates of Jerusalem? What, Jerusalem [Lam. 2:15], "the perfection of beauty, the joy of the whole earth?" ' As if one should hereafter pass by and see all the towns burnt up here in this land (which God grant may never be); but if it should be so, and one should pass by and see all the houses burnt up, and the churches burnt, would he not be amazed at it, and say, 'Why, what means this fierce wrath of the Lord?' Would it not make our hearts ache, brethren, to pass by these places and see the houses of God burnt down to the ground, and think with ourselves, 'Oh, the good exhortations and admonitions we have heard here!'

Then secondly, here is the reason and cause why the Lord dealt thus with them [Dt. 29:25]: "Then men shall say, because they have forsaken the covenant of the Lord their God." So brethren, if this should be our case, poor little ones would say then, 'I remember my father said thus it would be, for the land forsook the covenant of the Lord, and the minister told us of this stubbornness and rebellion against the Lord, that this would be the end of it.'

Then lastly, here is the testimony of the nations concerning the equity of the Lord's dealing: the standers-by justified it and said, 'The Lord is just, for they have forsaken the covenant of the Lord their God.' And so people would do here if the Lord should do with us as he did with the Jews.

First, of the judgments which the Lord threatened against them, 'What means the fierce anger of the Lord?' Why, it was the fierce anger of the enemies, was it not? Yes, but there is no enemy but is in God's hand; it is his wrath that they execute. The wicked of the world are but the Lord's instruments: the sword is thine, Lord, though thou usest them as the hand to strike with. The Lord commanded destruction to come upon them; hence observe God is the author of all those punishments and judgments that ever come upon a nation or people, family or person. It is his will that is the worker; he is the bringer of all sorrows, troubles, and judgments upon any.

It was not the Babylonians that overthrew them; it was not Nebuchadnezzar; it was the fierce anger of the Lord that did it. You know what God himself says, Is. 45:7, Am. 3:6: "Is there any evil in the city, and I have not done it?" And he, Is. 7:18, "hiss for an enemy"; all places are at his command. He commands deliverance for them that serve and obey him, as it is in the Psalm [44:4], and plagues and destruction for them that disobey him and rebel against him.

To make this then our own, brethren, by application, briefly; for I mean to fasten upon nothing in this verse, but to pass on to the other wherein is contained the main point which I intend to stand upon, as thinking it in my thoughts most fit for this congregation. If this be so, then here is a cooling card [2] for the wicked. All you that hear this word this day, whose consciences accuse you, that you are enemies to God and goodness, hear and fear and tremble forever. If God bring judgments, who shall feel them and find them? Surely, his enemies be them that shall feel them. It is the collection that the Psalmist makes, Ps. 10:16: "The Lord is King forever." And what then? "The heathen are destroyed," says he. If all judgments be at his command, then his enemies shall be sure to feel them. You that have wicked husbands or wives, fear every night when you go to bed lest the judgment of the Lord should come upon them, yet ere morning, and cut them off and send them to destruction. And you that are careless of your ways and go on in your wickedness, understand the Lord hath vengeance for you. He hath rods enough; they are not all burnt. He will bring them out against you, and, Ps. 68:21, "will wound the hairy scalp of him that goeth on in his sins." Mark what the apostle says, I Pet. 4:18: "If the righteous scarcely be saved, where shall the ungodly and the sinner appear?" If the righteous, brethren, hardly get to heaven, but [one] loses an arm, another a right eye, as it were, and with many prayers and sighs and grapplings with God, and through many temptations hardly come to heaven in the end, and a poor humble soul beg for power against his corruptions, as if he would pluck mercy from the Lord by strong hand, and yet scarcely subdue sin and obtain salvation, what then will be-

[2] A term of some unknown game, applied to anything that "cools" a person's passion or enthusiasm. *New English Dictionary*, II (Oxford, 1893), 111.

come of a company that are enemies to God and godliness? A company of unrighteous men, where shall they appear? The day will come when they that stand against the gracious voice of the Almighty now, shall hear the thundering voice of the Almighty, and shall call and cry, Lk. 23:30, Rev. 6:16, "to the mountains and hills to fall upon them and cover them," that they may be hid from the presence of the judge.

Secondly, observe that the text says [Dt. 29:24]: "What means the fierce anger of the Lord against this nation?" What nation? Why, the nation of the Jews, God's own people, his peculiar, his "first born," Ex. 4:22, his "beloved," Cant. 1:14, 15 and 5:1, 2, to whom the oracles of God were committed, to whom the prophets came in his name. That nation that had all means of good, that had all mercies, privileges, and all encouragements, the Lord showed his fierce wrath to them. Learn: no outward privileges in the world will free any nation under heaven from the judgments of the Lord if they sin against him and be stubborn and rebellious. If any people might have been exempted and freed, surely the Jews might. They might have said, 'Why, Lord, wilt thou plague us? What, wilt thou destroy us? Why, we are thy people; we have thy sacrifices and thy prophets; and thy temple is amongst us. That is all one.' "What means the fierce anger of the Lord against this nation?," says the text. Be the man what he will, the means never so excellent, and the privileges never so great, if he sin he shall be sure to be plagued. Jer. 7:12: Brethren, you may see there that when the prophet threatened the judgments of the Lord against them, Jerusalem began to brag of her privileges and the mercies of God which he had bestowed on them. [Jer. 7:12]: "Go to Shiloh," says the Lord to them, "the place where I set my name at first, and see what I did to it, for the wickedness of my people Israel." The case is clear and plain: no privileges, though the word of God and his ordinances and the means of grace be there, will keep away judgments. If people sin, God will proceed in wrath against them. Am. 3:2: "You only have I known," says the Lord, "of all the families of the earth." What then? Therefore will I cocker[3] and dandle you? No, but "therefore will I visit you for all your iniquities."

[3] To cocker means to treat with excessive tenderness and care.

If this be so, brethren, this teaches us this instruction: not to depend upon our privileges, not to boast of them and rest in them, and go away and say, 'What the Spaniards come into England! What, the enemy overcome England! We have the gospel, the means of grace. No nation under heaven [has] so many in it that fear the Lord as our nation hath.' O trust not to lying vanities, saying, Jer. 7:4, "The temple of the Lord, the temple of the Lord," as the Jews did when the Babylonians came. What good did their temple do them? Your outward profession will be your bane if you trust to it when time of trouble come. Rom. 2:9: "Tribulation and anguish shall be upon every soul that sins, upon the Jew first." Mark that, brethren. The highest in preferment, the first in punishment. You that have enjoyed great means, the Lord will proceed more heavily against you than against others when he begins to execute his wrath once. To have the name of outward profession is nothing; it will leave us in the dust if we trust to it. Privileges are like to paper walls; if a man rear up a paper wall against cannon shot, will that defend him, brethren? They are good in their place and kind, but if we put our confidence in them as if they should keep us out of trouble, it is like as if a man should put on a cut satin suit or coat of silk to go in the wars withal. Will that preserve him against the cannons and the enemies? Your outward appearance of profession is just so, brethren. A hypocritical, fine smooth coat, will not keep off the wrath of the Lord, but that will seize upon the soul, which hath no other defense but such.

Rev. 2. And the beginning Ephesus,[4] a church that lived gloriously and performed duties comfortably, mark what the Lord says of them, Rev. 2:2: "I know thy works and thy labor, and how thou canst not bear them which are evil." Verse 4: "Yet I have somewhat against thee, because thou hast left thy first love." 'And what of that?' might some say, 'I may be an honest man, I hope, and go to heaven too, though I have declined a little and be not so zealous and forward as I have been, as long as I am sincere and upright-hearted.' Aye, but what says the Lord, brethren? Verse 5: "Remember from

---

[4] By "beginning Ephesus" Hooker means the early church at Ephesus, which after the departure of Paul was injured by false teachers, Acts 20:29,30. Rev. 2:4 admonishes this church for having "left thy first love," or forsaken Christ.

whence thou art fallen, and repent and do thy first works, or else I will come unto thee quickly, and remove thy candlestick out of his place." Let no man trust in his own strength, depend upon his own privileges, and shadow himself under the name of religion and Gospel.

I Sam. 4. When the Philistines came against Israel, and Israel was smitten before them, the next time they came into the camp they sent for the ark that that might save them out of the hand of their enemies; and when the ark came into the camp, I Sam. 4:5-11, "all Israel shouted, so that the earth rang again. And the Philistines were afraid and said, Woe unto us, for the like was never heard of before; the God of Israel is come into the field. Who shall deliver us out of the hands of these mighty gods? These are the gods that smote the Egyptians with all the plagues that came upon them. Be strong and quit yourselves like men, O ye Philistines, that ye be not servants unto the Hebrews. And the Philistines fought, and Israel was smitten. And the ark of God was taken." They brought the ark of the covenant into the camp, but the ark would not defend them but was taken. Brethren, the ark was a type of Christ. You bring the name of Christians and the outward profession of religion into the field, and you think that this will save you out of the hands of your enemies; but you and that will sink under your enemies if you put confidence in that. Was any nation greater than Babylon, or more glorious than Jerusalem? But what is become of them, brethren? Hath not the Lord brought desolation and destruction upon them? "Oh," say the disciples, when they were at Jerusalem and saw the temple, Lk. 21:5, Mt. 24:1, 2, Mk. 13:1, 2, "what goodly buildings are here!" Verse 2: "I tell you," says our Savior, "a stone shall not be left on a stone." It skills not [5] what we are, brethren, in outward profession, but what we are in sincerity and holiness. Depend not on the privileges which God hath given you, but pray for grace to answer him according to the means which he hath bestowed upon you; and then this love may be continued, and there may be some hope that you shall enjoy these blessed privileges still.

Now we come to the place where we would be [Dt. 29], the 25th verse, wherein is the reason why God deals so with his own people.

[5] "It skills not" means simply that it matters not.

The text gives you to understand the ground of it was because they had forsook the covenant of their God. This we will fasten upon. And first I will open the words, and then draw some collections[6] from them for our benefit.

First, I will show you what is meant by covenant. Secondly, what is meant by forsaking of the covenant. Brethren, there is a double covenant in the frame of scripture. First, a covenant of being in God, which is called the covenant of faith. Jn. 3:15, 16; 5:24, 11:25, 26: "He that believeth shall live." Secondly, a covenant of walking before or with God. When we have received mercy and grace through the goodness of God in acceptation of our persons, in and through Christ, then the Lord requires that we should walk in new obedience before him, answerable to that grace bestowed. Brethren, mark that; and this is the covenant of new obedience or of thankfulness, which the Lord reveals, requires, and exacts of all that have given their names unto him. I take it that the covenant of the second sense is here meant. The other is supposed and included, but this is the main: the covenant of his law, whereby we should be obedient unto him. That is the mind of the holy man in this place, and the scope of the words.

Secondly, to forsake this covenant is this: when we keep not touch with God in sincere, exact, and holy obedience, answerable to the means and mercy he bestows upon us, and the care and kindness of the Lord toward us. When we, fleeing away from the command of the Lord, Ps. 2:3, "break his bands and snap the cords a pieces," when we walk after our own ways, are not governed by God and content to be ruled by his holy word in all things, then are we said to forsake his covenant. Nextly mark here: he says [Dt. 29:25], "they forsook it"; that is, the general frame of the nation. The general, not the naughty packs only and some few, but *they* [the whole nation] forsook it.

Now, brethren, having opened the words unto you, I will come unto the points of instruction; and first in that he calls his commandment and law his covenant. Observe a main point of great use and benefit, and that is this: that the commandments of the Lord are the

---

[6] Conclusions.

covenant of the Lord with his people, the covenant of new obedience. This is the covenant that God makes with his people; not of life, but of thankfulness. Dt. 5:2, 6: That one place will cast the case clear enough. In the second verse he saith, "The Lord our God made a covenant with us in Horeb"; then in the sixth verse and so on there is the covenant itself set down: "I am the Lord thy God which brought thee out of the Land of Egypt, out of the house of bondage. Thou shalt have none other gods before me." Famous is that place, Ps. 103:17, 18. There are two phrases used which serve to one purpose, and the one explicates the other. Verse 17: "The goodness of the Lord endures forever and ever." But upon whom, brethren? Verse 18: "Upon those that keep his commandments and think upon his covenants to do them"; so that his covenants and commandments are all one. As in a covenant there are articles of agreement between party and party, so between God and his people. Here are the articles of agreement, the ten words which God spake, the ten commandments. This Moses aims at here.

Now brethren, to set the truth upon his right ground, for the opening of the point, take notice of three things. First, what are the terms required in the covenant. Secondly, wherein this covenant consists, or what is the substance of this covenant. Thirdly, the reason why the commandment is called a covenant.

First, of the terms required in the covenant of us under the gospel. The tenure of the law is in a double consideration: first, a legal performance of the commandments; secondly, an evangelical performance and obedience. These are the two terms of conveyance of this covenant.

The law in the legal performance requires three things. [First], that a man out of his personal holiness keep it perfectly and exactly, and that to purchase and obtain life by this obedience. This is obedience according to the strictness and rigor of the law, wherein it will not abate a hair of what God requires; but it must be fulfilled every jot, and that out of a man's own personal holiness, and that in way of life. Thus it was a covenant between God and Adam only, Adam in his innocency. God gave him a good law, by virtue of which he should have lived if he had kept it; and by that holiness he had by gift and creation he was able to keep every minim[7] and title of the precepts of the Lord, and to obtain life thereby. But this covenant is not continued with us, is not required at our hands. No man doth or can perform the law out of his own holiness and goodness exactly, to obtain life thereby. Rom. 6:14: "We are not under the law, but under grace." That is, we are not bound to the strictness and rigor of the law, that a man should not live if he have in him any weakness and failings. Therein we are free from the rigor, and curse, and punishment of the law.

Secondly, evangelical obedience: obedience to the law of God according to moderation and the mitigation of the gospel, so far as God is pleased to accept of what we can do through Christ in way of thankfulness, not what we should do in regard of the exactness God looks for at our hands, though we have no power of our own. We cannot perform the law exactly, yet if we according to the measure of grace received walk in this obedience as well as we can in token of our thankfulness, this is the tenure of the covenant made with us.

The second part of the conveyance of the covenant: in it take notice of three things. First, we have not power of ourselves to keep it; secondly, we cannot perfectly perform it by that power we have; thirdly, when we walk in obedience to it, we look not for life and salvation thereby. The scope of evangelical obedience is to glorify God and to express the covenant by obedience in way of thankfulness, and to procure comfort to our souls. We are saved by the covenant of faith. "Believe and live," Jn. 3:15, 16, 36; not 'do and live.' This covenant whereof we entreat, and whereof the text is to be understood, is not the covenant whereby we shall obtain justification, but an evidence and sign we are justified and accepted of God. Rom. 8:3, 4: "That which was impossible to the law in that it was weak through the flesh, God sending his own son in the likeness of sinful flesh, and for sin, condemned sin in the flesh." That which was impossible to the law, etc., that can never bring any man to salvation, but only Christ redeemed us fully, and satisfied for us; and he performed what God required, and by that we stand just

---

[7] That which is very small in size.

in the presence of God. But being justified and made acceptable, the Lord requires that we express the covenant and walk answerable unto it, and express the virtues of him that hath called us. Brethren, you must not trust to your new obedience, to expect life from it; it is only an evidence that God hath showed mercy to you; it makes not you good, but shows that you are good. Evangelical obedience according to the measure of grace received is all that God looks for; not that there is worth in this to purchase salvation. It is an evidence to us that the Lord graciously looks upon us in Christ Jesus; it is the way that we must walk into salvation.

Secondly, wherein doth this covenant consist? It stands in three things: first, when in inward uprightness and singleness of heart we labor to be carried in virtue of God's command, not to do what God requires only, but because God requires it. Many of you come to the church not because God commands it; then you would not lie, or be drunk, or have secret base covetous humors, for God commands you should not do so as well as he commands you should come to the church. If a command carry in anything it will carry in everything. But the frame of an evangelical heart is to the covenant: that is the spring of a man's practice, the first mover, the weight that makes him strict in obedience to every commandment and approve inwardly of every commandment of God. Have not a secret distaste of some and a love of others: he is covetous to be drunk, but will not be covetous; covetous to come to church, but will not humble his soul privately. Though many failings be in him, and many rubs and hubs in the way, yet the bent of his soul is to God's commandment. Cast a bowl, though there be a rub here and hub there in the way which turn it out, yet it falls upon the bias: so an upright heart, though he meet with many hindrances within and without, yet the bias of the soul, the bent, is to God-ward still, to all his commandments, laboring to express the virtues of God which hath called him.

Secondly, there must be an answerable expression and putting forth of this inward disposition and frame of heart outwardly in tongue and life. If you had a good heart you would have a good life and a good tongue. If it be within, it will break forth. You that are fretful, proud, stubborn, peevish, stout, forward, and nothing but fiddle-faddle, and lament it not (and think your heart is good and you love the commandments), you deceive yourselves. If it were so, you would have a good tongue too, and be meek and humble. I will not give a rush for that man's religion that is not in some measure obedient this way. What saith the apostle? Jas. 1:26: "If any man seem to be religious and refrain not his tongue, that man's religion is in vain." There must be an expression of the inward goodness of the heart by the outward conversation: a good sap in the bottom, good branches and fruit on the top. Mt. 12:35: "A good man out of the good treasure of his heart bringeth forth good things."

If goodness be in the heart, brethren, it will be brought forth in life. If such bad ware be in the shop, there is as bad in the warehouse sure, if not worse. This we call the inward and outward covenant. Mark this you that think to smooth it over and carry it away with fair looks, and speak well and do well outwardly, but have dirty corners within. The heart is stubborn and rebellious against God; proud, stout, malicious, covetous. These are in the outward covenant, as those whom the Lord complains of, Is. 1:2: "Hear, O Heavens, and give ear, O earth; for the Lord hath spoken, I have nourished and brought up children, and they have rebelled against me." Verse 3: "The ox knoweth his owner, and the ass his master's crib; but Israel doth not know, my people doth not consider." The wicked are in covenant with the Lord outwardly, but not inwardly; the heart closes not with God, they are not humble. The Jews were God's people in outward covenant, but were disobedient and stubborn against the Lord.

Thirdly, there must be an answering the means of grace with the measure of our uprightness and obedience. He that hath received more must return more to God, brethren; he that hath received more helps from the Almighty must return more obedience. You know how farms and leases go, brethren. He that hath a lease of an hundred pound a year must not go and pay but fifty pound; and he that hath one fifty pound go and pay but twenty pound; and he that hath one of twenty pound go and pay but ten pound. The landlord will not be put off so for his rent: answerable to the lease, so must the rent be. You that live in this congregation sit at a high rate. Brethren, your leases are at an hundred pound a year; look that you pay God his full rent. The people that are in a town that have a good honest minister, and careful and painful, but he hath not those abilities that another hath (express not that diligent power, evidence of the Spirit, in his ministry), the people that are in such a place sit at a good rate. But they that have a faithful, eminent, powerful minister, they sit at marvelous high rents. To pray little and do little in good duties, the Lord will not take this of a Dedham Christian; that is for those that have small encouragements, and a sermon now and then (and that but weak neither), and creep out once in a month to a sermon. There is a fifty pound rent and a ten pound rent for such to pay. But you sit at an hundred pound rent.

Keep touch, brethren; come off, come off currently. Do you think the Lord will lend his mercies for nothing? No, he prizes the life, liberty, and pains of his servants, and their prayers, at an exceeding high rate: a hundred pounds for a prayer, and a hundred thousand for an instruction. And do you think with a prayer now and then, and with a sigh and a wish, that you could walk with the Lord, to pop off the Lord so?

No, you sit at heavy rents, and the Lord will call for accounts accordingly at the day of reckoning. Brethren, this will break some of your necks, if it break not your hearts now by repentance for your being behind hand with the Lord in his rent, and make you walk with the Lord better and keep touch with him for the time to come. But what is the reason that the Lord will call his laws and commandments 'covenants'? The reason is this (for I would have nothing untouched, that you may be wise and understanding Christians): because of the likeness between, and the resemblance of, a covenant that is made between two parties, and the law, which is the covenant which is given us of the Lord. In a covenant, first there must be conditions and articles of agreement between the parties offered and consented unto; and secondly, a binding one another to the performance thereof by bond (perhaps a pair of indentures are drawn between them), wherein is declared that they mutually agree: he to make good the land and to pay thus much rent; the other to let it him thus and thus. It is just so here. Mark the agreement between us and the Lord. He propounds the law, and saith, Dt. 28, Lev. 26, that if we will keep the law he will bless us abundantly in all things:

house and land, wife, children at home and abroad; in everything we put our hand unto. Then the people they agree, and say, 'Content, Lord; whatever thou sayest, we will do. The law thou hast given us, we will keep it; it is holy, just, and good.'

But then, for the binding of one another, you will say, 'How shall we know God will perform his part, and how shall the Lord know that we will perform our part to him? What bond is there for it?' The world is naught, and one cannot tell who to trust; and therefore God must bind us, brethren, to keep our covenant. And we are not to think much [of the fact] that he should. And we have bond of him too because of our unbelief. Now the bond is a corporal oath passed from the one to the other. The Lord takes a corporal oath that if we will keep his commandments, he will not be God if he bless us not. And so, brethren, you swear too (again on the other side to the Lord), and did when you were baptized, every one of you, that you would be his people and obey his laws and commandments.

The Lord's people take a corporal oath and a curse upon themselves if they do not keep covenant with the Lord. This belongs to us at this day, for we entered into a curse and desired that all the plagues and curses written in the book of God might light upon us if we keep not the commandments of the Lord, Dt. 29:10. When the Lord had propounded the covenant, mark how he deals with the people, Dt. 29:10: "You stand this day all of you before the Lord your God; your captains of your tribes, your elders, and your officers, with all the men of Israel." Verse 11: "Your little ones, your wives, and the stranger that is in thy camp, from the hewer of thy wood unto the drawer of thy water." Verse 12: "That thou shouldst enter into covenant with the Lord thy God, and into his oath" (mark that, brethren, the oath of the Lord), "which the Lord thy God maketh with thee this day": (mark that) "with us from Abraham to this day." The oath is taken in our baptism; we take the oath of allegiance, as it were, in this kind. All you that have given your names to the Lord Jesus, and have received grace from him, you all stand here this day before the Lord (and bring your children before the Lord in the day of a fast, else woe be to you) that we may renew our covenant with him. We are to enter into his oath, the oath of the covenant between the Lord and us, that the Lord may

stablish us today for a people unto himself, and that we may curse
ourselves if we do not walk with God, both ourselves and ours. And
woe to him that hath no care to keep his oath: no wonder he is a
beggar; no wonder his debtors run from him and leave him in the
lurch.

It is a wonder that the earth doth not open her mouth and swallow him up, Num. 16:32, as it did Corah, Dathan, and Abiram, and
all the plagues written from the beginning of Genesis to the end of
the Revelation. Amen. Fall not upon his soul and body. Why, you
have entered into a curse, man, and an oath with the Lord, Neh.
10:29. See how the holy man continued this course, how they entered
a covenant there with the Lord, as if they should have said, 'The
Lord curse this tongue if I speak not graciously; the Lord curse
this hand if I do not yield obedience to his will and command.' Look
to it; the curse will dog thee and follow thee if thou break covenant,
as it did the Jews in Nehemiah's time. Now when he had returned
the people out of captivity, he brought them all before the Lord
to enter into a curse, and into an oath, to walk in God's law. It was
a sweet course; every soul here stands bound to do as they did.
They took a solemn oath: whatever they had been, they would now
walk in God's law. Give me your hand, brethren, or at least let
me have your heart in the meantime, because that cannot be. Are
you the servants of God entered into covenant with the Lord?
Then know you are bound to keep covenant by virtue of that oath;
and when you are in your families, remember your oath. You are
bound hand and foot to the Lord; and therefore when you are drawn
by anything to break covenant with the Lord, think thus with yourselves: 'What, an honest man and lie, and forswear myself?' You
have all sworn to the Lord, brethren, your little ones and all. Cursed
shall you be in all that you take in hand if you do not walk precisely
and exactly in his law and covenant. Husbands, call upon your wives;
and parents, call upon your children, when you see them break
covenant, and say: 'Wife, or children, what, shall we bring a curse
upon ourselves?' When you begin to be careless of the Sabbath, and
cold, and luke-warm, and dull; call upon one another, and say: 'You
know the plague was near at hand, husband, at such a time; but the
Lord kept it from us. For God's sake, husband, let us take heed that

we do not bring the curse upon our family. No marvel though one run away with this from us, and another with that, and the Lord lay this sickness and that affliction upon us. What, wilt thou be a perjured man? For shame; keep thy oath; God will never trust thee else hereafter.'

Now the Lord swears to us by himself, Heb. 6:13, because he hath no greater to swear by. It is a sweet thing that the Lord hath bound himself by oath to us, to keep covenant with us. If you have an honest and an able man bound to you for a debt, you go away content; you have enough. Why, we have the Lord in bonds for the fulfilling [of] his part of the covenant. He hath taken a corporal oath of it, that he will do it; and shall we not take the Lord's bond and rest content with that? Let us now, Heb. 13:22, "suffer the words of exhortation" with patience and meekness. Oh, brethren, this point concerns us nearly this day! Covenants go far, especially if they be for weighty matters, when a man is in covenant for more than he is worth. Think of it seriously.

The first use shall be of examination. If this be so, we may have a touchstone from the form of doctrine delivered, to discover to us who is the sound professor indeed. There are a great many formal professors, but few true ones indeed. A man can scarce tell who[m] to trust, you say, for trading; I say, for living; you say, for buying and selling; I say, for professing. Would you know whether you are sound at root, and not have a name only, Rev. 3:1, "to live, and yet are dead." Let him that keeps covenant, that deals squarely (you know what that is, brethren), that keeps touch with the Lord, let him be the sincere man; he is worthy [of] the name of a Christian.

There are many fadling[8] patching Christians that are off and on, here and there (there is no hold of them; a man knows not where to have them), that will say fair and bid well, but do nothing in the end. Go you home to yourselves; see whether you keep touch with the Lord. You think you are bound to keep covenant in nothing but in your money. Rich men think all honesty is in paying of money.

I will not speak of the misery of them that must patch up and down in that fashion, and hang on every bush. But, 'Oh,' says the rich man (that is careful to give every man their due and to keep

[8] Faddish.

his day), 'what times do we live in! A man knows not where to lend
to have it again at his time; there is no honest dealing to be found.'
Mark the villany of his heart, because he keep touch with men and
is as good as his word. 'Oh,' says he, 'we live in very ill times, and
there is scarce a man to be found that one may trust of his word!
There is such unhonest dealing in all places that there is no hold of
men's words; but yet [man] oppresses and grinds the face of the
poor, and looks for his gain altogether.' Where is your honesty? So
some [are honest] that are careful of the body, and give it its due.
But the soul whines within for mercy, mercy that it may have
something to refresh it withal. But that cannot be heard; that is
starved (the body is fat but the poor soul is lean enough). Where is
your honesty? Do you not owe repentance, hearing, reading, and
praying to your souls? Your poor soul cries, 'Oh, remember me!
Let me have some mercy and forgiveness sought for me at the hands
of the Lord; let me have some time employed for my good.' But
you cannot hear it. Is this honesty, brethren? If a man starve his
servant so that he pine away till he is scarce able to go, and at last
come to the grave, everyone cries out shame of him. But, Oh,
brethren, the poor soul that is starved; but no man cries shame of
that! When did the Lord hear of many of you here present? Alas,
never, brethren, never! But when the soul said, 'Now pray for help
against this corruption, and for mercy for such a sin; now awake out
of thy secret worldliness,' you went away and would not hear that.
You have no leisure nor no time for that, but starve your poor soul;
and the devil he hath one part of your time, and your lusts another.
Is this honesty, brethren? This is the man God esteems as an honest
man: not a Protestant at large that hath a good purse and is good in
his kind and will deal honestly with men and pay them their due and
at their day, but he that will pay God and their soul their due too.
Ex. 19:5: "If you will obey my voice indeed and keep my covenant,
then you shall be a peculiar treasure unto me." If your debtors keep
day with you, you will trade with them rather than with any other
man. Let it be so in your dealings with men, but remember that you
do it with God. Think not to put off the Lord with fair speeches.
Good words pay no debts, brethren. We come here and give the
minister hearing, and God a glossing, but we walk not according to

God's commandments. You give God good words, but you go home and are as unprofitable, as vain, and frothy, and idle, as ever you were. If one owe you money, and take this day and that day and promise it and not pay it, you would not think well of this dealing. What may the Lord think of your hearts, when you have made so many promises to him, and had so many resolutions to perform your part of the covenant to him, but have not yet kept promise with him? Good words are good in their kind. God likes them well, as it is in Dt. 5:28: "This people have said well." But these are not sufficient; we have enough of this, says the Lord, Dt. 5:29: "O that there were such an heart in them, to do as they have said!" There is the point, brethren. If we have a debtor that comes oft to us and promiseth us payment, but keeps not day, we say, 'You give me good words, but I cannot pay debts so and keep my family so. Where is my money?' So brethren, you come and hear cheerfully and pretend that you will do that you hear. Ah, but give God his money: "Oh, that there were such an heart!" Know what God calls for: good money. Will he be paid with counters and shows? [9] No, but current money of England, when the heart is changed, the soul turned, and the affections moved to what God calls for; and that is good, equal, and righteous, and we desire with all our heart to perform it.

Brethren, when you are gotten home, call to mind what you have said this day, and this covenant which you have entered into with the Lord, and say, 'Oh, Lord, that I had such an heart! Good words are well, but oh, a heart! A heart, Lord, is that which thou requirest and I would have!' And it must be always and in all things. You must not pick and choose, and say, 'I will not be a drunkard,' yet be covetous. I wonder that you will not game, and be drunk, and yet gripe[10] the poor. Oh, that there were an heart to keep the commandments of God always! This is an honest man with God, a man after God's own heart, I Sam. 13:14, Acts 13:22, a man of God's mind, as we may say. If ever there were a saint, thou art. When the Lords says, 'Oh, that they had such an heart!,' the heart answers and says, 'Oh,

---

[9] A "counter" is an imitation coin of inferior metal, a token used to represent real coin. "Shows" is used here to mean anything of an unreal or illusory appearance.
[10] The action of grasping or seizing with the hands something from someone else.

Lord, that I had such an heart!' When the Lord says, 'Oh, that thou wouldst keep all my commandments!,' 'Oh, that I could!,' says the soul again. This is upright fair dealing indeed; current money. Your tongue and outward appearance is nothing. That sturdy and peevish heart, let it be humbled, and your untoward and rebellious heart be brought into subjection; and you servants, Tit. 2:9, not answer your masters again;[11] and you little ones, be not sturdy against your parents and disobedient unto their commands. Remember the little ones, 2 Kg. 2:23, that mocked Elisha.[12] 'Oh,' but you will say, 'we cannot do what we would!' No, it is pity you should; for then some of you would be without sin, which cannot be here. But do you endeavor to do what you can? And are you humbled and grieved for that you cannot do? And do you strive toward perfection and say with David, Ps. 119:4, "Thou hast commanded that I should keep thy statutes"? 'Oh, that I could, Lord!' Verse 5: "Oh, that my ways were directed to keep thy statutes!" And dost [thou] labor to mend thy pace because thou hast been slow and art cast behind in the way to happiness and hast lost thy time? This is all God requires of thee. If one that is in debt to you fall into decay and come to you and say he is not able to pay you your money, but he desires you to go to his house and take whatsoever is there that is worth anything to satisfy you, I appeal to your consciences, is he not an honest dealer? Yes, you will not deny it; but you will pity his case and say, 'The Lord may cross any man.' And you will be favorable unto him because he shows an honest mind in that he desires every man should have his own to the utmost he can, either in money or in money worth. So, brethren, observe what the soul wants in obedience, that it may pluck it out in repentance. That is the money worth, that when the poor sinner finds a dead heart, a sluggish endeavor, weakness in performance, and he cannot do as he should do, yet what he wants in obedience he fetcheth out in repentance. Step but in at the entry door, or under the wall, or under the window, and hear how he will break his heart, bewail his abominations, cry out

---

[11] "Exhort servants to be obedient unto their own masters, and to please them in all things; not answering again." Tit. 2:9.

[12] "And he went up from thence unto Bethel; and as he was going up by the way, there came forth little children out of the city, and mocked him, and said unto him, Go up, thou bald head; go up, thou bald head." 2 Kg. 2:23.

of himself and say, 'Though much means and grace have been offered me, yet, good Lord, this wretched world, that I should dote upon "lying vanities," Jn. 2:8, so as to "forsake mine own mercies!" Good Lord, subdue this earthly mindedness! Good Lord, take all away rather than this should take my soul from thee and from happiness!'

Oh, thus, brethren, he labors to please the Lord in sorrow and grief and mourning for the shortcomings of his payment in obedience! He lays load upon himself in this case. This is an honest heart; this is very good pay; it is money or money worth. He is humbled and ashamed and confounded because he cannot do what he would. In this case he deals squarely; he is an honest Christian, an honest man. If he be cast back in his estate, he will intreat liberty of his creditors, and resolve and promise them, too, that if ever God make him able his family shall not gain by it, but he will pay them to the utmost farthing. So is it with an honest heart, brethren.

I look not that a man should not have temptations and corruptions, and that sometime prevailing over him. But this thou must have (and thus thou beg earnestly of the Lord): godly sorrow and grief of heart for thy failings, and that he would recover thy strength, Ps. 39:13, before thou go from hence and be no more. Though thou lose this week, that thou mayest gather it up the next week work so much the more and the harder. The Lord be merciful to us. Where are those honest men to be found, brethren, that desire to do thus? Methink I hear you in your souls now saying, 'Good Lord, what will become of our town? Good Lord, what will become of our neighbors? They talk of honesty, and this is honesty; but alas, their life agrees not to it!' You complain of trading in the world: almost no trust to be put in any; every man almost is turned bankrupt. I am sure, brethren, it is true in religion: he that was a forward Christian a while ago is a drunkard now, or a gamester now; and he that was a forward professor and would go to a sermon four or five miles in a morning, and come home again, and to work hard to get up the time again, but now God hath given him a pretty estate in this world, he is turned a very muckworm,[13] become covetous, or a loose one. Though I do not know you, brethren, I am sure, brethren,

[13] A miserly person.

there are a number such abroad in this land, and I doubt not but you can point at such here in this congregation, and say, 'That is such a man, and that is such a man! He still seeks to hold in with his minister, and would fain be counted a professor; but O there is no life, nor heart, nor power of godliness in him! He is grown stark cold since I knew him; the world hath a part of his heart, his pleasure another, his profit another, idleness and ease another. He may even lay the key under the threshold.[14] For any sound religion and true grace indeed he is quite down the wind.' [15] But you will say, haply, that I think too hardly of you, I know you not. I hope, brethren, there are many of you godly. The Lord increase your number and his graces that are in you. But I am sure if you come to the balance, you shall find few that are sound and godly Christians indeed that will hold weight.

Let us search a little. 'Why,' you will say, 'I hope we are honest men the most of us; we pay every man his due.' It is well you do so; but I will bring in a bill now, brethren, which, if you cannot prove to be canceled, woe be to you.

This doctrine casts out abundance in all places, at this door and at that door, and packs them out, and will leave poor thin congregations. We will scan the case a little, brethren.

First, hence it is clear that the poor ignorant creature is gone; he is quite blown up if he so continue. He knows nothing in this kind; he knows not how to count twenty shillings. How shall he satisfy a debt of twenty pounds? That is to say, brethren, they know not God, nor understand the prayers that they make. They say the Lord's Prayer, and it is good to be used in its time; but do you please God in so doing, when you understand not what you say? One says, 'Hallowed be thy name,' when he knows not what God's name is, and what it is to hallow it. Another says, 'Thy kingdom come,' when he knows not what it is to have his kingdom come. You cannot count your money yet; you cannot discern a sixpence from

[14] To lay the key under the door, or threshold, is to shut up the house and go away.
[15] The expression "down the wind" is used here to mean moving toward decay and ruin, falling into evil plight. "To go down the wind" is to decline.

a groat.[16] That is to say, brethren, you know not what it is to pray and to hear the Word; you know not what it is to take the name of God reverently into your mouths. And so some will call God 'Father,' but they know not how he is their father, nor how they come to be his children. These are gone, they are carnal; they have not pay, therefore certainly cannot pay the Lord his due.

Secondly, there is another generation worse than these, and those are profane ones that set themselves professedly to run arrearages with the Lord, scorn all means God hath appointed to bring in his debts by. They will be drunk, swear, profane the Sabbath, scoff at such as [Pr. 1:15, 16] "refrain their foot from evil." Tell them God requires other things of them, and that they keep not touch with him; and he expects other things at their hands, and that they run in arrearages with the Lord for his rent; and that he will arrest them and confound them if they do not pay him his rent for the time to come. They say they purpose no other payment than he hath already at their hands; but let God get his own as he can. They will take their own course still. Is there any such here, brethren? There are too many such in the world; and I fear, too, some among you. Though you pretend fair and say not so openly, yet you say so by your deeds, brethren; for you will have this privy haunt and that secret evil way (take this and that wicked course). You resolve of it and will do it; let the Lord get his own if he can.

So he will I warrant you. Look to it, you that think to brave it with the Lord (when you are among your cups and companions), and to make your part good with him, to outbrave all judgments. And who shall arrest you? The Lord will pluck the cup out of thy hands and arrest thee with death, and a thousand devils shall lay hold on thee and drag thee to hell to torment thee forever. God will have his rent one way or another. Think of it, you that set your mouths against heaven. And what hath the minister to do to speak against you? You will outface God and minister and gospel and all (and think to go away scot-free). Look to it. God will get his own;

---

[16] The English groat, first coined in 1531, ceased to be issued for circulation in 1662. It was originally made equal to four pence.

he will have it of thee as he had it out of Julian the Apostate.[17] I will allege but one place to you for this purpose, and that is Dt. 29:18. The text says, "That if there be any root of bitterness among them," verse 19, "that when he heareth the curse of the Lord, [he] shall yet bless himself in his heart," [18] saying he shall escape and do well enough for all that. The text says, verse 20, "That the wrath of the Lord shall smoke against that man, and he shall blot out his name from under heaven." Oh, that this verse were imprinted upon the palm of the hand of every drunkard and every scoffer and profane one that walks after the stubbornness of his own heart, and, verse 19, "adds drunkenness to thirst"! And yet you think to go away with it, and so you may for a time, and these words break no bones, and all this wind shakes no corn with you. You hope to go to heaven as well as the best; you will drink and whore and yet [you think that] it shall go well with you in the end. And you are proud and stout and stubborn and stiff-necked against the Lord and the voice of his word; and yet you bless yourselves and promise to yourselves peace.

Mark what the God of heaven saith, verse 20: "The anger of the Lord shall smoke against that man, and all the curses that are written in this book shall lie upon him, and the Lord shall blot out his name from under heaven." Verse 21: "And the Lord shall separate him unto evil out of all the tribes of Israel." All the vengeance of the Almighty that ever was made known shall light upon the head and heart of that drunkard and that contemner of God and the word of his grace. "He will separate you from the tribes of Israel." You think to run away from your country and to fly from his judgments, as some bankrupts do escape from men (to run to Amsterdam and other places). No, the Lord will separate that man from all the tribes of Israel. Wherever he be, in France, Germany, Amsterdam, or

[17] Julian, emperor of the Roman empire, A.D. 332–361, renounced his Christian faith to become a cruel apostate. His death, by murder, was said to be an act of divine will. Theodoretus, *History of the Church*, Bk. III, Chap. 25 (London, 1854).

[18] In these verses Moses tells the Israelites that they will be cursed if they turn to other gods, or if "there should be among you a root that beareth gall and wormwood" (verse 18). A member of the tribe who hears the threat nevertheless blesses himself, saying, "I shall have peace, though I walk in the imagination of mine heart, to add drunkenness to thirst" (verse 19).

wherever; he will separate him and set the damned spirits on the back of him, and say, 'Take hold of that man and execute vengeance on him!'

Brethren, you may think I deal something harshly with you, but I deal for the best for you. Is it not better to hear of this now, in time, than hereafter, when the Lord hath arrested you, and you are locked up in close prison forever? You should think, 'Oh, if such a denunciation had been told me; if such an exhortation had been wrought upon me; if such a man had pressed hard upon my conscience, with such and such things, I had never come here!' Consider this: God will have it out of you as he had it out of Julian the Apostate that had blasphemed Christ before in the field. An arrow came from God and smote him that he died; and then he said, "Thou hast overcome me, O thou Galilean!" [19] You that are mates in this kind, go home to your fellow drunkards, and to your fellow whoremasters, and scoffers, and those that side with you against God and goodness and such as are godly, and tell them God will have his debt of them. Know it now to your humiliation and amendment, lest you know it to your cost, when there will be no prevailing with the Lord for mercy. The Lord persuade your hearts that there is no way to escape but by coming in and acknowledging your debt, and craving pardon though you cannot pay.

Thirdly, the close-hearted hypocrite: he comes here to be discarded. He thinks his penny good silver, and the world esteems of him as a sincere, honest, upright-hearted man. Tell him that he keeps not covenant with the Lord; he takes it in great indignation. If any be here (as this age begetteth a world of close hypocrites), understand and know: if you keep back some of the payment, [if you] have a secret haunt, do [not do] as Ananias and Sapphira did, Acts 5:2, that laid down a part of the price for which the possession was sold, and said it was all. "Is here all?," saith Peter to them. "Yes, all," saith he, verse 8. So when the Lord saith to you, 'Dost thou pray?' 'Yes, Lord,' 'And dost hate all sin?,' 'Yes Lord,' say you, why

[19] Hooker's source, Theodoretus, describes the emperor's death as follows: "It is said that directly after he had received the wound, Julian took some of the blood in his hand, and threw it up toward heaven, saying, 'Galilean! thou hast conquered!' " *History of the Church*, Bk. III, Chap. 25.

dost [thou] lie to the Almighty? Do you not know a company of secret haunts and back doors that you have to this lust, and that lust, and many secret corruptions you have, and yet come into the presence of the Lord as if you were upright with the Lord and there were no such matter? O ye hypocrites, why hath Satan filled your hearts [Acts 5:3] "to lie to the Lord"? Do you not know what Elisha said to Gehazi, 2 Kg. 5:20, 21, when he ran after Naaman for a bribe? Verse 25: "Where hast thou been, Gehazi?" [Gehazi answered] "Thy servant hath been nowhere." He thought to wash it away and make it over so with a lie. Verse 26: "Went not mine heart with thee," saith Elisha, "when thou rannest after Naaman for a bribe?" If any close hypocrite be in the congregation, let him know the Lord will find him out, and will say to him: 'Whither went thy heart all this while? Where hast been dodging? Was not my heart with thee (verse 26) when thou wentest after such a secret haunt, and such a close lust?' 'Oh,' but you will say, 'it is no such matter!'

You desire to be upright. I say, be so, brethren. The Lord goes with thee whither soever thou goest, and he sees all thy Delilahs and Herodiases[20] of pride and self-love. He seeth how thou seekest to Him in the pride of thy heart, and how thou professest to get a name and to hold in with others. These are base abominations, cursed hypocrisy; this is falseheartedness before God and shall be plagued by God at the day of account. There is not an honest woman that hath but one other man besides her husband. He is not an honest man that will not pay one bond of ten, or many. A penny is due as well as a pound. My hand is on your heart, brethren, for I fear many of you have some one back door which you mean to keep. And you will be proud or covetous a little, or unclean only; and all the rest of that covenant ye are content to keep. Is this honest: to scrape out what you please and leave what you please still? There is no honesty in this, brethren. But you will say, 'Who can lay anything to my charge?' I say, thou art a covenant-breaker, and the Lord could never get his own of thee yet. Well, yet thou wilt put it off as Saul did when Samuel came to meet him as he returned

[20] Delilah, Jude 16, who betrayed Samson; and Herodias, Mt. 14, Mk. 6, who planned the death of John the Baptist.

from slaying the Amalekites, I Sam. 15:13: "Come, thou blessed of the Lord." But what said Samuel to him? "Ah," says he, verse 14, "What means the bleating of the sheep and the lowing of the oxen?" [21] So you say you make conscience of all the commandments of the Lord; but what mean these secret corners and haunts? I mean those which conscience and God hear of, not what I hear of; for I know nothing but by them. What mean all these secret conveyances that you have to make away and hide your lusts with, that you may live in them and not be known so to do? What means your drunkenness in a corner; your adultery in a corner; your hypocrisy and covetousness, lukewarmness and coldness and earthly-mindedness?

Yet men will not be out-faced; they will bear a man down still, that it is so. Then I have no other way but this with you: look what a man doth by a debtor that saith the debt is paid, and will face him down that it is so, yet the book is not crossed; what will this creditor do now? Why then to your books he goes, and calls in the servant that takes in the reckonings, and saith, 'Do you remember it?' 'No,' saith the servant [to the debtor], 'you gave me good words divers times when I called on you for it, but no money was paid. [That is] why, then, I never had it.' So brethren, you say that you are holy. We will call for the books and for conscience, God's auditor and the keeper of his accounts, and ask that: whether you make conscience of private prayer and humbling your soul in secret; whether you make conscience of your stubbornness to your husband, of your peevishness and untowardness; whether you be a covenant-keeper, and whether you did ever perform that God hath required of you? He hath required much of you, that you should pray, read, be sober, humble, meek, dutiful to your husband. But you have been light, froward, undutiful, wayward. Why, did you pay this debt to the Lord, then?

The conscience will say, 'No Lord, I urged him to it, and said, Is. 26:16, "Now get alone, and pour out a prayer to the Lord; now go and read, and meditate on the word of God." And I told him, Lord, when he began to be so eager of the world [I Cor. 5:10], "Now you will be covetous and worldly;" but he would not hear me. He

---

[21] Because Saul did not destroy the sheep and cattle of the Amalekites, as God had commanded, he was punished with the loss of his kingdom (1 Sam. 15:26).

promised me, Lord, he would leave it and would do so no more, and he would take up this duty and that duty; [but he] put me off this time and another time, [and] he never did it.' Then you see the case clear, for you never kept day; you have a show of godliness, 2 Tim. 3:5, but where is the power of it? The power is to subdue inward lusts, secret corruptions, base thoughts that rise in the mind. This is not to be found in the most; therefore they are but hypocrites and falsehearted. At last, when the case is so clear by the book of the servant, this bad debtor doth confess it, and saith, 'It was a hard time and it was but little, if you had had it. I thought it could do you no great good; I hoped you would have borrowed it if you had had any great need of it. So many a cursed hypocrite confesses the conversation is good, and the course is holy which he should take and which God requires of him; but I feared the loss of my liberty, of my ease, or my honor and credit, if I had done it. I feared I should have suffered for it, and it was but this. I hope it was not such a matter.'

Is this honesty? When God and the gospel call for truth and for sincerity, you put off and say this is no great matter, you hope; there are worse matters than so in the world. Thou are not upright. God will have the utmost farthing, Mt. 5:26. There is truth in a penny. He that will not suffer in one kind, I will never believe he will suffer in another. But you will say, 'What if a man be covetous? He hurts none; it is his own that he holds so fast. He is but close-fisted a little.' I hope this is not such a matter. This is a great sin, brethren, in such a place as this is. What, not keep touch here? That man's sin that lives under the gospel is the greatest sin of all, of more weight than the sins of any besides. And therefore look to it, brethren. If a man forfeit a bond of twenty pound, or forty pound, perhaps he may recover it; but if of forty thousand pound, we say it will crush the greatest merchant in the land, and break his back. An hypocrite, a false-hearted one in the place where the gospel is, it is a heinous foul sin, it will sink him deep. A drunkard where the gospel is not, and an adulterer where the gospel is not, shall go to hell; they shall all perish without repentance. But he that lives under the means, yet is covetous, loose, proud, vain, oppressing, and gripping of his poor brethren (worldly or the like), that bond will break thy back; it is an hundred thousand pound bond. Take heed, brethren, a man that runs in arrearages with the Lord here, it will be heavy for him. Mt. 11:23: "And thou, Capernaum, which wert lifted up to heaven, shalt be cast down to hell." Some live at great rents. A Dedham man, God will not have him have a stomach only to a good duty, and now and then to pray, or to read, or confer; but he requires great debts of him. A Dedham drunkard, or hypocrite, careless carnal gospeller, or covetous one, the devils will rejoice for him when he comes to hell. They will make bonfires, and make it holiday for him, stand upon their tiptoes to look on him, and say, 'What, are you come hither after all prayers and sermons and sacraments and admonitions, and so many labors of God's servants that have worn out their lives to keep you from hence?'

This bond will break your back, brethren. An hundred thousand millions worth of exhortations you have had, and you owe the Lord for them all still. You have paid him nothing for them yet; you are not one whit the better for them. What shall become of you? The Lord will set a thousand devils to torment you when you drop into the pit, specially ancient men. Woe to your souls if once God lay hold of you. If a man that is in debt, for I know not how many bonds, be arrested but upon one, it will cast him into prison; but then if after that comes another and another in upon him, it will go very hard with him. He played fast and loose, and fair, and far off all this while. But now one hath clapped a writ upon his back, comes another and arrests him for an hundred pound at such a man's suit; and another arrests him for an hundred pound at such a man's suit. Oh, think of this! Your reckonings will be fearful when God casts you on your sick bed, and death comes to fetch away your souls, and you are going to the chains of darkness. Then there will come in one bond after another upon you, one indictment after another against you. Item: for the sins of your youth, your disobedience and stubbornness to parents and governors when a child. Item: for following your profits and pleasures, and minding nothing else when you were a young man. Item: for your worldliness since you were an old man. One bond after another the Lord will lay upon you. You would think such a man that hath so many bonds come upon him, in a hard case, quite undone, and that there is no recovery for him out of prison, but there he must lie till some part of him rot off, perhaps, and till he die in the jail. Oh, how you would pity such a man's case, and how you would be grieved for him! But oh, brethren, you that are husbands, or wives, or parents, when you see your children or your husbands arrested by God — not to go to an earthly jail, but to go to hell forever — oh, how should it grieve your souls for such a one! How should you pity such, and desire the Lord (while there is help and hope) to show mercy upon them!

Thus you see these sorts are cashiered for not being sound; and the Lord be merciful unto us, what a few are there besides these? Think of this, carry it home with you; and examining yourselves, know the Lord will have sincerity from you.

Secondly, it is a word of consolation. This is a marvelous comfort to those that love and fear the Lord, all you whose hearts answer. It is thus with you: lift up your heads with joy, for this will uphold you and make you, Lk. 21:28, "lift up your heads with comfort in all your troubles," and in the day of the Lord. "When your redemption draweth nigh," Is. 3:10 say, "it shall go well with the godly." I say to that man, whatever come, it shall go well with him. We use to say, without doubt, without danger. A man that owes nothing, he cares not for any pursuant,[22] or sergeant, or bailiff; he fears them not, for he knows they have nothing to do with him. This is a marvelous comfort to him; so it ought to be to a sincere heart that hath paid his debt to God, when trouble seizes upon him. You know what Hezekiah said, 2 Kg. 20:3, Is. 38:3: "Good Lord, remember how I have walked before thee with an upright heart." If a man be arrested upon a false ground, the law will bail him; there is no law against him. Think of that, brethren, Gal. 5:22, 23: "The fruits of the Spirit are love, joy, peace, longsuffering, gentleness, goodness, faith, meekness, temperance; against such there is no law."

There is no law to punish or condemn them or accuse them. Therefore blessed are your souls that are sincere and upright in heart and conversation always to all God's commandments. In public, in private, in ordinary times and extraordinary, there is no law against you. Whatsoever Satan or the world say against you, there is no law in the book of God to condemn you. Ps. 119:6: "Then shall I not be confounded when I have respect to all thy commandments."

[22] One who prosecutes an action at law.

In the times of all dangers and of all miseries, which are like to seize upon us soon, if the land should be overrun, and friends and means fail, here is comfort to every faithful soul. Ps. 103:15-17: "All flesh is grass; the wind passeth over it, and it is gone. But the loving-kindness of the Lord endures forever and ever." Upon whom, brethren? "Upon them that fear him, and think upon his covenants to do them." Mark how he sustains himself: life goes, friends go, means go. "All flesh is grass; the wind passeth over it, and it is gone." Means are gone. How then, brethren? Verse 17: "But the goodness of the Lord endures forever and ever." Though liberty be gone, the Spirit of the Lord endures; though means be gone, the mercy of God endures; though friends be gone, the favor of the Lord endures. Ps. 136: "The loving-kindness of the Lord endures forever." Upon whom? [Ps. 103:17, 18]: "Upon them that fear him, and think upon his covenants to do them." Though a poor soul fare meanly and live hardly (all helps gone), the wind hath passed over them. And liberty is gone, honor is gone, life is going, nothing endures; yet lift up thy soul in sickness, and say, 'My health is gone, my strength is gone, my life is going, "but the loving-kindness of the Lord endures forever upon every soul that keeps his commandments and thinks upon his covenants to do them." '

Lastly, for a word of exhortation. Is the commandment of God his covenant? And is the keeping of that the way to obtain mercy and happiness here and forever? Then go away if you will and be dishonest still, and break covenant with the Lord. The very name of dishonesty, methinks, should move you, brethren, to be faithful in your covenant, and to set on speedily, and to be exceeding watchful and careful, and to perform what you have promised to the Lord. Reason should move you. What? Not keep covenant, especially with the Lord? What? Shall we make promises to the Lord, and enter into covenant with him, and not keep it? Let it for shame never be said of us, brethren. Mark what David saith, Ps. 119:11: "I have hid thy commandments in my heart, that I might not sin against thee." His mind ran of them, and his tongue talked of them continually. Amongst men, brethren, you would not have your credit cracked for anything; and you do honestly. A good name is a jewel. But do thus with the Lord, brethren. Hath not the Lord kept touch with you in all his promises? Did you ever beg anything of him, and he not hear you? Why do you not keep touch with the Lord? Shame yourselves for this, I beseech you. Men in the world, if they break in their estates, they have this love and humanity in them, that if any lose then it shall be they that did deal most hardly with them and that got most by them when they were in trading. But this kind friend that was kind to him and lent him money sometime in his need, he shall not lose a penny by him. 'Oh,' saith he, 'I had a friend of him! I could never come to him but he would receive me.' This is honesty, and fair, and equal. Oh, consider of this, brethren! We have hard bargains at the hands of the world, and of the devil, and sin; many knocks of soul and girds of conscience with them. But the Lord hath been ever gracious, merciful, loving, and kind to us. Resolve therefore that the Lord shall never lose by you. Let the world lose if it will, and let carnal friends, and sin, and Satan lose if they will. Let not the Lord lose; but resolve, whatever becomes of it: 'I will pray constantly and read in my family morning and evening and upon every occasion, and reform my ways. It is not needful that I should be rich; it is that I be sincere, and faithful to the Lord. I will labor for a good conscience and endeavor to walk with God.'

DOCUMENT VII

The Danger of Desertion; c. April 1631

Introduction

The Danger of Desertion is commonly subtitled *A Farewell Sermon* and has been long understood to have been preached by Thomas Hooker in England on the eve of his departure for Boston harbor with John Cotton and Samuel Stone in 1633. Very prominent in it is the phrase ascribed to God: "Farewell England, or rather fare-ill." The text of the sermon is Jer. 14:19, "We are called by thy name, leave us not." And the message of the sermon is indeed the imminent departure of God's favor from England because of the failure of his people to reform the Reformation establishment. It is an extraordinarily moving sermon, which admirably sets forth the Puritan mood of desperation. Allusions in both versions to the Thirty Years' War in progress and the warning that God might desert even nominally evangelical Christendom and make of the Turks or Indians his people give an almost apocalyptic tone to the sermon.

It is understandable that the sermon would come to be thought of when printed in London in 1641 as Hooker's own farewell to England in 1633. It was transcribed and printed twice, Version T and Version F. We shall refer to the imprint of 1641 as the Traditional version (T). There is some evidence that T, transcribed by a somewhat less attentive listener, was a woman (see nn. 50, 88 of Document VII). At least references to wives, women, and children come out more amply in T than in F. The other version of the sermon is entitled "The Signes of God's Forsaking a People." It was printed in London as nineteenth among twenty-nine sermons of William Fenner and expressly ascribed to him by the editor, London, 1657. We shall refer to this as version F.

The two transcriptions differ from each other but not enough to suggest two separate deliveries. We are most fortunate in having

221

two versions of a sermon that Hooker could have delivered only in very special circumstances. The sermon is so clearly tied to a place and a moment in history with what seems also to be a specific reference to Passion Week ("day of atonement" at n. 150) and to a specific prophetic revelation to the preacher to warn England ("yesternight" at n. 135 f.) that it is inconceivable that the sermon would have been preached more than once without more substantial alterations. Any reconstruction of the original sermon quite properly, therefore, is a judicious composite of the two texts. Each one has preserved unique readings as well as minor variant phrasings.

The slightly fuller transcription is that ascribed to William Fenner (1600-1640). He was presented to the living in Rochford (Essex), southeast of Chelmsford near Southend-on-Sea, in 1629, serving there until his death. He was for a while chaplain of Robert Rich, the second Earl of Warwick, and it is plausible to think of this preacher, much younger than Hooker, as having been present at Hooker's farewell service either in Chelmsford or at the Earl of Warwick's seat in Old Park in Great Waltham, and as having transcribed the notable sermon, which was eventually found among his papers and ascribed to him because it was in his own handwriting.

A. The Date and Circumstances of the Sermon

It is clear that Hooker is preaching to a familiar congregation, referring to their return to their houses that evening. One has the impression of a late afternoon or evening service. The sermon is highly personal and emotional — with three remarks preserved by the transcribers recording the preacher's observations of the way the congregation was taking his awesome warnings (Document VII at nn. 120, 133, 140). It is quite plausible to think of it as a farewell sermon to a familiar congregation or gathering, and indeed to his wife and children (mentioned several times), as he was about to leave his family in England to explore the possibility of a freer ministry in Amsterdam. As we know he would arrive in the Netherlands in June, 1631 (Document VIII, Introduction, n. 5), that is the *terminus ad quem*.

In the sermon Hooker refers to "our" day of "atonement" and

"reconciliation," with explicit reference to the morrow, when practices not attractive to Puritans would be observed.[1] There is only one day in the liturgical year that could be called by a Christian, whether Anglican or Puritan, the "day of atonement" or "reconciliation," and that would be Good Friday. Easter in 1631 fell on April 20.[2] It is quite possible, therefore, to date the sermon as having been preached in or around Chelmford on the evening of Maundy Thursday, April 17, 1631.

Further evidence that Hooker's sermon was related to Maundy Thursday communion in Chelmsford or environs is as follows. Puritans, calling it an ordinance, or the sacrament, or means, observed communion by preference every Sunday.[3] It is, however, plausible to hold that Hooker would have observed the Maundy Thursday Holy Communion of the Church of England in a Puritan manner and that his followers in and around Chelmsford would have received it at the hands of their own lecturer after his final and defiant act of farewell and warning. (Hooker had already been obliged to leave Chelmsford for Cuckoos Farm with the suppression of Puritan lectureships in 1629.) [4] Moreover, Thursday in any week had, among earlier nonconformists, been the day for prophesying and may have retained a place in the weekly rhythms of Puritan Chelmsford, despite the attempted suppression of prophesying under Elizabeth.[5]

That Hooker was unusually mindful of a communion to follow upon his sermon is suggested by the frequent references in it to "means," "ordinances," and "sacrament." There is an allusion also

---

[1] Document VII at n. 150.

[2] Christopher R. Cheney, *Handbook of Dates for Students of English History* (London, 1945/61), p. 161. Easter in 1630, new style, fell on March 31; but there are reasons adduced below why 1630 is quite improbable.

[3] Horton Davies, *The Worship of the English Puritans* (London, 1948), p. 206.

[4] Samuel R. Gardiner, *History of England*, 10 vols., VII (London, 1886), 132; Daniel Neal, *The History of the Puritans*, ed., Joshua Toulmin, II (London, 1817), 226f., where Hooker is mentioned along with other deprived lecturers.

[5] For the Thursday observance, among Barrowists, see Champlin Burrage, *The Early English Dissenters in the Light of Recent Research, 1550–1641*, II (Cambridge, England, 1912), 158, 332. For the suppression, see Neal, *op. cit.*, I, 362. For the persistence, see Paul Seaver, *The Puritan Lectureships: The Politics of Religious Dissent, 1560–1662* (Stanford, 1970).

to worthy participation in the communion, when Hooker speaks of solemn and dutiful preparation for the visit of Christ as King and of appropriate royal "entertainment" with due thought on the part of the auditors to be given to pleasing his "tooth," to extending hospitality free of all superstition and error without any external bowing at his name and "stab at the heart." [6] That it is communion on Maundy Thursday is suggested further by Hooker's reference to Jesus' weeping over Jerusalem in Passion Week (Lk. 19:42) [7] and his appeal to clasp Jesus as did Mary after the crucifixion.[8] Moreover, the daring metaphor, sustained through several paragraphs, of the divine peddler, God or Christ, leaving England because people would not pay the "price" of his gospel or holy wares nor the cost of discipleship, would have been most appropriately developed in the context of traditional Passion Week expectations, however much Puritans in general strained to get away from all but sabbatarian worship and to suppress the other holy days of the ecclesiastical calendar. Though the metaphor of the divine peddler and his price is, to be sure, bold even for the deity as perceived by "a nation of shopkeepers in league with bourgeois capitalism," it is imagery that would come most readily to the mind and lips of a restless divine when he was sermonically reflecting on reconciliation/atonement/ redemption, the latter term itself presupposing a cosmic purchase or ransom:

God is packing up his gospel, because nobody will buy his wares, nor come to his price. Oh, lay hands on God! and let him not go out of your coasts, he is going, stop him, and let not thy God depart, lay siege against him with humble and hearty closing with him, suffer him not to say '. . . Farewell, or fare ill England.' [9]

In the sermon Hooker elsewhere urges his hearers to rally to the God of the covenant and to "plead" with him lest he "rather go to the Turks, and say: 'You are my people, and I will be your God.' " [10]

It is important to observe at this point by way of anticipation, that Hooker, in the intensity of his conviction based upon a vision of

[6] Document VII at n. 173.
[7] Ibid. at n. 181.
[8] Ibid. at n. 149.
[9] Ibid. at n. 144.
[10] Ibid. at n. 57.

the night, felt no theological embarrassment in making a prophecy that implied a private revelation. Later in New England, against Anne Hutchinson, he would forcefully argue against personal revelation subsequent to the Bible.

It is in connection with his dire prophetic warning that Hooker refers to the Thirty Years' War and specifically to Johann Tserclaes, Count of Tilly, in such a way as to suggest that he is a rising terror.[11] Tilly, who had become field marshal of the forces of the Catholic League under Maximilian of Bavaria, in November, 1630, also took command of the imperial Hapsburg forces from Albrecht von Wallenstein, Duke of Friedland, Sagan, and Mecklenburg. The region suggested by his ducal title was one of the first theaters of war in the third, the Swedish, phase of the Thirty Years' War. Gustavus II Adolphus had landed July 6, 1630, on Usedom Island in the estuary of the Oder River. Hooker and other Puritans could not have regarded the royal Lutheran warrior a pure Protestant, but they would have been relieved to learn of his taking Frankfurt-on-Oder amid great carnage in the imperial garrison; but by April 5, 1631, Tilly, who now combined the supreme authority over the forces of the League and of the Emperor, had withdrawn to join Baron von Pappenheim in the siege of the key city on the Elbe, Magdeburg, which would issue in fearsome fire and carnage in May. The battles in Mecklenburg, Pomerania, and Brandenburg, and the siege of Magdeburg, were closely watched and swiftly reported throughout Europe;[12] and it is in this setting of foreboding for Protestants that Hooker warns that a comparable pillage and devastation could befall an unfaithful England.[13]

Internal evidence that the sermon was not Hooker's own farewell

[11] *Ibid.* at n. 42.

[12] See notably Werner Lahne, *Magdeburgs Zerstörung in der zeitgenössischen Publizistik* (Magdeburg, 1931), with a map, p. 208, showing Amsterdam and The Hague among the many towns where *Flugschriften* on the siege were printed; and Joseph Frank, *The Beginnings of the English Newspaper, 1620–1660* (Cambridge, 1961), which points out the importance of English printers in the Netherlands.

[13] For Puritan views in general of foreign nations and continental events, 1618–1640, see Marvin Arthur Breslow, *A Mirror of England* (Cambridge, 1970), Harvard Historical Studies, LXXXIV, without specific reference, however, to Hooker.

on taking leave of England *for America* is the reference in F [14] to God's beginning to "ship away his Noahs" for New England as a refuge. The paragraph is cast in such a way as to make it difficult to hear in it an allusion to his own impending departure. It is, rather, a reference to the mass emigration for the Bay Colony which set out in five ships in the Thames beginning in late April, 1629.

Fitting into our evidence for April, 1631, rather than July, 1633, as the date of the sermon is the still discernible echo in it of the Joan Drake experience of April, 1625, where, near the conclusion[15] in the context of the call for the conversion of all England, Hooker individualized: "but that man that will bid God welcome to his heart [instead of refusing God's mercy, as Joan did so long] may go singing to his grave," as Joan did after her conversion.

B. The Complete Edition of F

The Edition of *The Danger of Desertion* (April, 1631), though it preserves the title of T, is basically that of F. The reader will have all of F before him. Where T seems to have preserved something not in F it appears in the main text in parentheses.[16] In several parts of the sermon where the texts of F and T are notably divergent, the Editor has run the two versions in parallel columns. In most cases he feels that F is probably closer to the original, but where not he has marked the T column with an asterisk. Where the divergence is less, the Editor has simply noted the alternate wording of T in a note.

Often the divergence is in the greater brevity of T. Some dis-

---

[14] Document VII at n. 144. The passage is absent in T. Whether it was also absent from the Ms on which T is based or whether its exclusion is editorial to make the sermon seem to be truly Hooker's farewell is 1633 cannot be determined.

Edwin Mead first recognized that the sermon was not preached in 1633, "Thomas Hooker's Farewell Sermon in England," *Massachusetts Historical Society, Proceedings*, XLV (1913), pp. 253–274.

Carl Bridenbaugh also recognized that the sermon was a farewell on leaving England for Holland, *Vexed and Troubled Englishmen, 1590–1642* (New York, 1968), p. 450.

[15] P. 19/262.

[16] Because of this convention parentheses are not otherwise employed in this Edition, commas or dashes being used in their stead.

crepancies are due to lapses in the auditor's original notation or in his or another person's transcription or to a conscious decision of the auditor or transcriber or printer to let go or summarize. Other discrepancies can be ascribed to mishearing. More commonly the discrepancies are due to divergent deciphering by the printer of manuscript problems. Still other discrepancies are clearly due to the stylistic preferences of the original notator or transcribers, and no doubt also of the later printer. For example, the tense, person, and number differ rather consistently throughout the two versions. T, for example, tends to pluralize, tends to have Hooker address the congregation as *brethren,* rather than *beloved* (F). Discrepancies in this range of oscillation have not been noted except where of possible significance. But other stylistic preferences between the two sets of notator-transcriber-printers have all been noted, as when F says *virgins* and T says *maids.* The last example is clearly stylistic and not the consequence of one transcriber mishearing the word spoken or of one printer misreading the word written.

DOCUMENT VII

The Danger of Desertion

Jer. 14:9   *"And we are called by thy*
Name; leave us not."

Two things, Brethren and beloved in Christ Jesus,[1] are intended and expressed by the holy prophet,[2] from the first verse to the thirteenth verse.

There is first a denomination[3] of a judgment, and that is: dearth or famine,[4] from the first verse to the seventh.

Secondly, the sword is threatened, to the thirteenth verse; he will send the famine, then the sword, and he will not be entreated.[5]

Then in the eighth and ninth verses, we have the importunate prayer of the Church to turn away these judgments. And the prayer is marvelous sweet, in confession, where they confess their sins, and seek to God for succor (against them, as if they should say: 'Lo, we are as base as base can be, and therefore help, for the Lord's sake.' And thus they make their supplication in the seventh and eighth verses; and this short prayer discovers itself, partly in the things prayed for, and partly in the manner; and the holy prophet, intending this, is very sweet in it.)

First, they desire God that he would not take his providence[6] from them: "Why stayest thou but for a night?," verse the eighth, as if they should have said: 'It is marvelous strange that thou behavest thyself so like a stranger; thou seest our sorrows and dost not help us. Thou perceivest our troubles and thou regardest us not.[7]

---

[1] T leaves out the address. Generally F prefers *beloved,* and T *brethren.*

[2] T has: *Holy-Ghost.*

[3] T has: *denunciation,* but *denomination* in the sense of *definition* is probably the better reading.

[4] T has: *sword.*

[5] T has not grasped the structure of the opening lines and reference to scriptural verses so well as F.

[6] T has: *preference.*

[7] T has: *succourest not.*

It is strange that the God of Israel [8] stands as a man astonished; that thou that hast heretofore received us should now stand as a man amazed and astonished, as if thou wert weary of this thy work, and couldst do no more, as if thou shouldst say, ' "Jerusalem cannot be saved, and Judah cannot be succoured." ' [9]

Secondly, they desire that God would not take away his presence [10] from them: 'Leave us not to ourselves,' say they. 'Let us see thy face. Though we die, yet let it be in thy presence. Yea, though thou help us not, yet it doth us good to look upon our Savior, and thou canst help us.' And thus you see the arguments wherewith they press the Lord, how sweet they are, viz: [11]

First, 'thou art the hope of Israel; alas, if thou forsake us we are all lost; our hope is not in the means only; but our hope is in thee, leave us not. For thou art the hope [12] of Israel. It is the task that thou hast taken upon thee, leave us not therefore.'

Secondly, 'thou hast made thyself a Savior, and now is the time of trouble, therefore now perform what thou hast undertaken.'

Thirdly, 'thou art in the midst of us, that is, thou art a great Commander [13] amongst us, always ready to succour us, and wilt thou now see us perish? Thou art more near to us than the Ark in the midst of the camp,' 1 Sam. 4:6. As if they should say, 'He lives in the midst of us, and will he not save us?'

Fourthly, ' " we are called by thy name," ' and therefore we have interest in thee. To whom should wives go, but to their husbands? To whom should children go, but to their fathers? To whom should servants go, but to their masters? To whom then should we go, but to thee, our God and Savior? [14] Leave us not therefore, and we will meddle with none but thee.' [15]

---

[8] T has: *thou the great God of Hosts.* F repeats, *it is strange.*

[9] T has the verbs reversed: *succoured, saved.*

[10] T has: *preference.*

[11] T lacks: *And thus . . . viz.*

[12] T has: *Saviour.* T also makes this line the beginning of a second point. F has the second point beginning below.

[13] T has: *comforter.*

[14] T has a different order and phrasings, leaving out *children,* and *us.* It is possible that Hooker in delivery did, in fact, leave out the children, because so imminently his own children would be going to their mother instead.

[15] T, puzzled by *meddle,* interprets it as *deal with* and says: *Now we will meddle only with the latter clause, 'Leave us not.'*

Secondly, though God might leave them, yet they beg that he would not. That is the Amen to their prayer: 'Though thou stand and wilt not help us, yet let us die in thy presence!' And this is the great request of the saints: they desire not to be left of God, although God might leave them, whence learn that God might cast off a people, and unchurch a nation.[16]

Israel did fear it and it is that which they prayed against, God might leave them.[17] I do not say that God will cast off his elect eternally; but those that are only in outward covenant with him he may.[18] See Is. 1: 2f.: "Hear O heavens, hearken O earth, I have nourished and brought up children,[19] but they have rebelled against me; the ox knoweth his owner, and the ass his master's crib, but Israel hath not known, my people have not understood, etc."; and verse the seventh, see the judgment: "Your cities are burned with fire, strangers devour your land in your presence, and it is desolate like the overthrow of strangers."

There is an outward calling, as well as an effectual calling. God may reject, "for many are called, but few are chosen," says our Savior [Mt. 22:14]. My brethren, cast your thoughts afar off, and see what is become of those famous Churches of Pergamum and Thyatira and the rest mentioned, Rev. 1:11. And who would have thought that Jerusalem should have been made an heap of stones, and a vagabond people? And yet we see God hath forsaken them, showing us thereby that, although God will never forsake his own elect ones, yet he may forsake such as are in outward covenant with him.

The Lord is said to dis-church or discharge a people, Hos. 1:9.[20] There God saith, "Call his name Loammi [not my people], for ye

[16] F does not have the last phrase.

[17] T has: *Israel suspected it, and feared it. It is that they prayed against, that God would not leave them.*

[18] Sentence as in T; version F has only: *but those in outward convenant;* but has *elect "ones".*

[19] T adds, *that is, the Jews,* but quotes no more from Isaiah.

[20] When Gomer, harlot wife of Hosea, bore a son, the Lord said: "Call his name not my people [Loammi], for you [Judah and Israel] are not my people and I am not your God."

T does not give the sentences *And yet we see God. . . discharge a people,* but gives as citation Hos. 7:9.

are not my people,[21] and therefore I will not be your God." And, as I may so say, he sues out a bill of divorcement, as it was in the old Law. They that had anything against their wives, they sued out a bill of divorcement against them, and so doth God. See Hos. 2:2[f.]: "Plead with thy mother, tell her she is not my spouse, nor my beloved; but let her cast away her fornications out of her sight, and her adulteries from between her breasts, lest I make her as at the first," that is, as she was in Egypt, poor and miserable. As if God should now say to England, 'Plead, plead with England, all ye that are my ministers in the way of my truth, and say unto her, let her cast away her rebellions, lest I leave her as I found her in the day of captivity and bondage under the blindness of popery and superstition.'

Objection: But how doth God cast off [22] a people?

Solution: I answer, first, when he takes away his love and respect from a people; and as his love, so the token of his love, which is[23] his word and sacraments, the means of salvation.[24]

Secondly, when he takes away his providence, I mean when he takes down his walls, that is, his magistracy and ministry.[25]

Thirdly, when instead of counseling, there comes in bribing; and instead of true teaching, there comes in daubing with untempered mortar when God takes away the hedge thereof [of the vineyard], Is. 5:5, or the stakes grow rotten, and are not renewed, then is God going away.

Fourthly, when God takes away the benefit of both these helps, they are signs of God's departure.

Use: May God un-church or discharge a people, and cast a nation off? [26] Oh, then let this teach us to cast off all security; for miseries are nigh at hand in all probability! When we observe what God hath

[21] T has: *Plead with your Mother, and call her Loammi, ye are not my people.* But the *plead* phrase appears in F, as below.

[22] T has: *depart from.*

[23] F reads: *in.*

[24] T has: *and as his respect, so his means too.*

[25] T has: *2. When he takes away his protection by taking down the walls, that is, these two great means of safety, Magistrates and Ministers.*

[26] Here T leaves out *a nation,* but cf. the reverse above at n. 22.

done for us, all things are ripe to destruction,[27] and yet we fear it not, but we promise to ourselves safety, and consider not that England is ready to be harrowed, and yet we cannot entertain a thought of England's desolation.[28] When there are so many prophesies in it of its destruction,[29] yet we cannot be persuaded of it. According to the conviction of our judgments, either it must not be, or not yet,[30] as if it were unpossible[31] that God should leave England, as if God were a cockering[32] Father over lewd (and stubborn) children. God may leave a nation, and his elect may suffer, and why may not England (that is but in outward covenant with him)?[33] England's sins are very great, and the greater, because the means are great, and our warnings are and have been great; but yet our mercies are far greater. England hath been a mirror of mercies.[34] Yet now God may leave it,[35] and make it [36] the mirror of his justice. Look how God spake to the people that did brag of their temple, Jer. 7:4. Saith God, "Trust not in lying words, saying, the Temple of the Lord, this is the Temple of the Lord." [37] But what saith the Lord by the prophet in the twelfth and fourteen verses? "Go now to my place which was in Shiloh, where I set my name at the beginning, and behold what I did unto it for the wickedness of my people Israel," etc.[38]

Even so England: 'Thou hast the temple and the priests, and yet may not God that destroyed Shiloh, destroy thee? Go to Bohemia, and from thence to the Palatinate (and so to Denmark)[39] and from

[27] T has: *ruin*.

[28] T has: *that England shall be destroyed*.

[29] T has: *so many professors in it*.

[30] Preferring the reading of T. F has: *but in our judgments it must not be, it must not be as yet*.

[31] T has: *impossible*.

[32] i.e., *pampering*.

[33] The phrase *that is but. . . him* comes from T, but it is a phrase that appears in F above at Is. 1:2, at n. 18.

[34] T has: *mercy*.

[35] T has: *us*.

[36] T has: *us*.

[37] T summarizes the foregoing as *sacrifice and offerings*.

[38] The passage, actually only verse 12, is not given by T.

[39] T adds *and so to Denmark.*, but leaves out *to other parts of Germany*.

Hooker refers to devastation in Bohemia, 1618–1620, in the Palatinate, 1622. On the Danish phase of the War, 1625–1627, see, in the Introduction to Document II, the last half of the sixth paragraph.

thence to other parts of Germany. Do but imagine that you were there, or do but mark what travellers say. God's churches are made heaps of stones, and those Bethels wherein God's name was called upon, are now defiled Temples for Satan and superstition to reign in. You cannot go three steps but you shall see the head of a dead man.[40] And go a little further, and you shall see the heart[41] picked out by the fowls of the air, or some other sad spectacle. And then surely you will say, '[Count von] Tilly hath been here or there.' [42] Now are these churches become desolate, and may not England? Do but go into their cities and towns, and there you may see many compassed about with chains of captivity, and every man bemoaning himself. Do but look under a tree,[43] and there you may see a poor fatherless child sending out his breath and crying unto his helpless mother.[44] Step but a little further, and you shall see the helpless wife, the sad wife,[45] bemoaning her husband, and this is her misery, she cannot die time enough.[46]

| But she shall see greater misery; for either she shall, as she thinks, see her little ones dashed against the stones, or tossed upon the pikes, or if they live, that then they shall be brought up in Popery; | And withal she makes funeral sermons of her children within herself, for that the Spaniard may get her little ones, and bring them up in Popery and superstition; |

and then she weeps again, and thinks that if her husband be dead it is well, but it may be he is upon the rack, or put to some other torment,[47] and then she[48] dies an hundred times before she can die. (Cast your eyes afar off.) [49] Thus if you can set your souls in their souls' stead, and imagine you were in their condition, and say: 'May not this be the condition of England, and who knows but it may?

[40] T pluralizes *head* and *man*.
[41] T pluralizes *heart*.
[42] Johan Tserclaes Count von Tilly, Flemish field marshal on the Imperial side in the Thirty Years' War.
[43] T has: *cast your eyes abroad.*
[44] T pluralizes *mother.*
[45] T has only: *sad wife.*
[46] T has: *soon enough.*
[47] T has: *cruel tortures.*
[48] T adds here for the second time: *then she makes Funeral Sermons.*
[49] Only in T.

(Who knows but it may be my wife,[50] when he hears of some in torment?)'

Oh, my beloved,[51] be not high-minded, but fear; for as we have God's bounty on the one side, so, for ought I know, we may have his severity on the other side! Prank not then yourselves with foolish imaginations, saying: 'Who dare come to hurt England? The Spaniard[52] hath his hands full, and the French are too weak.' But, beloved, be not deluded. Who would have thought that Jerusalem, the Lady City of all Nations,[53] whither the tribes went up to worship, should become a heap of stones and a vagabond people? But yet you see it was, and is to this day.[54] And I pray, why may it not be England's case? Learn therefore, hear, and fear God; for assuredly God can be God without England's prosperity.[55] Do not say: 'Here are many good Christians.' Do you think that God is beholding to you for your religion? Surely not. For rather than [that] he will preserve[56] such as profess his name, and yet hate to be reformed,[57] he will raise up of these stones children unto Abraham [Mt. 3:9]! He will rather go into Turkey and say unto them, 'Thou art my people, and I will be your God.'

But wilt thou let God go, England? Are you so content, and will you let Christ go and God go? [58] Oh, no, no; lay heart and hands upon him, as they did upon Paul [Acts 8:17]! [59] Every one of you lay hold on him and say thou: 'Thou shalt not go from us, "for we are called by thy name, therefore leave us not" ' [the sermon text: Jer. 14:9]. And for my part I will pray that he doth not take his leave of us.[60]

---

[50] See n. 88.
[51] T has: *ah, brethren.*
[52] T pluralizes *Spaniard.*
[53] T has: *the Lady of Kingdoms.*
[54] This sentence missing in T.
[55] T has only: *England.*
[56] T has: *maintain.*
[57] T has simply: *hate him.*
[58] T has only: *to let him go?*

Hooker's reference to *"into* Turkey" might well be an allusion to the Calvinist confession of faith, in Latin, 1629, in Greek, 1631, of the philo-Protestant Patriarch Cyril Lucar (1620–1638) in Istanbul.

[59] The comparison with Paul is missing in T.
[60] T leaves out allusion to sermon text and following sentence.

| Do you think that Rome will forsake or part with her Gods? No, they will rather lose their lives. And wilt thou let thy God go, O England? Plead with thy God and let him not depart, but part rather with thy rebellions. We are "called by thy name, leave us not." | Do you think that Rome will part with her religion and forsake her gods? Nay an hundred would rather lose their lives. Will you let God go? Oh, England, plead with your God and let him not depart! You should only part with your rebellions; he will not part with you. "Leave us not." |

You see the Church is very importunate to keep God with them. They lay hold on God with cords[61] of arguments: 'Oh, thou hope of Israel, do not leave us!' They beset God with their prayers; and, as it were, they watch him at the town's end that he should not go away; and they say: '(No, thou shalt not go away.) Thou shalt still abide with us!' They are importunate that he do not leave them.

Whence observe [this] doctrine: That it is the importunate desire of the saints of God still to keep God present with them. They[62] cared not so much for sword or famine, as they did for the loss of God's presence. 'O Lord, leave us not,' say they. This was their prayer.

| And blame them not, for consider what a grief it is that God should stand by and not help them. 'Good Lord,' say they, 'leave us not; we cannot abide to think that God should leave us, much less can we endure to feel it or taste it.' | And we cannot blame them, all things being considered; for it was their grief that God stood by, and would not help: 'Why standest thou as a man astonished? But, good Lord, leave us not.' They cannot abide to hear of that, much less to bear it. |

Thus they did, and thus the saints of God should do. (For the proof, see) Ex. 33:14-15. Moses saith: "If thy presence go not with us, carry us not hence." [63] Alas, Moses might have gone upon fair terms. 'Ye shall,' saith God, 'possess the land in peace with prosperity.' But what saith Moses? 'Though we might have Canaan and all the delights there, yet carry us not hence unless thy presence go with us.' This is the stay and the strength that he sticks to. So Ps. 80:18, 19: [64] "Turn us again, O Lord of hosts; make thy face[65] to shine upon us."

---

[61] T has: *words*.
[62] Whom Jeremiah was addressing.
[63] T does not quote the passage.
[64] T gives Ps. 80:7,19, which is also correct, for v.19 repeats v.7.
[65] T has: *cause*.

Here is a man, a David, a heart worth gold. He makes not many suits, but he comes home, he sues to the purpose. "Make thy face," saith he, "to shine upon us;" as if he should have said, 'that is prosperity enough, for it endureth forever.' [66]

[Objection:] But what is the presence of God?

[Answer:] In a word, it is the particular favor of God which he expresseth in his ordinances; it is all the good and sweetness that flows from the purity of God's worship, whereby God reveals himself unto us.[67] It is not gold, wealth, nor prosperity, that makes God to be our God; for there is more gold in the West Indies[68] than in all Christendom. But it is God's ordinances purely administered that brings God's presence to a people.

God forsook Shiloh because his ordinances were not purely kept there.[69] When the people left the Ark, viz, his pure worship, then God left the people. When the Ark of God's presence was among them, the word in the purity of it, then his face was there, and there God was principally present (where his ordinances are in the purity of them). Hence it was that Cain is said [Gen. 4:14] to be cast out of God's presence, because he was cast out from the Church; he was cast out from God's ordinances.

If a people do outwardly reform, and sincerely worship God, they may remain.	If that a people do outwardly worship God, and sincerely mend things that be amiss, they may continue.

If Sodom and Gomorrah had but legally repented, they had remained, they had not been destroyed [Gen. 19:24f.].[70] And hence

---

[66] After the quotation of a portion of Ps. 80:7(19), T reduces all the foregoing to: *as if he should say, here is prosperity*. T has preserved the point but without the vividness of adding the words and mood of the Psalmist.

[67] T preserves the same thought somewhat differently: . . . *and all the good and sweet that followeth there. The purity of God's word and worship, is that which God reveals himself in.*

[68] An allusion to the Spanish dominion.

[69] Joshua moved the tabernacle and the ark of the covenant from Gilgal to Shiloh (Jos. 18:1ff.). During the war with the Philistines, when Eli and his two sons were custodians of the shrine, it was carried into battle and lost, but then regained (1 Sam. 4–6). Jeremiah refers to the divinely punitive destruction of Shiloh and the permanent removal of the Ark (7:12–14; 26:6–9).

T at this point cites Ps. 78:5, which is not related.

[70] T has simply: *remained to this day*.

it is that the saints are so urgent for God's ordinances[71] in the purity of them. But the wicked say: 'Once a Sabbath is enough and once a week is too much.' [72] By this we may see that England is ripe. And is she not weary of God? Nay, she is fat fed to the slaughter. But it was not so with the saints and people of God in former times. It was David's grand request, Ps. 27:4,[73] that he might dwell in the house of the Lord. And [in] Ps. 42:1-4 he said his soul did pant for God's ordinances.[74] Thus you see that the saints of God are marvelous[75] importunate to keep God in his ordinances.

Question: But may not a man be saved without preaching? [76]

Answer: I answer, the argument is clear. The saints maintain God in his ordinances, the want[77] of which is under the penalty of death and damnation,[78] because we have more need of God in his ordinances than of all the gold in the world. For all the gold in the world[79] will not satisfy a hungry man.

It is bread that he must have, because he hath need of it; so the saints have most need of God, and of Christ, for though they have but ragged coats, and their bodies pinched with hunger, yet God is he that they stand most in need of.	But bread he would have, because that he hath need of: so the saints of God are marvelous importunate to keep God in his ordinances, so that though they wear a ragged coat, or be pinched with hunger; yet they want God more than these, either food or raiment.

In Ps. 73 David fretted[80] at the prosperity of the wicked, but at the last, verse 25,[81] he breaks off kindly, saying; "Whom have I [in] heaven but thee?" As if he should have said, 'Let them have what

---

[71] T has: *services.*

[72] Attendance at one Sunday service is enough and even that too much. T, for the reading, has a summary: *Hence it is that the saints of God are so urgent for God's services, and in that most men so slight them.*

[73] T faultily cites Ps. 34:4.

[74] F gives Ps. 42:1; T gives 42:4. It is the latter verse, with its reference to thanksgiving in the house of the Lord, that justifies Hooker's interpretation of "ordinances" as the object of panting thirst.

[75] T has: *wondrous.*

[76] T has: *But what if a man want preaching, may not he want it, and yet go to heaven?*

[77] The absence of the ordinances in the sense of the neglect thereof.

[78] T does not have *because . . . world.*

[79] T has simply: *Gold.*

[80] T has: *fretteth* and cites Ps. 37, which has indeed much fretting.

[81] F gives the v. where he gives the number of the Psalm.

they will, I will have nothing but thee." And why so? Why? [verse 26]: "Thou art my strength and my portion forever." He saith that God is his strength, yea the strength of his heart, hereby showing that all the helps in the world cannot help the heart of man, if God and Christ be wanting.[82] You were as good offer a journey to refresh a weary man, or the air to feed a hungry man,[83] as to offer riches, honors, and ease to help a distressed soul.

These will never help a man; he may well dote upon them, but his soul and conscience will be galled and troubled still. It must be the God of peace that must speak peace to troubled souls. It must be the God of peace that must speak peace to a distressed soul, to a soul that is damned in itself;[84] it is he that must say [cf. Ps. 73:26], 'I will be the strength of their hearts and their portion forever.' No marvel then if a poor soul cries to God, when happily the heart is full, when the soul gnaws and cries within itself, 'I am damned, I am damned.' Happily the palate is pleased with delicates, when the poor soul for aught it knows must go down to hell. Oh then, beloved, if you will have safety, go where God is, for every good gift comes in with him. If once a man hath got God into his company, he hath all good things with him.

These will never establish a man, he may hope to have comfort in them; but his soul shall be gravelled and troubled. It must be the God of peace that must speak peace to a troubled soul. It must be the God of salvation that can comfort a damned soul; that kindness will comfort, that is, strength of the heart, and portion forever. And then no marvel the soul call for God. The soul cares not, though happily the purse be filled, for it cries and sighs, 'I am damned.' Happily the palate may be pleased; but the poor soul cries, 'I may go to hell, and to the devil.' Now God comes, and he supplies all, for where he comes, there is every good gift. If once a man hath God, he hath all good things with him.

God blessed Obed Edom's house for the Ark's sake [2 Sam. 6:11].[85] Now the Ark was a type of Christ, and where it came, many blessings came with it.[86] Even so when God come unto a

[82] T has simply: *the heart without God.*

[83] T has: *A man were as good offer yron to a hungry man to refresh him, or air to feed him.* The fact that in the divergent reading of T and F, we have *yron* (iron) in T and *journey* in F, shows clearly that one or both are transcriptions of a Ms, because the differentiation is a matter of reading rather than of hearing. It would seem that journey is the better rendering. It goes with *air.*

[84] One is reminded here and elsewhere in the sermon of Joan Drake, of the self-damned soul, whose conversion was a model for Hooker ever thereafter.

[85] T has: *Obadiah's house.* Obed Edom was a Levite in whose house the ark lay for three months, 2 Sam. 6:10–12; 1 Cor. 13:13f.

[86] T has: *where he comes all good things follow.*

people, they are married unto him in righteousness, in judgment, in lovingkindness, and in mercies forever, Hos. 2: 19.[87]

When a man is married to a wife, all is his; so get Christ and all is thine.[88]

As when a wife is married, her husband is hers: so God and all is thine.

And then what wouldst thou have more?

God speaks to the rain, and it hears; God speaks to the corn,[89] and it hears; but if thou be in Christ, hell and death are thy servants (rather than thine enemies, for they have been subdued by Christ); but they that have outward things only, as profits, pleasures,[90] or the like, they have their ruin,[91] unless they have Christ[92] with them. Get Christ [93] therefore, for if he be wanting, all outward and inward dangers[94] befall that man, or that nation. "Woe be unto him or them that are without God." Hos. 9: 12f.:[95] "For, though they bring up their children, yet will I bereave them, that there shall not be a man left; yea, woe also to them, when I do depart from them! Ephraim, as Tyrus, is planted in a pleasant place; but Ephraim shall bring forth his children to the murderer." True indeed, woe be unto that heart, county, or kingdom,[96] that God is departed from. When God, who is the God of mercies and all consolation,[97] is departed away,[98] who can but pity that soul, county, or kingdom:[99] who will not submit to God's peace, consolation, and salvation?

[87] T has simply: *When God comes, we are married unto him, Hos. 2:19.* T has the citation, however, correctly, while F has incorrecctly 2:9.

[88] The conjugal point of view is different in F and T. In this connection it is of interest that T, above, n. 50. has a whole sentence about the wife, missing in F. Could this coincidence be a clue as to the sex of the transcriber? It is in any case quite possible that Hooker, on the point of leaving his wife and children for Holland, extemporaneously put these references into his farewell sermon, even though they were not in his Ms. In that case again, F would appear to be the quite fuller transcript of the original Ms., while T would be what could be actually taken down by a listener.

[89] T adds: *and the wine, and that hears Israel.*

[90] T has: *prosperity.*

[91] T has: *you have them with a curse.*

[92] T has: *God.*

[93] T has: *God.*

[94] T has for both simply: *all miseries.*

[95] T incorrectly says 9:13 and confuses the reference to *him.* T does not quote 13f. fully.

[96] T omits *county or kingdom.*

[97] T has only: *mercy.*

[98] T has: *gone away from him.*

[99] T has only: *who will pity that soul.*

When God (de)parts, all miseries follow (on amain:[100] when the banks are broken down, the sea breaks forth) for that man that makes no conscience of outfacing[101] God in the congregation.[102] Mark what the text saith, [cf.] Dt. 28:15,[103] "I will forsake them, and many miseries shall overtake[104] them." And (if God be gone) when the flood-gates are once up,[105] then come in all evils.[106] And then they shall say: 'Are not these things come upon us,[107] because God is not with us?' If therefore we would avoid woe and sorrow, slaying and killing one another,[108] if the wife would not see her husband killed[109] before her tender eyes, and the man see his wife snatched out[110] of the world by the hands of wicked men, then leave not God, but hold him fast, and then evil days will depart from us.

It is our holding of God that keeps miseries from us. [*Use*] Oh then what shall we think of them that are weary of God, and that say to the Almighty, Job 22:17: "Depart from us."? [111] [Objection:] But are there any amongst us that are weary of God? I hope there are none such amongst us.

And so holding God, he will keep us from misery. Use: To condemn two sorts of people. If the saints be marvelous importunate to have God with them, what shall we think of those that are weary of the Almighty, who say to him, depart from us. But you will say, such are to be chronicled, we have none such among us.

I answer: Thou art a servant, and rejectest the command of thy Master.[112] In it thou dost reject God. And [concerning] all such as have a mean conceit[113] of the worship of God, and the word of

[100] i.e., *violently*.

[101] i.e., *defying impudently*.

[102] T has: *his ordinances*. This is his preferred reading, cf. above. Another indication that the texts differ through misreading by at least one transcriber of the Ms.

[103] T has incorrectly: Dt. 3:37.

[104] T has: *befall*.

[105] T has, surely incorrectly: *drawn dry*.

[106] T has: *and in comes all misery*.

[107] T has: *all these things against us, seeing*.

[108] T reverses: *killing and slaying*.

[109] T has lost the structure of the sentence. The previous phrase being left incomplete, the next proceeds: *their husbands killed. . .*

[110] T has: *taken out*.

[111] From the speech of Eliphaz: "They [wicked men] said to God, 'Depart from us' and 'What can the Almighty do to us?'"

[112] T has: *Master's command*.

[113] i.e., *conception*.

God, and think that prayer or preaching is continued too long, I say, these men know not what they think or say, but certainly it is because they would be freed from the ordinances of God. Well, God will free thee from them one day, I will warrant thee! And then thou wilt be in a miserable condition! Oh, that thou wouldst pity thy poor condition! [114] But thou art weary of God's ordinances, and of his mercies, his presence, and patience.[115]

Know thou that thou shalt be deprived of God's goodness, and thy portion shall be with those that hate God in this life here; and after this life, if thou repent not, thy portion shall be with them in Tophet, where the worm dieth not, and where the fire goeth not out, and then crying will not avail.	Thou shalt one day be deprived of his presence, and shut up with the haters of God and goodness in the black Tophet, where the worm never dies, nor the fire never goes out. Then the crying will do thee no good.

God will be God over thee in destruction, yea, when he hath spurned thousands and ten thousands into hell, such as thou art, then shalt thou be the everlasting object of his never-dying wrath. Then (though thou couldst scale the heavens with thy tears) notwithstanding all thy shrill cries, though thou couldst be heard out of that dungeon, yet were thy help never the near(er); for God is God still.[116] I advise thee therefore what to do, whilst thou art here in this life, make thy peace with God in Christ, and lay thyself low before him, and bear patiently his hand in his wrath which thou hast deserved.[117] And mark what I say.

Thou has deserved to be in hell a hundred times, that is the least; and therefore be contented with thy condition.	A hundred hells thou hast deserved, and in those hells to lie a hundred years, nay forever. Hold theyself contented with thy condition.

[114] T has all the preceding but more briefly and at one point less clearly: *Why should a man say that they be so long and so long in prayer, and say, what man knows not what he says. He speaks this because that he is weary of the ordinances, and would be freed from them, and God will do it one day! Alas, poor soul, that thou couldst pity thy condition!*

[115] T reverses the last two of the four and repeats *weary* throughout, which sounds plausible for oral delivery.

[116] T has: *thy God is gone.*

[117] T has all this more briefly: *I admonish thee what to do lay thee down and patiently endure his deserved wrath.*

For thou hast chosen death rather than life, Jer. 31:8;[118] and God should wrong himself and thee also, if he should not let thee have[119] thy choosing.

Will not these things move you, my brethren? Methinks I see your colors rise.[120] I am glad of it. I hope it is to a good end. You may be wise, and happily so wise as to choose life rather than death. Now the Lord grant it, for he delights not in your destruction.

I will add[121] one word more, to leave the more impression in your hearts. My desire is the health of your souls.

| Though my meat seem sour, yet my mind is the will of God. | Though my meat seem bitter, yet it is the mind of God it should be so. |

Thou, man or woman, that canst not abide so much preaching, but standest upon thorns whilst it is preaching:[122] 'Too much of one thing,' you say, 'is good for nothing.' You do as much as say you will not have God with you; you will have a little of God, but you will have more of your pleasures.[123] Is this your desire, your delights? [124] Know then, whosoever thou art, that hast an ill will to God and his ordinances, and wilt not have the gospel in the purity of it: thou shalt have thy desires. Thou sayest, 'Depart, preaching.' And so it shall. Thou shalt have thy desires.[125]

| When thou shalt hear the trumpets sound, and when thine ears shall tingle with the sound of war; then depart forever. You that are weary of God, get you down to hell forever. Fulfill your base lusts. | When the trumpet shall blow, thy ears shall tingle with that sentence, 'Depart from me.' Thou that art weary of God, get thee down to hell, I say; God will set his teeth at thee, and stamp thee down to hell with thy base lusts. |

[118] T has incorrectly Jer. 31:8; F has no reference.
[119] T has: *give thee.*
[120] Presumably the flushed faces of anxiety. These three short ejaculatory observations are not recorded by T. Perhaps himself too much affected! It is almost certain that these lines are extemporary, based upon the preacher's observation of his congregation's reactions.
[121] The printing is unclear. It could be *would.*
[122] T has: . . . *on thorns, to have the sermon done.*
[123] T is not quite so clear.
[124] T reverses the two and keeps *delight* in singular.
[125] T has the same thought from *Know* on, but summarized.

Then will God say: 'For I have fed you on earth this twenty, thirty, forty, fifty, nay sixty years and upwards, and my mild word [126] could not rule you, nor prevail with you, and therefore now get you to hell, and there remain forever.' Think thus with yourselves. Will God serve me thus? Yea, that he will, for he hath prepared a place for the proudest kings, princes, monarchs, captains, etc., that are, or ever were in the world, if they will not be ruled nor guided by God, and his word. See Is. 30:33.[127] The text doth as good as say, he delighteth to make bonfires (upon their bones) about their ears.[128] And must this be the way to glorify God?[129]

[Objection:] But some may say: 'Surely kings and monarchs are exempted, they need not fear that such torments shall come upon them.' [130]

[Answer:] To this I answer: That God will say unto them, 'Reign there if thou wilt.' And then they shall know that there is a King that laughs at their destruction. Take notice of this, I beseech you, and reason thus with your own souls:

But God will say, be he a King that rules or reigns, yet as he hath rejected God, so God will reject him. He is a King of Kings, and Lord of Lords, and therefore such a one as will laugh at thy destruction. Take notice of this, and say thus to yourselves:

Is he a good son that cannot abide the presence of his own father? Is she a good wife that cannot abide the company of her husband? And is he a good Christian that cannot endure the company of Christ in his ordinances? [131]

Use: This may serve to rebuke God's people for their neglect. You see the gospel is going (brethren), Christ is departing, he is going to seek better entertainment.[132]

[126] T has: *words*.
[127] T has the same thought from *Think* on, but more compactly.
[128] Is. 30:30 is not so specific about the punitive fire.
[129] T makes the thought clearer and not in the form of a question: *Thus he will get himself glory by your destruction.*
[130] T has: *But you will say to me being a King or Monarch, I do not fear any such punishment shall befall me.* The F version is palpably closer to the original, for it is scarcely conceivable that Hooker or the transcriber would imagine Charles I talking back from the congregation!
[131] T has: *the presence of his Creator.*
[132] T omits what follows *going*.

But I marvel you give no better attendance; I pray hearken what I say, and have to say, stand up and hear, and the Lord give you grace to believe.[133]

I wonder you hear no better, better stand up and hear, and God give you grace to understand.

I will deal plainly with you. As sure as God is God, God is going from England. [134] Shall I tell you what God told me? Nay, I must tell you on pain of my life.[135] Will you give ear and believe me? I am a poor ambassador sent from God to do his message unto you; and, although I be low, yet my message is from above, and he that sent me is great, and from above; and O that he would grant that this my message might be believed (for his sake)!

What if I should tell you what God told me yesternight that he would destroy England and lay it waste? What say you to this, my beloved? It is my message, by meditation in God's word, that he bid me do to you, and he expects an answer from you. I do my message as God commanded me. What sayest thou unto it, England? I must return an answer to my Master that sent me, yea, this present night I must return an answer; for the Lord hath appointed a set time, saying, Ex. 9:5: "Tomorrow the Lord will do this thing [the plague on the cattle of the Egyptians] in the land."

Suppose God hath told me this night that he will destroy England, and lay it waste, what say you brethren to it? It is my message that God bade me do, he expects your answer, what sayest thou, Oh England, I must return an answer to my Master that sent me tonight.

Why speak you not? An answer you must give. Do you think well of it? Will you have England destroyed? Will you put the aged [136] to trouble, and your young men to the sword? Will you have your young women widows, and your virgins[137] defiled? Will you have your dear and tender little ones tossed upon the pikes and dashed against the stones? Or will you have them brought up in Popery, in

---

[133] These exhortations sound extemporary. In the F version they are enclosed in parentheses.

[134] T omits: *as sure . . . England.*

[135] T has: *pain of damnation.* Here begins Hooker's account of a personal revelation. Later, in the Antinomian Controversy in New England, he would oppose Anne Hutchinson's claim to just such a private revelation.

[136] T has: *old men.*

[137] T has: *maids.*

idolatry, under a necessity of perishing their souls forever,[138] which is worst of all? Will you have these temples wherein we seem to worship God, will you have them and your houses burnt with fire? And will you see England laid waste without inhabitants? Are you well-contented it shall be so? (God bade me ask. Why do you not answer me? I must not stir without it, I must have it.) I am an importunate suitor for Christ.[139] Oh, send me not sad away, but speak comfortably and cheerfully! What are you resolved of? Are you willing to enjoy God still, and to have him dwell with you? (You are, are you not?) It is well, I am glad of it if it be so.

But you must not only say so, but you must use the means, and you must plead importunately[140] with your God; for, although his sword be drawn and in his hand, lifted up and ready to strike, yet suffer him not to destroy, but rather to sheath his sword in the blood of his enemies. (God grant it.) I would be glad to have England flourish still. (And so are you, are you not? You are.) But if desolation do come, thank yourselves for it, it is your own fault if you be destroyed, and not God's; for he delights not in the death of any. We may justly take up the complaint of the prophet Isaiah who saith, 64:7: "No man stirreth up himself to lay hold on God." But this is our comfort, or rather our misery, that we have quiet prosperity, with ease and commodity, our bellies full, our coffers full, and our backs curiously[141] clothed, etc., not remembering the afflictions of our neighbor nations; but all is well with us, and it will serve our turns. And if we do humble ourselves a little, we think it is well.[142] And thus we play mock holiday with God and with his gospel, in making it our packhorse.

Well, look to it, for God is going, and if he do go, then our glory goes also. And then we may say with Phineha's wife, I Sam. 4:22: "[The] glory is departed from Israel." [143] So glory is departed from England; for England hath seen her best days, and the reward

---

[138] T has: *up in idolatry under the want of preaching.*

[139] T has only: *ambassador.*

[140] T omits: *importunately.*

[141] i.e., *with care.*

[142] T summarizes thus: *For this is our misery, if that we have quietness and commodity we are well enough.*

[143] T omits the quotation from I Sam.

of sin is coming on apace; for God is packing up of his gospel, because none will buy his wares (not come to his price). God begins to ship away his Noahs, which prophesied and foretold that destruction was near; and God makes account that New England shall be a refuge for his Noahs and his Lots, a rock and a shelter for his righteous ones to run unto; and those that were vexed to see the ungodly lives of the people in this wicked land, shall there be safe.[144] Oh, therefore my brethren, lay hold on God, and let him not go out of your coasts. (He is going!) Look about you, I say, and stop him at the town's-end, and let not thy God depart! Oh, England, lay siege about him by humble and hearty closing with him, and although he be going, he is not yet gone! Suffer him not to go far, suffer him not to say farewell, or rather fare-ill, England! Am. 4:12: "Therefore, because I will do thus unto thee, prepare to meet the God of Israel," O England.

Now God calls upon thee, as he did sometime upon Jerusalem, Jer. 6:8: "Be thou instructed therefore, O England,[145] lest my soul depart from thee, and lest I make thee desolate like a land that none inhabiteth."[146] And thus we see what the godly have done before us,[147] and now let it be our copy.[148] And let us, with Mary, clasp close about Christ.[149] They [the saints of old] have broken the ice. Let us follow them. This is our day of atonement. This present day is ours. We have nothing to do with tomorrow. We are at odds with God; and this is the day of our reconciliation.[150] This is the day wherein we are to make our peace with our God, and to end all controversies.[151] Let us labor, therefore, to prevail with God, and, that we may not lose his presence, do as the spouse [in] Cant. 3:1: 'She sought him, but she could not find him, yet she gave not over,

---

[144] The Massachusetts Bay Company expedition of five "arks," (the first carrying mostly cattle), destined for Salem, moved out of the Thames in late April, 1629. None of the voyage references appear in T.

[145] Jeremiah, of course, at this point addresses Jerusalem.

[146] T is shorter and fails to note the shift of text from Amos to Jeremiah.

[147] T has: *done and this must be our care.*

[148] i.e., *pattern.*

[149] T has: *clasp about the Lord Jesus as Mary did.*

[150] T reverses the phrases, *reconciliation* before *odds.*

[151] Of this sentence T catches only the phrase after *God.*

but she followed him till she found him.' [152] So our God is going, and shall we sit still (on our beds)? [153]

Would you have the gospel kept with [these] lazy wishes? Oh, no, no; arise, arise from off your downy beds, and fall down upon your knees, and entreat God to leave his gospel to you and to your posterity.[154] Shall we, by our sins, disinherit our infants and posterity[155] of such a blessing (shall we bereave them of the gospel), which is, or should be, the life of their[156] lives, and so have them brought up in superstition? No, no; Lord, we cannot abide[157] this. Oh, give us neither wealth nor any other blessing but thy gospel! This is our plea, Lord. And when we have found God, then let us bring him home to our houses,[158] and there retain him, that so he may be our God, and the God of our posterity, in all our and their afflictions.[159] (We will cry, "Lord have mercy upon us.") [160] And this will make you to rejoice exceedingly. Oh, my beloved, carry God home with you. (Lay hold on him. Let him not go. Say he is our husband. Let him not go for your little ones [sake].)[161] And let him be a father to you, and to your posterity.

[152] In the cited verse the beloved does not yet find the Beloved:
> Upon my bed by night
> I sought him whom my soul loves;
> I sought him, but found him not;
> I called him, but he gave no answer.

The citation of this passage might throw light on Hooker's momentous experience "yesternight," "this night [previous]," above at n. 135. We can picture him indeed upon his bed, thinking about his farewell sermon, thinking about his impending departure for Holland, leaving his wife now at his side behind.

[153] T has cast the phrasing in the second person plural and we have had, therefore, to alter his *on your beds* to fit the F version.

[154] T is not quite so full or dramatic.

[155] T has only: *infants*.

[156] T has: *our*.

[157] T has: *endure*.

[158] T has: *families*.

[159] T in the foregoing is briefer.

[160] A faint echo of the Kyrie eleison of the Prayer Book.

[161] T, from which we have taken the material unique to that version, finishes the sentence thus: . . . *and so let us leave God to be a Father unto thee.* It has already been noted several times that T seems to reflect a woman's point of view in the transcription. We can well imagine Hooker in his farewell addressing his wife and children with special poignancy, while speaking generally.

Question: But how may we keep the Lord? It would be worth our labor.[162] (It is comfortable.) For at his right hand are pleasures for evermore.

Answer: (If you will come to the price, you shall have him. The means are these:) First, we must be sure to prepare a room for him; for he is a King; and a King, you know, sends his harbinger before him to prepare a room for him (against he come to any place— so must you do by cleaning yourselves from every evil course), —[a harbinger], saying, 2 Cor. 6:[16], 17: "Come out of her [the unclean people, nation, church], my people, touch no unclean thing, and then I will be thy God, and thou shalt be my people.' " [163] So my beloved brethren, come out of all sinful courses,[164] pleasures, and practices, and you may expect God's coming unto your houses. And when you sit down by your fires, or lie down in your beds, think thus with yourselves: 'What an equal[165] condition doth God propound? It is but only to part with a sin, a lust, a Delilah,[166] which we may very well spare, as well as I may spare water out of my shoes, or a [hot] coal[167] out of my bosom. I say think thus with thyself, and in thy heart, 'Will God keep company with me, if I will not keep company with sin?' [168] (What is this his proffer?) 'Are the terms no harder? This is a good offer. I will at once bid sin adieu; for now I am upon another bargain. Here is an offer that I was not aware of. I will quickly dispatch this bargain, and make my peace with my God.' [169]

And thus if you would have God to be yours, then let your souls and bodies be his by forsaking all sins;	*Would you have God to be your God, and will you not keep out of sin? If not, he will not be your God. But

Indeed the concluding phrasing of T quoted at the head of this n. but not included in our main text, may well be the original oral wording at this point, understood to be addressed to Mrs. Hooker, even though elsewhere in the sermon Hooker can use *thou* and *thee* for each listener before him.

[162] T has: *the while*.

[163] The passage is itself an echo of Is. 52:11. T incorrectly cites Rev. 18:19.

[164] T omits: *courses*.

[165] i.e., *fair*.

[166] Both F and T spell the name Dalilah. She is the Philistine woman who enveigled and betrayed Samson, Jg. 16:4ff.

[167] T omits: *coal*.

[168] T has: *Will God keep company in the paths of sin?*

[169] T does not carry the imaginary soliloquy beyond *adieu*.

and, Is. 58:9, when you shall call, God will come and say, "Here am I."

now let every soul forsake his uncleanness, and God will come to that soul; and therefore that place is marvelous sweet, Is. 58:9. You shall call, and God shall say, "Here I am," if that you will forsake your evil courses. Thus you see you have as fair an offer, as fair a warning, as God can propound.

Secondly, as you must prepare a room for God, so you must give him content too. Let God have his will, cross him not.[170] Where the King is[171] he will have all things to his mind. Even so it is with God. If he may have his own worship, you please him wondrous well. You must dress his dishes according to his tooth; but if you put poison into his meat, if you mingle the traditions of men with God's worship,[172] then you discontent him. (Then you do not give him his mind.) Lay aside, therefore, all your superstitions, and erroneous opinions of God and his worship, and do it according to his will in his word revealed. And then you please him, indeed,[173] when a nation or a soul submits to God and to his truth in all things.

To bow at the name of Jesus [Phil. 2:10] is not meant at the word *Jesus;* for so to give him the bow is to commit syllabical idolatry;

*[Phil. 2:10] "At the name of Jesus every knee shall bow." This is not meant of the word *Jesus,* to give a bow with the knee, and a stab at the heart. If so, why do we not bow at the word *Jehovah,* as at the word *Jesus;* but the bowing at the word, the syllable, is idoltary. And here we do not give him his mind;

but the meaning is, we should worship him in spirit and in truth [Is. 4:24], humbly subjecting ourselves unto Christ.

Thirdly, as we must give him his mind, so we must give him welcome (also and entertainment). If you displease God and look loweringly,[174] or sourly upon him, and grudge at God or at his

---

[170] T omits: *cross him not.*

[171] T has: *comes.*

[172] T omits the phrase with *mingle.*

[173] T has instead of *erroneous opinions* the briefer *errors* and omits all up to: *then you please. . .*

[174] T omits: *displease, sourly.*

truth, no wonder then if God go away. And surely this is the sin of England. We bear an ill will unto God and his word, and God hath done well for this land.[175] And what could he have done more than he hath done for this land, as he saith, Is. 5:4, of his vineyard. But it brought forth contrary fruit. Even so we do all contrary to God's expectation. Mark therefore what God saith, Is. 5:5f., he will take away the hedge, and it shall be trodden down; and for aught that may be collected.[176] So it is like to be with us, if his mercy prevent it not; for, are we better than the old world? [177]

The same sins that were found in the old world, are found in us. Sodom's and Gomorah's sins were but straws in respect of ours! And yet God rained down fire and brimstone upon them. Tell me, are there not as great sins amongst us as were in Jerusalem, who were carried captives, and their city destroyed, and they a vagabond people unto this day? [178] Are we better than other brethren and neighbor nations, that have drunk so deeply of God's wrath? [179] I tell you truly, we are a burden to God; he cannot long bear us, and he will think his burden well over when he hath destroyed us. You know all men are glad when their pain is over. Even so it is with God. We are a pain and a trouble unto him, and why should God go continually pained [180] with us, which are worthy to be destroyed? (If his decree once come forth) then shall England seek peace, but shall not find it, God shall not pity us [as in Is. 7:25]. Oh, my beloved brethren, what a pitiful thing it is, when a merciful God shall show himself unmerciful? When his patience shall be turned into impatience? (O beloved,) there is a hard time ere long befalling England, if God in mercy prevent it not; [181] but we do not consider it. Lamentable is our time. Christ wept over Jerusalem: "Oh,"

[175] T has: *much for us of this Land*.

[176] The final phrase is obscured and not supported by the text of Is. 5:6, which begins: "And I will lay it waste."

[177] The *old world* here means the world before the Abrahamic and Mosaic covenants. It will presently come to mean old Christendom, contrasted with the *new* world and in it *New* England.

[178] T has slightly compacted the destruction of Sodom, Gomorrah, and, much later, Jerusalem.

[179] The reference is to the Catholic and Protestant principalities amid the Thirty Years' War.

[180] T has: *in pain and trouble*.

[181] T has only: *there is a hard time befalling us of England*.

saith he, Lk. 19:42, "that thou hadst known in this thy day of visitation, the things that do concern thy peace! But now they are hid
from thine eyes."

Beloved, what do you think we shall do, when God's mercies are
turned into justice? [182]

| Look to it England, the Lord hath wept over thee in mercy many years. What shall we do when we have leisure to consider what once we did enjoy? For God's patience is never truly prized till we want it; and then the poor soul will thus say: | *So may I say to England, their Lord hath wept over it in mercy and patience a long time, but it hath not been taken notice of, God hath hid it from our eyes. What shall we do when his mercy is turned into fury, and his patience into frowning? What shall we do when we have leisure to consider what once we did enjoy? We can never prize God's patience till that we find the great want of it. Thus then the poor soul will say: |

'There was a time when we might have been at peace with this
patient God, but now he is hid from our eyes, now the gate is shut,
barred and locked up.' [183] And thus when a people doth abuse[184]
God's mercy, he sends the contrary judgments, and then it will
grieve and wound our souls to think what once we did enjoy; but
that soul that will bid God welcome to his heart may go singing
to his grave.[185]

Fourthly, you must be importunate with God to tarry, and account
it a great favor if he will stay; for God hath room enough in
heaven, and therefore you need not lodge him for want of lodging,
but you must be beholding to him to tarry with you. Yet in these
days men do not love to be beholding. Jacob wrestled with God
[Gen. 32:24], and by that means he held him till he blessed him.
(And thus must we do if we mean to keep him.) You live under the
means, and know the way, and will you not do it? What greater
condemnation can there be, and how great will your judgment be
unto you? More than unto them that have no means! [186] And, as

---

[182] T omits the sentence.
[183] T uses slightly longer wording.
[184] T has: *refuse*.
[185] Could this be an echo of the experience of Mrs. Joan Drake, so formative
in Hooker's life? See: *Life*, pp. 4ff.
[186] From *you live* on, T is briefer.

it was said of Capernaum [Mt. 11:21-24], so say I to England, "Thou England that wast lifted up to heaven with means, shalt be brought down to hell; thou shalt be abused for it; for if the mighty works which have been done in thee, had been done in India or in Turkey, they would have repented ere this time." [187] And therefore Capernaum's place is England's place, which is the most scalding tormenting place of all,[188] if it repent not. And mark what I say, the poor native Turks and Infidels shall have a more cool summer-parlor in hell than England shall have; for we stand upon high rates.[189] (We were highly exalted.) Therefore thy torment [O England] shall be the more intolerable to bear.

Now the Lord write these things in our hearts by the finger of his Holy Spirit for his Christ's sake, under whom I would we were all covered. Amen.

[187] Hooker conflates Mt. 11:21 and 23; cf. Lk. 10:13-15. Jesus rebuked three Jewish towns, including Capernaum, and refers to three Gentile places of wickedness: Tyre, Sidon, Godom. Here Hooker allows England to take the place of Capernaum, and India and Turkey the places in the text of Tyre and Sidon.

[188] T has: *insufferable torment of all.*

[189] T has: *at a high rate.*

ESSAY 3

The Transcription and Transmission of the
Hooker Corpus

BY WINFRIED HERGET

Thomas Hooker's style has often been praised, even though tradition has it that almost all his published sermons were not written by Hooker himself but were made up from notes, which his auditors had taken down in accordance with Puritan practice. These sermons were then published many years later, apparently without Hooker's consent. Thus, "Spiritual Munition," the funeral sermon for the Reverend Wilmot, for which we now have established June 22, 1626, as the date of delivery (Document I), was not printed until 1638. *The Faithful Covenanter*, preached at the lecture in Dedham in Essex about 1629 (Document VI), was not published until 1644. Hooker's so-called farewell sermon, *The Danger of Desertion* (Document VII) did not appear before 1641, ten years after the popular lecturer had left England for Holland. Most of the sermons in the lecture series on the *ordo salutis*, which had made Hooker famous while he was preaching at Chelmsford in Essex between 1625/26 and 1629, were brought out in 1637. Indeed, by the time he sailed for America in 1633, only the Preface to John Rogers' *The Doctrine of Faith* (Document IV), *The Poor Doubting Christian* (Document V), and *The Souls Preparation* (1632)[1] had been published.

The importance of auditors' notations for the transmission of sixteenth- and seventeenth-century sermons[2] bears directly on the

---

[1] The question of dating Hooker's sermons has been discussed in W. Herget, "Preaching and Publication—Chronology and the Style of Thomas Hooker's Sermons," *Harvard Theological Review*, 65 (1972), 231–239.

[2] Sermon note-taking has been discussed in W. F. Mitchell, *English Pulpit Oratory from Andrews to Tillotson* (London, 1932), pp. 30–38; Alan F. Herr, *The Elizabethan Sermon* (Philadelphia, 1940), pp. 75–86; Babette M. Levy, *Preaching in the First Half Century of New England History* (Hartford, 1945), pp. 81–85; and J. W. Blench, *Preaching in England in the Late Fifteenth and Sixteenth Centuries* (Oxford, 1964).

form and nature of Puritan preaching. The Puritan sermon was meant to be repeated in the family or in meditation after the Sunday services or the weekday lecture were over. The auditor's notations served this purpose, and the preacher had to keep them in mind; he had to structure the sermon in such a way that the notator would be able to follow. The familiar structure of doctrine, reasons, and uses helped to fulfill this function. The divisions in the sermon are clearly marked, and each new point is numbered. The new matter which continues the argumentation is usually contained in the initial sentence of a point, which will then be amplified, proven by scriptural quotation, and illustrated by analogies from common experience and the Scriptures. In this way a rhythm is established which can lead to a rather tiresome regularity with the less-gifted minister, but is variable enough for the more accomplished preacher. Each point in itself is virtually open-ended; further scriptural passages, illustrations, and/or direct appeals to the audience may be added at the preacher's discretion. Moreover, the preacher is free to go through the sequence of doctrine, reasons, and uses more than once in a single sermon; and while it is true that he must not abandon the conventional structure altogether, he can spread the required structural parts over two or more sermons, interrupting where time makes it necessary, and continuing the week after. In this way many a single sermon that is part of a week-to-week topical lecture series based on the same scriptural text, loses the organic unity which is usually associated with the progression from the doctrine and reasons to the uses, from that portion of the sermon that is mainly meant to convince the intellect to the part which addresses itself more to the will and the emotions. In one such sermon the preacher may finish the uses from the previous Sunday or lecture day, and then perhaps, if the time permits, go on to another doctrine and reasons from the same text, again breaking off at some point.

It is commonplace knowledge that a published sermon bears only a certain degree of resemblance to the sermon as it was preached. Yet the various facets of the transmission process from the delivery to the press become very important, when, as in the case of Hooker, we have only the printed end product, but know that its status depends on the previous stages of its genesis. It would be ideal if we could trace one and the same sermon from the preacher's notes through the notations of more than one auditor to the printed version, if we knew, moreover, who the notators were and who wrote out the notes and saw the sermon through the press. We lack, of course, such comprehensive source material. Only in a few cases and at various stages of the process do we have some material that can be compared and some information that can be helpful in determining what is involved in the transmission of Puritan sermons such as the Hooker corpus.

No autograph of the sermons that Thomas Hooker delivered in Europe or America has been preserved.[3] None of the notations by auditors in England or Holland has been found, although many must have been in circulation. The only extant notes were taken down after he had settled in Hartford. Two of his sermons, delivered October 4, 1638, and June 20, 1647, are contained in a diary that Mathew Grant of Windsor kept in a very difficult chirography. The first is a thanksgiving sermon on 1 Sam. 7:12. There are, in addition, more than forty sermons which Hooker preached between May 2, 1638, and March 16, 1641, contained in the notebook of Henry Wolcott, also of Windsor.[4] Many of the sermons which Wolcott heard at Hartford were to make up the two volumes of *The*

---

[3] Among the holdings of the Connecticut Historical Society in Hartford there is a small miscellanea notebook in Hooker's own hand. It has been transcribed and reproduced in Andrew T. Denholm, "Thomas Hooker: Puritan Preacher, 1586–1647." Unpublished Doctoral Dissertation, Hartford Seminary Foundation, 1961.

Other extant manuscript volumes of Hooker sermons are usually copies from the published works. Everett Emerson, "Thomas Hooker Materials at the Connecticut Historical Society," *Early American Literature*, VI (1971) 187f., has recently called attention to such a volume which to him does not appear to be a copy. The titles used in the volume are, however, mostly those of Hooker's books.

[4] The diary of Matthew Grant has been transcribed by Jessie A. Parsons. The thanksgiving sermon on 1 Sam. 7:12 is included in an appendix of Denholm, op. cit. It has been printed in Everett Emerson, ed., *Resources for American Literary Study*, II (1972), 75–89. The shorthand sermon notes of Henry Wolcott are at the Connecticut Historical Society. They have been deciphered by Douglas H. Shepard. Two of the sermons were transcribed by J. H. Trumbull and published in the *Collections of the Connecticut Historical Society*, I (1860), 19–21. Denholm, op. cit., reproduced nine of the thirty-nine sermons by Hooker. For a description of the notebook, cf. ibid., 41of.

Application of Redemption,[5] where for the second — perhaps even the third — time[6] Hooker devotes a long series of lecture day sermons to the *ordo salutis*. When he had done so as a lecturer at Chelmsford, Essex, many of these sermons were later printed from the notes of auditors.

A comparison of the earlier publication of the Chelmsford sermons with Wolcott's notation and *The Application of Redemption* is possible. On January 2, 1638/39 Wolcott heard Hooker at Hartford. His shorthand outline of the sermon, as transcribed by Douglas H. Shepard, is short enough to be fully quoted:

> text 57 Isaiah 15 and I will dwell with him also that is of a contrite— and humble spirit
> dwelling implies 3 things /1 when God holds[7] such as those in whom he hath a special interest /2ly dwelling implies a taking up as residence and abode /3ly dwelling when it is attributed to the owner[8] of the house implies ruling and ordering the affairs of the house
> [reasons] he that is in a settled contented condition cannot receive faith for he will not go out of himself /2ly when he sees his distress he will labor to relieve himself now a man must 1st come [to] contrition and humiliation
> use 3 fold /1 to dash the hopes of all proud self confident carnal secure sinners God will never dwell with them
> 2 use to teach all those that love God to prize broken hearted sinners
> 3 use / use of exhortation to all those that would have God with them to labor to be broken hearted[9]

Wolcott omits the doctrine, and he forgets to mark the "reasons" after the explication of "dwelling." But otherwise his head sentences

[5] *The Application of Redemption*, Books I–VIII and Books IX–X, was not published until 1656, many years after Hooker's death.

[6] Thomas Goodwin and Philip Nye in their epistle to the reader of *The Application of Redemption . . . The Ninth and Tenth Books* (London, 1657), sig C 4ᵛ, maintain that Hooker preached the sermons of the redemption cycle first at Emmanuel College in Cambridge, then again "more largely" at Chelmsford, and for a third time at Hartford because he was dissatisfied with the imperfect editions that had been produced from notes taken by his auditors at Chelmsford. Cf. also Cotton Mather, *Magnalia Christi Americana* (London, 1702), Book III, § 23, p. 65.

[7] 'owns' seems to be a more likely reading than 'holds,' which Shepard gives.

[8] 'honor' in Shepard's transcription should read 'owner.'

[9] Douglas Shepard typescript (Connecticut Historical Society), 69f.

bear a rather close resemblance to the initial sentences of each point in the ninth book of *The Application:*

> To dwell implies Three Things.
> First, That the Lord owns such as those in whom he hath a special interest, and claims a special propriety . . .
> Secondly, Where a man dwels, as he owns the house, so he takes up his abode there, it is the place of residence;
> [Thirdly] Dwelling, if it be attributed to the chiefest Inhabitant and Owner of the House, it implies also the ruling and ordering of the occasions that come under hand there, the exercising of the Government of the house and family where the Owner is, and dwells.

The uses are also very similar:

> 1 A word of terror to dash the hopes, and sink the hearts of all haughty and hard hearted sinners, God owns not such . . .
> (Use 2) Instruction, To teach us to delight in such, to desire the Society of such as are contrite and humble men, to dwel there where God dwels;
> (Use 3) Exhortation, To perswade us all, and to prevail with us to take the right way to enjoy Gods presence, not only to seek for mercy, but seek it in Gods Order, not only to covet Gods presence, but in God's manner; labor to be humble and broken-hearted Christians:[10]

Wolcott, of course, misses the amplification of each initial sentence. In the first explication of "dwelling," this amplification runs to some seventy-five words. It is followed by an elaborate analogy between the temporal and spiritual realms, three supporting scriptural quotations, and a conclusion. Wolcott's abstract could not have served as a copy text for a printer.

The Application of Redemption is attested by Thomas Goodwin and Philip Nye to be truly Hooker's, "not as preached only, but as written by himself in order to the press," [11] and although a certain amount of sales strategy may be involved in their epistle to the reader, it is true that later sermons in the *Application* appear to be closer to the conventions of written style than do the earlier sermons based on auditors' notes. Thus, the first reason for the doctrine — Wolcott's notation is given above — reads

[10] *Application. The Ninth and Tenth Books, 2.*
[11] Ibid., sig. C4.

in *The Application, Bk. 9:* The first
which stops the way and work of faith
is a setled kind of contentedness in
our corrupt condition, and the blind,
yet bold and presumptuous confidence
that a natural man hath, and would
maintain of his good condition. Each
man sits down willingly, well apaid
with his own estate and portion, sees
no need of any change, and therefore
[is] not willing to hear of it.[12]

in "The Broken Heart": The first let
which is a hinderance to the work of
faith is this: there is a settled kind of
contentment which the soule taketh
up in its owne estate: and the heart
of a sinfull creature sitteth down well
apaid in that sinfull miserable condition wherein he is, and he desireth
no other, nay he would have no
change in this kind.[13]

Hooker's own version — if we believe Goodwin and Nye — is not necessarily more readable. With the greater attention it pays to logic and exactness, with its self-conscious effort to have a more balanced syntax and a greater copiousness of words, it seems more labored where the earlier version is more direct and livelier, more "oral."

On a much larger scale similar differences can be noted between *The Souls Preparation* and the tenth book of the *Application of Redemption*. One example must suffice here:

The 17th doctrine drawn from the
text Acts 2:37 in *The Application*
presumably written by Hooker himself, after he preached it at Hartford:
(Doctr.) They who are truly pierced
with Godly sorrow for their sins and
willing openly to confess them, when
they are called thereunto. Or. True
contrition is accompanied with confession when God calls thereunto.
So do these converts here in the place,
they come here of their own accord,
they do not stay til they be arrested
and summoned to the court; but they
readily arrest, indite, arraign and accuse themselves before Peter and the
rest of the Apostles. Men and brethren
you have discovered many sins and the

The same doctrine in *The Souls Preparation* brought out while Hooker was
in Holland,[14] and probably preached
at Chelmsford in Essex:
When the heart is truly broken for
sinne, it will be content to make open
and free confession thereof: or thus,
Sound contrition brings forth bottom-
confession.

*Men and brethren, what shall we doe
to be saved?* as if they had said, The

[12] Ibid., 7.

[13] *The Souls Implantation* (London, 1637), 6.

[14] In *The Souls Preparation* (London, 1632) the table of contents is followed by this note: "Christian Reader, thou hast here some sermons brought to light, which by reason of the author's absence, are presented to thy view, both with some lesser escapes, and in more homely terms, than his judicious eye would have suffered."

dreadful condition of the sinners who are guilty thereof, loe we are the men, thus and thus we have done. By us the Lord was opposed and persued, by us he was derided, rayled upon and blasphemed, by us it was he was murthered, and we are they that have embrewed our hands in his most precious blood: we are they that cryed and desired it, Crucified him, away with him, not him, but Barabbas. Nay they roundly, readily told al . . .[15]

truth is wee have heard of the fearefull condition of such as have killed the Lord Jesus, and we confesse whatsoever you have said, he was persecuted by us, and blasphemed by us, we are they that cryed, Crucifie him, crucifie him; we would have eaten his flesh, and made dice of his bones; we plotted his death and glorified in it; these are our sins, and haply a thousand more that they revealed . . .[16]

In addition to *The Application of Redemption*, one other book of sermons, *A Comment upon Christ's Last Prayer* (1656), "preached in the occasion of the Lord's Supper towards his latter end," is also attributed to Hooker's "own papers written with his own Hand" by Goodwin and Nye.[17] We do not know the source of their knowledge, or by which means they or the printer had access to Hooker's own manuscripts. Cotton Mather reports that Francis Higginson transcribed nearly 200 of Hooker's sermons, which were then sent to England for publication; but he hastens to add that "scarce half of them have seen the light unto this day."[18] Which sermons these were, at what time they were sent, and which of Hooker's published works may be traced back to these transcriptions, remains undetermined. Higginson was the teacher at the school in Hartford between 1641 and 1643, while he continued his studies under Hooker.

Two other New England ministers were involved in the publication of Hooker's sermons. Thomas Shepard, his son-in-law, prepared *The Saints Dignity and Duty* (1651) for the press. Zachariah Symmes,[19] perhaps in collaboration with Shepard,[20] served as a

[15] *Application. The Ninth and Tenth Books*, 619f.
[16] *The Souls Preparation*, p. 206.
[17] Thomas Hooker, *A Comment Upon Christ's Last Prayer in the Seventeenth of John* (London, 1656), title-page and half-title.
[18] Cotton Mather, op. cit. Book III, § 23 (London, 1702), p. 66.
[19] It is probable that it was Zachariah Symmes who signed Z. S. under the dedicatory epistle to the reader of *The Christians Two Chief Lessons* (London, 1640). Cf. George Leon Walker, *Thomas Hooker: Preacher, Founder, Democrat* (New York, 1891), p. 189f.
[20] Walker, loc. cit., thinks that the person mentioned in the dedicatory epistle as one "that was inwardly acquainted with the author" can be identified as Thomas Shepard, Hooker's son-in-law.

redactor for *The Christians Two Chief Lessons* (1640). Because Hooker was still living, Symmes found it necessary to defend his own "meddling in another mans labours" by pointing out that had he "not taken some paines in the perusall and transcribing thereof, after it came into the Printers hands," the work "would have passed the Presse more imperfectly than now it doth." Symmes also assured the reader that he and his collaborators did not alter the author's phrases, or "adde any thing of our owne; onely we amended s[u]ch errours as would have beene imputed to the Authour through the oversight of the Scribe." [21] Exactly how much freedom this gave to Symmes would, of course, depend on the quality of the notation that he transcribed.

For most of Hooker's works we do not know who the redactor or who the note-taker was, but for the so-called farewell sermon (Document VII) we have two variant published texts, and it has been possible to identify the notator or transcriber of one of them. Published in 1641 as *The Danger of Desertion* (referred to in Document VII as T — Traditional version) this sermon was probably preached before Hooker went to Holland in 1631.[22] Because the same sermon (referred to in Document VII as F) can be found again in the works of William Fenner (1600-1640), published posthumously in 1657,[23] there is sufficient internal evidence to conclude that the two texts are based on notes taken at the same delivery.

The Fenner version (F) is more fully written out, and has therefore been used for the edition of Document VII. Significant divergences have been given in parallel columns or in the accompanying notes there, so that longer quotations are not needed here. But some features thought to be typical of the transmission process for many Puritan sermons should be considered. Because the manuscripts for Hooker's farewell sermon are not extant, it is possible that diver-

---

[21] *The Christians Two Chief Lessons*, sig A 2ᵛ, sig A 3.

[22] For the dating of this sermon cf. the introduction to Document VII.

[23] "The Signs of Gods Forsaking a People" is the nineteenth of the *XXIX Choice Sermons on Several Texts of Scripture* (London, 1657), bound in *The Works of W. Fenner*, printed for W. Gilbertson, 1657.

Cotton Mather, op. cit., p. 62 (Book III, para. 15) reports: "Amongst Mr. Fenner's Works, I find some imperfect and shattered, and I believe, injurious notes of a *Farewel Sermon* upon Jer. 14.9 . . . which *Farewel Sermon* was indeed, Mr. Hooker's at his leaving of *England*."

gences between the two printed versions have their origin either in the notation, transcription, redaction, or finally even in the printing itself. In which of these stages the divergences originated can only be surmised in a general way.

The Danger of Desertion goes back to what must have been a more condensed notation. The condensation can partly be explained as a kind of telescoping which results from the time that elapses between the utterance of a word by the preacher and its being written down by the auditor. While the notator is still taking down what has just been said, he is already hearing what follows, and in the process of writing continues with the later words instead of those which had originally made up a clause or sentence. That nevertheless a consistent text ensues in this way can be attributed to the working of oral style, especially when a certain redundancy is involved. Differences in word order[24] may also have something to do with the writer/hearer situation, although the re-arrangement may have been made by the redactor for stylistic reasons. Fenner, of course, also condenses, and sometimes he will have only one adjective where *The Danger of Desertion* has a series; but usually his wording is more copious. The notator for *The Danger of Desertion* may have been slower: he leaves out more than does Fenner, and often summarizes, particularly where the Fenner text has the preacher using imagined direct speech and engaging in a rhetorical dialogue with his congregation, which adds further to the dramatic effect of the sermon.

Differences in the stylistic make-up include alternate, but synonymous, wording.[25] It is difficult to make out which words the preacher actually used; for the substitution of words may have taken place in the notation. Moreover, differences in tense, person, and number may also have taken place in the notation. But the connectives are more carefully worked out in Fenner than in *The Danger of Desertion*, reflecting a greater stylistic determination that may be more Fenner's than Hooker's, close as the style of the two preachers ap-

---

[24] Cf. Document VII, p. 243. For other examples, ibid., p. 244, together with n. 84, and n. 19 together with n. 150.

[25] For examples cf. ibid., 4 and n. 27, 7 and at n. 56, 10 and at n. 75, 12 and at n. 98, 12 and at n. 106, 17 and at n. 136, 17 and at n. 137.

pears to be in their other works. Some alternate wordings stem from misreading the notation.[26] In some cases a mishearing by the notator is also possible, but generally a misreading of the notation by the transcriber is more likely. The fact that Fenner normally has the more sensible reading would support the assumption that he was indeed transcribing his own notation, whereas the transcriber for *The Danger of Desertion* must have encountered some difficulties in deciphering a notation that probably was not his own. It is apparent at the beginning of the sermon, for example, that he was not always able to make full sense of what he found. He clearly did not pay too much attention to what was said before the doctrine; and his scriptural references show that he was not always able to discover how the biblical text was linked with the preacher's argument.[27]

Variant versions were also published of Hooker's famous *The Poor Doubting Christian* (Document V). Originally included in *The Saints Cordials*,[28] which contained sermons mainly by Richard Sibbes, when it came out in 1629 no preacher's name was given. But Hooker's contribution, as we have seen (above, p. 148), proved immensely popular; it was printed again as a separate title in 1635, and reached its fifth edition in 1638.[29] Hooker's name, as we have observed (above, p. 149), did not appear on the title-page until the 1646 edition, although his authorship was recorded in the Stationers' Register on May 6, 1637, when the title was entered for Robert Dawlman and Luke Fawne as "upon John the 6th the 45th by Master Hooker." [30] At this time Dawlman and Fawne must have

---

[26] For examples cf. ibid., 2 and at n. 10, 7 and at n. 61, 10 and at n. 83, 10, parallel text, 24 and at n. 184.

[27] Cf. for example ibid., 3 and at n. 19ff.

[28] *The Saints Cordials* (London, 1629). According to the table of contents, two sermons on Jn. 6:45 can be expected. The separate title-page of "The Poor Doubting Christian" announces only "one sermon."

[29] The textual history of *The Poor Doubting Christian* has recently been studied by Sargent Bush, "The Growth of Thomas Hooker's *The Poor Doubting Christian*," *Early American Literature*, VIII (1973), 3–20, and before him by Frank C. Shuffelton, "Thomas Prince and his Edition of Thomas Hooker's *Poor Doubting Christian*," *Early American Literature*, V (1970–71), 68–75.

[30] Edward Arber, ed., *A Transcription of the Registers of the Stationers of London: 1554–1640*, IV (London, 1875–94), 357.

thought it necessary to protect their interest in the popular sermon, because two weeks earlier, on April 21, 1637, the printer Andrew Crooke had also entered "certaine sermons upon John the 6th verse the 45th." [31] When Crooke brought out these sermons as *The Souls Effectual Calling to Christ*,[32] the large volume contained on pp. 538-610 what Dawlman was publishing as *The Poor Doubting Christian*.

While the possibility of two separate deliveries of the same sermon, resulting in different notations and different printed copies, cannot be entirely excluded, it is more than likely that both the Dawlman and Crooke texts go back to the same delivery of the sermon within a long series of sermons preached by Hooker on Jn. 6:45. *The Poor Doubting Christian* as it is published by Dawlman cannot have been preached as one isolated sermon, as was the farewell sermon or *The Faithful Covenanter*, preached at the lecture in Dedham; for it is not structured in the usual way, with an explication of the scriptural text followed by a doctrine, reasons, and uses. Therefore it must have been preceded by other sermons on the same text, in which the preacher had begun in the conventional way and then continued the various parts, perhaps week after week. As many sermon notebooks show, a minister would frequently recall the context of an earlier sermon, and then begin where he had broken off the lecture day or Sunday before. And if he — like Hooker — was particularly bent on the practical application of his text, he could spend many a sermon making uses of a doctrine expounded in an earlier sermon of the series.

This is clearly the case in *The Poor Doubting Christian*, where after the quotation of the scriptural text a precis is given of what "we have formerly set forth at large," [33] thus summarizing the preceding sermon, which is not printed in *The Saints Cordials*, but

---

[31] Ibid.. 355. This is the first time that Hooker's name is spelled out instead of giving only the initials. *The Souls Preparation* was even entered as by "F. H." (October, 29, 1631).

[32] *The Souls Effectual Calling to Christ* came out in 1637, and was re-issued in 1638 as *The Souls Vocation or Effectual Calling to Christ* where it was bound with *The Souls Ingrafting into Christ*. 1637 was an important year for the transmission of Hooker's sermons. For details cf. Herget, op. cit., 233f.

[33] *The Saints Cordials*, 347.

which can be found in full, eight years later, in *The Souls Effectual Calling*, pp. 520-538. And if the two printed versions are based on notations from separate deliveries, it would mean that the whole series was preached twice: one notation would date from the time when Hooker preached at the University before 1620, and the other from his lectureship in Chelmsford.[34] It seems more likely, however, that the two printed versions are based on separate notations taken at the same delivery; for the divergences between the Dawlman and Crooke texts follow the lines we have come to know in examples of separate notations and transcriptions of the same sermon. One typical exchange of an objection and an answer reads

in *The Souls Effectual Calling:* But you will say, Aye, thats true, if I had but a heart to mourne for them: see my sinnes I doe, and I cannot but acknowledge my corruptions: but I am not sensible of the load that lyes upon me, I cannot be burthened with the evils that oppresse me, I have a heart not only that doth not, but that cannot mourne.

I answer, this hinders not neither, provided thou beest troubled, because thou canst not bee troubled; provided thy heart be weary of it selfe, because it cannot be weary of sinnes;

if this be thy temper and frame, this hinders thee not from the mercie of God which is offered and thou needest: for that Christ that freely pardons sinne, can, and will, and that easily, breake thy heart, and fit it for pardon:

Mic. 7.18 The Lord pardons sinnes and subdues ininquities; not because thou pleaseth him:

but because mercie pleaseth him: Wherefore did the Lord shew most mercie to *Saul* when he shewed most hatred against him. . .[35]

in *The Poor Doubting Christian:* Oh, that is true, saith the poore soule, had I but a heart to mourne for my baseness; see my sinnes I doe but this is my misery,

I cannot be burthened with them, I have a heart that cannot breake and mourne for the dishonours of God.

This hinders not neither, provided that

thy heart is weary of it selfe, that it cannot be weary of sinne;

(*Mic. 7.18*) *The Lord Shewes mercy because he will shew mercy* it is not

because thou canst please him but because mercy pleaseth him. When did the Lord shew mercy to *Paul,* even then when Paul did expresse most malice against him. . .[36]

[34] Cf. above at n. 6.
[35] *The Souls Effectual Calling* (London, 1637), p. 542f.
[36] *The Saints Cordials,* p. 350.

The Poor Doubting Christian is the more condensed version of the sermon; but fundamentally both texts agree in substance and structure, even though stylistic differences may be somewhat greater than in the example quoted. *The Souls Effectual Calling* provides more and fuller transitional passages. What is more, the redactorial and typographical arrangement may be divergent in the two texts. Sometimes one notator will summarize where the other uses imagined dialogue of "objections" and "answers." Some points may be marked differently. Thus at the beginning of the sermon the first hindrance mentioned rather briefly in *The Poor Doubting Christian*[37] is not recorded in *The Souls Effectual Calling*, which gives[38] as its first hindrance what in *The Poor Doubting Christian*[39] is the second. At what point *The Souls Effectual Calling* would have the second hindrance begin can be told only from the table of contents.[40] This hindrance provides the third part of an answer to an objection in *The Poor Doubting Christian*,[41] and in the text of *The Souls Effectual Calling*[42] it is also introduced as "thirdly." On the other hand, the third hindrance is clearly marked only in *The Souls Effectual Calling*,[43] and the confusion probably indicates that the notators were not able to follow the way the preacher subdivided and numbered his points. Notators of sermons were frequently confused by the elaborate branching of points, as the notebooks of the time clearly show.

The 1629 edition of *The Poor Doubting Christian*, as has been pointed out (above, p. 151), was never again printed in its original form; for it underwent some changes when it was brought out as a separate volume in 1635. The new edition contained five major additions[44] amounting to some 2000 words;[45] and these additions

[37] Ibid., p. 348.
[38] *The Souls Effectual Calling*, p. 538.
[39] *The Saints Cordials*, p. 348.
[40] *The Souls Vocation* (London, 1638), sig D 2ᵛ.
[41] *The Saints Cordials*, p. 351.
[42] *The Souls Effectual Calling*, p. 546.
[43] Ibid.
[44] *The Poor Doubting Christian* (London, 1635), pp. 29–33, before the third hindrance in *The Saints Cordials*, p. 351; pp. 51–55 are added before the second help p. 353; pp. 63–66 before the third help p. 354; pp. 74–79 before the fourth help p. 355; pp. 135–140 are added to p. 603.
[45] Bush, op. cit.

usually occur at the end of points such as the first, second, and third
"helps" or means of cure to overcome the hindrances that keep
man from believing in Christ's mercy. These appended passages are
not to be found in *The Souls Effectual Calling*. But in two instances
the Crooke text, when compared with Dawlman's earlier, 1629 edition, has different additions and important alternate readings in the
same places.[46] The additions are of a reiterative nature, providing a
further edifying or hortatory conclusion to a point. As such they
may have been written by an experienced redactor to increase the
volume of the book, or they may have been preached but were not
taken down by the auditor whose notes served as the basis for the
1629 edition. In any case, the additions do not alter the general style
of the book, and on that account could be considered authentic.
But it should be remembered that the question of authenticity cannot be answered unequivocally as long as we have to assume that
the printed texts were made up from auditors' notations.

The borderline between a necessary and legitimate redaction and
a tampering with a text is rather thin. It is not until the 1646 edition
of *The Poor Doubting Christian* and the editions that follow it,[47]
that definite signs of the latter can be detected. These editions incorporate also the later sermons on Jn. 6:45 which in *The Souls
Effectual Calling* followed the portion that constituted the earlier
editions of *The Poor Doubting Christian*. It seems that these new
volumes were not made up from yet another set of notes; rather,
they were "improved" editions which generally used Dawlman's
expanded *The Poor Doubting Christian* as a copytext for the first
two-thirds of the book, and Crooke's *The Souls Effectual Calling*
for the last third. Transitional passages are rewritten, and the wording
of some sequences is altered, presumably in order to clarify Hooker's meaning, sometimes to the point of rationalizing his mixed
figurative language. For example, the sentence "This very word is
like a Milstone about my necke, to sinke my soule for ever,"[48]

---

[46] *The Poor Doubting Christian* (London, 1635), pp. 51–55, pp. 135–140; *The
Souls Effectual Calling*, pp. 557–559, 603f; *The Saints Cordials*, pp. 353, 362.

[47] Bush, op. cit., was the first to demonstrate that this composition of the
augmented text goes back to 1646, and did not originate with Thomas Prince, as
had been assumed by Shuffelton, op. cit.

[48] *The Saints Cordials*, p. 350. *The Poor Doubting Christian* (London, 1638),
p. 22.

is altered to read: "This very Word is like a Milstone about my Neck, and I in the Sea, ready to be sunke for ever." [49]

When Andrew Crooke brought out *The Souls Effectual Calling* in 1637, he was not only competing with Robert Dawlman, but also with Robert Young, still another printer who seems to have obtained notations of sermons by Hooker. In *The Souls Implantation*, Young published under the title "Spirituall Love and Joy," [50] as a sermon on Gal. 5:22, what was largely contained in Crooke's *The Souls Effectual Calling*[51] as the elaboration of the seventh doctrine set forth from its scripture, Jn. 6:45. Again, both printed versions have a somewhat different stylistic make-up, but follow basically the same outline. Crooke's text breaks off, however, at a point where "Spirituall Love and Joy" continues for forty-six more pages,[52] possibly two further sermons for which Crooke did not have notations. On the other hand, at the beginning of "Spirituall Love and Joy" there are references to earlier sermons which clearly allude to Jn. 6:45, the scriptural text for Crooke's *The Souls Effectual Calling*, and to sermons that were printed there[53] but not in any work that Young had published. What is more, although Gal. 5:22 is quoted as the scriptural text for "Spirituall Love and Joy," the sermon does not refer to it. The reader is simply told by the preacher at the start not to take the following "as if I would place sanctification before justification." [54] In Young's second edition of *The Souls Implantation* three years later,[55] these introductory remarks are missing. The sermon that had formerly been called "Spirituall Love and Joy" is now entitled "Spiritual Love." Another sermon, "Spiritual Joy," [56] is added, for which Heb. 3:17-18, is given as scriptural text. It is rather incompletely written out, and it seems possible that portions

---

[49] Hooker, *The Poor Doubting Christian* (London, 1684), pp. 14f; *The oor Doubting Christian* (Boston, 1743, [Thomas Prince, ed.]), p. 11.

[50] *The Souls Implantation* (London, 1637), pp. 155–266.

[51] *The Souls Effectual Calling*, pp. 202–282.

[52] *The Souls Implantation*, pp. 220–266.

[53] Ibid., p. 159: "for the Father learns us the lecture, and (as I told you before of the mind enlightened) kindles this holy fire."

[54] Ibid., p. 155. Similarly, though less amplified: *The Souls Effectual Calling*, p. 202.

[55] *The Souls Implantation* . . . *Carefully Corrected and much Enlarged* (London, 1640).

[56] Ibid., pp. 295–320.

of it come from notes of yet another sermon that may have been preached on Ps. 126:5.[57]

In 1637 Robert Young and Andrew Crooke again competed with variant texts of a Hooker sermon. "The Souls Ingrafting Into Christ," which Young printed in *The Souls Implantation*,[58] was also printed as a separate title by Crooke; and in this instance Young's text is about twice as long as Crooke's. It is more fully written out, either because it goes back to a more complete notation or because the redactor made better use of the notes supplied to him. Moreover, Crooke's text is frequently so condensed that it remains almost obscure; although occasionally the condensation can lend a peculiar metaphorical charge to a passage. When, for example, Young has:

> All this while the poor sinner is like the children of Israel travelling in the wildernesse, partly in the valley of teares, and partly in a vast wildernesse, . . .[59]

the Crooke text reads:

> All this while the Soule is like the children of Israel partly wandering in the valley of Teares, partly wildring in the desert of Humiliation.[60]

Because Crooke in most cases does not provide scriptural passages, but merely citations, it is difficult to grasp their connection with the text. When Hooker, for example, speaks of Christ's willingness to make the sinner unsure of God's mercy, Crooke has merely:

> It is just with him to estrange himselfe from that Soule, that he may labour from his former strength againe, Cant. 5.2 Psalm 30.6[61]

It is only in Young's text that we see the full meaning:

> It is just with him to estrange himselfe from that Soule, that so you may strive to receive that mercy and comfort which formerly you had, and now have sleighted. Thus he dealt with the Church in Cant. 5.2,3 when Christ knocked at the doore, and said, *Open to me, my sister,*

[57] Ibid., pp. 309ff.
[58] *The Souls Implantation* (London, 1637), pp. 81–153.
[59] Ibid., p. 85.
[60] *The Souls Ingrafting* (London, 1637), p. 2.
[61] Ibid., p. 21.

*my love, my dove, my undefiled; for my head is filled with dew,
and my lockes with the drops of the night:*

She made answer in this manner, *I have put off my coat, how shall I
put it on? I have washed my feet, how shall I defile them?* Now when
Christ withdrew himself, then she found her feet againe, and followed Christ with much labour from place to place, and could not
be content till she found him. And so it was with the holy Prophet,
I said in my prosperity, I shall never be removed: (Ps. 30:6) but when
he saw God going away from him: see how he bestirred himself:
(2 Sam. 22:7) *Oh*, saith he, *I cried to thee O Lord in the time of my
trouble.* Then he could pray, and hear again, and recount Gods former
goodness, and perform his former duties.[62]

Both versions also differ in their structural outlines. Crooke omits
Uses II-V, but he has the questions and answers which are a sequel
to Use V in Young, before Use I. Both texts agree again in Doctrine
II and its first reason, but in the second reason Crooke gives different
particulars and omits the following uses in order to provide an easy
transition to *The Souls Effectual Calling*, with which *The Souls
Ingrafting Into Christ* often was bound and sold under the title of
The Souls Vocation. For this reason it appears likely that the discrepancies between the two versions result from the exigencies of
the printer, although such discrepancies may also suggest two separate deliveries of the sermon.

As we have pointed out, a comparison of variant texts does not
yield an easy answer as to which should be preferred as being closest
to Hooker's meaning and to what he may actually have said at the
time of preaching. Considering the state of our knowledge, almost
any attempt at an answer is almost certain to raise new questions.
Too much depends upon the skill of the notator, the abilities of the
transcriber, the stylistic skill of the redactor who cast the sermon
notes into the proper written form, "and the willingness of the
printer to tender the author's reputation and the reader's benefit to
have the copy reveiwed and corrected," as Symmes has put it.[63]
Nevertheless, the complementary character of variant texts has to

---

[62] *The Souls Implantation*, pp. 130f.
[63] *The Christians Two Chief Lessons*, loc. cit.

be recognized, and through careful collation we can in some cases try to arrive at a new composite text, such as in Document VII. In any case it should be remembered that most of Hooker's early sermons had no variant texts, and that most depended upon a process of transmission similar to that which has herein been described.

DOCUMENT VIII

John Paget's XX Questions (Propositions) and Thomas Hooker's Answers; October, 1631

Introduction

Thomas Hooker had been invited by a large faction within the congregation of the English-speaking Reformed Church in Amsterdam to become the junior colleague of John Paget, who had been minister there since the organization of the congregation in 1607 (and would continue till his death in 1637). Paget's assistant, Thomas Potts, had died c. April 1631; and even before his impending death members of the congregation and the elders in particular had been on the lookout for an eventual successor. They had even tried to approach Hugh Peter, by now established as the minister of the English church in Rotterdam. Although both he and Potts had left England with nonconformist records, each served a turn as chaplain to the English garrison in Vlissingen.

John Paget was, for his part, eager to keep himself and his congregation in the good graces of the local authorities; and the congregation of which he had been so long the sole or senior minister was fully integrated into the Classis of the municipality of Amsterdam and hence also of the Synod of North Holland. Paget had even subscribed to the Belgic Confession and had stoutly resisted the effort of John Forbes, now of Delft, to organize the Synod of English-speaking churches, known more commonly as the English Congregational Classis, 1621-1635.[1] Paget's church, meeting in the former Catholic chapel of the Begijnhof,[2] was one of only two English-speaking congregations (the other in Utrecht) which had chosen

[1] See Raymond Phineas Stearns, *Congregationalism in the Dutch Netherlands: The Rise and Fall of the English Congregational Classis, 1621-1635* (Amsterdam, 1964).
[2] Alice Clare Carter, *The English Reformed Church in Amsterdam in the Seventeenth Century* (Amsterdam, 1964).

to be fully integrated into the state church of the host country. Paget's wariness with respect to various candidates for ministerial association with him and to Hooker in particular was prompted by an understandable desire to have his church considered by his colleagues who sat with him in the municipal Classis, as in no way different from their own congregations except for the difference in the language of worship. Paget's uneasiness was due to his fear of Independency. Both Peter and Hooker had a reputation for Independency, and after them (in 1634) John Davenport. Paget was, moreover, aware of the tendency toward Independency on the part of many members of his congregation who had come over from the local separatist "conventicles," notably the Brownists (from the Ancient Church of Henry Ainsworth, d. 1622).[3] The very man who wrote to Hooker in Chelmsford to come to Amsterdam, Stephen Offwood, who would later print a volume by William Ames with a preface (our Document X) by Hooker, was, as it happened, a convert from Brownist separatism; and his wife continued to attend upon the Brownist services.[4]

Hooker, for his part, ever since receiving the letter of invitation from Offwood, had insisted upon a proper call, by which he meant, no doubt, the duly formulated call of the whole congregation in concert with its sole minister. Arriving in the Netherlands in June, 1631,[5] Hooker stayed with Hugh Peter in Rotterdam, preaching both there and in the Begijnhof church in Amsterdam. On July 2 the consistory of the Begijnhof congregation, made up of the minister and three annually elected elders (occasionally assisted by the deacons), extended to Hooker a formal call.[6] Hooker preached in Amsterdam, but as the arrangements for his state salary were not completed, and he needed specialized medical help, Hooker went to The

[3] By his preaching Paget had drawn over many ex-Brownists, the most active group in his church. Carter, *op. cit.*, p. 59.

[4] Keith Sprunger, "The Dutch Career of Thomas Hooker," *The New England Quarterly*, XLVI (1973), p. 20.

[5] The basis of the dating is a summary of events related to Hooker in the Register of the Begijnhof English Church, vol. 3 (1628–1700) in the Gemeente Archief, Amsterdam. Mrs. Carter prints the relevant extract, dated November 1631, *op cit.*, p. 192; but she incorrectly read "in Junij" as "in January." See Sprunger, "The Dutch Career of Thomas Hooker," *loc. cit.*, n. 5.

[6] *Ibid.*, p. 21.

Hague.[7] While there, two elders of the Amsterdam church were dispatched with a gratuity for his past services among them and with an invitation to return to Amsterdam that they "might have a more perfect trial of his gift." After Hooker complied and to their satisfaction the consistory proceeded to elect him as the second minister.

It was at this point that the senior minister insisted on having his own lingering doubts about the call responded to by Hooker. Paget, whose salary came in part from the municipality and whose clerical status in the municipal Classis depended upon his abiding faithfully by the standards of the state church, deemed it appropriate to interrogate his prospective new associate, who had been pressed upon him by a large faction in the congregation working through the lay elders of the consistory. He accordingly asked his fellow members of the consistory to permit him to put questions to Hooker in a session of the consistory. But the consistory disclaimed competence, arguing, somewhat disingenuously, that such an inquiry into faith and polity lay with the municipal Classis. Whereupon Paget proceeded to act on his own and extracted from Hooker a promise that he would comply as one cleric to another. Hooker requested that Paget put his questions into writing. Paget wrote out twenty questions on the current issues, indicating his own agreement or disagreement with the propositions or queries with an *affirmatur* or a *negatur;* and he requested of Hooker that he write out his answers in four copies.[8] The lay elders, perceiving that the proceeding would 'breed dissensions" and prudently hoping to keep the matter from getting to the municipal Classis so that they could promote Hooker's candidacy at a more oppportune moment, in vain tried to persuade Paget to release Hooker from the promise to write out his answers, some of which they rightly recognized would jeopardize his position and theirs with the municipal and classical authorities.[9]

Paget brought out *The Answers to the XX Questions,* translated into Latin, to the Classis, where Hooker was predictably found insufficiently in accord with Dutch Reformed usage in faith and polity to be confirmed as the second minister in the English-speaking

---

[7] *Ibid.,* p. 21.
[8] Document VIII at n. 54.
[9] Sprunger, *op. cit.,* pp. 23f.

congregation of the state church. From Delft John Forbes made assertive inquires with the Amsterdam Classis in defense of Hooker. As Hooker wrote out his answers he became increasingly clear about where he differed with Paget,[10] and by the time he had come to answer the last questions, he acknowledged seeing "the opportunity to depart." Although Hooker remained for a time in Amsterdam, while his angered supporters sought to assert congregational authority against the municipal Classis, he declined an invitation to preach again; and in November, 1631,[11] he left Delft to become the associate of Forbes and as such also a member of the large consultative (rather than authoritative) English Synod or Classis.

Of the four copies of the *Answers* Hooker wrote out, two seventeenth-century transcriptions survive. (A fifth copy, a transcription, was also at the time sent to John Davenport in London.) [12] One of the four primary copies was transcribed in the William Boswell Papers (B). It was printed in part by Champlin Burrage (1912) and complete by Raymond P. Stearns, *Congregationalism in the Dutch Netherlands* (Chicago, 1940), appendix viii, pp. 105-113. Another copy was transcribed into the Register of the Begijnhof Church Consistory at the time of the controversy (R). The Register was not accessible to Burrage or Stearns. It was printed by Alice Clare Carter, *The English Reformed Church in Amsterdam in the Seventeenth Century* (Amsterdam, 1964). These two versions (B and R) going back to two different copies of the original four from the hand of Hooker are in a sense equally valid. As he copied what he had first written out, the spirited controversialist could not wholly restrain himself from making editorial changes. There are also slight

---

[10] John Paget in *An Answer to the Unjust Complaints of William Best* (Amsterdam, 1635) later characterizes the "congregationalism or Independency" of Hooker as drawn from his *Answers*. Paget's key section from Hooker is quoted by Sprunger, *op. cit.*, p. 29.

[11] Sprunger, *op. cit.*, p. 34. He freely calls the majority of the Begijnhof church "Hookerites," who not only desired Hooker as their co-minister but also became quite clear about the right to congregational decision-making. Although Hooker himself, while tarrying in Amsterdam, could not take an active part in the debate, he must have further refined his congregational ecclesiology in the light of the acrimonious controversy in his behalf.

[12] When polity was later intensively under discussion in London in 1633 among John Cotton, John Davenport, Thomas Goodwin, and Philip Nye, Hooker's *Twenty Answers* must have been very influential.

changes imported into the original in the two seventeenth-century transcriptions and again into the two twentieth-century decipherments and printings thereof. Mrs. Carter's printing of R includes in italics in parentheses the most important variations from B, which occasionally correct Stearns' reading and printing of B.

The text of our Document VIII is intended to render Hooker as fully as possible. It is a composite of R and B with R as basic, although where the transcriber B occasionally seems to have preserved Hooker more faithfully than R, then the reading of R is given only in the notes. Where B has something in addition to R, this is included in our text in parentheses, which punctuational marks therefore throughout the Document *exclusively* signalize the presence of B. Where B has less than R, this is merely recorded in the notes, if at all notable. Where the difference between R and B differ in a phrasing of several words or more, the two versions are printed in parallel columns, each having equal validity as coming ultimately from Hooker himself.

The Questions and Answers deal with the problem of the local separatists (1-3), of set prayers (4-5), of baptism of the progeny of non-members (6), of worship and sermons therefor on days other than the Sabbath (7), of unordained readers (8), of the authority of the elders apart from the whole congregation to determine discipline and membership (9-10), of the relative power of the congregation and the Classis in deciding on congregational controversies, censure, and excommunication (12-16), of the relative authority of ministers and private members in the interpretation of Scripture (17), of the relative power of public authority and congregational or intra-congregational disposition to engage in fasts, prayers, and other religious exercises (18), and justification and sanctification (19-20).

However, abstracting from the details and their immediate context in Amsterdam, we may characterize Hooker's *ad hoc* and gropingly imperfect formulation as a crucial and, indeed, even formative document in the evolution of the ecclesiology and polity to be known in recent scholarship as Non-Separating Congregationalism, but known in the seventeenth century as Independency, which many within and without the movement were not at all times able to distinguish from conventicular or separatist congregationalism (of both the pedobaptist and the believers' baptist basis for belonging to a church). Neither Paget nor Hooker, though they had been episcopally ordained, acknowledged a scripturally sanctioned distinction of a threefold ministry as in the Established Church of England: deacons, presbyter-priests, and bishops. They instead recognized deacons (deaconesses), lay elders, and clerical elders (seldom called presbyters; most commonly called ministers or pastors), as the principal functionaries of the church or congregation. In addition, they had from the New Testament evangelists, readers, and prophets. The last had been construed by John Calvin as teachers in his theory of a fourfold ministry (deacons; teachers; and elders, lay and clerical, the latter being pastors); and, accordingly, Hooker and Paget, too, used the term teacher, sometimes with special reference to the second or assistant minister. But nomenclature was not fixed.

There were three fundamental points of ecclesiology and polity at issue between Paget and Hooker. Both understood that some elders (presbyters) were elected laymen for a term, others were clerics for life. The lay elders were elected by the congregation. (1) Were the clerical elders (presbyters) also creations of the congregation? Hooker at the time was not prepared to go so far. But that the congregation should extend the call to a prospective minister had for him become basic. (2) Paget, sitting in the Amsterdam Classis of fellow divines, held with the Dutch Reformed Church and with Presbyterian polity in general that other congregations and other ministers through the deliberations and enactments of a classis (presbytery) or a synod could confirm or overturn the disciplinary and other decisions of a local congregation and its minister(s). (3) Paget was also much less open than Hooker to the spontaneous activities of lay preachers or evangelists, gathered in conventicles. As Amsterdam was filled with English separatists of various kinds and as the Begijnhof Church had within it a number of former separatists, Paget was very wary of countenancing fissiparous tendencies.

Interrelated though most of the twenty Questions are, the details are best taken up in the annotations on Hooker's Answers.

DOCUMENT VIII

John Paget's XX Questions[1] (Propositions)[2] and Thomas Hooker's Answers; October, 1631

Q. 1 Whether it is lawful[3] for any[4] to resort unto the public meetings[5] of the Brownists,[6] and to communicate with them in the worship[7] of God? *Negatur.*[8]

[1] Mrs. Carter calls them Questions.

[2] Stearns calls them Propositions.

[3] The term *lawful* involves for both Paget and Hooker the law of England and the law of the municipality of Amsterdam in the Province of Holland. But for both men the primary concern is with the order of the Church of England. Yet herein lay precisely the problem: whether the Canons of 1604, which had not been approved by Parliament; whether the bishop of London; whether episcopal, presbyterian, or congregational, or even separatist congregational government of English Christianity should prevail.

[4] Many members of the Begijnhof English Reformed Church had been members of the Ancient Church of Henry Ainsworth, like Stephen Offwood. Mrs. Offwood kept up her old connections.

[5] R has *meeting*. Although the attraction to the Ancient Church was no doubt the strongest, Paget was almost certainly casting his question in general terms. He also, by calling the separatists' gatherings public meetings, intentionally eschewed *churches*. There were in Amsterdam three different separatist conventicles or churches, the Ancient Church going back to Francis Johnson (d. 1618), that of John Smyth (d. 1612), and that of John Robinson (d. 1625), which well before the arrival of Hooker had removed to Leiden, whence to new Plymouth (1620).

[6] *Brownists*, a common designation at the time for separatist congregationalists, took their name from Robert Browne (c. 1550–1633). A relation of William Cecil, Lord Burleigh, a graduate of Corpus Christi College, Cambridge, where he came under the influence of Thomas Cartwright, Browne eventually organized separatist congregations in Norwich and elsewhere. Imprisoned but then freed through the intervention of Cecil, Browne betook himself to Middelburg with his Norwich flock. There he wrote *A Book which sheweth the Life and Manner of all True Christians* (Middelburg, 1582) and *A Treatise of Reformation without Tarrying for Any* (ibid., 1582). Browne submitted to the Church of England in 1584.

Hence the separatists in Amsterdam might better have been called Barrowists. Henry Barrow (c. 1550–1593), a lawyer identified himself with John Greenwood, and gave his name to that kind of pedopaptist separatism, in which the elders held a certain preeminence above the congregation. The Ancient Church of Johnson, Ainsworth, and, after a period without a ministry, of John Canne in Amsterdam, was Barrowist in that it did regard the elders, lay and clerical,

A. 1 To separate from the faithful assemblies[9] and churches in England as no true[10] churches is an error in judgment, and a sin in practice, held and maintained by the Brownists, and therefore to communicate with them, either in their opinion or practice, is sinful and utterly unlawful. But for a Christian renouncing both their opinion and practice, to hear amongst them occasionally and to communicate with them in that part[11] of God's worship[12]—which I conceive to be the meaning of the first query—is not, so far as I can yet see simply unlawful, but may prove occasionally offensive, if either by going, we shall encourage them to go in their course of separation or else by our unwise expressions might seem to weak ones to like of it ourselves, and so to draw them to a further approbation to

---

as having authority in the congregation. In that intra-ecclesial sense the Barrowists were presbyterian, whereas Brownists were wholly congregational. But both Barrowists and Brownists were one in refusing to acknowledge the authority of any other congregation or eldership therein or any presbytery or classis made up of the elders from several congregations in a region. John Smyth's General Baptists and Particular (fully Calvinist with respect to the decrees of election and reprobation) Baptists were also congregational in the Barrowist sense. And all three kinds of congregationalist (Baptist, Brownists, Barrowists) were separatists in contrast to the true Independents (Non-Separating Congregationalists), whose congregations were indeed independent of each other and therefore acknowledging only advisory or consultative synods or classes but whose sense of unity among the congregations of the Church of England was in a sense secured in the unity of a reformed magistry. In the end, failing of making England Independent, the Independents felt that they could achieve their goal best in New England.

Hooker, in pondering discreet answers to the essentially Presbyterian Paget, is groping for a Congregationalism different from that of Baptist, Brownist, Barrowist congregationalism.

[7] B has: *Word*.

[8] At the end of each of his Questions Paget indicates in Latin whether the specific proposition is by him denied or affirmed.

[9] It is to be observed that Hooker, coming to Amsterdam from Chelmsford, where he had indeed participated in and indeed led gatherings for prophesying, i.e. preaching, and also, it would appear, for irregular communions, is careful to enlarge Paget's *public meetings* into *faithful assemblies* in order that he may speak accurately about his own understanding of what he regards as true churches in England.

[10] B omits *true*.

[11] R has: *the part*. But it would appear that B is correct. Hooker, aware of the triple sense of *communicate* (converse with, consort with at worship of the Word, commune with in the Lord's Supper), seems to be suggesting that aspects of worship, namely, a preaching service but not communion, may be occasionally participated in.

[12] B has: *Word*.

that way than was (before)[13] meet. Whereupon it follows, if we give those occasions of offense we sin, if we do not abstain; but, if these occasions of offense may be removed by our constant renouncing of their course on the one side, and by our free and open expression of our intents, on[14] the other side; if we go only to hear some savory point opened, and to benefit by the gift of some able minister, that may come amongst them; if, I say, the giving of any just offence by this or any other means may be avoided,—I conceive then it is not a sin to hear there,[15] occasionally. And that some even[16] may prevent such occasions, it is to me a very disputable question, not having ever studied this point before.

Q. 2. Whether those members (of the Church)[17] who sometimes hear them and stiffly maintain a liberty therein are to be tolerated or rather censured. Censured.

A. 2 The practice of members according to the former caution and interpretation, being taken up and maintained though stiffly, with[18] argument, because it is but questionable and disputable before they be convinced of their sin, they [the members of Begijnhof] ought rather to be tolerated than censured; and this moderation in things which are disputable and not yet absolutely necessary unto salvation the Apostle enjoins (Rom. 14: 12 f.). And here must be remembered[19] also [that] the same degree of pains for convincing is not so sufficient in one disposition as in another.

Q. 3 Whether such of Brownists as have not renounced their separation from the Church of England nor yet allow communion with the public state thereof may lawfully be received for members of our Church. *Negatur.*

[13] We draw attention to the first of frequent instances where in parentheses we include what B has more than R.

[14] R has: *of.*

[15] B has: *them.*

[16] B has: *men.* Since Hooker in and around Essex was well acquainted with special meetings for Puritan prophesying, he is truly baffled that Puritan Paget would have become so much a part of the Dutch Reformed establishment that he would be troubled about occasional visits on the part of the Begijnhof congregation to hear good preaching at other English-speaking gatherings in Amsterdam.

[17] i.e., the Begijnhof English-speaking Reformed Church of Amsterdam.

[18] B has: *which.*

[19] B has: *here also remember.* R gives a faulty reference to Heb., not Rom.

A. 3 The not renouncing of separation from the faithful assemblies in England and the not allowing of communion with the public state of the Church of England, this mere opinion can in no wise make a man unfit to be received a member of this [Begijnhof] congregation, unless we say that such a man, being in his judgment and life otherwise altogether unblameable, is not a (visible Christian), which is a more (rigid) censure than the wisest of the separation could give way unto in a proportionable time.[20] As[21] I suppose a pious heart will not dare to affirm, and if in the judgment of charity he may be accounted a member of Christ and so a saint, by the same reasonable[22] charity he may be accounted fit to be a member of a congregation, I Cor. 1:2.[23] Besides, to judge a man unfit to be received a member for an erroneous opinion or practice (in such a kind), not yet through weakness,[24] is to confirm the Brownists in that insupportable and absurd censure, which now they maintain touching those who hold the churches in England[25] to be true churches and profess they will occasionally communicate therein. For it is easy for them [the Brownists] to infer thus if we think them unfit to be members of a true church, because they[26] hold against the Church of England. It's equal, will they say, that they should think these [us] unfit matter for a true church, who hold against them for the Church of England, since they judge the Church to be as bad as any can judge their cause and separation[27] to be. So I judge of this third query.

Q. 4 Whether it be lawful for ministers to use set forms of prayer

---

[20] B has: kinde.

[21] B has: And.

[22] B omits.

[23] I Cor. 1:2: "To the church of God which is at Corinth, to those sanctified in Christ, called to be saints together."

[24] B omits: not yet through weakness, but has instead: in such a kind. The two imprecise phrases are really alternate ways in which Hooker said the same thing: Somebody who continues to hear sermons occasionally at the Ancient Church may be received as a member of the Begijnhof Church, since it is not weakness that makes him wish to hear a good sermon occasionally in his own quarter of town.

[25] R has: Church of England.

[26] B inserts here: who.

[27] B has only: theirs.

and to read them out of a book in the public worship[28] of God? *Affirmatur*.

A. 4 [R] This nothing concerns this church in that there is no such use prescribed, unless men seek and would fain find differences of opinion.

[B] But since there is no use of it in this church, why it should be questioned I see not, unless men desire to find differences of opinion.

Secondly,[29] I say some set form of prayer may be used and read out of a book by a minister, if he do it in a right reason, in a right measure, and after a right manner. So I affirm.

Q. 5 Whether in the conclusion of other prayers you be content to use the Lord's Prayer before or after sermon. *Affirmatur*.[30]

A. 5 The Lord's Prayer may be used, and as occasion serves, I will use it; but it is confessed by all men[31] that it's lawful at several times not to use it when we pray; and therefore I will take my own liberty as I see fit; the Commissaries in England[32] are contented with so much, and the most of the best ministers do no more, so I affirm.

Q. 6 Whether[33] infants whose parents are not members of the Church may lawfully be baptised according to the manner of these Reformed Churches. *Affirmatur*.

A. 6 The manner how these churches do baptize children, whose parents are of no church, nor yet resolved to join any, I do not now[34] by experience know nor in this short time can tell how to learn fully in all the particular circumstances thereof. Yet if it be such as I understand by relation, I judge it unlawful for me to follow

---

[28] B has: *word*.

[29] Except for the first three words of this sentence, B has the same as R.

[30] R omits.

[31] B has: *on all hands*.

[32] Agents of the Court of High Commission.

[33] Paget's question on the baptism of infants touches upon the essence of a territorial as distinguished from a gathered church. Puritans did not like the medieval Catholic and the continuing Anglican practice of having sponsors or godparents to vouch for the faith and nurture of the infant baptized. At the same time Hooker was opposed to Anabaptist and Baptist insistence on believers' baptism. The compromise between a territorial and a gathered church would find expression in the Congregational Puritan insistance that only the children of members might be baptized. But in the following Answer, Hooker is not wholly clear.

[34] R has: *noe;* B omits. It could be: *not,* and hence a mistaken double negative.

leaving the churches to their own judgment. So I conceive[35] of this sixth query.

Q. 7 Whether it be lawful to preach as at Christmastide, Easter, Whitsuntide, as is used in these countries.[36] *Affirmatur.*

A. 7 [R] To[37] choose a text for the sermon of the day, after the same manner as upon the Lord's Day, to proceed in public worship without any manifest difference, this is unlawful; but a minister protesting publicly against all superstition and popish holiness placed in the day, teaching also the liberty that people have to labor and to do their six days ordinary work of their calling without giving any just scandal upon any of these days which are not Sabbaths, with these cautions and expressions I judge it lawful then to preach. This then to the seventh query.

[B] A minister publicly professing against all superstition and popish holiness that is placed in days, and as instructing the people teaching also the liberty that people hath to labor and do their ordinary works of their calling without scandal upon any of these days, which are not Sabbaths, with these cautions and expressions I judge it lawful then to preach.

Q. 8 Whether it be lawful to use a reader in [*sic*] publicly in the church which is no minister. *Affirmatur.*

A. 8 It is lawful to use a reader publicly in the church who is no minister. *Affirmo.*

Q. 9. Whether[38] common and ordinary offences are to be judged

---

[35] R has: *affirm;* but it would appear that B has the better reading in that Hooker is groping in his Answer and has said that, so far as he has understood the situation in Amsterdam, he considers it "unlawful" to leave so important a matter to the individual churches.

[36] In 1578 Amsterdam changed over (*Alteratie*) in accepting Calvinism as the official religion and in support of William I the Silent, Prince of Orange, Count of Nassau (assassinated, 1584). The bulk of the municipal population remained, however, Catholic; and the tolerant municipal government did not interfere with the observance of traditional religion in moderation.

[37] R, longer at this point than B, still does not make Hooker's point as clearly as it might. He does not object to having an extra day for preaching now and then, but he wants the reformed and the old way of observing the day to be marked by non-traditional sermon texts, if necessary, to manifest difference.

[38] The question as stated is the issue between Brownism and Barrowism. See above, n. 6. But Paget is also thinking of the congregational eldership (the consistory, the church session) and its relation to the territorial eldership (classis, presbytery). Hooker proceeds, however, to answer wholly in the context of the Brownist-Barrowist debate.

and determined by authority of the eldership without public cognition of the church. *Affirmatur.*

A. 9 This and the next query are of so general expression that they may not admit of an answer in a large manner suitable to the word in general. Though happily[39] it will not afford a satisfactory explication[40] thereof, but because it's only to be expected that any answer should be no otherwise expressed than the question is propounded, it shall suffice, then, to answer: *Affirmo.*[41]

Some controversies, common and ordinary offences, may be judged and determined by the eldership without the public cognition of the church.

[R] So[42] offences common and ordinary in their own nature yet in some cases, and accompanied with some occurrences, which may fall out, cannot be decided without the public cognition of the church.

[B] Some offences, common and ordinary in some cases, which may fall out,[43] cannot be decided without public cognition.

Q. 10 Whether it be lawful to receive any as members into the church, without public examination of them before the whole congregation? *Affirmatur.*

A. 10 The question admits of a like answer with the former. Some members may be received without public examination and yet the case may so fall out that some cannot without public examination.

[R] Thus in general to general queries. For it is endless to bring in all answers.

[B] If they had more particularly propounded, they should have so been answered.

Q. 11 Whether a particular congregation hath[44] power to call a minister, without the approbation of the Classis under which they stand. *Negatur.*

A. 11 Before I answer this query I would ask one thing, which

---

[39] i.e., *perhaps.*
[40] B has: *explanation.*
[41] B has: *to affirm.*
[42] Hooker or the transcriber failed to complete: *some.*
[43] Hooker or the transcriber of B clearly let a phrasing fall; R is the valid reading.
[44] B has: *have.*

may[45] give a little light to that which shall be said afterwards, namely, how the first Classis that ever was upon the face of the earth came to be constituted. And I presume[46] it cannot, nor will be denied but that it was made up by the combination of several ministers and elders, yea of several congregations? Whence it must needs follow that their particular congregations had power from Christ for to call (a minister) and so did by that, their power, choose and call their ministers fully and completely before there was a Classis, and therefore had their power not derived from a Classis, or by it, but from the direct ordinance and appointment of Christ, which power they may not give away and none can take it away, it being a legacy left them by the Lord Jesus,[47] as Dr. [William] Ames disputes and determines in his fourth book of his *Cases of Conscience*, p. 165.[48]

Touching this query,[49] then, my opinion is this, a particular congregation[50] hath complete power by Christ's institution to give a complete call unto a minister without any derived power from a Classis.[51] They who had complete and perfect ministers before any Classis had power to call them fully without any Classis.[52] But particular congregations had perfect and complete ministers or minister, i.e. perfectly and completely called before any Classis. *Ergo:* [I hold] that, if by mutual consent the congregation hath freely combined itself with the Classis, they shall do[53] piously and

[45] B has: *might*.
[46] B has: *conceive*.
[47] Hooker has throughout eschewed making a distinction between the elective eldership of the congregation and the congregation as a whole.
[48] *De Conscientia, eius jure et casibus* (Amsterdam, 1630); translated as *Conscience with the Power and Cases thereof* (London, 1643).
[49] Hooker now touches upon the central issue between himself and Paget. Hooker is saying that, though the Begijnhof congregation through its elders (consistory), of whom Paget is one, may consult the Classis, since they have freely entered into a relationship with it, the congregation, desiring Hooker to be the second pastor, is not bound by the judgment of the Classis.
[50] Again, Hooker thinks of all the members and not preeminently of the elders (lay and clerical).
[51] In effect, Hooker repudiates the constitution of the Begijnhof Church as an English parish of the state church of the province of Holland.
[52] Actually, the granting of the Begijnhof chapel to the English congregation and the establishment of Paget as minister of the English Reformed Church lodged there were concurrent.
[53] B has: *do*.

expediently: freely to crave the approbation of the Classis, that they may be more confirmed or, if doubts should arise, better directed in their course, always provided that, if the Classis should not approve, they may lawfully and without sin choose without or against the approbation of the Classis if they saw good reason, by the convenient fitness of the party to induce them thereunto. And so I judge of the eleventh query.

Q. 12 Whether Classis and Synod have authority, not only of administering and counselling but also of judging and deciding, the contoversies of particular congregations. *Affirmatur.*

Q. 13 Whether it be lawful for a particular congregation to excommunicate any offender whom they judge to be obstinate either without or against the judgment of the Classis under which they resort? *Negatur.*

Q. 14 Whether [1] there be any superior ecclesiastical power to censure or judge either a whole congregation, or the greater part thereof, erring in matter of faith and religion, or whether [2] in such a case, after admonition, their souls are to be left to the immediate judgment of Christ and their bodies to the sword and power of the civil magistrates. *Prima pars affirmatur; secunda pars negatur.*

A. 14 These three queries [12–14] desire a large explication, if they should be clearly and fully opened, without exception, which if I should do, my answers would grow too tedious for me to write four copies of[54] in this short time, and maybe for thee[55] and the brethren to read. Therefore, shortly and plainly thus: In all of them I concur with the judgment of Doctor Ames [in] the 4th book of his *Cases of Conscience*, pages 179–180; of Mr. [Robert] Parker, the 3rd book of his *Ecclesiastical Polity*, in several passages of sundry chapters between the (2nd) and 14th;[56] of Mr. [Paul] Baynes' *Diocesans Tryall*, page 13; conclusion 4, page 21.[57] Wherein how far they differ from you I doubt not but you fully know. And this

---

[54] B omits *four copies of.*
[55] R has: *they;* B has: *you.*
[56] *De politeia ecclesiastica Christi, et hierarchica opposita* (Frankfurt, 1616).
[57] *The Diocesans Tryall* (London, 1621).

I suppose may (serve or) suffice for the present. Yet if you desire more particular expression, give me notice and time, I shall give more explications.[58]

Q. 15 Whether [1] the church hath any authority[59] over him who, being privy to himself of any crime, doth therefore of his own accord depart from the communion of the church and holy things lest he should be cut off and whether [2] such a one is to be left to the civil magistrates and to other who have obtained power over him, by nature or law. 1. *Affirmatur;* 2. *negatur.*

A. 15 The scope of this query I do not fully understand and therefore happily[60] shall not give that perfect satisfaction thereunto, but[61] express what I perceive. The difficulty as far as I can guess lies in these words: [1] "being privy to himself" departs;[62] [2] "of his own accord." For they seem to me to imply a fault which the church neither did nor could take notice of, and therefore did not or could not proceed against him. If now he depart from the church, his own heart moving him thereto firstly, and after [he] got[63] consent also from the congregation that he might so do by joining[64] [as] a member of another church—if then his fault should be found out, I conceive the church from whence he came, having dismissed him and not then knowing any offence against him, cannot now proceed to lay any censure. The church hath power only over[65] those who are members of the church. Besides, to what purpose[66] should the church which he hath left excommunicate him, when the church wherein he is a member ought to do it and maybe will? Therefore, to them he is brought[67] for ecclesiastical censure and to the magistrates for his corporal punishment if his fault so deserve. But, if he shall wilfully depart and not upon good grounds and join himself either to no assembly or to a false one, and by the church's

---

[58] B has: *upon notice shall have it.*
[59] B has: *power or jurisdiction.*
[60] i.e., *perchance.*
[61] R has: *to.*
[62] R has: *to despatch.*
[63] R has: *yet.*
[64] B has: *becoming.*
[65] R has: *other;* B has: *of.*
[66] R has: *project.*
[67] B has: *lost.*

authority is not evacuated by such a departure[68] and therefore they[69] proceed with him, according to order by Christ prescribed [Mt. 18:15–17], and so either reform him or censure him as such a fault and the expression of his impenitence shall deserve.

Q. 16 Whether suspension from the Supper of the Lord may lawfully be used in some cases, as a lesser excommunication.[70] *Affirmatur*.

A. 16 Suspension[71] from the Supper of the Lord may lawfully be used in some cases as a lesser excommunication. So I affirm.

Q. 17 Whether[72] it be lawful for private members of the church to interpret the Holy Scriptures, at such set days and places, where sundry members of divers families do ordinarily assemble themselves together. *Negatur*.

A. 17 The[73] answer to this query depends upon the explication[74] of two things. 1. What it is to interpret Scripture. 2. Upon what grounds it may be done.

1. To interpret Scripture is to judge aright of the sense and meaning of the words and thereafter to express our judgment to others and to cause them[75] to understand.

2. This may be done from a double ground partly *ex officio*, from place of authority, which is conferred upon us by the church and

---

[68] B has: *by such dealing*.

[69] The sentence at this point would read better: "But, if . . . departure, they therefor may proceed with him . . ."

[70] In canon law a distinction was drawn between the lesser and the greater ban: between exclusion from communion without exclusion from divine service and banishment or at least shunning. The greater ban involved action by the magistracy.

[71] Suspension from communion would not exclude from the divine service. Indeed, every effort was expected of the suspended member to rectify his behavior or opinion to qualify himself for readmission to communion.

[72] In the scriptural background of this question is the *lex sedentium* of I Cor. 14:23 ff., which is the sanction for lay participation in interpreting Scripture in a duly constituted assembly for study and worship.

[73] Hooker is at pains to give a careful answer. He is confident that ministers are vouchsafed special grace to instruct magistrates scripturally as to their Christian duties. See Document X, at n. 154. At the same time, he is aware that unlicensed and sometimes unordained preachers participated in "faithful assemblies" outside the parochial structure and Prayer Book regulations.

[74] B has: *explanation*.

[75] R has only: *and cause men*.

by which we have commission thus to do[76] as teachers appointed by
the church, partly this action[77] may arise *ex dono*, from the gift,
that Christ [cf. I Cor. 12:12–31] doth dispense to several members
according to the measure, and the place they hold in the body. This
Dr. Ames in his fourth book of *Cases of Conscience*, cap. 25, page 162,
disputes and concludes, page 162, (both) by Scripture and reason
that it was the lawful practice of (all able) Christians indifferently
upon occasions to teach

[R] and to interpret—his word is— *preach* the gospel, as it appears by Acts 4 at 11; 19 at 18 and 24.	[B] in a right sense to preach the gospel in all places privately as opportunity and expedience served, to which purpose he judiciously allegeth Acts 3:14 + 11:19 + 18:24.[78]

So this being a duty founded in Christianity, as there he shows,
there needs no public approbation of the church to call, thereunto,
as the church doth[79] to call her officers, but only direction and
information by the minister of the Word and private advice, as
occasion serves, to teach men [lay exhorters] not to go beyond their
gift. But, as they may lawfully do it, so they must look in their
particular practice to the expediency thereof.[80] Much less needs
there any public officer to be set over them or to go along with them
to moderate the action (in this kind). But if there be any miscarriage
in this, as in any other Christian practice,[81] as others shall observe it
who are present, or as others of the church shall understand it, they
are to deal with them according to the rule of discipline [Mt. 18:
15–17]. Briefly, then, if it be a Christian duty thus allowed by
Scripture and practised by the saints to interpret the gospel unto
all, as opportunity calls or invites,[82] occasionally thereunto, the same

---

[76] B has: *interpret.*

[77] B has: *course of interpretation.*

[78] The reference to Ames is to the Amsterdam 1630, esp. headings 1–3 of
answer to Question 1. The scriptural references of R are more accurate than B.

[79] B has: *useth.*

[80] B has: *practices that they do it expediently.*

[81] For what follows R has: *as others shall observe it, which one present, as
others;* B has: *as any shall observe it who are present or others.* For the end of
the sentence B has: *brotherly according to the rule set down by Christ for the
reformation of sin.*

[82] B has: *serves.*

Christians, still keeping the proportion of their gift, not crossing their places, employment, and finding[83] other expedients for the action, they may at set times and in set places do it ordinarily. Being an ordinary duty of all Christians, their[84] gifts, opportunities, and expediencies serve. If any other distempers accompany the persons as

[R] if they contemn the public min-istry, if they violate discipline, if they break the rule of the apostle Jude, v. 4,[85]

[B] if they unlawfully join with any who are counted wandering stars by Jude and break any rule of direction there delivered,

if wives demean themselves disobediently and unwarrantably to[86] their husbands, if (lastly) any dissemble or color over their courses —these, I say, and the like failings issue from the folly of men's minds and corruption of men's hearts but are not caused by the (practice of this) duty,[87] the cautions of expedience, order, and such like being attended therein.

Q. 18 Whether in a Reformed Church[88] it be lawful for ministers and people of divers families without public authority to set apart occasionally days of fasting and humiliation wherein they may meet (together) for religious exercises and signify the same unto ministers and some families of other particular congregations that they may do the same in like manner.[89] *Negatur.*

A. 18 [R] For[90] ministers thus to meet upon extraordinary occasions to their extraordinary duties it is not only lawful but in some Reformed Churches necessary. Nor need we to

[B] For ministers so to meet as is specified their ordinary particular oc-casions pressing thereunto or extra-ordinary necessities of the church calling them to fasting and prayer,

[83] R has: *providing.* Hooker has a strong sense of calling in both church and society. Cf. his Answer 7.

[84] B has: *as the.*

[85] "For admission has been secretly gained by some who long ago were designated for this condemnation, ungodly persons who pervert the grace of our God unto licentiousness and deny our only Master and Lord, Jesus Christ."

[86] B has: *disobediently demean themselves towards.*

[87] The long sentence of "ifs" comes to an important conclusion ill formulated. Hooker is saying that all these admittedly unsatisfactory actions or attitudes are not the consequence of the cautions and discreet fulfilment of a lay *duty*.

[88] Paget seems to have in mind the special status of the Begijnhof Church as an English parish of the municipal Reformed Church of Amsterdam.

[89] B has: *that they in like manner may do the same.*

[90] Hooker in both versions seems to be including under "religious exercises" not only fasting but also the Lord's Supper, without leave of the magistrates.

expect public authority should join, this being a private Christian duty, no more than we should look [to it] that magistrates should make a law to press Christians to take up the private communion of saints before they [the faithful] should dare to address themselves to the practice thereof.

such meetings I say are not only lawful but necessary in some churches. Nor is it needful that we should expect that public authority should enjoin this Christian private duty, no more than we should look that the magistrates should make a law to press Christians to the communion of saints before they should dare to address themselves thereunto.[91]

Q. 19 Whether[92] true repentance or any saving work[93] go before true faith in those that are regenerate? *Negatur.*

A. 19 There is a double repentance.[94] The first is of preparation, wrought by the almighty and irresistible power of the Spirit, causing the sinner to go out of himself (and sin) in humiliation before he can go to

[R] Christ by believing in the work of vocation; and this goes in order of nature before faith and in the true work of it cannot be the reprobates. And it's nothing, as I apprehend, but the stroke of the Spirit in the conversion of a sinner under which the soul hath itself passive, as one divine useth to speak. This is a repentance in sanctification, the word here strictly taken; and that comes after faith. So I affirm; so also Mr. [John] Rogers in his treatise[95] of the nature of firm faith.

[B] God in Christ by faith in vocation; and this goes before faith and I conceive it to be nothing but the stroke of the Spirit in the very first work of conversion wherein the soul make itself merely passive as our divines used to speak, and in the true nature of it, cannot be in any reprobate. Second, there is a repentance in sanctification, that word being strictly so taken; and it comes after faith. So Mr. Rogers of Dedham in his treatise; so Mr. Chibal [Sibbald][96] in his treatise of the *Trial of Faith.*

[91] B, as printed by Stearns, has *are* for *dare*, as corrected by Carter, but in her printing of B in italics, she has inadvertantly dropped more than a line therefrom and altered the sense.

[92] Both Paget and Hooker are at pains to be on the high Calvinist side of the debate which shook the Netherlands and ended in the extrusion of the Remonstrants after the international Synod of Dort of 1618.

[93] B has: *Grace.*

[94] On the distinction, see further Everett H. Emerson, "Thomas Hooker and Reformed Theology: The Relationship of Hooker's Conversion Preaching to its Background," Ph.D. dis., Louisiana State University, Baton Rouge, 1948; cf. also quotation from Hooker, Essay I, at n. 73.

[95] Hooker wrote the Preface to this work, our Document IV.

[96] Of Nijmegen.

Q. 20 Whether we be justified by the active as well as by the passive obedience of Christ. *Affirmatur*.

A. 20 We are justified as well by the active as by the passive obedience of Christ. So I affirm also. These are my poor thoughts for the present touching all the opinions[97] propounded and as my judgment so likewise my practice is like to be so far as (my) conscience calls me hereunto, giving wiser and better than myself, loving leave to think and do otherwise, being ever willing to hear better arguments and any converting[98] reason, and to stoop[99] thereunto.

And because I do apprehend your opinion and affections[100] to be so far settled that you apprehend[101] there cannot be a peaceable concurrence in such distances of judgment to deliver you from all fear either of any molestations that might come unto your spirit or division to your congregation, I am resolved contentedly to sit down and suddenly as I see my opportunity to depart, wishing that the God of Peace would[102] provide so comfortable an assistant[103] as might suit with you in all truth and godliness[104] for your mutual comfort and the building up of the body of Christ.

[97] B has: *those Questions.*
[98] B has: *convincing.*
[99] B has: *to stop.*
[100] B has: *assertions.*
[101] B has: *conceive.*
[102] B has: *could.*
[103] R has: *assistance.*
[104] B has: *holiness.*

DOCUMENT IX

An Undated Letter to John Cotton [in London?]
From Thomas Hooker in Rotterdam; c. April, 1633

Introduction

There is but one letter, written in Europe, surviving from the pen
of Thomas Hooker, or rather a quoted paragraph of a letter to John
Cotton.[1] The fragment, however brief, is useful testimony as to
Hooker's familiar relationship with Cotton, supplying also a glimpse
into the mood and spirit of Hooker while sojourning in Holland.

The letter is preserved in Cotton Mather's *Johannes in Eremo*
(Boston, 1695). This was a series of lives of John Cotton, John Norton, John Wilson, and John Davenport, with an appendix on Thomas
Hooker, whose name did not directly fit into the caption "John"
crying "in the wilderness" of the New World.[2] The series was reprinted in *Magnalia Christi Americana* (London, 1702).[3] In intro-
ducing Hooker into his narrative, Cotton Mather says: "I have at
this time in my hands his letter from Rotterdam to Mr. Cotton."

The letter in his hands was presumably one preserved in the library
and archive of Increase Mather (1639–1723) in the parsonage of the
Second Church of Boston. Increase Mather had married Maria Cotton, one of the six children of John Cotton (1584–1652) by his
second wife, Sarah. This Sarah, a widow at the time of her marriage
to John Cotton in England in 1632, survived him; and she took as
her third husband in 1655 the widowed father of Increase. As the
son of Increase Mather and himself second minister (1685–1723) in
the Second Church, Cotton Mather would have had access to the

---

[1] From Cotton we have an insightful poem on Hooker, occasioned by his
death and prefixed to Hooker's *A Survey of the Summe of Church-Discipline*
(London, 1648), along with another poem by Hooker's Hartford associate
Stone.

[2] Each of the five biographies is separately paginated. The letter of Hooker to
Cotton appears in § 13, pp. 2of.

[3] Volume I, Third Book, Appendix.

Hooker-Cotton letter as handed down by way of either his grand-mother (Maria Cotton) or of his step-great grandmother, Sarah Hawkridge Story Cotton Mather! To be sure, John Cotton himself had left most of his library, not with Maria, but with his two minis-terial sons, Seaborn and John.[4] It is also true that some hundred books and perhaps papers in the library of Increase Mather were destroyed in the fire that burned the parsonage and meeting house in 1676. But whatever the intermediate line of transmission, Cotton Mather had in his hands in 1692 the letter Hooker wrote to John Cotton from Rotterdam.

As for the date of the letter, we have only (1) the internal evi-dence of the fragment of the letter, (2) the external evidence of the introductory and concluding remarks of Cotton Mather, which seem in part, at least, to derive from the portions of the letter not tran-scribed, and (3) Hooker's *curriculum vitae* in the Netherlands, as known from other sources.

Hooker resided in Rotterdam at least during two roughly datable periods. After he received c. April, 1631, an invitation from the English-speaking Reformed Church in the Begijnhof in Amsterdam to consider the newly opened position of assistant pastor, he chose to make his base the home of Hugh Peter, pastor of the English church in Rotterdam. Although he preached as candidate in Amsterdam on several occasions from June through October, he seems to have re-sided much of this time in Rotterdam. The memory of another Rot-terdam period in Hooker's life, of uncertain duration, is preserved wholly in the New England tradition, without any documentation in the Rotterdam municipal or English church archives. This would be after March, 1633, when Hooker is documented as having left Delft,[5] and before July, 1633, when Hooker and Cotton sailed from The Downs for Boston. Of course, Hooker could have been briefly on visits in Rotterdam at other moments during his Dutch sojourn.

As for the contextual evidence of Cotton Mather's transcription,

[4] J. H. Tuttle, "The Libraries of the Mathers," American Antiquarian Society, *Proceedings*, n. s. XX (1910), 269–356 with chart, esp. 274.

[5] *Boswell Papers*, I, 68, 114 indicate Hooker had departed from the land by March 20/30, 1633. Sprunger, "Dutch Career," p. 19, construes this notice as final. But it is quite possible that Hooker merely slipped away to England and came back to Holland unnoticed. See further, Document X, Introduction, at nn. 20 and 21.

there are several phrases relevant to the date of the letter. Mather introduces Hooker's letter thus: "But having tarried in Holland *long enough to see the state* of religion in the churches there, he became satisfied that it was neither eligible for him to tarry in that country, nor convenient for his friends to be invited thither after him." Surely the brief sojourn of Hooker in Rotterdam while awaiting the formal call from Amsterdam would not have been thought of by Hooker himself as "long enough" to pass a judgment. As this phrase leads directly to "the state of religion" in the provinces of the Netherlands, one might well conjecture that the sentence just reproduced from Cotton Mather is a paraphrase of a sentence or more in the letter of Hooker, just preceding the point where Mather quoted it directly. After the quotation of the fragment, Mather goes on in his own words: "Wherefore, about this time [of the Hooker letter], *understanding that many of his friends in Essex were upon the 'wing'* for a 'wilderness' in 'America,' where they hoped for an opportunity to enjoy and practise the 'pure worship' of the Lord Jesus Christ, in 'churches' gathered according to His direction,[6] he readily answered their invitation to accompany them in this undertaking. Dr. Ames had a design to follow Mr. Hooker; but he died soon after Mr. Hooker's removal from Rotterdam."

In Essay I, "The Life of Thomas Hooker," and in the Introduction and Notes to Document X, we have advanced reasons for speaking of a New England tradition as distinguished from Dutch documentation concerning a sojourn of Hooker in the spring of 1633 in Rotterdam, whither Ames moved from Franeker some time after August 7.[7] Therefore the spring of 1633 seems to be the most likely moment in Hooker's life in which to place a letter to John Cotton, namely, as he was being apprised of the gathering of his Essex friends and of their being "upon the wing for a wilderness" in America. Very likely the words in quotation marks in the passage from Cotton[8]

[6] Both these words are capitalized in the 1695 edition, making it clear that Mather, presumably paraphrasing Hooker, intended divinely/scripturally ordained congregational polity.

[7] Keith Sprunger, *The Learned Dr. William Ames* (Urbana, 1973).

[8] The words are in italics in *Johannes* and *Magnalia;* but Mather's erratic use of italics, like that of his contemporaries, makes it uncertain whether he implies quotation.

actually come from the Hooker letter; and if the letter was written as late as the spring of 1633, then Cotton himself would have been no longer in old Boston but hiding with John Davenport in London or with Henry Whitfield in Ockley. In this case, the reference to its not being "convenient for his [Hooker's] friends to be invited" to the Netherlands, which we have conjectured paraphrases what Cotton Mather saw in a part of the letter not transcribed, could refer to the plan of the London enfoeffees (after their failure in the daring plan to establish plenary congregational polity in parts of London by buying proprietorships of several parish churches) [9] to implement an alternative plan of resettling in the Netherlands. John Davenport actually came (1634) to the second post in association with John Paget in Amsterdam, for which Hooker himself had proved to be an unsuccessful candidate.

The internal evidence of the letter also points to a later rather than an earlier date. Hooker would scarcely have presumed to generalize about the state of religion in the Provinces after but a few weeks or months in the country. Moreover, he speaks of his ague as something familiar to John Cotton, which "yet holds," and goes on to speak of "the long time" of his sickness. The whole fragment suggests a weariness and discouragement that would only have been appropriate in so stalwart a man as Hooker after he had been turned down by John Paget in Amsterdam and had been obliged to leave John Forbes in Delft. It is not the letter of one who had but recently ridden on horseback alongside the addressee to Sempringham (July 25, 1629).[10] It is that of one who has been long enough in the Provinces to know that they could no longer be a place of refuge and experimentation in pure worship and polity either for him or for his friends in Essex and elsewhere. It was surely written in Rotterdam in the spring of 1633 (rather than, say, the summer of 1631, soon after his arrival). Yet it could not have been written after Hooker had made up his mind to join John Cotton for the sailing from The Downs in July, 1633. The tone of the fragment itself and even the contextual material of John Cotton's emplacement of the

[9] Isabel M. Calder, *Activities of the Puritan Faction of the Church of England, 1625–1633*, edited and with an introduction (London, 1957).
[10] See Essay 1, "The Life of Thomas Hooker," at n. 42.

letter in his narrative show that the writer has not yet committed himself to the long and perilous journey overseas with the addressee. As a firm conjecture, one could date the letter, Rotterdam, c. April, 1633.

DOCUMENT IX

Letter to John Cotton From Rotterdam; c. April, 1633

The state of these Provinces[1] to my weak eye[2] seems wonderfully[3] ticklish[4] and miserable. For the better part [with respect to]
heart religion[5] they [the Dutch] content themselves with very
forms[6] though much blemished; but the power of godliness [cf. 2
Tim. 3:2], for aught I can see or hear, they know not.[7] And if it
[heart religion, as distinguished from the form thereof] were thoroughly pressed, I fear lest [8] it will be fiercely opposed. My ague[9]
yet holds me. The ways of God's providence, wherein he has
walked toward me, in this long time of my sickness, and wherein

---

[1] During Hooker's sojourn (June, 1631–c. April, 1633) in the Netherlands the
seven United Provinces of Gelderland, Holland, Zeeland, Utrecht, Friesland,
Overijssel, and Groningen (Drenthe was only a "territory" without a delegation
to the States-General) were under Frederick Henry (brother of Maurice of
Nassau, d. 1625), who, as prince of Orange, was elected stadhalder in most
Provinces and was head of the Council of State (1625–1641). Of the seven
Provinces, Hooker knew only one well, which for ecclesiastical purposes was
divided into the Synod of North Holland (Amsterdam) and the Synod of South
Holland (Rotterdam).

[2] The self-disparaging remark is of a piece with the general discouragement
evidenced in the letter, connected with physical disability.

[3] i.e., *remarkably*.

[4] In the sense of *easily overturned*.

[5] i.e., *experiential religion*.

[6] i.e., *true forms*, possibly, *mere forms*. The text of 1695 has *very*, which could
be a misprint for *mere*.

[7] Hooker's experience while staying with Hugh Peter in Rotterdam, waiting
for a decision of the congregation in Amsterdam to formulate a call to him
thither against the opposition of John Paget, could be the basis for the phrase
"see and *hear*." Still Hooker would not have been long enough in Holland to
have made the generalization elsewhere in the letter. Hence we have dated the
letter toward the end of his Dutch sojourn rather than near the beginning.

[8] The text has *least*, which could be either *at least* or *lest*, our preference.

[9] Hooker speaks of his illness as something familiar to John Cotton. During
the period of waiting out the decision in Amsterdam, Hooker is known to have
gone to The Hague to seek relief from some ailment. Keith L. Sprunger, basing
his statement on the records of the Begijnhof chapel in Amsterdam, "The Dutch
Career of Thomas Hooker."

I have drawn forth many wearyish hours under his Almighty hand (Blessed be his Name) together with pursuits and banishment, which have waited upon me, as one wave follows another, have driven me to an amazement, his paths being too secret and past finding out [cf. Is. 55:8] by such an ignorant, worthless worm as myself. I have looked over my heart and life according to my measure, aimed and guessed as well as I could, and entreated his Majesty[10] to make known his mind, wherein I missed. And yet methinks I cannot spell out readily the purpose of his proceedings, which, I confess, have been wonderful in miseries and more than wonderful in mercies to me and mine.[11]

[10] An unusual way for the exiled English subject to refer, not to his king, but to his God.

[11] Hooker's wife and children remained safe in Essex under the protection of the Earl of Warwick.

DOCUMENT X
The Preface, Spring, 1633

To the Posthumous *Fresh Suit Against Ceremonies*
(Amsterdam, 1633) of William Ames

Introduction[1]

William Ames died in Rotterdam in November, 1633, before his *Fresh Suit Against Ceremonies* came completely from the press in Amsterdam. His posthumous work was the climax of a series of his writings on the subject, this one taking the form of a refutation of a prolix defense of three Anglican ceremonies by Dr. John Burgess. Thomas Hooker did not really supply Ames' volume with a preface in the ordinary sense of helping the reader into his colleague's book. The Preface (Document X) is, rather, an independent work that makes no reference at all to the ensuing *Fresh Suit* but defends and quotes Ames in his earlier phase of opposition to ceremonies, namely, in two anonymous *Replies* (1622 and 1623) to Bishop Thomas Morton. With more on this controversy, below, it suffices here to say that Burgess came in 1631 to the defense of Morton against the anonymous Ames of the *Replies*. Then in the Preface Hooker defended Ames against Burgess in parallel to Ames' own defense of himself against Burgess.

As Ames was the more important controversialist, so his *Fresh Suit*, in terms of the basic issues, probably deserves more attention

---

[1] In preparing the Introduction the Editor has been helped, by way of correspondence, by three scholars currently working on related projects: Professor Stephen Foster of the University of Northern Illinois at DeKalb, who is at work on congregational polity, as it was developed in England and in Holland among the refugees; Professor Harry Porter of the Faculty of History, Cambridge, who is preparing an introduction to a reprint of an earlier work of Dr. John Burges(s) than that central to the present text; and Professor Keith L. Sprunger of Bethel College, North Newton, Kansas, who published *The Learned Dr. William Ames* (Urbana: University of Illinois Press, 1973), and "The Dutch Career of Thomas Hooker," *The New England Quarterly*, XLVI, (1973), 17–44. A facsimile edition of *A Fresh Suit*, with a brief introduction by Richard Simmons, was published by the Gregg Press, London, 1971.

than Hooker's Preface. But because of Hooker's subsequent American career, the Preface turns out to be a precious document in that it registers the views of the only American Puritan to have been directly involved in the Anglican-Puritan controversy over ceremonies, which by 1633 was already well merged with the controversy over polity, that is, over the authority of the bishops who were imposing the ceremonies.

The development into which Hooker's Preface fits is the Jacobean-Caroline phase of the Vestiarian Controversy. This earlier controversy over clerical dress with all its implications for the meaning of Holy Communion in the Church of England began under Edward VI, when in 1550 John Hooper refused to be consecrated Bishop of Gloucester wearing the surplice and rochet as prescribed in the First Book of Common Prayer (1549).

After the Roman Catholic interlude under Mary, the restoration of Anglican vestments in the Chapel Royal under Elizabeth in 1559 and elsewhere excited strong opposition, especially among the most highly reformed of the returned Marian exiles and notably in the Convocation of Canterbury of 1563. After the subsequent failure of Archbishop Matthew Parker to reach a compromise with the opponents of any vestments that would perpetuate even the suggestion of a priestly as distinguished from a purely ministerial action at Holy Communion, he issued *The Book of Advertisements, partly for due order in the public administration of Common Prayers and using the holy sacraments, and partly for the apparel of persons ecclesiastical by virtue of the Queen's Majesty's letters commanding the same* (March, 1566). Among some thirty-nine items, *Advertisements* required the use of the surplice by the celebrant at Holy Communion, required the kneeling of the recipient at Communion, but disallowed the sign of the cross at baptism. Although the use merely of a surplice in place of the traditional Mass vestments represented already a move in the Reformed direction, by the Stuart period Puritans found even the surplice too much of a relic of popery; and in the meantime the use of the cross at baptism had been reinstated (in canon 20 of *The Book of Canons*, 1604) and defended by High Churchmen. Thus the ceremonies against which Ames and Hooker were contending in 1633 were precisely three: the surplice, the kneeling, and the sign of the cross. But by 1633 much more was at issue than the three ceremonies.

There was, of course, the lingering vestiarian concern as to whether a distinction could be drawn between, on the one hand, scripturally enjoined (or prohibited) liturgical actions as the essence of divine worship and, on the other, "circumstantial," "accidental," or "indifferent" procedures in the interest of "good order and decency." More fundamentally, there was by now the issue whether bishops as representatives of the Crown could properly impose these minor regulations on the ground that they were external matters within the competence of the state to the end that the whole established Church might show forth pleasing conformity in usage as well as in faith. Finally, there was the basic ecclesiological issue as to the propriety of separation from an insufficiently reformed or a recidivist established Church. This issue does not clearly surface in the Preface, but both Ames and Hooker in Holland were keenly, even nervously, aware of a certain precariousness in their position; for they, over against pedobaptist and believers' baptist English separatists sharing exile in Holland with them, knew that they were clinging to at least one ceremony, namely, the baptism of infants incapable of articulate faith (without sponsors), which practice could not be easily demonstrated from scripture — their alleged sole norm in eliminating surplice, kneeling, and the cross as a sign. They knew, further, that unlike the separatists who were willing to risk apprehension or exile for reforming in conventicles without tarrying for any, they, as non-separating Congregational anglicans, as it were, did fully countenance the role of King and other magistrates in giving unity and order to a national Church, which practice and theory therefore were also difficult to demonstrate from scripture alone. But on this ecclesio-political issue, Ames, appropriating, prefacing, and Latinizing the work of William Bradshaw (1605) as *Puritanismus Anglicanus* (1610), was surely more of a statist than Hooker, as some remarks in the Preface bear out.

A. The Book of which the Preface is a Part.

The book of which the Preface is a part, *A Fresh Suit*, has been bibliographicallly described by Charles E. Sayle[2] and by A. F. Johnson in his "The Exiled English Church at Amsterdam and its Press." [3] The most usual arrangement of the several components of the book is as follows: a page indicating that it was published by S. O. [Stephen Offwood]; a portrait of William Ames; Advertisement to the Reader; Epistle of John Laski to Edward VI (in English and Latin); the Preface [by Thomas Hooker]; Alphabetical Table, List of Books by Ames; second title page; direction to the reader; Part I (156 pp.); Part II (531 pp.); A Table; An Addition (64 pp.). The book was put together differently, and extant copies differ considerably; and its various parts, as printed in Amsterdam and separately sent to Rotterdam, were noted by the informers of the English ambassador in the Netherlands, Sir William Boswell, who sent the book in two installments to Sir John Coke, Secretary of State.[4] The publisher of the book, as distinguished from the printer(s), was "S.O.," Stephen Offwood (variously referred to also as Ostwood; Oswood). An innkeeper (victualler), "dwelling near the old Church at Amsterdam," and a former Brownist, Offwood had headed the faction of the church of John Paget that wrote to Hooker, asking him to come to succeed Thomas Potts (see introduction to Document VIII).[5]

---

[2] *Early English Printed Books in the University Library, Cambridge 1475–1640*, 4 vols. (Cambridge, England, 1900–1907), III, item 7015.

[3] *The Library*, 5th series, V (1951), 219–242, esp. 242f. See also Sprunger, "Dutch Career," and Stephen Foster's forthcoming "Notes from the Caroline Underground: Alexander Leighton, Clandestine Puritan Printing, and the Laudian Reaction to Nonconformity."

[4] Boswell, The Hague, November 18/28, 1633: "I have heretofore sent your Honour a book in 4to : called A fresh sute against Ceremonies, very virulent in divers passages against the Ordre & honour of our Church whereof your Honor shall herewith receive the second part as waspish & sophisticall as the former: both printed at Amsterdam being written by Doctor Ames. . . . [T]he whole Impression, (I heare) is in the hands of one Stephen Offwood (an ignorant victualler of Amsterdam) who will part with no more Copies of this second part untill he hath Doctor Ames his picture (as he pretends) en taille douce, with a brief relation of his life, to be bound up, & sold with this irrefragable piece." He then goes on to characterize the Preface. See below at n. 17. State Papers, 84, V. 147, f. 174.

On Offwood (Ostwood), see below.

[5] Offwood is referred to above in n. 4. His habitation, profession, and letter to Hooker are in British Museum, Boswell Papers, Add. Ms 6394, 1, fol. 139. Documents relating to Offwood and his activities are further described by

The book as a whole may be seen as concerted action on the part of the Prefacist (presumably at the time of composition still in Delft) and of Ames, first in Franeker, then in Rotterdam, to stay the attempt of William Laud, the bishop of London (1628–1633), to impose ceremonies at Delft and in the garrisons, and in due course to extend the authority of the diocese of London to all Englishmen in all of Holland.[6] The English church in Delft under the Scotsman John Forbes (? 1568–1634)[7] was the principal recipient of the pressure being brought by Edward Misselden, a tractarian on the economics of the staple trade, by the Anglican conformist chaplain Stephen Goffe, and by the perhaps half-reluctant Ambassador Boswell.

B. The Background of the Hooker Preface

In 1618 Thomas Morton (1564–1659), at the time bishop of Lichfield and Coventry with a doctorate in divinity (1606), published *A Defence of the Innocencie of three ceremonies of the Church of England, viz. the surplice, the crosse after baptisme, and kneeling at the receiving of the blessed sacrament*. In two closely related

---

Champlin Burrage, *English Dissenters*, I (Cambridge, England, 1912), 30, 109, 179–181; II, 272f., 284; Raymond Phineas Stearns, *Congregationalism in the Dutch Netherlands. The Rise and Fall of the English Congregational Classis, 1621–1635* (Chicago, 1940), pp. 27, 64, 116, 118; Alice Clare Carter, *The English Reformed Church in Amsterdam in the Seventeenth Century* (Amsterdam, 1964), pp. 59, 77, 79, 88.

[6] There were, very broadly viewed, three groupings of Englishmen and Scots in the Protestant Netherlands. The older grouping were the members of the Company of English Merchant Adventurers, chartered in the fifteenth century to handle the staple trade with their principal factory in Delft and with other merchants based in Rotterdam, Amsterdam, Middelburg, Flushing, etc. The second grouping were the regiments of English and Scottish soldiers sent first by Elizabeth in the 1580's and maintained by the Stuarts to assist the Dutch in securing their independence of Spain. In the 1620's these British soldiers consisted of sixty-eight companies under the four standing Colonels in the Low Countries. The third grouping, overlapping in part with the first and second, were religious refugees of varying degrees of Puritanism. See further Stearns, *Congregationalism in the Dutch Netherlands*.

[7] Forbes was pastor of the English Church in Delft, 1631–1634. He had been earlier pastor in Middelburg, 1621–1631. He was the third son of William Forbes of Corse, Aberdeenshire. Exiled from Scotland in 1606, he spent time in France. He may have become acquainted with Hooker at Esher. See Biographical Essay.

pamphlets William Ames (1576–1633), at the time entering upon his
duties as professor of theology and in due course rector at the University of Franeker (1622–1633), argued against the legitimacy of
the three ceremonies successively in *A reply to D. Mortons generall
defence of three nocent ceremonies* (1622) and in *A reply to D.
Mortons particvlar defence . . .* (1623).

Somewhat less than a decade later, Dr. John Burgess (1563–1635),
sometime imprisoned (1604) Puritan but now conformist, came to
the defense of Bishop Morton in a large volume, *An Ansvver reioyned
to that much applauded pamphlet of a namelesse author* [Ames],
bearing this title: *A reply to Dr. Mortons generall defence of three
nocent ceremonies, etc., the innocency and lawfvlnesse whereof
is againe in this reioynder vindicated* (London, 1631).[8] Burgess was
now a beneficed clergyman at Sutton Coldfield, Warwickshire, and
a prebend in Lichfield as well as, on the other side, a practicing
physician (M.D. Leiden, 1610). In his preface Burgess says that he
had had his *Answer* or *Rejoinder* in manuscript for some time (since
about 1625) and apologized to His Majesty for having delayed defense of his "Father in God," Bishop Morton. It is quite possible
that Burgess had delayed the publication because he knew who had
written the anonymous two *Replies;* for that person was none other
than his son-in-law! In fact, William Ames had not only married
(1613) one of the daughters of Dr. Burgess but had also succeeded
him briefly as chaplain to the English governor, Sir Horace Vere,
and the garrison in Brill, until under pressure from authorities in
England he was dismissed as not sufficiently conformist.

As a sometimes nonconformist who had suffered, as a reluctant
conformist, Burgess understood himself as a spokesman for the middle way, regarding ceremonies as acceptable, especially when enjoined by Church or State, but always hoping that moderation might
be maintained on both sides:

[8] The Gregg Press, London, is doing a reprint of *An Ansvver* with a preface
by Harry Porter, which rehearses the life of Burgess. The book is divided
arbitrarily into two unequal, separately paginated parts: 1–75; 1–654. As
Hooker's refutation of Burgess concentrates on the second, longer part, most
of his references and hence ours, are to Part ii without further notice in our
notes. When Hooker retorts to the first part, he calls all of it "The Preface,"
although only a portion thereof is so entitled. In our notes we shall sometimes
be saying "Preface," more commonly "Part i."

Yet is not this all the hurt that cometh of this distraction: for some men, who doe discover the ground of this opposition against Ceremonies, to be nothing but a rigid precisenesse, whereby that is made sinne which God never made so to bee, and find the same in some men to bee seconded with a masterly over-weening of their owne sinceritie, do grow easily into dislike of such men: and not considering warily, what other things in some of them are good, doe easily fall into suspition and dis-regard of their very moralities and vertues, as if all were either hypocrisie or nicenesse. . . .—Such men therefore as truely haue discerned the fayling of judgement in matter of *Inconformitie*, haue disesteemed first and after despised that strictness also of conversation, which Christian men ought to follow. As for example, diligence in hearing or reading the Word of God, exercise of Prayers, and singing of Psalmes in the family, care of keeping holy the Lords day, especially in private, modestie in apparell, meates, drinkes, and mirth, forbearance of vaine oathes in communication, drinking of healths, and idle talk, etc. From vvhence hath come that vvhich now vvee groane vnder, that all good behaviovr is scorned of many, as a matter of *Puritanisme*, and so termed.—Moreover, divers in detestation of the strictnesse of some men in these matters of Ceremonies, haue declined also all strictness of conversation, which some such men doe follow, and imagine their damnable loosenesse to bee defensible, by the onely accusation or scorne of some mens preciseness vvhere it needeth not. And they againe, who obserue the vnexcusable debosheries of many which oppose their Inconformitie, doe strengthen themselues the more in that their precisenesse. So as each partie is the worse for this opposition, and the more confirmed in their mistakings, which should be reformed in each of them.—And hence also hath it come, that while men haue receded further and further one from another, without due circumspection, some of both sides haue fallen into fearfull extremities, such as lay neerest to their way: some on the one side to Separation, and to Anabaptisme; others to Poperie, or Newtralitie, and, in effect, Atheisme, in words confessing a Godhead, in deeds denying it. (*Answer*, part i; pp. 6f.)[9]

Two years after Burgess published the *Answer* in 1631, Ames replied to his father-in-law in print. That was in 1633, the year he left Franeker because of the adverse effect of its climate upon his

[9] In this highly characteristic and revealing passage from Burgess, the paragraphs are here compacted and indicated by dashes.

asthma and because of the "Implacable controversy" between him and a professor at Franeker.[10] Ames established himself in Rotterdam with a view to serving as co-pastor with Hugh Peter (1598– 1660) and to presiding over a soon to be founded English college. The date of his arrival in Rotterdam is variously given.[11] He was still in Franeker August 7, writing about packing and moving. There is a letter of his from Amsterdam dated September 23. As there is a strong New England tradition that Hooker was actually for a brief period a pastoral associate of Ames in Rotterdam, it would be helpful if the Dutch and other sources documented an earlier arrival. He must have settled in Rotterdam sometime in August and gone to Amsterdam briefly on the matter of his *Fresh Suit*. Whatever the date of the arrival of Ames in Rotterdam, the internal evidence of the Preface to *A Fresh Suit* makes it clear that Ames and Hooker were independently refuting Burgess.

Ames' work was entitled in full *A fresh svit against human ceremonies in Gods vvorship or a triplication unto D. Burgesse his rejoinder for D. Morton, The first Part.* It was apparently printed by Sabine Staresmore, in parts, in Amsterdam; the first section is paged separately from the rest with its own title page. The English ambassador at The Hague wrote Sir John Coke, Secretary of State, on September 20/30, 1633, that he was sending on what would turn out to be the first part of *A Fresh Suit*, which he characterized as "whollie directed against the Ceremonies of our Church and in many poyncts very scandalous against the same." [12] He gave as his reason

[10] The source mistakenly calls him "Paconius a Palonian Professor." Letter from Boswell to Coke, November 18/28, 1633; *State Papers,* 84f.; 174 r.–v. This was the Polish Calvinist professor of theology, a strong drinker, Johannes Maccovius, Jan Makowski (1588– 1644), several of whose posthumously published works were later used as texts at Harvard. Cf. Sprunger, *Ames,* p. 93.

[11] Sprunger, *Ames.* pp. 92f. A distinction must be drawn between his receiving a call while in Franeker, his arrival in Rotterdam, and his beginning to function as a co-pastor with Peter. Sprunger, *Ames,* noting that Ames is not recorded in the archives of the church in Amsterdam, opts for August or September. Stearns, *Peter,* says simply the summer of 1633. Stephen Foster in correspondence with the Editor says July. In the article on Ames in J. P. de Bie and J. Loosjes, *Biographisch Woordenboek* (The Hague, n.d.), I, p. 114, there seems to be some information derived from the University of Franeker archive that would indicate that the confirmation of the call from Rotterdam was on April 9, 1633.

[12] State Papers, Domestic, Charles I, Vol. 246, art. 56; reprinted with notes as item 65 "Bibles and Other books Smuggled in as Blank Paper, 1633," in Walter

for not notifying the Dutch authorities his intention of being un-
obtrusively on the lookout for the author. Boswell was aware in his
letter that Dr. Ames "had the second part prepared if not already
in the presse." He remarked that it was being "perus'd by divers
of the Classic men." Boswell's agent, Alexander Brown, wrote to
him November 1, 1633, that "Doctor Ames his prefaice to the fresh
suit, is printed." [13] Before Ames could see the second half of his
work, Rotterdam was inundated; and in escaping from his house by
night he became ill from exposure and died; he was buried November 4/14.[14] Boswell, who had already sent Secretary Coke a copy
of the first part of *A Fresh Suit*, in a follow-up letter November
18/28 sent on the second part and informed Coke further about the
book. Since Hooker had already arrived in Boston September 3/4,[15]
we must establish Hooker's authorship of the unsigned Preface well
before that date.

C. Hooker's Authorship of the Preface

To be sure, there is no name or initial attesting to Hooker's authorship of the Preface; and the earliest biography of Ames, the *prae-
fatio introductoria* of the Utrecht theologian Dr. Matthew Nethen
in his edition of the Latin works of Ames (Amsterdam, 1658) merely
refers to the Preface thus: "Qui liber [*A Fresh Suit*] autore vivo
excudi coeptus post mortem ipsius, cum inserta post praefationem

---

Wilson Greg, *A Companion to Arber, being a calendar of documents in Edward
Arber's Transcript of the register of the Company of Stationers of London,
1654-1648* (Oxford, 1967), p. 291.

[13] British Museum, Boswell Papers, Addl. Ms 6394, I, fol. 153r. Incompletely
and defectively printed in Burrage, *Dissenters*, II, 273f. The "prefaice" must be
that of Hooker for Ames' *Fresh Suit*. Boswell had possession of "sheets" of the
Preface, November 7/17. Staresmore on November 18/28 was still at work on
A Fresh Suit, adding the portrait of Ames and the binding. The Preface may
not have been printed by Staresmore, since it has an end piece (a bear) used by
another Amsterdam printer, J. F. Stam. Stam and Staresmore may well have
worked in collaboration. On the Brownist Staresmore, see Burrage, *Dissenters*, I,
175–181, and more fully in the forthcoming study by Professor Stephen Foster.
[14] Ms dates by Thomas Prince, based upon an inscription in a book from
Thomas Shepard, Jr. See further below at n. 22. Boswell to Coke, November 18/
28, *loc. cit.*, says that Ames had died "about 12 dayes since of Apoplexie." His
date for the death would thus be 6/16. But see Sprunger, *Ames*, pp. 94, 247.
[15] Two slightly discrepant Ms notes in the Prince copy of the *Fresh Suit*.

satis longam autoris effigie, in lucem prodiit." [16] Since the account of the life and of the book is very brief, there is no reason to expect Nethen to have identified the author of "the fairly long preface." To be sure, Ambassador Boswell suspected Hugh Peter of Rotterdam rather than Thomas Hooker, associate of John Forbes at Delft, as the author of the Preface.[17] But now it remains to establish Hooker's authorship.

There are two distinct testimonies in New England to Hooker's authorship of the Preface. New England, though remote from the scene of the action, was peopled with those who could have left reliable reports, not least of whom would have been Hooker himself and his family, including his son-in-law in Cambridge, Thomas Shepard. As it happens, one of our two witnesses is Thomas Shepard, Jr. by way of Thomas Prince; the other is Richard Mather by way of Cotton Mather; and in Cotton Mather's accounts there may well have been the testimony of both his paternal grandfather and also his maternal grandfather, John Cotton.

Dr. Increase Mather (1639–1723) in the preface to the work of his son, Cotton Mather, *Johannes in Eremo: Memoirs relating to the lives of the ever-memorable Mr. John Cotton, Mr. John Norton, Mr. John Davenport, Mr. Thomas Hooker* (Boston, May 16, 1695), wrote (p. 11): "I remember, my Father [Richard, 1596–1669] told me, that Mr. Hooker, was the Author of that large Preface which is before Dr. Ames his Fresh Suit against Ceremonies." [18]

---

[16] The Life by Nethen is available in English translation by Douglas Horton, *William Ames* (Cambridge: Harvard Divinity School Library, 1965), p. 20.

[17] State Papers 84, V. 147, f. 174 v.: "The long & seditious preface. . . is of another stile [from the book as a whole] & lookes like Mr. Peters of Rhotterdam, as well in the heads of the same, which are his ordinary discourse, as in divers homely proverbs, (which are familiar likewise with him) & in the distinction in it of covenanting members & subjects of a church; for this he practiseth in his congregation." Boswell also encloses a copy of Peters' "Covenant of Articles given me by a Parishioner: whom he keepeth from the communion, for no other reason known but not subscribing to the same." The Covenant has been printed several times, most conveniently in Raymond Phineas Stearns, *The Strenuous Puritan Hugh Peter, 1598–1660* (Urbana, 1954), p. 76.

[18] *Johannes in Eremo* (Boston, 1695) became the first part of the Third Book of the *Magnalia Christi Americana* (London, 1702). As an owner of a copy of *A Fresh Suit* and related works, Increase Mather had the interest of an antiquarian joined to that of a possessive bibliophile. Julius H. Tuttle, "The Libraries of the Mathers," American Archaeological Society, *Proceedings*, n.s.

Thomas Prince (1687–1758) in 1708 bought the copy of *A Fresh Suit* which is now in the Boston Public Library. He already had a copy "bo't out of ye Library of ye Rev Mr Thomas Shepard [Jr.] of Charlestown." But it was inferior to his newly acquired one, as he remarks of the new one that it was the fairest he had ever seen. Before parting with the inferior copy, perhaps once belonging to Thomas Shepard, Sr., he transcribed to the new copy opposite the title page what he regarded as valuable data *from the hand of Thomas Shepard, Jr.* Prince's full-page inscription[19] begins, "Put this among ye New England Books [instead of European]; because The Large Preface before it was wrote by ye famous Mr. Thomas Hooker afterwards of Hartford in New England." Hereupon he cites the already quoted place in Cotton Mather. He then continues: "And in a Mss note at ye Beginning of sd Preface in a Book bo't out of ye Library of ye Rev Mr Thomas Shepard [1635–1677] of Charlestown are these words—'written by Mr Thomas Hooker; as I have heard.' " This Thomas Shepard, Jr.[20] was son of the Rev. Thomas Shepard of Cambridge. The latter had taken as his second wife the daughter (Joan) of Thomas Hooker. The phrasing preserved by Prince sounds like what the younger Shepard would have written down in his copy of the book on the basis of information received indirectly from his step-grandfather, Thomas Hooker, by way of his father and/or stepmother.

Prince was no doubt correct in assuming that he had two independent testimonies to the Hooker authorship from at least two, perhaps even five or six, English-born persons: Richard Mather, Mrs. Ames, possibly John Cotton, Thomas Shepard, Sr., Thomas Shepard, Jr., and John Eliot, formerly Hooker's usher at Little Baddow.

XX (1909–1910), pp. 269–356, esp. 284. Increase Mather it was who insisted, as the son acknowledges in his own introduction, that Thomas be included among the four Johns, despite the asymmetry. Increase seemed to know quite a bit about Thomas Hooker. It was he presumably who supplied Cotton with the tradition that Ames and Hooker were intimate. Just before what is quoted in the text above, Increase wrote: "Mr. Cotton in his Preface to Mr. Nortons Answer to Apollonius, sayes of Mr. Hooker, Dominatur concionibus. Dr. Ames used to say, He never knew his Equal."

[19] This page is reproduced in Appendix 2.
[20] Thomas Shepard, Jr. was born in London and was graduated from Harvard in the class of 1653. John Langdon Sibley, *Biographical Sketches of Graduates of Harvard University*, I (Cambridge, 1873), 327–335.

There is some discrepancy in our meagre evidence about when Hooker left Holland for England and thence to New England (in July, 1633). The New England sources, which also identify Hooker as the author of the Preface, allow him to have remained longer in Holland than the information provided by a letter of Edward Misselden from Delft on March 20/30, 1632/3 to Boswell would suggest:

> I think I told you when I was with you that mr. Hooker went out in Norman [writing obscure]: belike to heare how the squares [affairs] goe in England & soe do give diligent advice to mr. F[orbes] & himself to resolve of his owne way, to returne hither or haply for new England.[21]

Although the obscure *Norman* cannot be made out to be *Rotterdam*, the notice does not preclude the possibility of Hooker's passing through Rotterdam *en route* to England and tarrying there for a longer time than the foregoing note of Misselden would suggest. It is also possible that Hooker went to England in late March, as Misselden reported, and then returned to Holland, though this seems less likely.

Over against the implications of Misselden that Hooker left for England in March is the testimony in New England of Thomas Shepard (transcribed by Thomas Prince [Appendix 2]), and of Cotton Mather, himself in possession of at least one Hooker letter (Document IX). The New Englanders seem to have had information that allows Hooker to have remained in Holland into the spring beyond March, thus giving him more time to have become involved in the writing and the printing of the Preface.

We have already adduced the full-page of notation from Thomas Prince opposite the title page of his "superior" copy of *A Fresh Suit*. The following further information was inscribed by Thomas Prince from his inferior and now lost copy, once owned by Thomas Shepard, Jr.

> . . . at ye end of 2 years [with Forbes in Delft], viz in 1632, He [Hooker] remov'd to Rotterdam & Preached There with Dr Ames, & There wrote sd Preface. In ye Spring of 1633, He returns to England.

---

[21] British Museum, Boswell Papers, Addl. Ms 6394, I, f. 114; located and transcribed by Professor Stephen Foster.

in July sails cu [*sic*] ye Downs: On Sep. 4, lands at Boston in. N E.[22]

It is, of course, possible that precisely the foregoing lines in the handwriting of Prince and once presumably located opposite the title page of Shepard's copy of *A Fresh Suit* and now situated on that page between transcriptions of historical data expressly taken from Shepard's inscriptions *in other of his books*, comes not from Shepard but from Prince himself on the basis of what he knew from Cotton Mather in the *Magnalia* (1702), which we now adduce as our second New England source:

> At the end of two years, he [Hooker] had a call to Rotterdam; which he the more heartily and readily accepted, because it renewed his acquaintance with his invaluable Dr. Ames, who had newly left his place in the Frisian University [summer, 1633]. With him he spent the residue of his time in Holland, and assisted him in composing some of his discourses, which are his *Fresh Suit against Ceremonies*. . . . Dr Ames had designed to follow Mr. Hooker; but he died [November] soon after Mr. Hooker's removal from Rotterdam.[23]

It is true that Mather and Prince alike say "at the end of two years." Thus Prince could well be dependent upon Mather instead of upon Shepard at this point in his rather extensive transfer of historical data on Ames and Hooker from the Shepard into the new copy of *A Fresh Suit*, merely making more specific Hooker's relationship to *Fresh Suit* on the basis of Shepard's saying of the Preface, "written by Mr. Thomas Hooker, as I have heard." But in defense of the independence of the whole testimony supplied by Prince and in that case going back to Shepard (along with the specificity respecting

[22] That this information is supplied by Shepard is suggested by the fact that Prince continues with information on the burial of Ames, this time derived from another book, owned by Shepard, Ames, *Explicatio utriusque epistolae Divi Petri* (Amsterdam, 1635). From a blank leaf thereof Prince transcribes the following: "Thomas Shepard's Book, 1656"; and presumably written by Shepard therein: "Dr. Ames Died in Rotterdam: & was Buried Nov. 14, 1633 Stilo novo."

[23] *Magnalia Christi Americana: The Ecclesiastical History of New England* (London, 1702); critical edition based on the original folio volume of 788 pp. by Kenneth Murdock and Mrs. Perry Miller, I (Cambridge: Harvard University Press, 1974). Documentation for Ames' intention to leave Holland for New England is contained in his letter to John Winthrop from Franeker in 1629; published *Collections of the Massachusetts Historical Socciety*, 4th series, VI (1863), 576f.

the Preface) are the following points: (1) Prince(/Shepard) says only that Hooker "preached there with" Ames, while Mather speaks more formally of his having "had a call to Rotterdam" (unsupported by the rather extensive archival material) and (2) Prince does not take from Mather the datum that Hooker returned to England "in the spring of 1633." [24]

The best way to reconcile Misselden, on one side, and, on the other, Shepard/Prince and Mather is to conjecture that though the hostile Misselden was informed of the expressed intention in March of Hooker to leave for England, Hooker did not immediately carry out his plan. We know that he wrote John Cotton *from Rotterdam* (Document IX); and this and perhaps other correspondence with other friends, planning "to wing for the wilderness," [25] may well have effected the same purpose which in Misselden's letter to Boswell was to be achieved by an actual visit to England. In any case, Hooker wrote from Rotterdam and may well have "tarried" there[26] well into the spring (as Shepard/Prince indicate). Although he certainly could not have tarried into August when Ames presumably settled in Rotterdam, surely his later befriending of the widowed Mrs. Joan Ames and her children in Cambridge might well indicate much more than merely epistolary contact between Hooker and Ames respectively in Delft and Franeker. It is, then, plausible to assume that Mrs. Ames, who survived until 1644, could have been one of the sources of the New England tradition that Hooker composed the Preface to her husband's *Fresh Suit*.[27]

It is quite sufficient, however, for our main purpose — to prove

---

[24] It might also be observed that the dates of Prince/Shepard for Hooker's departure from the Downs in July and for his arrival in Boston on September 4 do not come from Mather either. In Prince's hand at the end of the Preface (not reproduced in Appendix 2) the date is given as September 3.

[25] Mather's phrase, after giving an excerpt from the letter.

[26] Again, a phrase from Mather, reporting a bit of the content of the letter before transcribing an excerpt.

[27] The information that Hooker helped Mrs. Ames when her house burned down is from the *Magnalia, loc. cit.* Mrs. Ames with her children settled first in Salem in 1637 and then removed to Cambridge so that her son William could attend the College. Mrs. Ames brought her husband's library with her. In November, 1637, the General Court of Massachusetts gave forty pounds to her as a pension. Sibley, *Graduates of Harvard University*, pp. 107 ff. William Ames, Jr. was born c. 1623.

Hooker's authorship of the Preface — to substantiate enough of the New England tradition about collaboration between Hooker and Ames to be able to assume that Ames, while still in Franeker, had already asked Hooker, while still in Delft, to prepare the Preface.[28] The fact that the author of the Preface makes no reference to *Fresh Suit* and only to the earlier works of Ames and to Burgess' *Answer* is a clear indication that the Prefacist and the principal Author were, indeed, not at the time of composition in close contact. We may even allow that Hooker left his Ms "Preface" with Peter in Rotterdam, or with Stephen Offwood, before the arrival of Ames, and that either Peter or Offwood prepared it for printing. Hence Boswell's ascription of it to Peter,[29] though he was also aware of the entrepreneurial activity of Offwood. Though Ames and Peter were indeed in spirit and friendship very close, Ames dying in the arms of his younger colleague and protegé,[30] it is not likely that Ames would have asked a man more than two decades his junior to write a preface. Hooker, in contrast, was only ten years his junior.

The clerical status of the Prefacist excludes any known nonconformist printer in Amsterdam from consideration as possible author. Moreover, internal evidence for Hooker's authorship of the Preface is not wanting: it is clear that the Prefacist is a minister ("our calling," at n. 164) and that for conscience's sake he had left England and had left his family there (at nn. 175, 183), in contrast to Peter.[31] The University education of the author is attested by his highly developed polemical style, his extensive use of classical Latin phrases and Greek in some of his scriptural references. There are several characteristically Hookerian words or phrases like "daubing," (at n. 52), "flashes of comfort" (at n. 8), nautical and commercial imagery (at n. 12), vivid householder's imagery like "snuffing of the candle too near" (at n. 47), toiling at the fireplace when the thatch above is aflame (at n. 176), the appeal to experience (at n. 148), and the presentation of the *ordo salutis* in a few words (at n. 142).

[28] This is the surmise of Sprunger, "Dutch Career," at n. 65.
[29] Above, at n. 17.
[30] On the close relationship, see Stearns, *Peter*, esp. ch. 3.
[31] Hugh Peter had his wife (a sometime widow of wealth, whom he had in 1625 married when only twenty-seven and she about fifty) come to join him in Rotterdam in 1629. Stearns, *Peter*, p. 56.

There are numerous conceptual contacts between material in the Preface and in the Hookerian corpus. The Preface deals (p. 426–430) with the carnal hypocrite, to whom Hooker elsewhere devotes a complete discussion (Document III: *The Carnal Hypocrite*). The Preface deals *inter alia* (at n. 178) with kneeling at the name of Jesus (Phil. 2:9f.), which he explains in a Puritan sense even more explicitly elsewhere (Document VII at n. 173). There is reserve about sudden flashes of religious emotion, also characteristic of Hooker; and there is a reference to recent news of an action in Leicester of the Court of High Commission (at nn. 42, 44) that would appropriately have come to Hooker, who had been wont to make an annual visit there. In the possession of the Prefacist was a document from the hand of Arthur Hildersham (d. 1632), who had encouraged Simeon Ashe to go into the ministry, who in turn became an influence in the life of Hooker at Cambridge. Ashe might well have been the one to send to the Prefacist in Holland the Hildersham document (n. 126).

Still unexplained is why the Preface was printed unsigned. Indeed, at the time of its appearance about November 1, Boswell's agent called it "Ames his prefaice." It would seem scarcely possible that the lack of a signature was the oversight of the printer. More likely, with the less famous Hooker out of the country and presumably known to be headed for the New World, the printer simply credited the more famous Ames with the whole book, although the Preface indeed clearly refers to Ames in the third person as the Replier. The printer in Rotterdam could not have known at the time of the illness and impending death of Ames and of his burial on November 14.[32] To be sure, Hooker was not *persona gratissima* to all in Amsterdam in view of the earlier controversy over his candidacy for the co-ministry there with John Paget (see Document VIII); but surely the *Fresh Suit* was intended for sale and influence far beyond Amsterdam, Rotterdam, and Delft; far beyond Holland. Indeed, precisely because its principal prospective sale would be in England, Hooker, when he left Holland for England, conceivably urged that not even his initials be subscribed to the Preface for prudence' sake, for he

[32] See above, nn. 14, 22.

could not have been sure, on leaving Holland, exactly when he would be able to get away to New England.[33] But once safely settled there he would have had every reason to share the fact of his authorship with Richard Mather (d. 1669) and with his son-in-law Thomas Shepard and hence, no doubt indirectly, with Thomas Shepard, Jr. (d. 1677), who at some point came into possession of a copy of the *Fresh Suit*.

The evidence for Hooker's authorship of the unsigned Preface is cumulatively so convincing that we can no longer allow Misselden's letter to Boswell to be adduced as virtual proof that Hooker left Holland in March, 1633. He must have been in Rotterdam, if not Delft, long enough to finish the Preface and to write to John Cotton in England (Document IX). Indeed, it is even possible that Ames himself arrived in Rotterdam earlier than he is recorded as a co-pastor there (possibly August or September). Perhaps the New England tradition has something to it in that the sojourns in Rotterdam of Hooker and Ames may have briefly overlapped. Ames left the judgment that "he never met with Mr. Hooker's equal, either for preaching or for disputing." [34] There is no known place where Ames could have *heard* [35] Hooker preach or dispute. It could have been in Rotterdam. Although the internal evidence of the Preface makes it clear that Hooker did not know what Ames himself was writing — at least there is no cross-reference — the Preface with the attendant New England tradition of a sojourn of Ames and Hooker in the same place long enough for one to judge of the preaching and disputing skills of the other makes plausible a much longer stay in Holland and hence specifically in Rotterdam than our sole reliance on the Misselden letter of March would have indicated.

D. Hooker's Understanding of Authority, Ceremony, and Polity: His Disagreement with John Burgess, 1633

The defection of Dr. Burgess to conformity represented an immense threat to Hooker and Ames. No doubt the importance of the *Answer* for both men was heightened by the fact that Ames knew

---

[33] Misselden's letter *re* Hooker of March 20/30, is quoted above at n. 21.
[34] *Magnalia, loc. cit.*
[35] Implied, rather than having merely *read*.

Burgess as a kinsman by marriage, that Burgess had once shared a
Dutch sojourn as an exile for conscience' sake, that he had indeed
in 1604 and again in 1613 suffered for his dislike of ceremonies, that
he had declined, on his return to England, to subscribe to canon 36
when licensed by the University of Cambridge to practice medicine,
and indeed incurred the direct wrath of James even to the exercise
of the royal prerogative in prohibiting him from practicing medicine
in London. A man of such credentials could make a great impression
on many a would-be Puritan back home, wavering between conformity and nonconformity with respect to the three ceremonies.
Intensity of feeling or even animosity is often closest between persons or parties which have much or even most in common. What
separated Ames and Hooker on the one side from finally conformist
Burgess on the other, on the issue of ceremonies, was that the latter
argued massively that the disliked ceremonies should be observed
by all until by law or by canon conscientious objectors were ac-
corded relief therefrom.

The canon that held all clergymen to the strict use of Book of
Common Prayer and attendant ceremonies was canon 36 of *The
Book of* [141] *Canons* enacted under Richard Bancroft for the
province of Canterbury in 1604 (repeated for York, 1606.) [36] It
was, however, in canon 20 that one of the three "nocent ceremonies"
was expressly prescribed: the sign of the cross in baptism. The
crucial comprehensive canon with respect to ceremonies, it is divided
into three articles. The first declares: "That the Kings Maiestie
vnder God, is the only supreme Gouernour of this Realme, and of
all other his Highnesse Dominions and Countreys, as well in all
Spirituall or Ecclesiasticall things or causes, as Temporall: and that
no forreine Prince, Person, Prelate, State, or Potentate, hath or ought
to haue any Iurisdiction, Power, Superioritie, Preheminence, or
Authoritie Ecclesiasticall or Spirituall, within his Maiesties said
Realmes, Dominions, and Countreys." [37] The second article prescribes

---

[36] Published in Latin, it draws on medieval prescriptions, Matthew Parker's
Book of Advertisements (1566), and the Thirty-nine Articles (1563). J. V.
Bullard has edited a modern edition of the authoritative Latin and English texts,
London, 1934.
[37] The English text of 1604.

the use of the Book of Common Prayer; the third insists, among other points, upon subscription to the Thirty-nine Articles.

Both Ames and Hooker accepted in theory the first article of three in the 36th canon, although Puritans argued against the whole Book of Canons of 1604 that it was never approved by Parliament. It is clear that Hooker on this point is somewhat less compliant than Ames. Indeed, one of our interests in the Preface at this point is Hooker's criticism not only of the prudential "statist" (see at n. 19) but also any ordained minister who fails to understand his plenary task to include instruction of the magistrate out of scripture as to Christian responsibilities in government (see at n. 154) and no doubt as to the limitations on his exercise of magisterial and royal prerogative in the affairs of the Church. The reason that Hooker does not regard either the very low churchman Burgess (who personally disliked the imposed ceremonies even after conforming) or the very high churchman Archbishop William Laud (1633–1645) as valid instructors of magistrates or the King was that they mixed the word of God with human traditions from within and without the Church.

Because of the strength of his convictions about the impropriety of using scripturally unauthorized ceremonies, Hooker had become convinced that the only polity in the Church is that which recognized the ultimacy on earth of the congregation of experientially covenanted Christians spiritually under Christ, as distinguished from the parochially or geographically ambient nominal Christians morally and legally under the King and lesser magistrates (for Boswell to Coke on this item, see n. 17): that polity which recognized the only ministry in the Church to be that of virtual equals,[38] whether pastors or teachers, in no wise inferior in authority to bishops. But congregationalism (cf. Document VIII) is more assumed than expounded in the Preface, which is directed primarily against instrusive ceremonies, imposed by Laud as bishop of London (1628–1633) and as archbishop of Canterbury (1633–1645) not only in England but also on English subjects in the Netherlands.

[38] His reference is to the Preface, at n. 55.

E. Hooker's Composition of the Preface and its Place in the Hookerian Corpus

The Preface was composed in haste and apparently set in type without Hooker's having had a chance to see his work as a whole. Several of the announced subdivisions are not carried through satisfactorily and the whole piece abounds in confusing numerations in Roman, Arabic, and written-out English. To facilitate the reading the present Editor has introduced seven subdivisions of his own with appropriate capitalized titles of his own. All the other subdivisions are at least suggested by Hooker even if not fully or consistently carried out by him or his printer. Our Part IV appears to be, from the format in the originally printed text, leaves from Hooker's copybook filled with provocative quotations from Burgess and preserving Hooker's reactions at the time of reading. The leaves were presumably sent to the Amsterdam printer as they were. The present-day reader could well skip this Part, so hard to follow even with our notes, which fill out the context of Hooker's transcriptions from Burgess, although the section does give us some feeling for Hooker's method of reading and his temperament.

The first part of the Preface up to Dv, namely up to what appears to be the insertion of the copybook leaves, is printed with many marginalia. Thereafter there is only one other marginalium (a page reference). (One could conjecture thus at least three installments in Hooker's hastily composed and hastily typeset piece.) Because of the richness of the early marginalia, often adding substantive material as well as summaries and both scriptural and page references in Burgess, the present Editor has placed all this material (with one or two exceptions clearly noted) into the main text, either as centered headings or subheadings or in the main body of the text, where appropriate. In order to indicate that a marginalium has been introduced into Hooker's main text, the Editor has enclosed the material in parentheses (). The *centered headings*, though they also come from the margin, are not in parentheses; but any additional material introduced by the Editor for clarity's sake is enclosed in brackets [ ].

Although the specific issues debated by Hooker with Burgess

have largely lost the intensity of emotion and the sense of cosmic relevance with which they were once invested by both sides, the Preface has continuing interest in its spirited and sometimes imaginative style and as a nearly unique specimen of Hooker's expository, polemical, and apologetic writing; for the bulk of the corpus that has survived is sermonic, and indeed sermonic in compressed transcription by auditors. In the Preface we can almost hear Hooker debating in Holland just before he took ship for Boston.

Document X: The Preface

To A Fresh Suit against Human Ceremonies in God's Worship

[Introduction]

[(:) (:) 4r][1] They who put to sea, according to their several scopes and purposes, so do they steer [by] their compasses and proceed in their travels answerably.[2] Such as set out merely to satisfy their pleasure or some private end, when once the heavens begin to be beset with clouds, [when] the winds grow high and the storm approaching threatens apparent danger, when their companies are scattered and severed from them, or when the foulness of their stomachs and the noisesome humors there cause that they cannot brook the sea but [suffer] with much tedious disquiet and sickness, they turn their courses and make to shore with as much speed as they may.[3]

Others who seriously intend to make a voyage of it and are bound for some remote place and resolved to fetch some precious commodities from a far country, they reckon upon hazards, expect the common calamities of the sea and determine to undergo whatever [(:) (:) 4v] they do expect or shall befall. The conclusion is: Willing they are to adventure the loss of their lives, but not willing to lose their voyage. Therefore on they will [to continue]: Extreme necessities may overbear them, but no fears can discourage them in their course.

As thus it fares in traveling, so fares it also with men in professing the [revealed] truth; their aims are several and their proceedings suitable thereunto. Some take up the profession of the truth as a

---

[1] The pagination of the Preface is continuous with the unrelated previous matter of the *Fresh Suit*.

[2] The opening sentence is inadequate in syntax for modern usage: They who put to sea . . . do so by steering with their compasses and in other ways proceeding in a responsible manner.

[3] By slightly altering the punctuation and inserting a verb, an originally incomplete sentence has been syntactically righted.

voyage of pleasure, and such will be sure to sail no further than that they may see the smoke of their own chimneys. They will serve Christ no longer than they may serve their own turns, and therefore such will have no more of the gospel than they may have their own private[4] with it, not only within sight but within reach. And it's admirable to see what falseness they discover in their course, and yet what fair colors they put upon all their proceedings and would bear the world in hand. They wish nothing but soundness when indeed there is nothing but shows and appearances to please a sensual eye.

It's not amiss therefore to take the scantling[5] of both these kinds, that the judicious reader may be able to own them as they appear in his way, either in their writings or behaviors, for the lives of men are [Ar] [6] like living books which a wise man will search into and observe. To this purpose therefore we shall shortly consider: I: What is the cause of this declining?; II: What be the pretenses whereby they labor to excuse it?

[I. The Four] Causes of Declining, [cf.] Lk. 13:19
First Sort [of Decliners]

The cause of this declining is the entertainment of the truth upon false grounds. The apple which is unsound at the core will discover rottenness in the skin afterwards. When the foundation is not sure, the whole frame will sink when it's shaken by the least storm.

Some there be, like the stony-hearted hearers, who from the present apprehension[7] of the comforts and promises of the gospel are tickled with the sweetness [of] the rose, though but in general conceived, and have their hearts suddenly cheered with the confused

[4] Some such word as *advantage* may have dropped out here: but *private* as a noun has the archaic meaning of *personal interest*.

[5] *Scantling* means *measure*. Hooker, in view of his ship metaphor, could have better said *scantling number* or *numeral*, which is the computation of several standard ship's dimensions and structural materials to establish the classification of the ship and its seaworthiness.

[6] A new foliation begins at this point. The Editor indicates the pagination with *recto* and *verso*.

[7] i.e., expectancy concerning the comforts.

and unapplied grounds of good. And therefore they are said to receive it suddenly with joy, Mt. 13:20 (εὐθύς).

But as they flourish speedily, so do they fade as soon. For these flashes[8] of comfort, as they arise not from any deep root, Mt. 13:21, (οὐκ ἔχει ρίζαν) of an humbled and self-denying heart, so they leave no deep stamp or impression upon the spirit; and therefore when sad and heavy pressures of sorrow do seize upon the soul, these slight impressions of flashy joy vanish away.

[Av] These comforts in temporaries[9] are like the painting and complexion which is laid upon the face by deformed harlots which the least violence of cold or heat takes off immediately, whereas a sound joy issuing from grounded assurance is like ruddy complexion which ariseth from good blood and wholesome constitution [and] which the greatest heats or colds may increase but cannot remove as long as life and strength lasteth.

Second Sort of Decliners

Others again are brought to embrace the truth because of the company or multitude which they see give credit or countenance thereunto. Thus the Pharisee, Lk. 13:24, Mt. 8:20, would not to heaven unless he might go in the crowd or because of the safety and commodity which the Lord sometimes vouchsafes to sincere professors. Thus many turned Jews in Esther's time [8:17] not because they were the better, but the stronger party, not for the truth of their profession, but for the safety of the professors. These attend upon Christ for the loaves, Jn. 6:26, and follow the gospel no longer than profit follows them. The name of a prison, the noise of a chain, makes the truth so deformed in their eye that they dare not and therefore will not own it. As the leaves of a tree, while they be fed with moisture drawn up into the branches by the sun in the spring, they flourish; [A2r] and [when] cold frost drives back the moisture they wither and fall. Like the leaves is the love of these worldly gospellers. An instance of this temper is apparent

---

[8] The expressions "flashes of comfort" and "flashy joy" are characteristically Hookerian disparagements of momentary motions of grace. See above. Essay 2.
[9] In things temporal.

in many of our Elizabeth[an] professors,[10] as they are termed, who were hot at the entrance of the gospel when company, credit, and profit were attendants to it; but when the frowns and displeasure of authority like winter blasts plucked away their livings and dignities which were as the moisture to feed their desires, they dried away in their discretion[11] and retained nothing but the name of ancient professors like boxes in apothecaries' shops which carry fair titles on the outside and fill up room but have not one healing or useful drug in them.

Third Sort [of Decliners]

A third sort there be who at the first appearing of the gospel in a place are taken up with the strangeness and novelty, either of the doctrine or the manner of delivery and answerably with some affection make inquiry after it. This was their practice when John Baptist came preaching in the wilderness. Mt. 3:5: "Then went out to him Jerusalem, and all Judaea, and all the region about Jordan." This also our Savior acknowledged as their endeavor. Jn. 5:35: "John was a burning and a shining light and you would have [A2v] rejoiced in him for a season." It befalls the gospel in this case, as it doth with some strange commodity, when it first comes to view: many see and cheapen[12] until the price proves too heavy and then they depart and will not buy. So here. When our Savior sets upon the sale of the gospel in some obscure place, many will be comers, hearers, cheapeners,[13] until they find that the Word grows somewhat high rated and the conditions of the gospel seem too hard and then they forsake it. Herod welcomes John Baptist [Mk. 6:20] and observes him, but at last murders him.

Fourth Sort of Decliners

Others, lastly, after some sad conviction of the truth revealed, as

[10] In 1633 it would have been 75 years earlier that the Marian exiles returned under Elizabeth I (1558–1603).

[11] The word *discretion* is put in parentheses by the printer suggesting that a word may have dropped from Hooker's manuscript.

[12] i.e., bargain.

[13] i.e., bargainers.

also of the necessity and excellency thereof, hold it a point of honor to persevere in the defense and maintenance of it, and hence for their own praise may and do suffer heavy persecutions as poverty, exile in the profession of the truth, the power whereof they never approved in the exactness of it.[14]

Thus many in Queen Mary's days[15] were exiled for the gospel who afterward returned into England and opposed, yea persecuted, the power and accurateness [in the] practice of it, Mt. 13: [30] ($\kappa\alpha\iota\rho\acute{o}s$).[16] For there is a nick of temptation which suits[17] the humor of these temporizing hypocrites and discovers them [A3r] in their colors, and hence it is that these of Diotrephes' generation [cf. 3Jn.9] could endure banishment because that hindered not, but promoted, their honor in that kind of suffering; yet, when they came into place of supremacy, fell to beating of their fellow brethren, as conceiving the strictness of their [the Puritans'] course carried a condemnation of their [own] careless and pompous sensuality.[18]

[II. The Pretences, Excuses, and Pleas for Temporizing of Three Sorts of Men: Statists, Temporizers, And Hypocrites]

[i. The] Statist's[19] Pretence

We have seen the causes, consider we now the excuses they would pretend for themselves. And here as men's corruptions are diverse

[14] An allusion to John Burgess, among others, who did suffer in the Puritan cause for a season but did not at any point, according to Hooker, really approve of it in every exact particular.

[15] Mary Tudor (1553–1558) at first tried to be lenient toward Protestants, while proscribing their religion. Persecutions began in 1554.

[16] Hooker is here anticipating his strictures on the least Reformed of the Marian exiles; for those who felt the exacting explicitness of the Puritan version of Protestantism, as well as those who did not approve "the exactness" of the gospel in every respect, alike had to leave repapalized England and make the best of sojourning among the Reformed churches on the Continent.

[17] The text reads: stuttes.

[18] The poorly constructed sentence refers to those Marian exiles enstated or reenstated as prelates in the Elizabethan establishment who made it difficult for the more rigorously Reformed contingent among the returned exiles and others; and Hooker suggests that the liturgical and moral rigorism of the one carried a steady condemnation of the other party.

[19] It is not at all certain that Hooker means by "Statist" an Erastian, for he

and act more or less strongly, their shifts carry more or less appearance with them. Here first your statist is most gross to whom his religion is as his coin. All that goes for current gospel with him that is stamped with the authority and allowance of the state. He is hovering betwixt several religions that he may take any for his turn, waits, and eyes to see which side is like[ly] to prosper, that so he may be of the safest side. And he blesseth himself with the name of a Christian church and the substance of religion. And whatever things are like[ly] to prove troublesome, these he will make indifferent that he may take them or leave them as he likes best for his ease.

Discretion is Thy Statist's God and Gospel

He complains much of the restless strictness of men's spirits who cannot see when they are [A3r] well, put too great weight upon things that are of no worth, stand upon trifles. He crieth out for "discretion" as that which would umpire and determine all doubts. And therefore "he can run with the hare and hold with the hound" — by discretion! He will do anything rather than suffer anything — by discretion! He can solder[20] with the times and wink at the sins of men, yea, swallow them down, though with reluctance of conscience; and that he terms tolerating — and all by discretion! Authority is in stead of all arguments to this man; he inquires after no other ground or warrant.

[ii. The] Temporary Professor's Pretence[s]

The temporary gospeler, having had some touch of religion and

---

seems to have more in mind the prudential conformist to the regnant religion. But he could have intended to suggest the Erastian motif. Thomas Erastus (d. 1583), professor of medicine in Heidelberg (1558), held, against the extreme Calvinists in the Palatinate, that the state had ultimate authority over such a matter as excommunication. This was expressed in his posthumously published *Explicatio gravissimae quaestionis* (1589). Richard Hooker defended civil authority in his *Laws of Ecclesiastical Polity* (1594).

[20] The text reads: *soder.*

light of truth in his mind, can find no rest unto his conscience unless he have some show of reason to allege, for he remembers the charge of the Apostle, I Cor. 7:23: "Ye are redeemed with a price. Be not the servants of men." He recalls the limitation of God's command, I Pet. 2:13: "Obey in the Lord;" that, [cf.] I Cor. 11:2, we ought to be followers of the apostles no farther than they were followers of Christ, that the utmost extent of our Savior's commission, [cf.] Mt. 28:18–20, to teach and for men to obey was that men should be taught to observe all that he commanded, not that men commanded.

[1.] A Declining Heart Catcheth at Anything
that it may plead for declining

[A4r] Resolving therefore to decline, they [the temporary gospelers] seek to catch at any appearance which they may plead for their declining. And because they are most led by example and sense, these are the weapons with which they use to ward themselves and maintain their course.

Common example carries a persuading power with them; it's a sufficient reason for their doing because they see it is done. Here they take up their stand. All men for the most part do so, and why may not they? Thus like sheep they follow the drove though it be to the shambles. (*Non quo eundum sed quo itur.*) [21] Especially if they hear of any noted and famous for piety and godliness to go in such a way, they conclude forthwith it is the right way, reasoning thus: '*They* are wise and godly; and think you they durst do it, they would do it, unless it were good and pious?' When the truth hath told us, Rom. 3:4, that "all men are liars" and either do or may deceive or be deceived! Even the courses of the strictest saints have their crackings. Peter was a good man and yet dissembled, Gal. 2:12; and Barnabas was a good man, Acts 11:24, and yet was snatched away by example into the same dissimulation. What madness is it [that] because a wise man happily[22] falls into the mire that we should foul ourselves and wallow with him?

---

[21] "Not where they ought to go but where they are going." The text has not been further identified.

[22] *Happily*, i.e., by chance.

[2.] The Authority of the Church and the Canons of it, like wind and tide, carry the temporizer to any coast[23]

But the main bulwark whereby they beat back all assaults is if they [A4v] can hold out some ecclesiastical canon: The Church enjoins it, and are you wiser than the Church? This strikes it dead. No man must dare to dispute any further. Nay, they count it unreasonable once to demur or doubt anymore, but expect that all men should captivate their conceits presently and put off reason and pluck out their eyes to see by other men's spectacles, which is in truth not only to cease to be Christians, but to be men.

The extent of the Church's authority

Not that I detract any due respect and esteem which each man should have both in opinion and affection of the true Church of Christ. I know she is the spouse of Christ; yet but the spouse. It is enough that she is next to her head, the Lord Jesus. She must not usurp to be head; her power is subordinate, not supreme, Mt. 28:20; *ministerium*, not *imperium*. She must deliver the laws which she hath received from her King, not dare to make laws. And therefore we must beware, lest while for our own ends we would honor the Church too much, we dishonor Christ, wrong and grieve both. To crush therefore the former cavil and objection, I answer several things.

[A Refutatory Excursus]
The Pretence Taken From The Authority [of The Church]:
Dashed [Six Times]

1. [The pretence is dashed], (*a* because it [ecclesiastical authority] is a poisoned drug of popery.) [24] It is the Romish tenet to a hair and one of the most fulsome points and loathsome dregs of the filth

---

[23] Hooker's paragraph has been broken to make way for insertion of a marginal summary as a heading.

[24] The text has two marginal summaries numbered 1. To bring both of them into our edition, Hooker's material in the paragraph has been divided into subarguments *a* and *b*.

of popery, the Jesuits themselves, having no other bottom, [Br] to bear up to or to build up their blind obediences — an opinion constantly and unanimously opposed by all our divines, abhorred by all Christian self-denying, and sincere-believing hearts. [Daniel?] Chamier, *De Votis*, *lib*. ii, cap. 11.[25] [The pretence is dashed] (*b* [b]ecause it overthrows the sovereignty of Christ and his prophetical and kingly office).[26] For what is it else but to jostle Christ out of his prophetical and kingly office, to resolve out faith and obedience lastly into the determinations and commands of men?

2. Why are the Beroeans, Acts 17:11, commended for examining Paul's doctrine? [27] Why are all men enjoined, 1 Th. 5:21, "to try all things and to hold that which is good" if we be bound to take our religion upon trust from the authority of the Church?

3. (The Apostle would not challenge this power.) If Paul an apostle and doctor of the Gentiles disclaims all such sovereignty as tyrannical usurpation, what man or church dare challenge it? But disclaim it he doth, 2 Cor. 1:24: "Not that we have dominion over your faith, but are helpers of your joy, for by faith you stand."

4. Had men or churches power to coin ecclesiastical canons, to forge new articles of faith, to make these senses of the scripture authentic which suited their minds, and to charge these upon the consciences of men as necessary to be believed, believers should not stand [Bv] by their faith; but they, and their faith, should stand or fall according to the feeble determination of men.

5. (That the authority of the Church is not the rule, and the same rule which guides the Church doth guide each member.) If the faith of particular men depend upon the Church, upon what doth the faith of the Church depend? Either they be the rule, which is too loathsome to affirm, or else they are guided by the rule of the Word in their determinations, which begets both saving light in their minds and sound faith in their hearts: Eph. 2:20; Rom. 10:17. And if the

[25] The reference has not been found.

[26] Of the *triplex munus Christi*, popularized by John Calvin, Hooker has chosen to avoid mention of the priestly office.

[27] The Jews in Beroea received Paul and Silas, refugees from the uproar in Thessalonica, and were commended by Luke as "noble," because they eagerly examined the scriptures daily.

Word be able to give them light and faith, why not others as well as them?

6. The authority of the Church, unto which we must captivate our judgments, must either be the authority of the Universal Church, which acteth nothing but in the particulars and these have varied in opinion and practice, touching ceremonies, and therefore cannot settle us in a certain determination; or it must be the authority of a particular church. But particular churches have not only erred, but [also] departed from the faith. Who lorded it over the law? Did not the Church, Mt. 14:10?[28] Who condemned and crucified the Lord? Did not the Church? Who persecuted the apostles and forbade them to preach and publish the gospel? Did not the Church? And this [B2r] which is said of churches is true of councils of all kinds, as experience of all ages hath made it good.

[3.] Third Plea of the Temporizer is the Love of his People
and preaching, when indeed it is the love of himself and [his] living

Others of this rank [clerics] plead the love of their people, the necessity of preaching, and [the] hope of doing good, how precious men's pains are, and what need [there be] of laborers in the vineyard. And therefore [they] conclude: if all men should sit down[29] in silence, as some do, the ruin of the Church must needs follow. They confess, it's true indeed, [that] these popish relics, which are the bane of the churches' peace, being unprofitable and needless, nay scandalous and offensive, should be removed. But when they weigh that heavy charge: "Woe if I preach not the gospel" [1 Cor. 9:16], they are then willing to bear all rather than to deprive the Church of the benefit, and the souls of God's people of the profit and comfort, of their ministry! Whereas, alas, all this pretense of mercy is a miserable mistake and commonly that worldly watch-

---

[28] The reference is to Herod as head of the Jewish particular (!) church, commanding the decapitation of John the Baptist.

In the margin at item 6 is the dictum: *Universale nec existit, nec agit nisi in individuis*, "The universal neither exists nor acts except in particulars." Herein Hooker rests his Congregationalism in a nominalist view of the Church.

[29] The text reads: *dovvur*. The *corrigendum* at the end makes of this: *downe*. Nevertheless Hooker could indeed have also meant *dour*.

word of "favor thyself" [29a] lies closely covered under these curious
flourishes of care and compassion for the common good. For the
question is not whether preaching be precious,[30] or the pains of
faithful ministers profitable, but the doubt here is whether we may
come to do lawful things by unlawful means, to sin that we may
do service, as though [B2v] the Lord had need of my lie or else
that he could not bring his servants to his own haven without the
devil's boat,[31] or that Christ could not uphold his own kingdom
without the pains and preachings of some men. Now I conceive, it
is undeniably evident, that the suffering in the time of Queen Mary's
days did more settle and enlarge the bounds of the gospel than all
the preaching did in King Edward the Sixth's reign.[32]

[4.] A Fourth Plea of the Temporizer

Others speak out and deal down right. [They] profess it is against
the hair and their hearts to do this drudgery,[33] but they are not
able to undergo the extreme pressure which follows the refusal of
them. Nay it is certain, some have openly protested, that if it were
but half an hour's hanging, they would rather suffer it than subscribe.
(I speak but what I know.) But for them and theirs, to lie in the
ditch and to be cast into a blind corner like broken vessels, yea,
they and their families to die many hundred deaths by extreme
misery before they could come unto their graves, this they were
not able to undergo; a condition, I acknowledge, which needs and
deserves a great deal of pity and commiseration, since it is true
that some kinds of oppression make a man mad. But O that the
God of mercy would put it into the minds and hearts of those whom
it doth concern, that they would never [B3r]suffer such refuse

---

[29a] In the margin the phrase goes on: ". . . is the serious charge—whatever is
alleged to color it with."

[30] The text reads: *precions*. This could be a misprint for *precisian* (precise as
applied to Puritans) or for precious and as such possibly an allusion to I Sam.
3:1: "The word of the Lord was precious in those days."

[31] The phrasing sounds proverbial, but is not recognized as such. Cf. below,
n. 117.

[32] Not necessarily an allusion to Thomas Cranmer's *Book of Homilies* (1547),
under Edward VI (1547–1553).

[33] i.e., to observe the three ceremonies.

relics long to hazard not only the comforts but even the consciences and happiness of many distressed souls![34]

[iii.] The Close Hypocrite's Excuses

There is a third and last sort of men, more ingenuous than the former, who, when they see that such colors of excuses formerly propounded are not laid in oil, and therefore will not continue, nor can give them any encouragement in their course — such feeble pleas being like fig leaves which cannot cover the nakedness of their cause, being neither true in themselves nor honorable to their proceedings — they come to the main hold and profess [that] the things are lawful and commendable and therefore they do no more but what they may, nay what they ought. And whereas they have been of another mind, they diversely discover the causes of their change, as they are diversely affected or have a greater stroke of conscience and conviction of judgment.

1. Not willing to search

One man acknowledgeth he hath been long staggering about the things in question; but now he hath got greater light, sees more, and understands better. And yet no man could ever see his [the staggerer's] candle lighted, his arguments alleged, nor yet were his overswaying reasons ever offered to scanning.

[B3v] Nay if he be put hard to, it will appear he hath none. Yea, he is not acquainted with the things he doth if he come to give an account of what he hath done. Only, you must believe, he hath private arguments which do overpower his judgment. Otherwise he must grant he doth practice without ground and reason. The sum in short is [that] he hath gotten a perspective about him and perceives that ease and liberty is good and therefore, Issachar-like [Gen. 24:14f.], is resolved to sit under his burden. He sees the way

---

[34] The not quite clear sentence concludes ". . . refuse reliques, longe, to hazard, not only the comforts, but even the consciences & happiness of many distressed soules."

by swallowing of ceremonies, how to sleep in a whole skin and that course he takes.

[2.] His falsehood in his search; consult[s] with these only who are of his judgment

If some searching truth delivered in public press him, or some sincere-hearted friend persuade him to a further inquiry, he seeks after the truth as a coward doth for his enemy, being afraid to find it. Loath he is to be in the society of such whom he conceives to be either judicious in their dispute or zealous in their course against this trash. Secretly desirous that others should not occasion conferences or that such should not enter into serious communication of these things, and if they do he is weary of it and blames the author of the discourse — as[35] that more savory or seasonable talk were shut out — when he goes for counsel and direction, it is to some such authors who write for the things he would [B4r] practice, or [he] consult[s][36] only with those men that profess to maintain them, and so they make up the match at midnight.[37]

[3.] Or adviseth with those who are weak, if contrary they be in judgment

But if yet their own consciences, the arguments, or persuasions of others provoke to a more serious examination of both sides, how wearily[38] and unwillingly go they to the work? Commonly they make choice of the weakest whose opinion they know to be cross to their course, or if they advise with other of more able understanding, it is upon a start or sudden [so] that there can be no sad dispute. And if yet such arguments fall which they are not able to

---

[35] *As,* i.e., *so.*

[36] The emendation here improves the syntax; but Hooker no doubt intended *consult* as an infinitive in faulty assimilation to the prepositional phrase above: "when he goes for counsel. . . , it is *to* some such authors. . . or [to] consult only with those men."

[37] A marginal summary reads: "Consult with these only who are of his judgment." As this is so much like what is in the text, the Editor has not absorbed it into the main text in parentheses.

[38] The text reads "wearishly."

gainsay, they go their way and can tell how to forget or neglect them and profess they were with such but could not be convinced nor see any sufficient reason to settle their judgments.

[4. Or they seek out those with savory advice]

But when they consult with such whose opinions they know will please their palates, and persuade them to that which they are resolved beforehand to practice, though happily they propound no reason but only administer some grave counsel or savory advice to express their own resolution or allege that place, Rom. 13:1: "Let every soul be subject to the higher powers"; Oh, [how] they go away with abundant content! [They] admire and thank him for his advice, profess they [B4v] never heard so much and that now he[39] is fully settled and hath his doubts answered to his desire, gives it out that such a man is able to give satisfaction to any, when in the meanwhile he never asked any argument but took his bare opinion because it pleased him, and yet will reject the reason sometimes of another because it crosseth him.

[5. Dr. Burgess' *Answer* too easily satisfies]

May be, it so falls out, that some new book of great note and expectation is published which might clear the cause to these men's contents. After they have viewed it and wiped their eyes, all things then are so clear that there is not a cloud in the sky, nay not a mote in the sun. There was never said so much before. Oh, this book of Dr. Burgess hath made all things evident to them, even to admiration, and conclude it will do as much to any that reads it. So that if men be not obstinate they cannot but be convinced.

But alas, these men, have they taken the arguments into serious consideration? Have they labored to search and examine the strength of them? Have they propounded them to such who are held most able and judicious of the other opinion, who do not find themselves

---

[39] Hooker passes from a series of plurals to the singular. The *he* refers not to the person who gives savory advice but rather to each of the class seeking it.

yet persuaded? Alas, here is deep silence! Where is that ancient rule: "Audi alteram partem?" [40] Where is that [Cr] charge of the Apostle, 1 Th. 5:21: "Try all things"? Is it not likely [that] the man should be persuaded by his author who resolves beforehand never to question anything in him? He must needs be of his author's faith who purposeth to believe all he says or not to doubt of what he says.

[6.] This [kind of declining] was done at Leicester[41]

And while I was penning this Preface there was one curious prank of cleanly conveyance[42] of a declining heart brought to hand, and it was this: Pressures [were] growing heavy upon such that would not conform themselves. The Court censures of the Commissary,[43] proceeding to [the] excommunication of such as refused [conformity], and adding aggravations thereunto — to wit, forbidding to buy or sell with such that were so excommunicate upon pain of excommunication, — one[44] amongst the rest was not able to undergo the

[40] Listen to the other side.

[41] Hooker had close connections with Leicester. See at nn. 44 and 126.

[42] A legal phrase of the period is "innocent conveyance" of property as by deed.

[43] The Court of High Commission sat in London. Its responsibility was to check heresy and enforce the prescribed order of worship by visitation and hearings, to hear ecclesiastical suits, and to serve as the normal court of appeals for the venerable ecclesiastical courts of first instance. The Court originated *ad hoc* in 1549 in a congeries of ecclesiastical commissions, which were regularized in the Elizabethan Act of Supremacy in 1559. The name appears only c. 1570. Apart from the central court there grew up certain regional commissions for the north and west. Puritans and common lawyers deplored its arrogation of authority. It was abolished in 1641. Its records were largely destroyed.

[44] The preceding phrases, like an ablative absolute in Latin, supply the attending circumstances. Hooker had close ties with Leicester and would have been swiftly made privy to so important an episode there. The person in Leicester has not been identified; but a possible informant was Arthur Hildersham (d. 1632) of Ashley-de-la-Zouch, who was several times suspended from 1590 on. Ashley is just south of Leicester. The informant could have been Francis Higginson of Leicester, a friend of Hildersham and Hooker; but he had left for New England in April, 1629, on the *Talbot* from the Thames; and Hooker's sentence gives the impression of fresh news. See further n. 126 and cf. above at n. 41.

burdens, to profess he could not suffer,[45] was too shameful; and therefore he professeth his judgment was changed by Dr. Burgess' book and therefore he need not, nay he should not, suffer. Some of his partners or consorts, desiring satisfaction with him, entreat that he would point at the place, express the argument or arguments in this book that prevailed with him. To which he answers, no particular or particulars in the book persuades, but the whole. The English of which speech and practice is this: 'I am [Cv] resolved to conform, and I will be persuaded by Doctor Burgess' book to it, but neither I nor you shall know what persuades me, that so my grounds not being known they cannot be answered nor I unsettled anymore.' Oh, the desperate folly of a declining heart, to betray and deliver up itself unto the delusions of Satan!

[7.] The shifts of subtle disputers

There is lastly another sort of profound disputers in the world who, apprehending their reach to be beyond the reasons and writings of other men, have, out of the depth of their judgments, devised a way judiciously to deceive their own souls, and, out of their picklock subtility, count it easy to make way for themselves and maintain their way in any question. And this they do by making a maze of divisions and cut things in so many shreds, by multitudes of distinctions, that at length they lose[46] their cause, the truth, and themselves also in the issue, and must of necessity bewilder the reader unless he be of a searching judgment. This kind of distinguishing is like snuffing of the candle too near,[47] putting out the light wholly while they intend to make the light burn more clear. So do these men darken the truth, professing to discover more of it. Pregnable examples of this kind the Rejoiner [Burgess[hath expressed unto us, when to avoid the dint of the argument concerning [C2r] significant ceremony and worship, his distinctions are so many and

[45] The phrase would read better: "professed he could not suffer [excommunication]; [it] was too shameful."
[46] The text reads "loose."
[47] To put out the light by cropping the snuff on the wick of the candle too close.

intricate that one member destroys another and the true nature of worship also, as may appear in the 85th and 136th pages of the first part of this dispute.[48]

[III. Selected Objections to Dr. Burgess]

All this I speak, not that I would fall out with any who is not of the same opinion with myself, for I profess the contrary. In a word or truth, every man abounds in his own sense. Only this seems somewhat grievous, and I conceive also, injurious to the truth, that after all hard dealing she cannot get an indifferent [49] hearing, seeing it is the fashion of the world to have men's persons in admiration, to gain some countenance thereby to their own courses, and therefore to blow up the fame of men's abilities, as they do bladders, to the utmost greatness they can, that the greater warrant they may seem to have to follow their opinions and ways. And contrariwise the person must be disparaged when we would have his cause or work come into discredit, a fashionable but a shameless piece of rhetoric.[50] Thus the writings of the Replier [Ames] must be "a pamphlet," his manner of writing "scurrilous," that when both are thus disfigured by the dirt and soot which the Rejoiner hath flung upon them, it may be conceived [that] they [C2v] were so misshapen in their first frame, whereas the *Answer* of the Rejoiner must be lifted up and proclaimed worthy, learned, and judicious, which puts me in mind, Acts 19:24ff., of Demetrius' outcry, v.28: "Great is Diana of the Ephesians." The ground whereof was not so much the love of the goddess as the greedy desire of that great profit they reaped thereby. So here the *Answer* must be learned and judicious that men may conform learnedly and judiciously.[51]

[48] Burgess' *Answer* is divided arbitrarily into two unequal separated paginated parts: 1–75; 1–654. A portion of the first part is indeed called a Preface, and Hooker refers to the whole as such. Hooker's specific reference here has not been ascertained, but his general characterization is cogent.

[49] *Indifferent* in the sense of *disinterested*.

[50] Hooker is saying that Burgess has practiced a familiar but shameless rhetorical device in disparaging the person of Ames in order to discredit his cause.

[51] Hooker is, of course, being ironic. He implies a parallel between the craftsmanship of the makers of Diana trinkets and the scholarly workmanship of Dr. Burgess in defense of "papist" ceremonies.

Not that I envy the Doctor's honor or would diminish anything of his due, but I cannot endure daubing,[52] much less that the praise of men should be advanced to the prejudice of the truth. Laying aside, therefore, all prejudice and partiality, cast we the proceedings of the Replier and Rejoiner[53] into the scales of righteous consideration; and where the blame most appears, let the reader lay it on and let him bear it to whom it is due by desert. And in this search, let no man think I intend or seek the Rejoiner's dishonor, for my witness is in heaven: I do not, nay I dare not, do it. I know the righteous Judge would require it, but it is for the manifestation of truth and innocency wherever it is to be found.

That I may do the Doctor right, then, I will set down the rules [i] how far the failings of others may [C3r] be laid open; ii, how far and in what cases some kind of tartness and sting of indignation may be expressed in pen or speech as allowable in Holy Writ.

[i.] How Far Lawful to Lay Open Sins

That we may lay forth the limits of the first and see how far the compass of our Christian commission reacheth in the discovery of others' faults, we must wisely distinguish of persons and sins that so we may not be deceived.

Persons then undergo many conditions and relations. Some are members of the same congregation who have covenanted to walk in the fellowship of the faith of the gospel.[54] Others are subjects of the same commonwealth only, professing the truth.[55]

Both these[56] either are again repenting and pertinacious or incorrigible sinners.[57]

---

[52] "Daubing" is a favorite word of Hooker's: whitewashing (from *dealbare* through the French).

[53] Ames and Burgess.

[54] Experiential Christians who have in some way personally owned the covenant.

[55] Ordinary parishioners who in the eyes of Hooker are subjects only of the King and not of Christ.

[56] i.e., sinners in terms of the local congregation and sinners in terms of society at large.

[57] The sentence would read better: "Both these again are either repenting or pertinacious, incorrigible sinners." The imprint has *there* in the place of *either*, but a *corrigendum* is noted at the end of the Preface.

Sins also are of sundry kinds. Some are private: some are public. Both these again are lesser scandals or more heinous and capital crimes which threaten apparent hazard to the public good or a state or the prosperous success of the gospel. Now out of these distinctions such conclusions may easily be collected which may give answer to the first question so far as concerns our purpose, and these be three.

[Three] Rules of Direction
How we may discover the faults of others

[1.] In private offenses, the rule of our Savior takes [C3v] place [Mt. 18:15]: "If thy brother offend, tell him his fault betwixt him and thee alone. If he hear thee, thou hast gained thy brother." If our admonition attain the end in removing the evil, we need not then crave further help from any other to redress it. Beside[s], our brother having regained his honor by repenting, we should not cast the blot again upon him by any fresh report.

2. If, under private admonition, a brother prove obstinate and incorrigible, we may and should publish both person and fault to the congregation, as our Savior in that case enjoins it as a duty to be discharged and leaves it not to our freedom to omit. For the words run in force and [take the] form of a command [Mt. 18:17]: "Tell the church."

3. If the offense be public, either left upon record in writing and made so notorious to all that will attend and read it, or acted in some solemn assembly or in open view before many witnesses, laying aside malice and envy which may stir us to[58] sinful and sinister ends — which may carry us hereunto and spoil this and the best service, — it's very lawful, nay in case very necessary to speak of such miscarriages or write of them as occasion may require, and that with[C4r]out all breach of love. Whether we look at others who are but standers-by that they may not be scandalized, infected, or plucked away by the error of men, or if we look at the offenders themselves by way of caution and wholesome prevention, we stop

---

[58] The text has *or*. The text has a period after *service*, but this would make the sentence incomplete.

the poison of their practice — that so they do no more harm to others nor bring any more guilt upon their own souls. Than which what greater love and mercy can be shown to our fellow brethren?

And out of this ground and after this manner it is that we shall bring some of the Doctor's miscarriages to consideration and present them to the view of the reader, but such only which he himself hath made open and notorious either by writing or practice. And that for this end alone, that the false colors which he hath put upon his course and proceedings may not prejudice the truth in the hearts or judgments of the ignorant and unwary readers, or any that are willing to decline who would very fain have the Doctor's words without control, that so they might follow him without fear. And this may suffice for [C4v] answer to the first question and the warrant for our way to walk in.

[ii.] How Far Tart Speeches May Be Used

The second [question] admits satisfaction in short, to wit, how far and in what cases some kind of tartness may be expressed in pen or speech.

Answer: There be two instances in scripture which are plain and pregnant to this purpose and left for our direction in this case.

The first is the behavior of Elijah towards idolators and their idolatrous practices whom he jeers to their faces and out of a holy kind of indignation stings with a better and a deriding irony. For so the text, 1 Kg. 18:26: "And it came to pass at noon that Elijah mocked them and said, 'Cry aloud, for he is a god; either he is talking or is pursuing or he is in a journey and per adventure he sleepeth and must be awakened.' " And hence it is, the Lord casts such loathsome terms of detestation upon the idol that he besparkles the worshippers therefor with disdain.

The second instance is touching ambitious false teachers or idle[59] shepherds. So Isaiah's watchmen, 56:10, are "blind, they are dumb dogs, they cannot bark, they are greedy dogs, they can never have enough." So the Apostle Paul girds the consciences [Dr] of those

[59] The text has *Idoll.*

silken doctors of Corinth and their followers which slighted the
simplicity of the gospel, 1 Cor. 4:10: "We are fools for Christ, and
ye are wise in Christ; we are weak, and ye are strong; ye are honorable, and we are despised." These tart ironical speeches stable the
heart with a secret disdain of their groundless and ambitious folly.
And indeed when the Lord enjoins it as a duty and makes it a note
and argument of a happy man, Ps. 15:4, "that a vile person is condemned in his eyes," what expression of words can suit such a
contempt in the heart unless they carry some tartness of disdain
with them?

We now see our limits and allowance. Let the judicious reader
according to this rule consider of some keen passages of the *Reply*.
And I suppose it will be found that the most of them if not all are
pointed against the unwarrantable standings and places, the intolerable and ambitious courses of our prelates, or else their seeming and
self-deceiving arguments.

If in any he [Ames] hath exceeded the bounds of sobriety, I
profess neither to defend nor excuse it. I know the Replier [Ames]
himself will not allow it, for he hath silenced all such expressions in
this second *Reply*,[60] though he had never so just cause to provoke
him thereunto and [Dv] never so great advantage given him by the
miserable mistakes of the Rejoiner in many places, which if the Rejoiner had found in him, — he that can balk [61] after words with
such eagerness, — we should have had exclamations, proclamations,
and outcries enough to have filled up a wordy and windy volume.

However, was the Replier never so worthy to have the reproach
of scurrility cast upon him or his work, the Rejoiner was most unworthy and unfit to do it, who hath, I dare say, much exceeded in
this kind. (*Quis tulerit Gracchos?*)[62] How unseemly is it and how

---

[60] The reference "this second reply," could appear to be, to *A Fresh Suit,*
occasioned by Burgess' *Rejoinder*. But Ames published an anonymous first
Reply to Bishop Morton's *general* defense in 1622 and a second *Reply* to the
particular defense in 1623. The reference here would thus be to that second
Reply, for there are no other references in Hooker's Preface to *A Fresh Suit*
(Ames', in effect, *third* reply).

[61] To heap up in piles. A figure from ploughing. The balk is the earthen ridge
thrown up between two fields.

[62] Juvenal, *Satires,* 11.24: "Quis tulerit Gracchos de seditione querentes?" (Who
would have borne the Gracchi complaining of sedition?) The phrase is used of

ill sounds it to hear thieves complain of robbers; harlots, of adulter-
esses. The proverb is homely, but true: It's a hard world when herring men revile fishermen.[63] For proof whereof I appeal to thine
eyes to be witnesses, Christian reader. And that I may proceed according to *allegata probata*,[64] I will not look beyond my line. Only
that picture which the Rejoiner hath made of himself, I judge it not
only lawful, but in this case necessary, to present again to his view
that the world may know and, if God will, Doctor Burgess also may
know himself and what his spleen[65] hath been against the people of
the Most High God, blessed forever.

[D2R][66] [IV] CERTAIN QUERIES BY WHICH THESE [TART] PASSAGES
May Be Weighed in the Balance of Serious Consideration

Of all, in general, the queries are these: 1. If the Replier did anywhere give sentence of conformists' consciences? 2. If he uttered
any one bitter speech against all conformists? 3. The former being

---

those who criticize procedures they themselves have resorted to. Even if Ames
were deserving of the reproach of scurrility, how much more Burgess?

[63] The stench from herring is presumably stronger than that from other fish.

[64] Alleged proofs.

[65] There are several references to the spleen and to anatomy and medicine in
general, as Hooker makes the most of the fact that Ames' father-in-law and
antagonist on ceremonies is also a physician. The spleen, source of red cells,
was in medical theory the base of melancholy and in English religious theory a
partial explanation for the heat and vagaries of one's theological opponents. See
forthcoming article by John F. Sena, "The Melancholic Madness and the
Puritans," *Harvard Theological Review*, XXVI (1973), pp. 293–309.

[66] From pages D2r through E4r Hooker proceeds to deal with Burgess by
arranging materials in two columns. This material undoubtedly represents
Hooker's copybook sent in with the rest of his material without further editing
on his part.

In the right-hand column is a series of twenty-one queries. In the left-hand
column, Hooker refers to certain passages in Burgess and each of these is
numbered in correspondence with a query. The right-hand column is generally
fuller. The Editor has chosen to collapse the two columns in the interests of
clarity of exposition. Reference to the pagination in our edition will be confined to the location of the left-hand column of citation from Burgess followed
by Hooker's sharp query. The Editor is generally putting the passages from
Burgess in quotation marks whether or not the reference is verbatim or a paraphrase. He has introduced dots to indicate when Hooker has not fully transcribed Burgess.

negatively true, if the Rejoiner in his over and under-lashing was not overcome of his own evil, rather than the Replier's?

A Taste of The Tartness of Doctor Burgess' Spirit In The Several Passages of His *Answer*

This tartness will appear in three kinds: 1. His heavy censures and that of the very hearts and consciences of men. 2. His open reviling of the persons of the non-conformists, or secret inducements to bring them into distaste. 3. His keen and scornful jests, which are his pastime, frequently expressed through the whole.[67]

[i.] [His] Heavy Censures

i. "[T]hey who tell us that all . . . the Church may do touching ri[D2v]tes . . . is but the application of circumstances which are in nature civil . . . , adding that the church may not ordain any . . . ceremony . . . merely ecclesiastical, do manifest a spirit which lusteth after contradiction, p. 37 of [Ames'] *Manuduc[tion]*."[68] Query:

1. If a man upon probability affirm such a point, or out of ignorance and mistake conclude it certain and so relate it as by him conceived, doth he hereby necessarily manifest a spirit of contradiction or the weakness of his own apprehension? 2. If charity hopes the best that can be conceived in reason, to judge men's spirits by grounds weak and feeble out of which nothing can be concluded: query: whether it be not uncharitable censuring? 3. Do all those who contradict the like conceits of the Rejoiner as false manifest a sinful spirit in lusting after contradiction?

ii. In the *Answer:* "If it seem so to him [Ames] indeed, God

---

[67] These three kinds of tartness in Burgess have been partly capitalized to conform to their reappearance as subdivisions below. Kind 1 follows. The quotation from Burgess is put in quotation marks (Hooker not using such marks); and where Hooker leaves out some words, the present Editor indicates this always with marks of an ellipse (. . .).

[68] Burgess is quoting from the second of two works by Ames of this title: *A Manuduction for Mr.* [John] *Robinson, and such as consent with him in privat communion, to lead them on to publick* (1614) and, after Robinson replied with *A Manvmission to a manvdvction* (1615), *A second manvdvction* (1615). Burgess' sentence begins: "Wherefore they which. . . ."

hath smitten his contentious spirit with giddiness, for who but a man forsaken of all wisdom, etc.," p. 62. Query:

Whether may not a man mistake a thing plain and be of no contentious spirit? Whether, in such a mistake, is it certain God smites with giddiness? Whether is not this to judge men's consciences beyond warrant of any word of God or the nature of the work will bear? But is not this only unreasonable but intolerable if the thing be true?

iii. "The Convocation house[69] . . . is not so likely to conclude, etc. . . . as this libeller is to come to shame for his factious and intolerable comparison. . . . unless God humble him," p. 62. Query:

1. Whether these words come from a calm, loving, and merciful Spirit? 2. Whether God may not abate a man for his falls in executing judgments here, or may lay many punishments on him beside open shame? 3. Whether these definitive determinations of judgments upon men for some light differences and those not so clear be not to jostle God out of the place of justice and to cast thunderbolts where he doth not? But if the Replier make his expression good by his defense, as he hath, is not this a strange censure upon so small a thing and so strange a mistake?

iv. "For whosoever thinks not as [D3v] they must either be condemned of gross corruption or excused as having some good meaning, yet much weakness with all, scilicet in comparison of them. And this pride makes them so scornful," p. 65.[70] Query:

Whether this charge issues not out of a principle desirous to make the persons of nonconformists odious to all, proclaiming them as such whose intolerable pride scorns and condemns all men in regard of themselves? Whether the Rejoiner's passion did not transport him beyond himself in this accusation when it makes him contradict his own confessions? [See his] Preface, p. 5: "There be some mod-

[69] The Convocation of Canterbury differed from the provincial or archdiocesan synod in being made up of both diocesan bishops and priests, whereas the synod had only bishops. There was also a Convocation of York. The two Convocations virtually replaced synodal gatherings in England; and the Convocation of Canterbury under James I and particularly Charles I sometimes exercised quasi-parliamentary functions.

[70] The sentences start on p. 64. Hooker has certain words in parentheses, as though he might have supplied them, but, as the words so enclosed appear in Burgess, the indications for parentheses have been dropped.

erate, learned, godly, loving," etc.[71] Whether his spleen is not great that would spare none but even destroy the nation of nonconformists in the esteem of men, as Haman [Est. 3:13] [72] the Jews? For of all he speaks: "They," "Them."

v. "It is so palpably false that I should hardly believe any friar durst have set it down in print," [73] p. 67. Query:

Whether he be not more charitable to friars than nonconformists since he knows what they have printed? [74]

[D4r] vi. "And see how these men that walk and write in so haughty and magistral a fashion do but gull and deceive them with the names of worthy men, which is so great and shameful a sin, and in this Replier so frequent, that I wonder he dares dispute about ceremony before he have learned the substance of common honesty in his allegations," [75] p. 83. Query:

Whether if this Replier was faulty, was it reasonable to fly in the face of all nonconformists? Whether the Rejoiner's conscience in cold blood dare say that there is not amongst the nonconformists the truth of worthiness, but only the names, when in his Preface he [himself] thus writes, p. 3: "Some peaceable and very worthy ministers were cast out"? [76]

vii. "How can you believe any truth cross to your opinion when as you seek glory[77] one of another and presume of your new tradi-

---

[71] Burgess writes in the first part (Preface): "I would by no means have this understood of all which either use not or like not to use these ceremonies in question; for I know there be some such learned, moderate, godly, and loving, whom with all my heart I also love and honor."

[72] Burgess is compared to Haman, chief minister under Xerxes (Ahasuerus), who was determined to put to death "a certain people scattered abroad and dispersed among all provinces" of the kingdom because they would not bow down to Haman.

[73] Burgess complains that the Replier (Ames) wrongly asserts that Dr. Morton made no effort to prove Anglican ceremonies agreeable to scripture.

[74] Hooker is saying that Burgess is more charitable to Catholic antagonists, whose works he presumably has not read, than to nonconformists, whose work he knows.

[75] The quotation is accurate except that Burgess has *ceremony* in the plural and *quotations* instead of *allegations*.

[76] Burgess is referring to strictures on Puritan ministers after the Hampton Court Conference. See below, n. 90.

[77] Burgess has *honor*, instead of *glory*. Hooker reflects the original wording in the next paragraph.

tions as if the spirit of truth came to you or from you alone," p. 103. Query:

Whether they that cannot entertain truth cross to their opinion and seek honor one from another can have any truth of grace? Our Savior seems to gainsay it, Jn. 5[:44], and therefore whether there be any color of argument for the Rejoiner to condemn all nonconformists as such whom this charge condemns?

viii. "As for terms of excre[D4v]ments which he would be loath one should apply to the hair of his head,[78] it savoreth of a spirit . . . of rancor as doth the like foul speech in the *Scotch Dialogue*.[79] God will judge them for these reproaches by which they labor to breed scorn and abhorring of these in the minds of ignorant men," p. 131. Query:

Whether doth the vilifying of a relic which one conceives superstitious argue[80] a spirit of rancor? How came the Rejoiner to be sure that God will judge them for these? Whether may they not repent and then God will pardon them, not judge them? How if the relics be base and deserve to be scorned?

ix. "This flimflam Master [Henry] Jacob[81] lent you, and both he and you take it up merely for a shift,[82] not out of conscience or judgment, but of haughty desire of defending what you have once spoken," p. 207. Query:

How knows the Rejoiner but they might do it out of ignorance? And an error of ignorance may stand with a good conscience. How

[78] The text of Burgess reads: *beard*.

[79] The marginal reference to the *Scotch Dialogue* refers to p. 120 therein, quoting thus: "It were good either to recant and vomit them up or else let them pass with the excrements through the dung-port." The *Dialogue* has not been identified. Both Ames in his *Reply* and the author of the *Dialogue*, in distinguishing the accidental from the essential parts of "chief worship," identified the former as a kind of excrement.

[80] The text reads: *argues*, because Hooker has forgotten that he has begun with *doth*.

As for the substance of his retort, Hooker is saying that relics of popery are superstitions and should be gotten rid of with scorn and disdain.

[81] Henry Jacob (1563–1624), a moderate Brownist, was minister in Middelburg, Leiden, and London.

The "flimflam" which, according to Burgess, Jacob lent Ames was the allegedly false distinction between civil and religious acts. Burgess accused Ames of using a ploy when he claimed he was being misunderstood.

[82] A petty expedient.

knows the Rejoiner that it was a haughty desire and no other passion? But if all this be maintained, is not the Rejoiner extremely harsh in his censures when no room will serve him unless he sit upon men's consciences and, Pilate-like, condemn the innocent?

x. This Replier in a com[Er]mon course giving the name of "a good Christian" to some uncomformable,[83] the Rejoiner breaks out into these words: "This addition savors strongly of that spirit of separation which hath been hunted after in the chase of unconformity, for this shows that these men — the adversaries of ceremonies and bishops — are the only good Christians," p. 216. Query:

If one call a nonconformitant "a good Christian," doth he express a strong favor of separation? He that names a nonconformitant "a good Christian," doth he conclude that the adversaries to the bishops are the only Christians? Query: whether reason or passion against all color of reason make these consequences? And whether the Rejoiner would suffer us to make the like out of his words when he calleth conformists "the faithful servants of Christ" as he doth, p. 628.[84]

xi. "Doth this Replier and such as he who, without law, without calling, without reason, without conscience, do smite with their tongues and condemn to the pit of darkness the bishops and the conformed ministers and in a manner all that are not of their party . . . ," p. 219.[85] Query:

[1.] Would not the Rejoiner make nonconformitants monsters of men who shall commit so capital a sin as condemnation of men to hell, and being void of law, calling, reason, [and] conscience in so doing? 2. Where doth this Replier condemn all that are not his

[83] i.e., Ames is being criticized by Burgess for according the designation of "good Christian" as a courtesy ("in common course") to some unspecified separatist, not merely a non-conformist but, in Burgess' word, an "uncomformable." The strongest argument on Burgess' side would always be that nonconformity leads inevitably to full separation, a position stoutly opposed by both Ames and Hooker.

[84] Burgess had written: "These and such like *censures*, or rather *calumniations*, darted against the *Church*, the *State*, the *Pastors*, their *Brethren*, their owne *bowells* whereby they have wrought the faithfull servants of Christ out of the love, and estimation of many (not ill affected, but misguided Zealots of our Land), and brought the publicke prayers into contempt."

[85] In Burgess' text there is no *and* after *bishops*. The quotation is not a complete sentence.

party or all conformed ministers? Nay, if neither he nor any non-conformitant ever writ, spake, printed, nay, thought so unreasonably, query: Whence such an accusation comes and what ground it argues which exceeds the bounds of truth or reason, yea, common sense?

xii. "Nor is it rightly taken up that these men are counted factious for neglect of ceremonious canons upon conscience, but [rather] for stiff opposition to ecclesiastical laws[86] which they despitefully speak and write against, and for contempt of these[87] statute laws by which the Book of Common Prayer[88] . . . is established. For that they draw, as fast as they can, into a body of themselves, engrossing aforehand the name of "brethren," "the godly," "the Church," the "good Christians," as though[89] we had lost out Christ and they had found him quite away," pp. 221f. Query:

Whether those hundreds of ministers silenced at the beginning of King James[90] were despiteful speakers against the ceremonies or conscionable forbear[er]s of their use? Whether these who desire to subscribe according to law be despisers of the law, or those who deny them the benefit of it? Where is that body into which the nonconformitants gather themselves? How appears it that they ever engrossed such titles to themselves, so as to deny them to all others, or more than the Rejoiner engrosseth the title of "the faithful servants of Christ" unto conformists. [Cf.] p. 628.

xiii.[91] The terming of our ceremonies popish is done "out of faction and to make the imposers and observers [of them] [92] hateful with the people of God, which I believe no church would suffer. I am sure it should [93] not," p. 238. Query:

Whether this imputation be not to bring them [Amesians et al.] into hatred and distaste of the state? Whether ever profane drunkards,

---

[86] Burgess has *canons*.

[87] Burgess has *those*.

[88] The fuller text reads: "Common Prayer and these ceremonies in controversy are established."

[89] Burgess has *as if*. As for the substance of the preceding characterization of Puritan shunning, see another quotation from Burgess to the same effect in n. 21 of Essay I.

[90] After the Hampton Court Conference in January, 1604.

[91] In the text queries 12 and 13 are grouped together. For Burgess on p. 628, see quotation above, n. 84.

[92] Hooker has added to Burgess the phrase we have placed in brackets.

[93] Burgess has *ought*.

riotous adulterers, scoffing atheists, or the bitterest of the Jesuits, jeered more tauntingly against many faithful? And is it not loath-some to lick up their vomits? For the worst of men have not worse language against the nonconformists.

xiv. "This man [Ames] forceth his wit, and I fear his conscience also, and doth not believe himself when he saith that these cerem[onies] are imposed as parts of God's worship but only for faction and opposition [sake] [94] would fain have it thought so, that their opposition might be justified before men," p. 243. Query:

Whether the Rejoiner can judge of a man's heart any other way than by his expressions outward? Since the Replier's professions and expressions are plain one way, by what warrant can the Re-joiner conclude his conscience is other?

xv. "For a wrangling spirit, yea, an ill conscience, is so[95] plainly to be observed while he studies [E2v] to persuade what [he] him-self believes not," p. 243. Query:

Neither word, nor reason, nor love, nor religion learns or allows such inferences. What is the principle whence these proceed?

xvi. "But what, should I press these men with the authority of men who have themselves in estimation for soundness of judgment before all men?," p. 370.[96] Query:

Whether any man truly humble and gracious can prefer himself before all men? Whether the Rejoiner accounts all nonconformists void of all truth of grace when he layeth this to their charge?

xvii. "But the Replier, seeing no interpretation will help against the clear testimonies of the learned by us alleged, confesseth they were men — as if he and his partners were more than men! — and that there is a little variety. So willing are men rather to cast dirt in the faces of others than to confess any mistaking in themselves. Is this anything but the spirit of pride [E3r] thus masterly to judge the Lord's worthies?," p. 387. Query:

Whether he that says "the ancients were men" doth thereby infer

[94] Burgess has: *opposition sake. . .*
[95] Burgess has *also.*
[96] Burgess reads thus: "But what should I press these men with authorities of men who have themselves above all other men in estimation for soundness of judgment?"

that he himself is more than a man? Whether to affirm the "fathers to be men" is masterly to judge them or argues a spirit of pride when they themselves so judge and speak of themselves? Whether to affirm the ancients to be men argues a man resolved to sink all men's reputation, how holy and zealous soever they be, rather than to confess his own mistake?

xviii.[97] "This answer you think good to give because you are resolved to sink the reputation of all men, ancient or latter, how learned and zealous soever they were, rather than to confess your own mistaking." Query:

Whether there can be a heavier charge laid against a man than "rotten-hearted and unfit to live in the society of men"? And yet what lighter ground, and more insufficient, can be pretended to bear it up?

[ii.] [His] Open Revilings of the Persons of Nonconformitants or secret inducements to bring them into distaste[98]

[xix.] In p. 52 of the Preface: some nonconformists are brought in and said to be of that temper that when the removal of cerem[onies] only was mentioned, their answer was: "They must not leave one hoof[99] [E3v] behind them." And the note in the margin tells us: [100] "This S[i]r Fran[cis] Walsingham[101] told Mr. [John] Knewstubs[102] of whom I had it." Query:

[97] This quotation really belongs to the series in item xvii and is responded to in Query xvii, last sentence. It is possible that the quotation from Burgess, to which Query xviii is the response, got lost by the typesetter, who simply detached the last sentence of item xvii and made it into the present item xviii, to which, however, Hooker has already responded. Query [i.e., Retort] xviii appears to be a response to a quotation from Burgess lost perhaps by the typesetter.
[98] This subdivision ii within the series of quotations from Burgess retorted to by Hooker goes back to the announced three-point assault on p. D2r (at n. 66).
[99] We at this point render Burgess correctly. Hooker or his printer has at this point: *have a hoof.* . .
[100] The following sentence is indeed a marginalium in the *Rejoinder.* Hooker or the typesetter has numbered it as item 1 and assigned to each of the subsequent paragraphs the numbers 2 through 8. His Query xx seems to be a response to items 2–4. The typesetter then breaks the sequence of queries and starts after xx with a bunching of responses: *Quaere 5,6,7,8.* The Editor numbers this bunching xxi and drops the misleading numbering of the paragraphs 1–8.
[101] Francis Walsingham (c. 1530–1590), who lived abroad under Mary, was

[1.] What if no man should have known that Mr. Knewstubs told Dr. Burgess in private, conceiving him of the same judgment? Ergo query: Whether it be safe for fellow brethren to betrust their secrets to the Rejoiner's keeping [E3r]? 2. Whether the Rejoiner did not rake up all the blind corners of his memory to fetch out what might be to bring nonconformers into distaste?

[xx.] It "is a ridiculous supposition," it's "a malicious surmise," "all this scurrilous bundle is of no use unless it be to ingraft himself into the affections, which he calleth the consciences, and applause of his own party," Preface, p. 63. "These two notes note you to be an egregious wrangler," p. 6. "Did ever sober man reason thus?," p. 61.[103] Query:

Whether this be not downright railing?

[xxi.] "I should be sorry to find so much waywardness and false-hood in any man of our religion, but cannot but wonder at it in [E4r] a man pretending more than ordinary sincerity," p. 15. "How ever these men, who in effect say to all other men: 'Stand back, I am more holy than thou,' etc., what a shame is it for men to glory of sincerity for refusing cerem[onies] and use no sincerity in al-leging authors," p. 284. "But that use which the learned divines call historical, these men call religious, that they might by a false ear-mark bring us into suspicion abroad and into hatred with our re-ligious people at home, and yet they would be counted sincere men," p. 303. Query:

Whether the Pharisees in their ceremonies did not practice more holiness than other men? And whether conformists be not therein more like the Pharisees than nonconformists? Whether this be not to leave the persons and to jibe at sincerity itself? Whether do the

---

English ambassador in France (1570–1573) and secretary of state (1573–1590). Of Puritan sympathies, he favored English colonialization, induced Elizabeth to throw her support to the Dutch against Spain, and was instrumental in bringing Mary Stuart to trial and execution.

[102] The reference is presumably to John Knewstub(s) (1544–1624), who among other things published *An answeare unto certayne assertions, tending to maintaine the Church of Rome to be the true catholique church* (1579). Knewstub(s), rector of Cockfield in Suffolk, was one of the four "Agents of the Millene Plaintiffes" at the Hampton Court Conference.

[103] This series of three quotations from Burgess is numbered in the left-hand column 2, 3, and 4. For the first, Hooker or his printer incorrectly gives p. 633.

professed enemies against the power of godliness use any other language when they would jeer at the sincerity of God's servants? Is not some historical use religious? What want of sincerity then is it to distinguish that historical use of images which is to stir up devotion from other civil use by the term religious? Nay, what sincerity is there in branding such a declaration with a false affected ear-mark?

[iii.] His Tart Jests and Taunts are not as Grains of Salt
but so frequent that they seem as pickle in which the passages of his book are laid to steep, and therefore I will but point at some number of places to ease the reader and myself

Page 71, line ; Preface, p. 14, line 29; p. 19; p. 33, line 22; [Preface] p. 15, lines 1f., 11; p. 37, lines 24f.[104] And he not only takes but seeks an occasion, yea, is content to go some miles about to reach men a blow who were of godliness and worth by some slighting taunt to disparage their persons or works.

That judicious and painful laborer and faithful servant of Christ he slights on this manner (Preface, pa[ge]4): "Mr. [Robert] Parker's gaudy and passionate treatise on the cross," [105] a work in truth of that strength and beauty that it blears and dazzles the eyes of envy itself. And therefore men out of hope either to imitate it or

[104] Hooker's allusions here to part i ("Preface") and part ii in the Burgess pagination are not exact, but three that are certain may be adduced:
Preface, p. 14, lines 13–15; 29f.: "[F]or no man ever hath credit with them, who was once against Conformity [like] Burgess in any degree, and comes after to speake for it. . . . It will be sayd, I hunt after preferment in my old dayes."
Preface, p. 15, lines 1 ff.; 10 ff.: "[I]t hath beene bruited, that my Lord the Bishop of *Coventry* and *Lichfield*, hath promised to giue me a Prependeraie, in regard of this work [*The Answer*] . . . . [T]his is the vncharitableness of some men, that they would haue all men esteemed corrupt and carnal, who accord not vvith them in all their Periods."
Part ii, p. 37, lines 24–27: "I see no cause of this outleap [Ames' ridicule of certain preposterous scriptural proofs] but either to ease his stomacke, or to please those of his side, whom he hath lately smitten, as children are sometimes pleased by smiting of others in their sight."
[105] Robert Parker, *A Scholasticall discourse against symbolizing with Anti-christ in ceremonies, especially in the signe of the crosse* ([Amsterdam], 1607), frequently cited by Burgess. The remainder of the sentence and what follows summarizes Burgess' disparagement of the book.

answer it would bear the world in hand. It was not worth the while to spend the labor in it.

But the Rejoiner wisheth some would (pa[ge]75, Preface) "reduce it to [Fr] logical arguments," and then he doubts not but it would soon be answered.

Which is such a mere put-off and so unbeseeming the skill of a logical disputer, much more the champion-like confidence of Doctor Burgess, that had not his heart secretly misgiven him in this seeming bravado, such an expression would never have fallen from his pen.

For let any rational man be judge in this case. Are not logical arguments plainly expressed in a continued discourse and by a logician easily collected? And what needs a reducing to a form then?

Beside[s], Mr. Parker's *Discourse* is either empty and void of sinews of sound reason — and then the weakness of it is soon discovered and may be confuted, yea, disgraced with more ease, — or else there be arguments of that solidity and strength which either the Rejoiner cannot reduce, or else is not able or not willing to answer. To say he cannot reduce them to form is a thing too mean to imagine, nor will the Rejoiner grant, nor will I, [n]or do I think. To say he is not willing to answer is to gainsay his own course, the profes[Fv]sion of his care, to traverse[106] this cause and his love to our[107] cerem[onies] and the peace of our Church so much pretended in his *Answer*.

The third[108] therefore must be concluded, for I do not see what fourth thing can be given. Only, did ever any answerer, serious and judicious amongst divines of any kind, Protestant, Papist, Lutheran, propound such conditions? Did ever any grant such? Nay, is it not to common sense ridiculous for any Lutheran to send to a Calvinist, any Protestant to a Papist, having printed some serious treatise against them, to send I say this message? 'Well, you have printed a

---

[106] *Traverse* in legal sense: to deny formally an allegation of fact made by the other side. Cf. below at n. 182.

[107] The "our" from Hooker is ironic. He surely did not feel possessive about the required ceremonies of the Church of England!

[108] Hooker is saying that in addition to the two possibilities set forth in the preceding paragraph, namely that the Rejoiner cannot reduce his argument to form or that he is unwilling to answer, there can be only a third explanation (surely not a fourth) to which he now proceeds.

treatise here, and you place some, yea, great confidence in it. If you will reduce it into syllogisms you[109] shall be soon answered, and [the answer will be] that there is nothing but bombast and painted vermillion put upon it! *Spectatum admissi risum?'* [110] Would not the Papists laugh in their sleeves at such an answer? I will say no more, but only propound this form to the Rejoiner and save him a labor to reduce it.

He that propounds such terms of answer, which never were yet asked or granted and indeed are unreasonable to yield, professeth he can[F2r]not make an answer, being willing thereunto.

But such terms the Rejoiner craves. The like jerks[111] he lends to Mr. Jacob,[112] p. 16 [and] to godly learned [Dudley] Fenner,[113] p. 38.

And he hath such a mind to chide that upon the occasional mentioning of one word "excrement" he fetcheth a vagary into Scotland, as it were, and sits in judgment upon the author of the *Scotch Dialogue*,[114] p. 131, line 20, without any confutation of any ground,

---

[109] The text reads: "wil (reduce it into sillogismes) you. . ." The matter in parentheses in the text is indispensable to the sense and may have been added by the printer.

[110] Horace, *Ars poetica* 5: *Spectatum admissi risum teneatis, amici?* (Would you not laugh such pictures to behold?) Horace is referring to incongruous juxtapositions in a painting. Hooker is placing the line of query from Horace on the imagined lips of Burgess, addressing Parker in scorn for having put together such laughable bombast and demanding that he simplify the argument.

[111] Strikes as from a lash.

[112] Burgess says, p. 16: "Calvin never meant to put as you [Ames] doe into M. Jacobs new pinfold [confine], 'onely to dispose of such circumstances as are in their kind necessarie,' etc., as you affirme."

[113] Burgess, p. 38, refers respectfully to "that good man" Dudley but notes that even he could overpress Scripture for what he wants to find; e.g. in Canticles 4:2 "Thy teeth are as a flock of sheep" as a sanction for deacons! *Song of Songs, translation into English meeter* (1587). Dudley Fenner (1558–1587) was a major exponent of Puritan views.

[114] We have not identified the *Scotch Dialogue*, from which, indeed, Burgess has a marginal quotation with references to p. 120 therein. See above at n. 79. The word "excrement," as used first by the Replier, Ames, was with reference to the hair of the body as in a sense excrement. In the debate over what constitutes the circumstantial or accidental in worship as distinguished from the substantial or essential, certain small matters are like the accidental hairs on the body. Burgess, in carrying the point further, turns from body hairs to something more distinctive of personage, namely, his beard. It is true that Burgess then moves on to the more common sense of the word with his marginalia on the dung port.

which I suppose had better suited his place, being an answerer and not a judge.

In like sort, he vilifies Mr. [William] Bradshaw,[115] a pamphlet *Of Things Indifferent* of Mr. Bradshaw, p. 188, "your Mr. Bradshaw," whom we are not ashamed to own and suppose the Doctor would have been afraid to have grappled with him in an arg[ument] had he been alive.

Venerable Mr. [Thomas] Cartwright [116] he taketh up sometime, as if he had written upon prejudice, without judgment. Thus much I thought good to add in short to wipe away that supercilious disdain cast here by the Doctor upon divers of the Lord's dear servants, many thousands of [F2v] whom together he accuseth after of stupidity or prejudice, even all that allow not of organs in divine service or psalm-singing. We shall now summarily point at the rest of the places as an inventory or treasury of the Rejoiner's taunts: p. 47, line 22; p. 50, lines 7f.; p. 52, lines 33–35; p. 55, line 26; p. 113, line 32; p. 120, line 12; p. 130, line 10; p. 141, last line; p. 180, line 32; p. 182, lines 16f.; p. 213, line 18; p. 247, lines 21f.; p. 312, lines 6f.; p. 315, lines 11f.; p. 316, line 10.[116a]

These are some of the many commonplaces of scoffs to be found in his book and all are contained within the compass of the three first chapters. As for the last, I had neither leisure nor list to trouble thee, good reader, or myself, with writing them out.

Only to give thee a guess how prettily the Rejoiner can play with words, find himself talk, and fill up pages, I shall take so much pains as to transcribe a place or two. Thus he writes, p. 66:

So this and those rules after added are, as the proverb[117] is, like a

---

[115] William Bradshaw (1571–1618) published, among other items referred to by Burgess or Morton, anonymously, *A treatise of the nature and use of things indifferent* (Amsterdam?, 1605).

[116] Thomas Cartwright (1535–1603), the principal English Presbyterian opposed by Richard Hooker in his *Laws of Ecclesiastical Polity*, Books I–IV (1594), V (1597), was a supporter of the *Admonition to Parliament* (see n. 118) and the presumptive author of the *Second Admonition*.

[116a] Examples of the taunts cited are: p. 47, l. 22: "This poore distressed man knowes not what to doe"; p. 50, ll. 7f.: "So I see here Master *Cartwright* holding the head of their Negative Argument till it dye in his hands."

[117] The original Burgess text reads: ". . . are (as the byword is)." The proverb is documented by Morris Palmer Tilley, *A Dictionary of the Proverbs in England in the sixteenth and seventeenth centuries* (Ann Arbor, 1950), R 174.

rope and butter, that "if the one slip, the other may hold." [So again pp. 73f.] The truth is Mr. Jacob could never get over the block which Mr. Cartwright and the Admonitors[118] [F3r] had laid in his way. However, Mr. Cartwright himself, a man of more activity, made a shift to leap over it, namely this: Whatsoever is not commanded in the Word must not be in the Church. And yet Mr. Jacob, that he might seem to hold fair quarter with Mr. Cartwright and other learned divines, who acknowledge that certain ecclesiastical rites and ceremonies appropriated to holy actions were left to the determination of the Church under some general rules of the Word, will seem to allow somewhat, he cannot tell what, some circumstances only civil or occasional as the time and place [of worship], which he rather calleth circumstances than ceremonies, that so if any shall say he alloweth nothing to the Church's determination to be squared by some rules, he may answer for himself and say: "Yes, certain circumstances are, namely such as are necessary in civil as well as sacred actions." If, on the other side, one challenge him to give some liberty to men for the ordaining of rites which are but extrinsical circumstances about the worship of God, he may answer for himself that he hath protested against all mere ecclesiastical rites which are ordained by men and not left so much as one to their determination.

[F3v] Thus, as he that by turning of his picture of a horse made it running or a tumbling horse, which you would, so hath Mr. Jacob provided for himself there to square some circumstances by four rules, or, to cut off all by another, as the market shall require.[119]

This is the substance, Christian reader, of a whole page almost, touching which I would propound these [two] queries to thy consideration: [1] Whether it was not easy to make us a massy volume

[118] The *Admonition* of 1572, composed by the London clergymen John Field and Thomas Wilcox, and the *Second Admonition* by Cartwright, demanded a non-episcopal constitution for the Church of England. These Admonitors were expressly opposed by Richard Hooker (n. 116). See Donald Joseph McGenn, *The Admonition Controversy* (New Brunswick, 1949).

[119] The Editor has followed Burgess' text. Hooker's transcription is exact except for a *thus* for a *this,* a missing *that* and *of,* and in the last line: *put of* for *cut off.*

Burgess' point in the foregoing hostile excerpt from him by Hooker is that the moderate Brownist (separatist) Jacob is able to keep in the good company of Presbyterian Cartwright *et al.* by construing as "circumstantial" rather than "ceremonial" certain regulations he is willing to accept from the state, while refusing to accept anything ceremonial from the established Church, which is not literally sanctioned by scriptures.

with such talk as this? 2. If a man should set down such like passages word for word and add an answer suitable, filled with such wind, would it not rather be accounted, and that justly, a blotting of paper and abusing the reader, than rendering an answer of any worth and satisfaction?

And by the survey of these particulars collected out of the three first chapters and comparing the *Reply* therewith, I am confident it will soon appear to any not forestalled with prejudice whether the *Reply* or *Answer* may most justly challenge and bear the name of scurrilous? And it will be as evident that the Rejoiner had no cause to accuse the Replier of scurrility unless he would con[F4r]demn himself not only of the same crime but of somewhat beside far more sinful. For[120] though it be easily incident, I confess, to our corrupt natures, out of a pang of pride and passion, to cast unbrotherly contempt upon such who seem to cross us in our opinions and practices — when it comes to point of opposition betwixt some particular men and ourselves, — yet to vent such a mass of venom in heavy censures, harsh revilings, slighting scorns — and that not against one particular which may appear in competition and opposition against us, but even against the generation of those which refuse human ceremonies in divine worship, many whereof our pens and consciences acknowledge worthy and godly, — nay not only to vent these expressions, but [also] to keep them souring[121] and leavening[122] by us,[123] in our hearts and writings, many years[124] — wherein [i.e., during which time] we have been persuaded by

[120] The long, syntactically loose sentence which follows reads succinctly thus: "For though it be easily incident . . . to our corrupt natures . . . to cast unbrotherly contempt. . . , yet to vent such a mass of venom . . . nay, not only to vent these expressions but [also] to keep them souring . . . many years . . . and yet after all this [delay] . . . to print them . . . — how such a man's heart is principled and whether it was a root of bitterness or godliness whence such things [could] issue I leave . . . to the Almighty to judge and to the wise-hearted to discern."

[121] The text reads: sovvring, cf. the pickling and steeping charged to Burgess above.

[122] i.e., fermenting.

[123] i.e., in respect to us.

[124] Hooker alludes to the Address to King Charles, in which Burgess expresses regret for "my suppressing what I had written some years past."

Burgess had written *The Answer* four years before publication. Richard Simmons, facsimile reprint of *A Fresh Suit*, introduction, p. 4.

friends and, after persuasions, resolved rather to have them burned by others or to burn them ourselves — and yet after all this in cold blood, in saddest consideration, upon review so far to "approve" of them as to print and publish them to the world: — how such a man's spirit is principled and whether it was a root of bitterness or godliness whence such things [could] issue I leave it to the Almighty to judge and to the wise-hearted to discern.

[V. FURTHER WITNESS OUT OF BURGESS' OWN BOOK,
ESPECIALLY ITS PREFACE OR PART I]

These be the witnesses which I have to produce out of the Rejoiner's own writings. All that I desire is that their depositions may be impartially weighed and in this desire and endeavor there is no wrong done to any rule of piety or charity.

We have also the Rejoiner's open practice as an apparent evidence to contradict what [he] himself professeth in his Preface touching the constancy of his opinion about the inconveniency only of these ceremonies. However, he bears the world in hand to the contrary, and that with great confidence, to which purpose we entreat the following allegations may be indifferently[125] heard from those who as witness can testify [to] his walking by their experience.

That faithful servant of Christ, Mr. Arthur Hildersham,[126] now at rest with God, upon his sick bed with great regret and grief thus expressed himself to a fellow brother: [127] "Doctor Burgess' conscience knows that I know he speaks untruly." And that it may appear these words were neither spoken passionately by him nor

[125] e.g., disinterestedly.
[126] Of royal descent and Catholic parentage, the Puritan divine Arthur Hildersham (1563–1632) was, after graduating M.A. at Christ's College, Cambridge, appointed lecturer in September, 1587, at Ashley-de-la-Zouch (Leicestershire) by his mother's second cousin, the third earl of Huntington. In June, 1590, he was suspended from the ministry by the Court of High Commission. He was eventually reinstated, this time as vicar. On the accession of James I he was active in the Millenary Petition, 1603. He was suspended from his ministry several times. Among men whom Hildersham encouraged to enter the ministry was Simeon Ashe, important in Hooker's life in Cambridge. On Hildersham as a possible source of information about an excommunicated person in Leicester who was converted to conformity by Burgess' *Answer* (1631), see above, n. 44.
[127] Unidentified.

forged by me, he hath left the proof of them under his own hand upon record which I now have by me and shall be bold, for fuller satisfaction, to set down his own mind in his own words.

In the 19th page of the Preface the Rejoiner expresseth himself on this manner, "I do ingenuously[128] confess two errors in that my *Apology*,[129] one[130] that I trusted too much to the quotations of the *Abridgment*[131] which then I had in writing." To which Mr. Hildersham thus replies in his notes:

> How false the quotations are in the *Abridgment* will be seen hereafter. But this is manifestly false that he was, before the writing of his *Apology*, deceived thereby or that he had a copy of it in writing before that time. For the *Abridgment* was not made until after he was deprived.[132] And therefore no man could have any copy of it, either in print or writing. Nay, the large book, whereof it is an abridgment, was not delivered to His Majesty[133] before that day he was deprived and the *Abridgment* was made sundry months after.

He [Burgess: error two] proceeds, *ibid.*, p. 19:

> It's true that the ministers [of Lincoln] were resolved to have chosen him [Burgess] for one of those three that should have disputed for

---

[128] The text reads *ingeniously*.

[129] In connection with developments leading to the proclamation of July 16, 1604, requiring all ministers to conform to the new ecclesiastical canons, Burgess preached a sermon before James at Greenwich on June 19, 1604, to which the King took offense and had him put in the Tower. He sent the King a copy of his offending sermon, which had recognized the lawfulness of ceremonies but which urged against forcing their use; and he submitted. After his release he drew up his *Apology*, addressed to his ordinary, Bishop William Chadderton of Lincoln. Burgess' *Apology* was not printed.

[130] The second of Burgess' self-confessed errors is not expressly noted.

[131] *An Abridgement of that Booke which the Ministers of Lincolne Diocesse Delivered to His Maiestie upon the first of December 1605* (Lincoln 1617). This was an apology for those who refused subscription and conformity. *An Abridgement* was reprinted by William Brewster at the Pilgrim press in Leiden, 1617.

[132] Burgess was deprived of his living in November, 1604, when he refused to subscribe to the canons. See above, n. 129. He thereupon went to Leiden and studied medicine. After his rehabilitation as a minister in the established Church, Burgess published in the same year as his *Answer* a single piece on the subject of ceremonies, which had occasioned his exile: *The Lavvfulnes of knealing in the act of receiving the Lords Svpper, wherein also somewhat of the crosse in baptisme* (1631).

[133] James I.

them—such profession he had made unto them of his full consent [Gr] with them in judgment— and he had been one of the disputants if that not the dean of the chapel,[134] but the King himself had not expressly, in his message, excepted against him, which also argues that his Majesty did hold him to be fully of the mind that the rest—who had sent him the aforesaid book—were of.

In his notes of the 20th page he [Hildersham] hath these words:

That there is no color of truth in this that he [Burgess] saith here, that is—

That when he [Burgess] was chosen to be one of those that should maintain their cause by disputation, he professed to his brethren that he could not speak against the things as unlawful, but only as inconvenient. . .[135]

may appear evidently to any reasonable man. For seeing they had in their book delivered to his Majesty, our King's father, stated the question not against the inconveniency but the unlawfulness of these things, who will imagine they would even have chosen him to be one of the three to dispute for them if he had professed to them at that time that he had nothing to say against the unlawfulness of them?

These be the dying words of that dear servant of God as I have them to show in black and white.

If yet the witness of the dead deserve no credit, [G2r] the Rejoiner may with some small consideration recall to mind how after the revolt of change of his former opinion in an occasional concurrence and meeting of many fellow brethren[136] when they out of

[134] John Rainolds (1549–1607), dean of Lincoln Cathedral, was the chief spokesman of the Puritans at the Hampton Court Conference of January, 1604. Burgess was, of course, not one of the four Puritan representatives. See William Barlow, *The Svmme and Substance of the Conference . . . at Hampton Court . . .* (London, 1604), p. 2; see above, n. 102 and Mark H. Curtis, "The Hampton Court Conference and its Aftermath," *History*, XLVI (1961), 1–16.

[135] Hildersham, quoted by Hooker, is quoting presumably from Burgess' unpublished *Apology* (summer, 1604) with reference to the Hampton Court Conference earlier in January.

[136] The date of Burgess' self-deprecation before a meeting of Puritan brethren is not known. But see n. 137. It is known that on July 10, 1627, Burgess was one of fifty-nine Cambridge men who incorporated at Oxford, "at which time liberty was allowed to him by the venerable congregation that he might study in the public library." *DNB*, p. 311B. But this does not seem to fit the Hooker reference. It may be to a Banburyside in Westminster or to such a district in Hackney.

human civility desired him to take his place according to his years and gifts, I say, he may, if he will bethink himself, easily recall what words he then openly uttered to this or like effect. He told them he was unworthy to sit with them, to have respect from them, since he had betrayed them and their cause. Now the cause which they maintained was not inconveniency but unlawfulness in these things. If the Rejoiner's memory serve him not about this particular, let him repair to Bamburyside,[137] to his ancient friends there and they can testify so much to his face. If, then, the construction that the King and state made of his course, [if] the apprehension his fellow brethren had of his practice, nay, [if] his own profession may be trusted, let all the world and Dr. Burgess' own heart judge whether he hath changed his opinion yea, or no?

In his Preface there is not much that expects answer. For to omit his biting language and devouring words wherewith we have cloyed the reader in the foregoing catalogue, and unto which rank many gibes here may be referred, as that [on] page 5: "These do commonly call any small company of their party [G2v] 'The church and the Christians of such a town.' As if Christ were, I say, not divided amongst us but wholly taken away from us to them; and what wants this of schism in the heart." [138] And that [on] page 9: "[T]he glory of suffering for, as they call it, the good cause." [139] And that [on] page 12: "Others aim at 'schism' and 'anabaptistical delusions.' " [140] To let pass these pangs of spleen[141] and other distempered carriages which he himself cast upon some passionate people and strongly conceited, all which being justly blamed, it neither

---

[137] Banbury in Oxfordshire. Burgess' first living was in Norwich. The allusion is not clear.

[138] Cf. above at n. 89. This passage from Burgess is quoted somewhat more fully in n. 21, Essay 1.

[139] This phrase concludes the following sentence in Burgess: "Nor do I conceive, that pressing the vtmost rigour of Lawes against all that refuse Conformity, is the way to vhite vs; because this is so farre from altering the judgement, that it rather confirmeth it, in such as will adde the glory."

[140] Burgess was concerned with keeping open a *via media*. The whole quotation is: "And besides, as way is not to bee given to such pretenders of *Conformitie*, so not to the progresse of Schisme, or inclination to Anabaptisticall Delusions, which others ayme at vnder the covert of opposing Ceremonies, as corruptive in the Church."

[141] See above, n. 65.

hurts the cause against which he writes, nor helps that which he defends, since the most glorious gospel of Christ hath such blots cast upon it by reason of the sinful weaknesses of some who take up the profession thereof. Leaving, I say, all these as not worthy the consideration, we shall entreat the Rejoiner at his return to give some satisfaction to these [three] queries:

1. Why atheists, Papists, profane varlets, brutish drunkards, hellish blasphemers, together with the accursed crew of the most riotous wretches, yea, the generation of neutralists, moral formalists, ignorant sots of all sorts are so zealous for these ceremonies, are so violent to urge, so careful to practice them, who never had care of piety in all their lives?

[G3r] 2. After the Lord hath cast in some saving illumination into the mind, convicted the conscience, and converted the hearts of scandalous sinners; after such have gained sweet peace of conscience and assured evidence of God's love sealed unto their souls,[142] why do the hearts of such rise in some strong indignation against these popish relics when they have never been persuaded thereunto by teachers nor had time from their own inward troubles to consider of them? That this is the disposition of many I can speak by proof. I would have the Rejoiner speak to the reason of it.

3. When it is notorious to all the English world that the most of the people, who live in the bosom of the Church and profess the faith, be wholly taken up with conformity, both approving and practicing of it, countenancing those that do it, why is the Doctor so troubled that a few silly despicable people, void of wisdom — nay, if his former charges be true — void of grace, should distaste the ceremonies, when I know no judicious nonconformer is disquieted that the crowd of the formal gospellers should embrace them? While the Rejoiner is searching the reason of these things, it

[142] In the foregoing we see clearly outlined Hooker's *ordo salutis*. See Essay 2. On the Puritan views on conscience, see Coleman C. Markham, "William Perkins' Understanding of the Function of Conscience." Unpubl. Ph.D. dis. Vanderbilt University, 1967; Kevin T. Kelley, *Conscience: Dictator or Guide?: A Study in Seventeenth-century English Protestant Moral Theology* (London/ Dublin, 1967), which, as for Puritans, deals only with Perkins and Ames; and Thomas Wood, *English Casuistical Divinity* (London, 1952).

may chance he may either search or see his own heart somewhat more clearly.

Leaving then these to his consi[G3v]deration, proceed we a little to survey the Preface, and the substance of it may be referred to three heads: 1, he chargeth nonconformity to be cause of many mischiefs; 2, he debates the cure and administreth that which he conceived most meet for redress; 3, he makes a defense for himself and writing. Against all which we [take] except[ion] thus: 1, that his charge is not just; 2, his dealing in the cure not plain and thorough; 3, his defense in that where the stress lies either not equal or not sufficient.

[I. The Charges of Separation and Profaneness are not Just][143]

Come we to scan the particulars, the mischiefs which he conceives to issue from nonconformity are no less than separation and profaneness. A heavy charge, I confess, but the best is his reasons have not the weight [144] of a rush.

1. That of separation, p. 5, is supported upon so slender a ground that he betrays[145] only his desire to have surpassed his power, therefore rhetoricates instead of reasoning. 'If these,' saith he, 'be idolatrous will-worships, how can you, how dare you, join with us in those acts of religion wherein these are used?' Wherein he neither concludeth the question because a man may refuse to join in such acts without separa[G4r]tion, or utter condemning and renouncing all church communion. Neither doth he prove that which he concludeth about joining in such acts by any other argument but only by 'how can you, how dare you?,' to which I answer: We so can and dare join in good acts to which something participating of idolatry is added, [just] as Christ, our teacher, and his apostles did join in the Jews' worship, unto which were added many superstitions as unlawful as we hold our ceremonies [to be]. Nay, I will add one thing further, that if Doctor Burgess be resolute in this point, i.e.,

---

[143] Item 1 here is that in the first set of three heads at the top of p. G3v rather than that in Hooker's three objections, although heads and objections are closely related.

[144] The text reads *vvayt*.

[145] The text reads *bevvrayes*.

that he must separate from all churches and church actions in which any superstition is exercised, then he must be one of the greatest Separatists in the world. For he, holding error of judgment to be superstition, and those superstitious brethren that abstain for conscience' sake from things lawful, though only upon error in judgment, must upon the former ground separate from all those churches in whose religious acts anything in his judgment lawful is so abstained from and much more if anything in his opinion unlawful be put in practice from one of which faults few or no churches will be found wholly free. Yet I would have another opinion of Doctor Burgess and think that though he hold bowing to the altar[146] to be superstitious or idolatrous, yet would [G4v] he not therefore separate from the good prayers that follow that ridiculous ape of idolatry.

[2.] That other charge of profaneness, p. 6, pretended to come from preciseness[147] is so strange a consequence that it can hardly with deliberation be fathered upon nonconformity without nonconscience. For strictness in matters of ceremonies hath no more force to bring forth looseness in matters of substance than zeal in matters of faith and charity hath to bring forth carelessness of both, nay, than pure religion hath to breed atheism.

Go we to experience. View the places where nonconformists live, the people whom they teach, the ways of those with whom they

[146] It is somewhat surprising that Burgess and Hooker following him would so readily acquiesce in calling the communion table against the east wall an "altar." The movement of Archbishop William Laud, while well under way by 1633, was, of course, resisted by the more Protestant heritage as well as by the Puritans. See David L. Clark, "The Altar Controversy in Early Stuart England," Ph.D. thesis, Cambridge, Mass. 1967. On Burgess and bowing, see above, n. 132. The logic of Hooker's sentence would be improved if he had left out "or idolatrous" and made superstition (kneeling) the ape of idolatry but not quite idolatry.

Clark, *op. cit.*, shows that the Puritans insisted on the Table close to the congregation to allow for the "affective" role of the visible fraction of the Bread in a truly scriptural "ceremony."

[147] Proto-puritans and Puritans already in the sixteenth century were called disparagingly "Precisians" for their restraining strictness in matters of ceremonies. See a substantial quotation from Burgess, Part i, p. 6 f. in Introduction to the Document, at n. 9, wherein Burgess makes, in fact, a good point, namely that a polarization in the established Church makes for separatism at the one extreme and profaneness (atheism) at the other—the conformist extreme.

walk, who they be that have reference to and dependence upon their persons or ministries; and I suppose[148] the walls of the churches and the stones of the streets [cf. Lk. 19:40] will give testimony against this accusation. Nay, I suppose I may speak it truly, as I profess I think it, that some one nonconformable minister hath been a means under God to bring more souls to grace and heaven than all the cloisters or cathedrals in all England in the same time where all conformity hath been the daily diet and livelihood of the people.[149]

[Hr] Go we to reason. The best that either the Rejoiner or any beside can make of our [Church-established] ceremonies is that they are things indifferent. Now, that weak ones may doubt and stagger about such; that doubting they ought not to practice them, Rom. 14:23,[150] is made a duty; that men's walking according to conscience should be the cause of others' disobedience; that keeping the law should be an occasion in itself of profaning the law; that stopping the very appearance of the least evil should set open a gap to the greatest — I appeal to any reasonable man whether it be not a consequence void of common sense unless men have a miraculous skill to solder quicksilver or tie sand together or make heaven and earth meet!

Last of all, it is remarkable that Doctor Burgess himself, p. 8, doth impute these mischiefs unto civil war about ceremonies, which if it be well weighed, it will manifest too much prejudice in his former discourse. For in civil wars, the mischiefs ensuing on them are not wont to be charged upon one part alone, and that [the] poor [part], passive, overpowered, obnoxious[151] to the suffering of whatsoever pressures their opposites please to lay upon them, which is the case of the nonconformists in these commotions.

---

[148] In the obsolete sense: *conceive as true.*

[149] Hooker is referring to the numerous Puritan lectureships. See Seaver, *op. cit.*

[150] Rom. 14:23: "But he who has doubts is condemned if he eats [meat sacrificed to idols] because he does not act from faith; for whatever does not proceed from faith is sin."

[151] i.e., exposed to the punitive consequences of the suffering. Exactly nine years after Hooker penned this line the Civil War would break out in the drawn battle of Edgehill, with "ceremonies" indeed among the great issues of rebellion.

Tell us, I pray [Hv] you: If in your conscience the prelates, canons, courses, courts, and proceedings have had no hand in working mischief? Nay, divers of these mischiefs, which you have affectedly placed on the other side? If non-residents, double-treble-beneficed men, unable, perverse, scandalous, half-popish ministers have not had a finger in them? If those trumpeters and drummers who proclaim the innocency and justness of our prelates' proceedings have not brought something to the furtherance of these mischiefs?

If you speak your conscience it must needs say, yes, and so confess, it was your passion, not your judgment, that obtruded all upon non-conformity.

The state of this war is this: We, as it becometh Christians, stand upon the sufficiency of Christ's institutions for all kind[s] of worship; and that exclusively the Word, say we, and nothing but the Word [rules] in matters of religious worship. The prelates rise up on the other side and will needs have us allow and use certain human ceremonies of religion in our Christian worship. We desire to be excused as holding them unlawful. Christ we know and all that cometh from him we are ready to embrace. But these human ceremonies in divine worship we know [H2r] not, nor can have anything to do with them. Upon this they make fierce war upon us and yet by the pen of Doctor Burgess lay all the fault of this war and the mischiefs of it upon our backs. Now all ye that pass by, consider and judge what equity is used in such dealing? They will say all things are to be done 'decently and in order,' to which we willingly consent, but allege again that we cannot apprehend these ceremonies to be necessary for order and decency. They, as our [spiritual] lords, tell us it is enough for our consciences that they esteem them so. Our consciences tell us this is to usurp the place of God. What can we say less than we will follow our consciences rather than their wills? [152]

To conclude, the Rejoiner, p. 285, maketh circumcision lawful

[152] This paragraph best summarized Hooker's position in the debate on ceremonies. He regards the bishops as usurping churchmen. He does not directly challenge the state. Like the ministers of the Lincoln *Abridgement* (1604), above, n. 131, Hooker does not contest the first of the three article of canon 36, namely, that the King is supreme in all matters, even spiritual. But see also at nn. 154 and 155.

to be imposed upon the same grounds that our English ceremonies stand on. Now if it should please our prelates in a Convocation to appoint that all English men should consent to the cutting of their foreskins and denounce war upon those that should refuse this goodly canon, was it not a grave accusation to lay all the mischiefs of such a war upon those which would not conform to such a ceremony? But the weakest must always go to the wall, and the lamb H2v] must die for troubling the water if it please the lion so to determine it.

[II. Burgess' Remedy is not Clear]

We have done with the disease and mischief together with the cause of it. We are now come to consider the remedy the Doctor administers, and we except against his dealing herein as not plain, nay not profitable, even by his own rules.

1. He deals not plainly. For making the abolishing of the ceremonies by authority to be one and the chief course for cure [and] as despairing to obtain that, he refuseth to persuade thereunto: because forsooth to judge what is most convenient and to determine thereof belongeth only to those who, together with power of doing what they shall well like, have judgment to make choice of the best way — which is a weak and a very unworthy conceit.

For Dr. Burgess cannot deny that those[153] who impose, urge, and with capital punishments enforce these ceremonies upon Christ's ministers and people do therein abuse that authority which they received for the procuring of the quietness, peace, and safety of those that desire to serve God according to his word and not for the troubling, vexing, and scandalizing of them by opposing [H3r] their mere wills in religious affairs to men's consciences. Depending wholly and only upon God's word, he cannot, I say, deny this to be a grievous sin of those in place, and yet refuseth seriously to admonish them of the same, being called to give counsel and advice about this very cause.

2. It is to be supposed that worthy ministers of the gospel are not

---

[153] The bishops, particularly Bishop/Archbishop Laud.
   Hooker inserts in this sentence after *For* a superfluous numeral, 1.

destitute of wisdom and judgment concerning religious affairs. By this reason, therefore, Doctor Burgess might as well have forborne to judge what they should choose as to determine so peremptorily thereof.

Lastly, [3] I would gladly know of Doctor Burgess: Whether the scriptures be not able as well to make magistrates and governors perfect to every good work as they can do ministers? Whether either minister or magistrate should do, or ought to do, anything which God hath not commanded them? Whether a faithful minister in his office ought not to understand what that Word reveals, ought not to teach all magistrates what out of the Word one so understands? [154] If all which particulars be plain and undeniable, it will appear that it belonged to Doctor Burgess, being called to give counsel declaratively, to judge and determine what was convenient to be done, [H3v] which if he durst not declare he durst not do his duty. And that I may fasten this nail yet more fully, I thus force the conclusion:

Whatever [the] duty of any calling, the Word teacheth that the minister by the Word ought to judge, determine, and deliver. Else how can he teach the whole counsel of God? How can he give everyone his portion?

But the duties and doings, if good, of all magistrates the Word teacheth.

Ergo the minister ought to judge and determine of those by the Word and so deliver them. *Ergo* it doth not belong to those only who have power and are in place to judge and determine, which was the Doctor's assertion.

Again, whatever God commands, that, and all that, the minister should teach and so judge and determine else the trumpet should give an uncertain sound.

But whatever men or magistrates ought to do, that Christ hath commanded. Both the parts of the argument are in Mt. 28:20.[155]

[154] Hooker's Calvinist congregational polity is so determinitive here that, while he can argue that "the faithful minister" may "teach all magistrates" "out of the Word," he does not see any problem in denying that a prelatical "minister," like Laud, may instruct the chief magistrate, the King, out of the Word and Tradition. Cf. below at n. 155.

[155] Jesus' commandment to the disciples to *teach* all Christians *to observe all* his commandments is extended by Hooker to every minister. And the minister must declare to the magistrate his duties.

Therefore the conclusion follows: whatever men or magistrates ought to do, ministers should teach [H4r] and consequently judge and determine.

[III. The Unprofitableness and Insufficiency of Burgess' Plea] [156]

And as thus the Rejoiner dealt not plainly in his cure, so neither[157] hath he dealt profitably in that his receipt is against his own rule as it shall appear in the scanning of his defense, which we except against as insufficient in those particulars wherein the stress and weight of the plea lies. And those appear in three special objections he makes, the dint of none of which he is able to decline.[158] The objections are [on] pp. 12f. and the sum of them in short is: [i.] "this writing [*The Reply*] stirs strife, objection two: [ii] exasperateth authority, objection three, [iii] hinders the removal of the ceremonies, objection four." [159] Hear we now his defense to each of these, in order:

[i] To the first [i.e., objection two] he answers in truth by denial, that this course of his is so far from stirring the fire of contention that it's casting on water to quench it and to this also belongs that, p. 11, there is a necessity that some should speak for the cause unless we shall suffer ourselves not only to be rooted out of our livings but, which is worse, out of the hearts of our people, whom we serve in the Lord.

Answer: Bare denial without reason yields small [H4v] relief to a cause but when it is contrary to the Word and itself it betrays a cause, doth not defend it, and such is this.

1. It is contrary to the Word and that staple rule delivered by the Apostle which he sets down as a station and shelter for the weak in the faith to betake themselves unto, Rom. 14:1, where the non-

[156] The inserted subtitle derives in part from the last of three heads announced at the top of p. G3v.

[157] The text reads, no doubt incorrectly, *whether.*

[158] The blow of none of which is he able to parry.

[159] Hooker, transcribing Burgess, passes over Burgess' objection 1, assigns his own numbers to the last three of Burgess' four. To avoid confusion and for general symmetry, we have designated the three objections to be dealt with as i, ii, iii.

toleration[160] of those who are weak in the practice of things indifferent is ever the ground of contention and disturbance in the Church. And therefore this course of forebearance he infers, verse 19, as the way to follow peace. Sense teacheth it also: when a company of passengers are confined to one way to pass or one door to enter it causeth them to crowd and jostle.

2. This denial[161] is contrary to the Doctor's own doctrine delivered in page 3 where it's granted by him and proved by the experience of three score years,[162] that opposition begets opposition and that which was given to stir the humor did only sharpen it.[163] Put we now the case to the College of Physicians,[164] nay, let Doctor Burgess himself be judge. Is it a rational course? Or like[ly] to work a cure that, when the body hath been distempered many months with physic, we should still continue the same receipt? [165] [Ir] And it's marvelous to see how conviction wrests truth from a man even against his own passion and purpose. Weigh these two passages and see if they will accord? [166]

The Doctor must write that he may not be wrought out of the hearts of his people, p. 11, and yet he confesseth by writing, he hath wrought himself out of the hearts of the godly.

[160] The text reads "the not toleration." Hooker is not scripturally congruent. In Rom. 14:1, which Hooker does cite, the weak with respect to Jewish dietary laws, comparable to ceremonial laws of the Church of England, are not to be decisive; but in the parallel in I Cor. 8:10f. the weak are in effect decisive because those who know that the (dietary) ceremonial laws are not binding (the Puritans) should yield to the timid sensibilities of the weak (conformists)! To be sure, Hooker *here* cites only Rom. 14:1–19 and its principle of mutual toleration of both non-scriptural ceremonies and the avoidance thereof in the same established Church.

[161] Burgess' denial, namely, that he has raised up contention.

[162] Three score years before would have been 1573, but Hooker is probably referring to the sequel to the *Advertisements* of 1566.

[163] On spleen, bile, and humor, see above at n. 65.

[164] In June, 1613, James I complained to the University of Cambridge that Burgess had been admitted to the doctorate in medicine (after training in Leiden) without subscription to the three articles of Canon 36. He continued to practice medicine without a license during his ministry. (In August, 1634, he would be admitted an extra licentiate of the College of Physicians.) Hooker in any case is making an allusion to Burgess' efforts to practice.

[165] i.e., prescription/remedy.

[166] The two passages, Burgess on pp. 11f. and on p. 3, are by Hooker contrasted. Burgess had first said that opposition begets opposition, and then later, that his Rejoinder puts an end to strife!

[ii] His defense to the second objection [i.e. Burgess' objection three, above] is yet more feeble, though more ingenious, for his answer is nothing but yielding the cause in some compass and circumlocution of words. For, firstly, when he grants that he forbore some years this course of writing that he might not exasperate authority, he privily,[167] yea, plainly yields the objection had such rational face in it that it did not only press him but prevail with him also. Whereas, secondly, he adds that by this means he hath some hope to persuade some to conform and so to avoid the lash of authority. By this he doth not only yield the objection but confirm and establish it. For if only those who are persuaded by his *Answer* shall avoid the lash, therefore they who will not be persuaded must expect the blow, and shall be sure to feel it. [Iv] Thirdly,[168] he adds for his own intention: "Sure I am that I desire not the vexation of any sober man." But his own bond will not be taken because he hath so often broken his word he must seek for other sureties. *Quid verba audiam, cum facta videam?* [169] "Little power have words to persuade any of common understanding when the practice goes the contrary way." Not yet can I discern how to judge of any man's desire but only by his endeavor. Those heavy accusations [and] uncharitable censures whereby he chargeth and that with much bitterness the generation of nonconformists — from what root they come and what desire they imply — let any rational man determine. For it cannot be to ingratiate them or procure favor for them [the nonconformists] in the affections of the governors when he makes them appear such as deserve none, nay, such as ought to receive none but the contrary at their hands.

[iii] Lastly, when it is objected [Burgess' objection four, above] that this course [nonconformity] hinders the removal of these things [ceremonies] which authority otherwise might possibly remove, his defense is that he will never believe that authority will remove them with dishonor of it[I2r]self, as yielding the things to be unlawful which it hath so long maintained.

---

[167] See above at n. 124.
[168] The text reads with an Arabic 3 beginning a new paragraph; but this numeration could be confused with a subdivision 3, introduced below as simply "Lastly."
[169] Cicero, *Tusculanae disputationes* III, 48.

In which answer these two particulars offer themselves to consideration: 1. To remove ceremonies as unlawful, being long maintained, is a dishonor to authority; 2. Doctor Burgess believes authority will not thus dishonor itself.

Answer [to 1]: The first of which is a most dangerous assertion and is made a chief bar to stay Papists and others from re-forming of anything that others have opposed and they defended. And it's usual in the mouth of false flatterers and back-friends[170] to all reformation.[171] And I would hope that Doctor Burgess did utter more in this by his pen than he meant in his heart. Beside[s] the consequences are not so dangerous but the ground is as weak. For the long continuance or maintenance of a thing if evil and unlawful is so far from bringing dishonor upon any for the removal of it that retaining thereof increaseth both his sin and shame, and it argues a greater measure of humility and power of grace to abandon it.

Nay, were the thing lawful if yet by circumstances it did appear that God's honor, the common good, [I2v] [and] the edification of our brethren might more be promoted by the removal of it, though it were hoary-headed with antiquity and continuance, it argued greatest love to God and man to alter it rather than to keep it in use. And that would bring greatest honor to him that should so do since by the verdict of God's spirit he is most honorable that most honoreth God.

[Answer to] 2: From these grounds, how rotten and unsavory the second particular of the Rejoiner's defense is will easily be granted. For if in such a removal the duty of authority doth consist, the power of grace doth appear, the glory of God and good of the Church and Commonwealth will be advanced. To be of that belief with Doctor Burgess that magistrates will never be brought to do what they ought, how uncharitable is it thus to lay their honor in

---

[170] Archaic for *secret enemies*.

[171] Burgess would be willing to have the offensive ceremonies made optional in order to appease the Puritans but he would not wish them to be revoked as unlawful, lest the Reformation itself be one day declared by another Mary unlawful. Hooker objects to this argument as inhibiting "the reformation of the Reformation." When Hooker speaks of a "bar to stay Papists," he may mean, however, no more than what he might have called the national Catholicism of Laud. See below at n. 173.

the dust? And not to press them hereunto when we may, and by our calling[172] ought, how unconscionable is it? And how contrary to that love we owe to the Almighty and our governors?

The crowd of objections which he makes concerning himself, I conceive, as so many strugglings of spirit which stood in the way to withstand him in his course. His conscience, as it should seem, gave the onset and let in some such intimations as these to him.

[I3r] Why, is not Popery coming in fast enough, but you must make a preparation thereunto, yea, become a purveyor and harbinger to make room and lay in provision for it? [173] Is it not sufficient that the wicket is set open, that the popish pack may be drawn in, but you must set open the great gate that a sumpter[174] horse may amble in with a load of relics and ceremonies? For if the patent of the Church be so enlarged [as] to appoint ceremonies at their pleasure to admonish and teach, and it is in their power to appoint what and how many as seems good to them, why then let images be erected, let crosses and crucifixes be set up in every corner! These are lawful admonitors and instructors, and we cannot have too many good companions to put us in mind of our duties!

Consider beside[s] how many poor ministers are under pressure, some fled, some imprisoned, many suspended, themselves and families undone.[175] Why, will you not suffer them to lie in the dust, but will you trample upon them even unto death? Is it not enough they make brick but must they be beaten also [Ex. 5]? Oh, consider as before the Lord to whom you must give an account! Do you[176] in the chimney while the flame is in the thatch? Is not the fury of the bishops[177] yet fierce enough, their rage sharp enough, but you

[172] The possessive "our calling" makes clear, if we needed any further proof, that the author is a minister, not, for example, the printer or some other layman. See further at n. 183.

On the duty of the minister to instruct the magistrate out of the Word, see above at nn. 154 and 155.

[173] An allusion to the Laud's high church reforms.

[174] Archaic for *packhorse*.

[175] Hooker had left his family in England: cf. n. 183 below.

[176] i.e., work you, or do you continue at your work at the chimney while the roof is on fire?

[177] The text reads *BB.*

must set them on and strengthen their hands to strike harder? Lastly, is not cringing at altars, bowing at the name of Jesus,[178] like[ly] to be brought in and practiced with great forwardness; and will you, dare you, encourage [them] in such courses, yea, give an approbation and commendation to them? For they will say, 'They are but significant[179] ceremonies. They place no merit, put no efficacy in them, only they are admonitors of our duties.' Thus is the foundation of superstition laid, the gospel stopped, and an open way made for Popery; and you are the persuader, the encourager, yea, defender of all these. How will you answer this at the Great Day?[180]

[VI. Conclusion][181]

Yet do I not speak this as though I were troubled with the weight of anything he hath writ. For I profess unfeignedly [that] the way of his traverse[182] finds welcome with me, wherein the nakedness and indefensibleness of his cause I hope will be discovered. Only

[178] Bowing at the name of Jesus, based on Philippians 2:10, was enjoined by Canon 18 of 1604. It is related to kneeling at communion, one of the principal three ceremonies at issue. Bowing at the name of Jesus had been popularized by the Franciscans in the fifteenth century; and the Feast of the Holy Name of Jesus was officially granted to the order in 1530, whence it spread. Puritan scriptural literalism and legalism were put to a test in their refusal to comply with a quite clear, apostolic injunction! Hooker gives a fuller answer in Document VII at n. 173.

[179] This could be a misprint for *insignificant* but more likely the word should be understood in the context of the scholastic (ultimately) Augustinian distinction between *signa* and *res*, in which case the defenders of certain innocuous ceremonies would be arguing that they but point to a transcendent reality which are not to be taken realistically, for example, that a sign of the cross at baptism merely betokens the banishment of Satan rather than effectuating it. The ceremonies are, in other words, allegedly only *signifying*.

[180] This is the only clear reference to the Last Judgment in the Preface. In general in Hooker's writings eschatology is not prominent in contrast to many of his contemporaries, e.g., Richard Sibbes and even John Cotton. See the forthcoming *A Study of Eschatological Thought in English Protestant Theology* [Anglican, Puritan, Separatist], *1640–1662, with special reference to the Second Coming of Christ and the End of the Age*, by Bryan William Ball, Studies in Late Medieval and Reformation Theology, edited by Heiko A. Oberman (The Hague, 1975).

[181] This is really the Conclusion of the three exceptions under Part V of our edition, but it may serve as the conclusion to the whole "Preface."

[182] In the legal sense of a formal denial of some particular matter of fact alleged by the opposite party in any stage of the pleadings. Cf. above at n. 106.

one thing I would most earnestly entreat, that he would show us but fair play in these proceedings, to wit, that he would not break our heads while others have bound our hands. Let him but grant us indifferent terms, even the common courtesy of the court, an impartial pleading. We desire no more favor than the cause by its own credit will procure. Let the law [I4r] be open as the rigor of justice allows. To which purpose shall he so far prevail with his lord bishops that we may enjoy the use of our books, the liberty of the press, and if not the benefit of our charges, yet freedom of breathing in our native soil and with our poor desolate families.[183] And I dare promise him he shall not want those that will join issue with him in this traverse either by writing or printing and that without any gaudy expressions, whereof he accuseth Mr. Parker,[184] but by plai[n] [185] dint of syllogism; and we will take our oaths as he so desireth, that each man of us shall write[186] his conscience, which I wonder why the Doctor put in, since it's openly known to all that will not shut their eyes that all conscience doth not live and die alone with conformable men. But if we neither have, nor he will procure us leave, or liberty, either to preach or write or print, yea, scarce to live, then he must know we are denied the benefit of the law and the courtesy of the court and in vain he brags of his traverse.

To pursue all the particulars objected and answered in his own behalf is not worth the while since no weight of the cause lies thereupon. Only the bravado here vented by the Rejoiner is not to be borne, which observably [he] set down in the fourteenth objection: [187] Doctor Burgess hath parted with more profit by taking up [I4v] conformity and a benefice than any now in England hath done by his unconformity and loss of a benefice! [187a] Surely he mindeth not so affectionately[188] as he should the affliction of his brethren. What did Doctor Burgess part with? Nothing but future contingent uncertain profit which made him liable to be envied, and

---

[183] Cf. above, n. 175.
[184] Above at n. 105.
[185] The text reads "playe."
[186] The sentence would read better with *right*.
[187] Part i ("Preface"), p. 20; Objection [14]: "Yet some say, I was of their mind against these ceremonies, till a good benefice brought me about."
[187a] Ironic summary by Hooker of Burgess' *Answer*.
[188] i.e., feelingly.

opposed by the College of Physicians,[189] — profit, which was not necessary to his life and being, depending upon extraordinary pains such as in all probability he could not have long endured, or at least with contentment of mind. His physic practice made that change which Tully commendeth in merchandize: *Satiata quaestu, vel contenta potius, ut saepe ex alto, in portum, sic ex ipso portu, se in agros possessionesque contulit*[190] — "after sufficient gettings it [the trader spirit] forsook both sea and sea-haven and betook itself to quietness and plenty in the country."

On the other side, what have not [men lost], what do men lose, by unconformity? Even all their means of living, all their liberty, not only of providing for themselves and their families but even of breathing in any air, saving only that which may be drawn out of stinking prisons. Nay, sometimes all the commodity of [Kr] their country or national habitation being [taken from them, they are] forced to flee even unto the Indians[191] for safety; to say nothing of their loss of life itself by cruel imprisonments. Now let our Savior judge betwixt us and Doctor Burgess. The poor widow, saith he, that parted but with two mites parted with more than they did who out of their plenty parted with many shekels because those two mites were all that she had [Mk. 12:41-44]. If this be true then, many and many a one hath parted with more profit for nonconformity than Doctor Burgess did for conformity, for so much as they

---

[189] See above, n. 164. Burgess was not wholly welcome in the College. James in 1613, n. 164, complained to Cambridge that he had been admitted to the doctorate in medicine (on the basis of work at Leiden) without subscribing to Canon 36 with its article on ceremonies. When, however, he continued to practice medicine, James prevented him from doing so in London at least, on the ground that he was in holy orders. He went to Isleworth (up the Thames towards Hampton Court), and acquired a lucrative medical practice. In July, 1617, he accepted a living at Sutton Coldfield (Warwickshire) but continued to practice medicine. He accompanied Sir Horatio Vere as chaplain in the war of the Palatinate in 1620. In 1625 he was made a prebendary of Lichfield by Bishop Thomas Morton, but he continued on at Sutton Coldfield as both minister and physician.

Hooker's argument here is *ad hominem* and not convincing.

[190] Cicero, *De officiis*, I, 151.

[191] The great Massachusetts Bay Company expedition of the *George*, the *Talbot*, the *Lyon's Whelp*, and the *Mayflower* had sailed from the Thames to what would be called Salem in April, May, June, 1629, with two clergymen, Samuel Skelton of Lincolnshire as pastor and Francis Higginson of Leicestershire.

have parted with all they had and he only with part of that which he had or might have hoped to get superfluous in comparison of that which others have lost. To conclude all, I suppose if we were willing to suffer, we should be more willing both to search and see the truth; and I doubt not but the Lord would settle the hearts of such and bless their endeavors in that behalf. All that I would crave at thy hands, Christian reader, is this, that thou wouldst read without prejudice and judge without partiality. Judge not the person or cause of the distressed the worse because of their pressure[192] or paucity.[193]

[Kv] Welcome Christ with his cross; any truth, though with trouble. Be willing the truth should fall on any side as worthy to be praised and loved for itself. That is all I desire for my money; and religion, conscience, reason will not deny this.

[VII] Rules for to Direct the Weak Reader: How to read the book[194] with profit

[1] Where these abbreviations occur, *D.B.* signifies Doctor Burgess. *Rej.* signifies Doctor Burgess. *Repl.* notes the Replier [Ames]. *Def.* signifieth Doctor Morton.[195]

2. Because the Replier is forced to follow Doctor Burgess in his far-fetched and new-coined definition and the maze of the multitude of his distinctions, the weaker understanding will be at a loss, as not able to comprehend or catch his meaning suddenly; and therefore if I were worthy to advise, I would entreat such to crave the help of some judicious minister[196] who is faithful not to betray him for having the book but willing and able to inform him how to conceive of it aright.

---

[192] i.e., *oppression.*

[193] i.e., *their fewness.*

[194] The "book" is, of course, the *Fresh Suit* by Ames. Our Prefacist, however, has done little to prepare us for it, for his has been an independent argument against Burgess. The abbreviations that follow, however, are the same used in the Preface except that Bishop Morton is not referred to. The Printer rather than the Prefacist (Hooker) may well have prepared this last section after Hooker's departure.

[195] Thomas Morton. See Editor's Introduction to Hooker's Preface.

[196] The reference would be not to English ministers in the Netherlands but back in England, where *A Fresh Suit* was expected to circulate.

[K2r] The Replier's [Ames'] manner of writing being press[197] and punctual [198] and [199] therefore set down so much of the Rejoiner's words as he conceived needful, if any difficulty arise therefrom, the reader is to be entreated to consult with the *Answer* at large.[200]

[197] i.e., *precise, exact.*

[198] i.e., *to the point.*

[199] It would read better: "*he* therefore set down . . . as he conceived needful. If any. . . ."

[200] Because of Ames' precise economy in his citation of Burgess, the reader will do well to follow the argument by occasional direct reference to Burgess' *Answer.* The Editor can say the same of Hooker's Preface!

The final paragraph is followed by more than a dozen *errata,* "the faults, escaped, correct thus." These have all been silently absorbed in our text of the Preface, a mere fraction of the *errata* corrected by the Editor with but an occasional rendering of the original spelling in a note, where there might be some doubt.

Establishing the Hooker Canon

BY SARGENT BUSH, JR.

Throughout the three and one-quarter centuries since Thomas Hooker's death there has been a curious imbalance between scholarly evaluations of his importance to the Puritan movement in England and America, and first-hand knowledge of the corpus of his literary canon. Perry Miller and Thomas H. Johnson, in their important early edition of Puritan writings, describe some of Hooker's works as "masterpieces" and call the author "the most impassioned orator in the first generation of [New England] preachers." [1] In his crucial studies of the New England mind Miller frequently expressed his high regard for Hooker, bowing to no one in his admiration of Hooker's writings. Likewise, Babette M. Levy, whose 1945 study, *Preaching in the First Half Century of New England History*, remains indispensable, wrote that Hooker, of all the first generation New England divines, was "the most capable and forceful in his preaching." [2] None of the recent scholars who has written about the Puritans, supplementing and sometimes correcting the conclusions of Miller and Levy, has seen fit to question these judgments. Yet neither Miller's generation nor ours has known exactly what works comprise Hooker's canon; nor has there been adequate access to the works. In effect, the substance of Hooker's surviving work remains largely unknown, even obscure, to most scholars in the field.

Until 1971 Hooker's works were out of print, and since then only three of his volumes have been made available, all as reprints. Moreover, it has been more than forty years since any scholar has seen fit to attempt a revision of the Hooker bibliography; and this absence

[1] *The Puritans*, ed. Perry Miller and Thomas H. Johnson (New York, 1938), p. 800.
[2] (Hartford, 1945), p. 138.

of accessible texts and lack of a satisfactory bibliography has no doubt contributed to Hooker's sometimes being undervalued, as in a recent bibliography of early American literature in which he was included among the "Lesser Figures," [3] which hardly seems appropriate treatment for a writer of "masterpieces." Even when full-scale listings of his writings have been attempted, however, they have typically omitted major works and included works that Hooker never wrote. Clearly the time has come to set the record straight.

What is known about Hooker's literary corpus can be briefly stated. We generally consider the most important of his works to be his extensive treatment of the stages in the process of regeneration. He minutely described the difficulties and joys as well as the psychological characteristics of this process in a long series of sermons known to have been repeated at least three times in his life as a minister. Certainly, in so far as the surviving sermon texts are a fair indication of what his career was all about, these works embody the central concern of his ministry. The books which comprise this series include *The Poor Doubting Christian*, *The Unbelievers Preparing for Christ*, *The Souls Preparation*, *The Souls Humiliation*, *The Souls Ingrafting*, *The Souls Implantation* (revised as *The Souls Implantation into the Natural Olive*), *The Souls Effectual Calling* and *The Souls Exaltation*. Late in his life Hooker began to rewrite the whole series, and the result of this revision is *The Application of Redemption: The first eight Books;* and *The Application of Redemption: Books Nine and Ten*. At this time he also wrote *A Comment upon Christs Last Prayer*, which takes up glorification — the final stage in the redemption process. Miller and Johnson summarized the significance of these texts in the remark that they "constitute the most minute and searching analysis of the soul and the process of spiritual regeneration, the most coherent and sustained expression of the essential religious experience ever achieved by the New England divines." [4]

While such important writings deserve close attention, there are other Hooker books which should also be noticed. These are of two

[3] Richard Beale Davis, ed., *American Literature through Bryant*. Goldentree Bibliography Series (New York, 1969), p. 52.
[4] *The Puritans*, p. 800.

types: collections of sermons, and non-pulpit literature written to be read. The sermon collections include *The Pattern of Perfection, Four Learned and Godly Treatises,* and *The Saints Dignity and Duty,* each of which contains writings of considerable value. One selection, "The Activity of Faith," has twice been singled out for inclusion in anthologies of great Christian sermons. Indeed, the quality of Hooker's works is consistently high throughout, though of course some note-takers, printers, and editors have represented him more successfully than have others.

The most famous of the published texts apart from the sermons is the treatise defending the New England Way of church government against English critics, *A Survey of the Sum of Church Discipline* (1648), which Hooker wrote at the request of his fellow elders. This work stands as the major defense of early New England Congregationalism. Until recently, however, it seems to have obscured the presence in Hooker's canon of other non-pulpit literature. His cathechism, *An Exposition of the Principles of Religion,* and his *A Brief Exposition of the Lords Prayer,* are clearly works intended to be read, not heard. Both were published during the convening of the Westminster Assembly, a circumstance which, together with the books' contents, may suggest Hooker's active interest in their publication.[5] The prefaces to the two books by his friends John Rogers and William Ames are also in this category of published works prepared for the press by their author. Finally, he prepared for his congregation aids to spiritual nurture, which were published as appendices to other works. *The Properties of an Honest Heart* and three "Miscellanies" on prayer, preparation for communion, and self-examination published at the back of *The Pattern of Perfection* were all intended to aid the struggling Christian in his personal spiritual life. These works, which were originally written as books, are smaller in combined bulk than are the sermon volumes (and perhaps are of secondary importance), but their presence is worthy of fuller notice than has usually been received.

There has never been a collected edition of Hooker's writings, although card catalogues in occasional libraries (the Connecticut

---

[5] See Bush, "Thomas Hooker and the Westminster Assembly," *William and Mary Quarterly,* XXIX (April, 1972), 291–300.

Historical Society and the University of Chicago, for example) list four-volume sets of Hooker's *Works*. These library listings merely indicate cases where some early bookbinder has bound several of Hooker's published works in four separate volumes. The editions included are from a variety of years and printers, so that the volumes thus manufactured by no means represent either complete or new editions. We still await such a collection.

The need for taking a closer look at the Hooker canon is demonstrated with abundant clarity in past Hooker bibliographies, which, though they have served for many years, are now obsolete. Because there has never been an adequate Hooker bibliography, numerous errors have been duplicated with distressing frequency. To take just one example, as long ago as 1875 Joseph Sabin, in compiling his monumental twenty-nine-volume bibliography, *Bibliotheca Americana*, included an anonymous work called *Heautonaparnumenos* in his list of Hooker's works. The attribution was picked up by subsequent bibliographers in 1891 and 1932 and continues to appear with relentless consistency in lists of Hookers' works, in footnotes in new studies of the Puritans, and in card catalogue entries in major research libraries on both sides of the Atlantic. There is, however, no good reason to believe that the book is Hooker's and several to believe that it is not, as more than one informed Hooker reader has said.[6] Present signs indicate, nevertheless, that many if not most libraries and scholars are unaware of any reason to doubt Hooker's authorship of the work.

Other errors — both more and less obvious than this one — persist. For example, *The Literary History of the United States* (*LHUS*)[7] includes only eighteen works instead of the twenty-nine known to be Hooker's when *LHUS* was published. One of the works included is not Hooker's at all. In addition, it perpetuates

[6] Two Ph.D. dissertations contain valuable comments on items of dubious authorship in the Hooker canon: Hubert R. Pellman, "Thomas Hooker: A Study in Puritan Ideals," University of Pennsylvania, 1958, and Andrew T. Denholm, "Thomas Hooker: Puritan Preacher, 1586–1647," Hartford Seminary Foundation, 1961. Both doubt Hooker's authorship of *Heautonaparnumenos*. The *Catalogue* of the McAlpin Collection at Union Theological Seminary also expresses this opinion.

[7] Ed., Robert Spiller, *et al.* (New York, 1948–1949), III, 568–569.

two errors in dating from earlier bibliographies and adds new mistakes in its observations on "Edited Texts and Reprints." The editors' candid observation that "no satisfactory bibliography of Hooker's works has been published" is thus all too clearly borne out by their own list.

The Hooker bibliography which has usually been considered the standard was compiled by the noted Hartford scholar of the nineteenth century, J. Hammond Trumbull, and published as an Appendix to George H. Walker's biography, *Thomas Hooker: Preacher, Founder, Democrat* (1891). This Trumbull list has had lasting usefulness despite its compiler's forthright uncertainty about many of its details. Its chief weaknesses are its omission of many editions of works and its inclusion of works on the dubious authority of secondary and sometimes unreliable sources.

A bibliography by H. Clark Woolley, which appeared some forty years later,[8] was a slight enlargement of Trumbull's work and has been until now the most comprehensive of all. As had Trumbull, however, Woolley relied too heavily on secondary sources of information about editions which he had not seen, and he often simply did not know of many extant editions. Like Trumbull, he derived his information mainly from the important holdings of Hartford collections of Hooker's works and published catalogues from British libraries. The apparent reason why Trumbull's and not Woolley's has been the standard statement is the relative scarcity of the Woolley list, which was published as a monograph by Center Church in Hartford, while the Walker-Trumbull volume is owned by most libraries.

The standard library reference short-title bibliographies by A. W. Pollard and G. R. Redgrave (covering books published up to 1640) and Donald G. Wing (post-1640 books) not only fail to note many editions, but also are sometimes misleading. Pollard and Redgrave include eighteen editions under their Hooker heading and two editions of *The Poor Doubting Christian* under the heading "E. C.", while Wing lists twenty-two editions, of which three are not actually Hooker works. On the latter point, it is worth noting

[8] *Thomas Hooker Bibliography (complete as known to date)* (Hartford: Center Church Monographs No. 1, 1932).

Donald Wing's disclaimer in the Preface to this important reference tool — a disclaimer all too often ignored by the bibliography's users: "I assume no responsibility for authority of attribution." [9]

The matter of attribution has been a lingering problem in establishing the Hooker canon, mainly because so many of Hooker's books were published anonymously and apparently without the author's immediate involvement or even consent. This has meant that we have been very slow to locate as Hooker's some of his books (four appear here for the first time in any Hooker bibliography) and almost as slow to eliminate works which are not his. Apart from the great increase in the number of editions included in the bibliography in the present volume, the most significant development lies in the purification of the list of acknowledged Hooker works. The revisions now incorporated into the Hooker canon involve the elimination of three titles frequently attributed to him and the addition of four others. All three of the false attributions date back to their inclusion in Sabin's bibliography. One of the works now excluded from the canon, *Heautonaparnumenos: or a Treatise of Self-Denial* (London, 1646), has already been mentioned. Presumably the subtitle of this work has something to do with the original assumption that it was by Hooker, whose book called *The Christians Two Chief Lessons* includes as the first "chief lesson" a sermon on "self-denial." [10] Both book are treatments of the same biblical text, Mt. 16:24, where Jesus tells his disciples, "If any man will come after me, let him deny himself, and take up his cross, and follow me." Despite these superficial similarities, however, they are entirely different works. *The Christians Two Chief Lessons* is a series of sermons while *Heautonaparnumenos* is a written treatise intended to be read. Furthermore, the latter is a self-consciously learned work which quotes Greek and Latin abundantly, sometimes discussing such matters as grammatical constructions of words and phrases in the Greek

[9] Donald G. Wing, "Preface," *Short-title Catalogue of Books Printed in England, Scotland, Ireland, Wales, and British America. . . 1641–1700* (New York, 1945), p. ix.

[10] Trumbull takes the entry from Sabin but precedes it with a question mark and speculates: "I am confident this *title* is not (our) Thomas Hooker's but the book may be a bookseller's make-up from 'The Christians Two Chiefe Lessons'" (p. 191).

original of the biblical text. At some points, moreover, its author presents the doctrine of atonement in such a way as to make it inclusive, giving the reader considerable benefit of the doubt in his own spiritual case. These were not the practices or beliefs of Hooker. In addition, the style of *Heautonaparnumenos* argues for non-Hookerian authorship. Though this anonymous author sometimes uses figures of speech which Hooker would have approved, he shows a tendency in his vocabulary and his insistently rational argumentation to speak to the learned, the "ingenious" as he calls his audience at one point, rather than to the simple man whom Hooker always kept in mind in framing his discourse. A direct comparison of the sermon on self-denial in Hooker's *A Christians Two Chief Lessons* with *Heautonaparnumenos* shows that, while the two authors agree on several points, they are clearly two distinct individuals in their ideas and writing styles.

Another work in the same category — published anonymously in the mid-1640's — is the book called *The Immortality of the Soul*, which appeared in London in 1645 and again the following year. Everett Emerson has correctly argued that the book's ideas and style are both somewhat inconsistent with Hooker's.[11] Both Trumbull and Woolley take the item from Sabin's bibliography, neither having seen a copy. The reader familiar with Hooker's writings will have no difficulty in agreeing with Emerson and others that "it surely is not Hooker's." [12]

A third book even more easily shown not to be Hooker's, though it has remained on lists of his works with surprising tenacity, is entitled *The Equal Ways of God: Tending to the Rectifying of the Crooked Ways of Man*. The first edition appeared in 1632 and listed the author as "T. H.," the detail which has led to the subsequent confusion. Few have noticed the second edition, published in 1639, where the author's name is spelled out on the title page: "Thomas Hayne." Pollard and Redgrave, the *Dictionary of National Biography*, the British Museum *Catalogue*, and several individual scholars including Emerson have all correctly identified the work as non-

[11] Everett H. Emerson, "Notes on the Thomas Hooker Canon," *American Literature*, XXVII (January, 1956), 555.
[12] Ibid.

Hookerian, although it has appeared in the Hooker listings of Sabin, Trumbull, Woolley, Levy, and *LHUS*.

While we are eliminating these works from our survey of the Hooker canon, we must now also add four new titles, all dated 1638. These works have recently been located in unique copies in the Sion College Library in London.[13] The titles of the books are *The Properties of an Honest Heart*, *The Sinners Salvation*, *Spiritual Thirst*, and *The Stay of the Faithful*. It was thought expedient to question whether or not these might be Hooker's because their biblical texts all coincided with four of those listed in a November 13, 1637 *Stationers Register* entry to the printer Robert Dawlman of "a Booke called *The Souls possession . . .* by T.H."; and, because *The Souls Possession*, which has long been assumed Hooker's, and *Spiritual Munition* (see above, pp. 41ff.) are written on only two of the scripture passages cited in the entry, it is logical to assume that each of the seven Bible references is the text for a separate book. Moreover, a reading of the contents of each of these works further corroborates the presumption that they are Hooker's.

A full justification for attributing these four books to Hooker requires more space than is here available, but it can at least be said that they fall into two main categories of Hooker works. Three of the books, *Spiritual Thirst*, *The Sinners Salvation*, and *The Properties of an Honest Heart*, are part of Hooker's preparationist message on the way the Christian believer comes to an awareness of his acceptance by God among the elect. *Spiritual Thirst* is organized around the biblical metaphor of true "thirsting," which Hooker also uses in other works to characterize the condition of a sinner newly entered into true humiliation. In Hooker's system of gradual progression toward grace (see Pettit, pp. 124ff. above), while the sinner's affections are reaching toward God through hope, desire, love, and joy, he is ever more actively "thirsting" for full assurance. In other words, this spiritual thirsting characterizes the post-humiliation stage of "vocation" or "effectual calling."

The Sinners Salvation deals at length with the author's description of four "antecedents" of faith, a topic which clearly places the

[13] Katharine Pantzer of The Houghton Library first raised the question of a possible connection between these works and Thomas Hooker.

work in the context of Hooker's preparationist theology; and *The Properties of an honest Heart* describes, so that the individual believer can evaluate his progress to grace, the characteristics of soul which identify the regenerate individual. This self-examination is of course a process to which Hooker and other Puritans were always exhorting their congregations.

The Stay of the Faithful is especially interesting to the reader of the present volume. Discovered after our edition of early Hooker works was well under way, it offers good reasons for assuming that it dates from Hooker's English ministry of the late 1620's. He makes frequent references here to the present "publique sinnes and calamities" and "the publike evils of the times that wee complaine of so much." Such references are of course closely related to similar allusions in *Spiritual Munition,* where the anti-Puritan policies of King Charles I and Bishop Laud provide the catalyst for bold allusions in the sermon and give a clear historical backdrop for the sermon being preached.,

Finally, each of these new works contains the characteristic turn of phrase, metaphoric plainness, and rhythmic pungency familiar to the reader of Hooker. Thus, on the basis of the Stationer's statement that the author of sermons on biblical texts identical to the texts for these works was one "T.H.," and the further circumstance of their inclusion in the same *Stationers Register* entry as two known Hooker works, together with their thematic and stylistic content, there seems no reason to hesitate in assigning them to Hooker, adding them, after nearly three hundred and fifty years, to our list of known Hooker works.[14]

It is a truism for any serious student that as he adds to his knowledge he becomes aware of his ignorance. This fact of the scholarly life, which can be both frustrating and energizing, is fully borne out by our present evaluation of our knowledge on the Hooker canon. While the changes in works included in our list of acknowledged Hooker books can be made and, one hopes, accepted with confidence, we are a long way from having answered all questions

[14] The reasons for assigning these books to Hooker are discussed more fully in Bush, "Four New Works by Thomas Hooker: Identity and Significance," *Resources for American Literary Study*, IV (Spring, 1974), 3–26.

on the subject. There are still some intriguing unknowns which ought to continue to provoke the curiosity of anyone interested in the work of this major Puritan preacher and writer. When we consider that for most of his career he showed relatively little active interest in publishing his work, we must acknowledge that a surprisingly large number of Hooker's sermons have survived to our day. We also know, however, of the supposed one-time existence of major manuscripts which were never published in spite of the likelihood that in these instances Hooker meant them to be. The English printer Peter Cole some nine years after Hooker's death brought out three substantial volumes of Hooker sermons which he called — perhaps because Hooker wanted them called — eleven "Books," announcing in advertisements printed in these volumes that "six more books" were "now printing" in the series. The eleven "Books" were published in three volumes as *The Application of Redemption: The first Eight Books, The Application of Redemption: The Ninth and Tenth Books,* and *A Comment upon Christs Last Prayer,* which was described as Hooker's "*Seventeenth Book made in New-England.*" This numbering certainly suggests that the printer had every intention of filling the gap in numbering by issuing "books" eleven through sixteen. Since Thomas Goodwin and Philip Nye tell us in their introductions to these published books that they have used Hooker's own manuscripts in their publication, and since the promised six remaining "books" never appeared, so far as we know, the whereabouts or fate of the manuscripts remains an intriguing mystery. In 1656, if these "books" were not actually then "printing," Peter Cole must at least have had additional Hooker papers in his possession or near at hand.

Another case of lost manuscripts is also part of the Hooker story. It was early reported that Hooker's sometime student and disciple in Connecticut and later the long-lived minister at Salem, John Higginson, copied out some two hundred of Hooker's sermons for transmission to a printer in England. This extensive labor was clearly brought on by Higginson's admiration for Hooker as a man and preacher, so that there is almost a tragic poignancy — if we accept the story of the manuscripts' existence — in their never having found their way into print. We now know no more of their fate or whereabouts than we do of the missing six "books" in the *Application of Redemption* series. They could centuries ago have gone to the bottom of the Atlantic Ocean, as did Hooker's first version of *A Survey of the Sum of Church Discipline*, or they could just as well have gone into someone's trunk. At this late date it is neither likely nor entirely impossible that they might turn up.

Further reason not to become complacent with our understanding of the Hooker canon can be found in the work of past scholars. Trumbull, for example, listed without visual verification other than a 1639 *Stationers Register* entry, a work by "T.H." called *The Garments of Salvation*. Trumbull had not seen the work. What is more, works entered by the Stationer were not always published, so that it is possible that this one was not. However, the existence of single editions of some of Hooker's books in unique copies suggests that the book may have been written by Hooker and actually published. The title, at least, should be kept in mind against the possibility that a copy might some day turn up. In the same category is the work registered with the Stationer at the same time as *The Souls Possession* and the other works discussed above, four of which have very recently been identified for the first time. All the biblical texts cited in that entry, with the exception of I Pet. 5:5, have been related to a known book. There is every reason to believe that this work was published and, if it should be found, could be proven Hooker's. The likelihood, then, that we will need occasional revisions of the Hooker bibliography is not at all remote, and we should certainly not become complacent about what we now know. The past history of Hooker bibliography ought itself to be enough to warn against such error.

Finally, we shall in all probability supplement our knowledge of the canon by discovering editions of already acknowledged Hooker books. Among the most recent discoveries have been the many editions of *The Poor Doubting Christian*, which show it to be one of the most popular Puritan books of the seventeenth century,[15] and the two editions of *The Souls Preparation for Christ* from the first year of its issue, 1632. Conspicuous for its absence from the Hooker

[15] See Bush, "The Growth of Thomas Hooker's *The Poor Doubting Christian*," *Early American Literature*, VIII (1973), 3-20.

bibliography, however, is the fourth edition of John Rogers' *The Doctrine of Faith*. We can safely assume that there was such an edition and that it included Hooker's Epistle to the Reader, but in keeping with our policy of including only verified editions, it has been excluded until a copy is located. Undiscovered editions of other works in the Hooker canon may also be one day found. It is important to ask, for example, whether or not the September 5, 1637, entry of *An Exposition of the Lords Prayer* in the *Stationers Register* points to a work actually published in 1637 or 1638. Such a work, if it exists, would replace the 1645 edition as the first to be printed. For these reasons, as well as unknown others, we have fair warning to continue the search. The questions about the Hooker canon are by no means all answered.

Our new awareness of the considerable size of the Hooker canon, both with respect to the number of separate works included and the number of editions now known to have been printed, indicates perhaps more substantially and concretely than earlier evidence Thomas Hooker's standing as a Puritan voice. The popularity of his best-known writings was enduring throughout his lifetime and beyond. For decades his works were published, sold, and widely read, and their presence at this time in scattered libraries in both Europe and America is a lasting tribute to Hooker's importance in his own day.

A Bibliography of The Published Writings of Thomas Hooker

Introduction

The following list of Hooker's published works is the most complete ever compiled, listing half-again as many editions as did H. Clark Woolley's bibliography of 1932, the longest heretofore. This list adds several works to Hooker's canon which have never before appeared in a bibliography of his writings, and it eliminates some which have been consistently included.

The intention throughout has been to make this a bibliography which will be highly usable, to the end that Hooker's canon may eventually receive the detailed attention and reading that it deserves. Details which the full-dress technical bibliography often includes—physical properties and exact dimensions of the bindings, number of end papers, types of paper, water-marks, have been excluded; but the length of each work is indicated by giving both the number of pages and the general size of the volume (duodecimo, octavo, quarto, etc.). Also included are indications of all line endings on the title pages, mainly because this information sometimes allows the reader to distinguish one edition from another, as for example the first from the second edition of *The Danger of Desertion*. Each title page, however, has not been fully reproduced, it being thought best to eliminate the scriptural passages which appear on the title pages of Hooker's sermon volumes. In most if not all cases these passages were selected by the printer rather than by the author. In any case, they are never the actual text of the sermon(s) in the books but are simply quotations on themes similar to those of the sermon texts. It is also impossible here to indicate accurately the typographical peculiarities of these books. In particular, the indication of capital and lower case letters does not show the great variety of sizes of the type face. A book such as *The Souls Preparation*, for example, has eight or nine different sizes of capital letters on the title page.

Because it is assumed that most users of this bibliography will be seeking information about the contents of particular works, each item has been annotated to indicate in a very limited space the major subject matter of the work and to point to places where the contents of some of the books are duplicated or paraphrased in others. Moreover, locations are indicated for each item. Major libraries in the United States, England, Scotland, Holland, and France have been consulted, and some have been discovered to contain editions entirely unknown before. Hooker's books have also been found in libraries which are not major research libraries; and there can be no doubt that other copies and perhaps even other editions have still to be located. In most instances the compiler has been able to consult the actual books and sometimes to compare multiple copies. Where it has not been possible to have at least one copy of an edition physically in hand, a photographic copy of the title page and of other selected details has always been obtained.

Finally, in order to allow this list fully to serve its function, reel numbers have been included for all Hooker books which have been filmed in the STC microfilming project through May, 1973. This information will of course need frequent updating as additional Hooker works become available on microfilm.

Where Sabin, Wing, Evans, and STC numbers are cited, the reference indicates that the edition is listed in one of the following well-known major bibliographies: Joseph Sabin, *Bibliotheca Americana. A Dictionary of Books Relating to America* . . . (New York, 1868–1936); Donald G. Wing, *Short-title Catalogue of Books Printed in England, Scotland, Ireland, Wales, and British America* . . . . *1641–1700* (New York, 1945–1951; Charles Evans, *et. al. American Bibliography* . . . *1639 Down to and Including the Year 1820* (Chicago, Worcester, Mass., 1903–1959); A. W. Pollard and G. R. Redgrave, *A Short-title Catalogue of Books Printed in England, Scotland & Ireland* . . . *1475–1640* (London, 1926).

Abbreviations for libraries are as follows:

AUB – Universiteits-Bibliotheek, Amsterdam
C – Cambridge University Library
CE – Emmanuel College, Cambridge
CLU-C – William Andrews Clark Memorial Library, UCLA
CSmH – Henry E. Huntington Library, San Marino, California
Ct – Connecticut State Library, Hartford
CtHC – Hartford Seminary Foundation
CtHCen – Center Church, Hartford
CtHS – Connecticut Historical Society
CtHWatk – Watkinson Library, Trinity College, Hartford
CtY – Yale University
DC – Dulwich College
DFo – Folger Shakespeare Library
DLC – Library of Congress
EN – National Library of Scotland, Edinburgh
HR – Royal Library, The Hague
ICN – Newberry Library, Chicago
ICU – University of Chicago
L – British Museum
LCL – Congregational Library, London
LSC – Sion College, London
LU – University College, London
LW – Dr. Williams's Library, London
MB – Boston Public Library
MBCong – Congregational Library, Boston
MH – Harvard University
MiU-C – Clements Library, University of Michigan
MWA – American Antiquarian Society
NcD – Duke University
NcU – University of North Carolina, Chapel Hill
NIC – Cornell University
NjPT – Princeton Theological Seminary
NN – New York Public Library
NNC – Columbia University
NNUT – Union Theological Seminary, New York
O – Bodleian Library, Oxford

PU — University of Pennsylvania
RPJCB — John Carter Brown Library, Brown University
ViU — University of Virginia
WU — University of Wisconsin

— 1627 —

1. "To the Reader." In: THE/ DOCTRINE/ OF/ FAITH,/ Wherein are practi/cally handled twelue/principall points, which/explaine the Nature/ and Vse of it./ By IOHN ROGERS,/ Preacher of Gods Word/ at *Dedham* in Essex./ The second Edition, newly cor-/ rected, and inlarged by the Author./ . . . . LONDON, printed for *Nathanael New-bery* and/ *William Sheffard*, and are to be/ sold at their Shops in Popes-/ head Alley. 1627. 9 pp. LW.

This nine-page signed ["THOMAS HOOKER"] preface was added to Rogers' work when it was revised and enlarged. The first edition, which had "practically handled ten principall points" rather than twelve and did not contain Hooker's essay, was also published in 1627. (Copies of the first edition are owned by the Folger Shakespeare Library and Dr. Williams's Library.) Hooker's essay briefly propounds a favorite topic of his entire ministry and a concern of Rogers' book: the location of faith in the stages of redemption, after contrition and vocation and before sanctification and full glorification.

Hooker's preface was neither revised nor reset for any succeeding edition. It is probably safe to assume that the essay appeared in the fourth edition as well as those listed below, but no copy has been located.

1a. The third Edition. . . ./LONDON,/ Printed for *Nathanael Newbery* and/ *Henry Overton*, and are to be/ sold at their Shops in Popes-/ head Alley. 1629. DFo, MH. STC 21187, Microfilm 1003.

1b. The fifth Edition. . . ./LONDON,/ Printed by *I.D.* for *Nathanael New-/ bery* and *Henry Overton*, and are/ to be sold at their Shops in *Popes-/* head Alley. 1633. DFo. STC 21188.

1c. The sixth Edition. . . ./LONDON,/ Printed by *G.M.* for *Nathanael New-/ bery* and *Henry Overton*, and are to/ be sold at their Shops in *Popes-/* Head Alley. 1634. DFo, NYUT. STC 21889, Microfilm 1287.

1d. The seventh Edition. . . ./LONDON,/ Printed by *Iohn Dawson* for *Ione* [sic.; i.e. Joan] *New-/ bery* and *Henry Overton*, and are to/ be sold at their Shops in *Popes-/* Head Alley. 1638. CE, L, MB. STC 21190.

1e. The eighth Edition. . . ./LONDON,/ Printed by *E.G.* for *Henry Overton,/* and *Samuell Enderby*, and are to/ be sold at their Shops in *Popes-/* Head Alley. 1640. DFo. STC 21190a, Microfilm 668.

1f. *Thomas Hooker: Writings in England and Holland, 1626–1633*, ed., George H. Williams, Norman Pettit, et al. (Cambridge, 1975) pp. 143–146.

— 1629 —

2. THE POOR/ DOVBTING CHRISTIAN/ DRAWNE VNTO CHRIST./ . . . LONDON,/ Printed in the yeare 1629. In: THE SAINTS/ CORDIALS./ AS THEY VVERE DELI-/ VERED IN SVNDRY SERMONS/ upon speciall Occasions, in the Citie of/ LONDON, and elsewhere./ . . . . LONDON,/ Printed for ROBERT DAVVLMAN dwelling at the Brazen-Serpent/ in Pauls Church-yard. Pp. 345–366. Folio. Ct, CtHC(2), CtHWatk, L, O, MB, MH. Sabin 32843. Microfilm 1083. STC 22503.

In its original form, this was a portion of a long sermon which was later published in full as part of *The Souls Effectual Calling* (1637). It is mainly a work of reassurance and encouragement to the timid believer who is too willing to doubt the quality of his belief. Biblical text: Jn. 6:45.

The most popular of all Hooker's books, *The Poor Doubting Christian* also has the most complicated publishing history. Significant additions and alterations to the text occurred in the 1635 and 1646 editions. For discussion of these changes see Bush, "The Growth of Thomas Hooker's *The Poor Doubting Christian*," *Early American Literature*, VIII (1973), 3–20, and Frank Shuffelton, "Thomas Prince and His Edition of Thomas Hooker's *Poor Doubting Christian*," *Early American Literature*, V (1971), 68–75.

2a. THE/ POORE/ Doubting CHRISTIAN/ Drawne to/ CHRIST./ . . . . The Second Edition. LONDON/ Printed for *R. Dawlman* and *L. F./* at the Brazen Serpent in Pauls-/ Churchyard. 1635. Pp. 1–163. 12°. DFo.

2b. THE/ POORE/ Doubting/ CHRISTIAN/ Drawne to/ Christ./ . . . . The Third Edition. / LONDON/ Printed for *R. Dawlman* and *L. Fawn/* at the Brazen Serpent in Pauls–/ Churchyard. 1636. Pp. 1–163. 12°. L.

2c. THE/ POORE/ Doubting/ CHRISTIAN/ Drawne to CHRIST./ . . . . The Fourth Edition./ LONDON/ Printed for *R. Dawlman* and *L. Fawn/* at the Brazen Serpent in/ Pauls Church-yard. 1637. Pp. 1–163. 12°. CtY.

2d. THE/ POORE/ Doubting/ CHRISTIAN/ Drawne to/ CHRIST./ . . . . The fourth Edition./ AMSTERDAM,/ Printed for T. L. for the benefit of our/ English Nation. 1637. Bound with John Preston, *The Doctrine of the Saints Infirmities*, Amsterdam, [n.d.] and Thomas Goodwin, *Aggravation of Sinne and Sinning against Knowledge and Mercy*, Amsterdam, 1639. 75 pp. 8°. O. STC 4266. Microfilm 1266.

2e. THE/ POORE/ Doubting/ CHRISTIAN/ Drawne to/ Christ./ . . . . The fifth Edition./ LONDON,/ Printed for *R. Dawlman* and *L./ Fawne* at the Brazen Serpent in/ Pauls Church-yard. 1638. Pp. 1–163. 12°. CE, DFo, MH. STC 4267.

2f. THE/ POORE/ Doubting/ CHRISTIAN/ Drawn to/ CHRIST./ . . . . The sixth Edition./ LONDON,/ Printed by *I. Raworth*, for *Luke Fawne*,/ and are to be sold at his shop, at the/ signe of the Parrot in *Pauls*/ Church-yard. 1641. PP. 1–163. 12°. CtHS, CT, DFo. Sabin 32844; Wing H2651B.

2g. THE/ Poor Doubting CHRISTIAN/ Drawn to CHRIST./ . . . . By THO. HOOKER./ . . . . LONDON,/ Printed by *Ruth Raworth*, for *Luke Fawne*,/ at the signe of the Parrot in *Pauls* Church-yard. 1646. Pp. 1–189 (much misnumbering of pages). 12°. CtHS.

2h. [Title page lacking.] Pp. 1–189. 12°. CtHS.
The text is the revised text of the 1646 edition, but the printer of this edition has eliminated some of the errors in pagination making this appear to be post–1646.

2i. THE/ Poor Doubting/ CHRISTIAN/ Drawn to/ CHRIST./ . . . . By THO. HOOKER./ . . . . LONDON,/ Printed for *Luke Fawn*, at the sign of the/ Parrot in *Pauls* Church-yard. 1652. Pp. 1–158. 12°. LW.

2j. [Title page lacking.] Pp. 1–152. 12°. CtHS [title page, pp. 23, 24 missing; pp. 1–22 damaged.]
This bears a closer physical resemblance to the 1652 edition than to any other. Contains the full text of post–1645 editions.

2k. THE/ Poor Doubting/ CHRISTIAN/ Drawn to/ CHRIST./ . . . . By THO. HOOKER,/ . . . . LONDON./ Printed by *John Macock*, for *Luke Fawne*,/ at the signe of the *Parrot* in *Pauls*/ Church-yard, 1659. Pp. 1–185 (last page misnumbered 158). 12°. Ct, MB. Wing, *A Gallery of Ghosts*, #O H2651C.

2l. De/ *Arme Twijffelende*/ CHRISTEN,/ genadert tot CHRISTUM./ . . . In't Engels beschreven door/ *THOMAS HOOKER*,/ *Dienaar das Woorts, in Chelmsford*,/ *in Essex*./ Ende nu vertaalt door H. H./ . . . . t'AMSTERDAM,/ By Gerrit Willems Doornick, Boeck-/ ver-hooper op de Lingel. in't groot Cantoor-/ Boeck. Anno 1660. Pp. (6), 227. 12°. AUB.
The entire work is in Dutch. Contains "Opdracht-Brief. . . ." (4 pp.) by Hendrik Hiddingh; "Bescheyde Leser" (1 p.); and a poem on Hooker by Johannes Roos (1 p.).

2m. THE/ Poor Doubting/ CHRISTIAN/ Drawn to/ CHRIST./ . . . . By THO. HOOKER, Late of *New-England*./ . . . .LONDON./ Printed by S. G. for *Nathaniel Ranew*,/ and *Jonathan Robinson*, at the *Angel*/ in Jewenstreet, 1667. Pp. 1–185. 12°. LSC, MWA.

2n. THE/ Poor Doubting/ CHRISTIAN/ Drawn to/ CHRIST./ . . . . By THO. HOOKER./ . . . . LONDON,/ Printed by *J. M.* for *Nath. Ranew* at/ the *Kings Arms* in St. *Paul's*/ Church-yard. 1674. Pp. 1–185. 12°. CtY.

20. THE/ Poor Doubting/ CHRISTIAN/ Drawn to/ CHRIST./ . . . . By *THOMAS HOOKER*./ . . . . *London;* Printed by *J. D.* for *Nath./ Ranew* at the King's Arms, and/ *Jonath. Robinson* at the Golden/ Lion in St. *Paul's* Church-yard,/ M.D.C.LXXXIV. Pp. 1-185. 12°. EN, L, MH, MWA, NjPT. Wing H2652.

2p. THE/ *Poor Doubting* CHRISTIAN/ Drawn to CHRIST./ . . . . By *THOMAS HOOKER*./ The Twelfth Edition./ *LONDON*, Printed by *R. J.* for/ *J. Robinson*, A. and *J. Churchill*, *J. Taylor*, and *J. Wyat*. 1700. Pp. 1-167. 12°. Ct, CtHCen, RPJCB. Sabin 32845; Wing H2653.

2q. THE/ *Poor Doubting*/ CHRISTIAN/ Drawn to CHRIST./ . . . . By *Thomas Hooker*./ With an *Abstract* of the Author's *Life*./ . . . . BOSTON:/ Printed by GREEN, BUSHELL, and ALLEN,/ for D. HENCHMAN, in Cornhil. 1743. [Thomas Prince, ed.] Pp. 1-14, 1-143 (1). 16°. Ct, CtHS, CtY (2), DLC, MH, MB, MBCong, MiU-C, MWA, NcD, NN, others. Sabin 32846; Evans 5214.
   Contains a 14-page "Preface" signed by Thomas Prince and dated "Boston, April 1, 1743."

2r. DE/ ARME TWYFELENDE/ CHRISTEN,/ genadert tot/ CHRISTUS./ . . . . *In 't Engelsch, beschreven door*/ MR. THOMAS HOOKER,/ En in 't Nederduits vertaalt door H. H./ . . . . *TE ROT-TERDAM,*/ By HENDRIK VAN PELT, en ADRIANUS DOUCI, p–z. 1761./ Boekverkoopers. [Apparently a translation of the London, 1684 edition.] Contains "Voorberigt van de Drukkers aan de Lezer". Pp. (2), 1-186. 8°. HR.
   Bound with *De Waare Ziels-Vernedering en Heilzame Wanhoop (The Souls Humiliation)*, Rotterdam, 1760. Each work has a separate title page and the volume has the following title page: TWEE/ UITMUN-TENDE/ PRAKTIKALE TRACTATEN/ van den beroemden/ THOMAS HOOKER,/ . . . . genaamt/ I. De Heilzame Wanhoop, en/ II. De arme twyfelende Christen. This is followed by a 10-page "Voor-reden aan den Heilzoekenden Lezer" by D. L. J.

2s. THE/ POOR DOUBTING CHRISTIAN/ DRAWN TO CHRIST:/ . . . . BY REV. THOMAS HOOKER,/ FIRST MINISTER OF HARTFORD, CONNECTICUT./ *With an abstract of the Au-thor's life.* /Also an Introduction, by/ EDWARD W. HOOKER, D. D./ PROF. SACRED RHETORIC IN THE THEOLOGICAL INSTITUTE OF/ CONNECTICUT, EAST WINDSOR./ . . . . HARTFORD:/ ROBINS AND SMITH./ 1845. Pp. (4), 5-8, 9-21, 22-23, 25-165, (1). Ct, CtHC, CtHS, CtHWatk, DFo, L. Sabin 32847.
   Contains one-page note by J. Hawes dated March 26, 1845, one page of illustrations of the first meeting house and of Hooker's home in Hart-ford, a four-page Introduction signed by E. W. Hooker and dated February, 1845, the "Biographical Sketch" of Hooker by Thomas Prince, a "Supplement to the Biographical Sketch," and at the end of the book, one-page "Contents."

2t. DE/ ARME TWIJFELENDE/ CHRISTEN,/ GENADERT TOT/ CHRISTUS./ . . . . *In't Engelsch, beschreven door/* Mr. THOMAS HOOKER,/ En in't Nederduits vertaalt door H. H./ . . . . beneven *vijftig plichten,* welke/ van een begenadigde dienen/ betragt te worden, door/ JACOBUS KOELMAN,/ *Bedienaar des H. Evangeliums.*/ Onveranderde Uitgave./ Te ROTTERDAM, bij R. C. Huge. Bound with *De waare Ziels-Vernedering, en Heilzame Wanhoop,* with a "Voorword" by P. Deetman dated 3 Augustus 1878. Separate title pages but consecutive pagination. Pp. 261–396. AUB.

2u. The Poor Doubting Christian/ Drawn to Christ./ BY THOMAS HOOKER./ With an Introduction by the/ Rev. D. M. M'Intyre./ Drummond's Tract Depot, Stirling./ London: S. W. Partridge & Co. n.d. [1904]. "An abridgement," with modifications of the prose as well. "Introduction" (16), pp. 21–95. L, O.

2v. *Thomas Hooker: Writings in England and Holland, 1626–1633,* ed., George H. Williams, Norman Pettit, et al. (Cambridge, 1975), pp. 152–186.
Note: The following entry, which suggests the possibility of yet another edition, appears in the *Stationers Register* for June 6, 1645:
John Stafford [Bookseller]. Entred . . . under the hands of Master DOWNHAM and Master PARKER warden a booke consisting of severall sermons, vizt, of Mr Fenner's *upon* ROM: 8th. 22th, *the first Epist. of JOHN,* 2^d, 6th, *JOHN* ye 3^d ye 20th, *LAMENT.* 3. 57.; Mr Hooker *upon JOHN,* 6.45; Mr Rogers *upon* ROM: 6:21, & M^r R *(?)* Hubberd *upon* GAL. 5:6. *HEBR.* 9.14.; 1 *PET.* 2.2; *EPH.* 4.30, 1 *CRON.* 28. . . . *HEBR.* 9.27., *reserveing every mans right to all or any of the said sermons.*
The biblical text for the Hooker "sermon" mentioned here is the same as that for *The Poor Doubting Christian.* We have not been able to locate or verify the existence of any such book.

— 1632 —

3. THE/ SOVLES/ PREPARATION/ FOR CHRIST./ OR,/ A TREATISE/ OF *CONTRITION./ Wherein is discovered/* How God breaks the heart/ and wounds the Soule, in the con-/ version of a Sinner to Himselfe./ . . . .LONDON,/ Printed for ROBERT DAVVLMAN, at the signe of/ the Brazen-serpent in *Pauls Churchyard./* 1632. Pp. (6), 1–258. 4°. Ct, CtHWatk, CtHS, CtY, DFo, L, LU, MB, MH. Sabin 32857, STC 13735, Microfilm 1026.
This is the first collection of Hooker sermons on the stages in the process of regeneration, which was the major subject of his published works. This work describes in detail the earliest stage, contrition. Hooker revised and expanded the work later in *The Application of Redemption: the Ninth and Tenth Books.* Biblical text: *Acts* 2:37.
Note that two separate editions appeared in 1632. The 258-page edition was apparently issued first. This edition contains "A Table of the

Contents", scripture reference index, and list of *errata*. Several of the errata listed in this edition have been corrected in the 241-page edition. Later editions reprint these corrections, though other substantive changes including deletions of entire sentences and paragraphs appear in the later editions. All editions include the following note just preceding page one: "Christian Reader, thou hast some Sermons brought to light, which by reason of the Authors absence, are presented to thy view, both with some lesser escapes, and in more homely termes, then his judicious eye would have suffered." In 1632 Hooker was in the Netherlands, a fugitive from the ecclesiastical justice of the Court of the High Commission. His name is nowhere mentioned in the volume.

3a. THE/ SOVLES/ PREPARATION/ FOR CHRIST./ OR,/ A TREATISE/ OF *CONTRITION*./ *Wherein is discovered*/ How God breaks the heart/ and wounds the Soule, in the con-/ version of a Sinner to Himselfe./ . . . .LONDON./ Printed for ROBERT DAVVLMAN, at the signe of/ the Brazen-serpent in *Pauls Church-yard*./ 1632. Pp. (4), 1–242. C. CtHCen, DLC, MH.

"A Table of the Contents" is printed in 3 1/2 instead of the 4 1/2 pp. of the preceding edition.

3b. THE/ SOVLES/ PREPARATION/ FOR CHRIST./ OR./ A TREATISE/ OF *CONTRITION*./ *Wherein is discovered*/ How God breakes the Heart,/ and wounds the Soule, in the/ conversion of a Sinner to/ Himselfe./ . . . .LONDON,/ Printed by *E. A.* for *R. Allot* and *R. Dawlman*,/ and are to be sold at the Black Beare, and/ the Brazen Serpent, in Pauls Church-/ yard. 1635. Pp. (9), 1–456. 12°. CtHC, CtHCen, CtHS, L. STC 13736.

3c. THE/ SOVLES/ PREPARATION/ FOR CHRIST./ OR,/ A TREATISE/ OF *CONTRITION*./ Wherein is discovered/ How God Breakes the Heart,/ and wounds the Soule, in the/ conversion of a Sinner to/ Himselfe./ . . . .LONDON, Printed by *E. A.* for *R. Allot* and *R. Dawlman*,/ and are to be sold at the Brazen Serpent,/ and the Black Beare, in Pauls Church-yard. 1635. Pp. (9), 1–456. 12°. CtY.

This is another issue of the preceding item.

3d. THE/ SOVLES/ PREPARATION/ FOR CHRIST./ OR,/ A TREATISE/ OF *CONTRITION*./ *Wherein is discovered*/ HOVV God breakes the heart./ and wounds the Soule, in the con-/ version of a Sinner to Himselfe./ . . . .The fourth Edition./ *LONDON*,/ Printed by the Assignes of *T.P.* for *T. Nickoles*, and/ are to bee sold at the signe of the *Bible*, in/ *Popes-head Ally*, 1638. Pp. (4), 1–242. 4°. Ct, CtHCen, CtHWatk, LCL, MH, MWA, NN. Sabin 32858.

3e. THE/ SOVLES/ PREPARATION/ FOR CHRIST./ OR,/ A TREATISE/ OF *CONTRITION*./ Wherein is discovered/ Hovv God breakes the heart,/ and wounds the Soule, in the con-/ version of a Sinner to Himselfe./ . . . .The fourth Edition./ *LONDON*,/ Printed by the Assignes of *T.P.* for *A. Crooke*, and/ are to bee sold at the Black

Beare, in Saint/ *Pauls Church-yard*, 1638. Pp. (4), 1–242. 4°. CtHS, DLC, LSC.
Bound variously with *The Souls Ingrafting*, 1637, *The Unbelievers Preparing for Christ*, 1638, *The Souls Exaltation*, 1638, *The Saints Dignity & Duty*, 1651. STC 13737.
This is another issue of the preceding item.

3f. THE/ SOVLES/ PREPARATION/ *FOR CHRIST:*/ BEING/ *A* TREATISE OF/ *CONTRITION*./ Wherein is discovered/ *How God breakes the* Heart, *and*/ vvounds the *Soule*, in the conver-/ sion of a Sinner to Himselfe./ . . . .PRINTED/ (For the use and benefit of the/ English Churches) in the/ NETHERLANDS./ Anno 1638. Pp. (4), 1–227. 12°. CtHWatk, O. STC 13738.

3g. THE/ SOVLES/ PREPARATION/ *FOR CHRIST:*/BEING/ *A* TREATISE OF/ *CONTRITION*./ Wherein is discovered/ *How God breakes the* Heart, *and*/ vvounds the *Soule*, in the conver-/ sion of a Sinner to Himselfe./. . . .PRINTED/ (For the use and benefit of the/ English Churches) in the/ NETHERLANDS./ Anno 1639. Pp. (4), 1–227. CE.
This is another issue of the preceding item.

3h. THE/ SOVLES/ PREPARATION/ FOR *CHRIST*./ OR,/ A TREATISE OF/ *CONTRITION*./ *Wherein is discovered*/ How God breakes the heart, and/ wounds the Soul, in the conversion/ *of a Sinner to Himselfe*./ . . . . The sixt Edition./ *LONDON*,/ Printed by *M. F.* for R. Dawlman. 1643. Pp. (6), 1–386. 12°. L, O. Sabin 32858, Wing H2656.
This is a new edition and contains "A Table of the CONTENTS" and a one-page advertisement for "Severall Treatises of this *Authour*" before p. 1.

3i. The Souls/ PREPARATION/ FOR/ CHRIST,/ OR,/ A TREATISE/ OF/ CONTRITION./ *Wherein is discovered*/ How God breaks the Heart, and/ wounds the Soul in the conversion/ of a Sinner to himselfe./ . . . .The seventh Edition./ *LONDON*,/ Printed by *J.G.* for *R. Dawlman*, and are to be sold/ by *Hen. Cripps*, at the entrance into Popes-head/ Alley, out of *Lumbard-street*./ 1658. Pp. (6), 1–386. C. CtHS, MBCong, NNUT. Sabin 32858, Wing H2657.
A reissue of the 1643 edition with a new title page.

— 1633 —

4. "An Advertisement to the Reader" and "The Præface" in William Ames, *A FRESH SVIT*/ Against/ HUMAN/ CEREMONIES/ IN GODS VVORSHIP./ OR/ *A Triplication unto*./ D. BVRGESSE HIS REJOINDER/ *For*/ D. MORTON./ *The First Part*./ . . . .Printed Anno 1633. n.p. [Rotterdam?] "An Advertisement to the Reader" (2 pp.), "The Præface" (77 pp.). DFo. STC 555. Microfilm 982.
"An Advertisement to the Reader" is a brief comment by Hooker announcing that William Ames was indeed the author of this and an

earlier work on the same subject, regretting his recent death, and observing Ames's increased concern over the English Church's attitude toward unauthorized "ceremonies" in worship at the end of his life.

"The Præface" offers character sketches of several weak types of people who, lacking sufficient will and principle, are swayed by others whose authority or reputation they respect. He is referring especially to those who have conformed to the English Church's dicta on "ceremonies" in worship, a subject of great importance to devout Puritans. He warns especially that the Church must not make laws but must be subject to those made by Christ. Hooker particularly exposes the illogicality and perverseness of certain arguments and passages in the book which Ames's work also answers, namely John Burgess, *An answer reioyned to that much applauded Pamphlet of a Nameless Author, bearthis title: viz. A Reply to Dr Morton's Generall Defence of three Nocent Ceremonies, &c*. . . . (London, 1631).

4a. Facsimile edition. Introduction by Richard C. Simmons (London: Gregg International Publishers, Ltd., 1971).

4b. *Thomas Hooker: Writings in England and Holland, 1626–1633*, ed., George H. Williams, Norman Pettit, et al. (Cambridge, 1975), pp. 320–377.

— 1637 —

5. THE/ SOVLES/ HVMILIATION./ . . . .*LONDON*,/ Printed by *I. L.* for *Andrew Crooke*, at the/ signe of the Beare in *Pauls* Churchyard./ 1637. Pp. 1–224. 4°. CE, Ct, EN, MB, MH (imperfect copy). STC 13728. Microfilm 1208.

The sermons in this work comprise the sequel to *The Souls Preparation* in the series on the soul's progression to grace and, like the earlier book, date from Hooker's ministry in England prior to his silencing in 1630. Biblical text: Lk.15: 14–18.

5a. THE/ SOVLES/ HVMILIATION./ . . . ./ *The Second Edition.*/ . . . .*LONDON*,/ Printed by *I.L.* for *Andrew Crooke*, at the/ signe of the Beare in *Pauls* Church-yard./ *1638*. Pp. 3–223, (9). 4°. Ct, CtHS, CtY, DLC, L, MH, MWA (2), NN, O.
Sabin 32851. STC 13729, Microfilm 1208.

Both this edition and the 1640 (see below) have, following the end of the text on p. 223: FINIS/ October 10. *Imprimatur*
1637 *T. Wykes.*
This is followed by a blank verso, "The Table" (4 pp.), an index to Bible passages mentioned in the work (3 pp.), and an advertisement for "Severall Treatises of this Avthovr" (1 p.). Immediately following the scripture passage index is printed: FINIS/ December 6. *Imprimature,*
1637 *Tho: Wykes.*

5b. THE/ SOVLES/ HUMILIATION/ . . . .*AMSTERDAM.*/ Printed for T. L. and are to be sould at his/ Chamber in Flowingburrow, neare/

unto the English Church./ ANNO *1638*. Pp. 3–302. 4°. CtHS, MBCong. Sabin 32853.

5c. THE/ SOVLES/ HVMILIATION./ . . . ./ The third Edition./ . . .*LONDON*,/ Printed by *T. Cotes* for *Andrew Crooke*, and/ *Philip Nevill*. 1640. Pp. 3–223 followed by "The Table" (4 pp.), scriptual reference index (3 pp.), and printer's advertisement (1 p.). 4°. Ct, CtHS, CtY, DFo, L, LSC, MB, MH, NjPT, NNUT. STC 13730, Microfilm 1243.

5d. DE WAARE/ ZIELS-VERNEDERING,/ EN/ HEILZAME/ WANHOOP./ In't Engelsch beschreven/ DOOR/ MR. THOMAS HOOKER,/ en in't Nederduits vertaalt/ DOOR/ JAC,OBUS KOEL-MAN,/ *Bedienaar des H: Euangeliums*./ . . .*TE ROTTERDAM*,/ By {HENDRIK VAN PELT, en} {ADRIANUS DOUCI, p. z.} 1760./ Boekverkoopers. 10-page "Voorreden", pp. 1–244. CtY, HR.
This translation is bound with Hooker's *De Arme Twyfelende Christen* (Rotterdam, 1761). See description of full volume in item 2r above.

5e. DE WAARE/ ZIELS-VERNEDERING,/ EN/ HEILZAME/ WANHOOP./ In't Engelsch beschreven/ DOOR/ Mr. THOMAS HOOKER,/ en in't Nederduits vertaalt/ DOOR/ JACOBUS KOEL-MAN,/ *Bedienaar des H. Euangeliums*./ Met een Voorwoord van Ds. P. DEETMAN,/ Predikant te Charlois./ Onveranderde Uitgave./ Te ROTTERDAM, bij/ R. C. HUGE, 1878. One-page "Voorwoord" by P. Deetman dated August 3, 1878, "Voorrede aan den heilzoekenden Lezer (pp. iv–xii), pp. 1–256. 8°. AUB.
This edition is bound with *De Arme Twyfelende Christen* (Rotterdam, 1878). See item 2t above.

6. THE/ SOVLES/ INGRAFTING/ into CHRIST./ By *T. H.*/ . . .*LONDON*,/ Printed by *J. H.* for *Andrew Crooke*, at the/ signe of the Beare in *Pauls* Church-yard./ *1637*. Pp. 1–30. 4°. Ct (3), CtHS, CtY, DFo, DLC, MB, MBCong, MH, NNC, NNUT. Sabin 32856, STC 13733, Microfilm 1072.
This is a short transitional work of pastoral encouragement which provides a link between the contents of *The Souls Humiliation* and *The Souls Effectual Calling* in the series on the stages of regeneration. It was printed to be bound with and immediately precede *The Souls Effectual Calling*, whose first page is numbered 33. It was bound with various works, however, including *The Souls Effectual Calling*, *The Souls Preparation*, and *The Souls Exaltation*. Biblical text: Mal.3:1.
A much longer version of this sermon is the second sermon in *The Souls Implantation: A Treatise* (1637), pp. 81–153, which was in turn reprinted in more carefully edited form in *The Souls Implantation into the Natural Olive* (1640), pp. 93–178.

7. THE/ SOVLES/ EFFECTVALL/ CALLING TO/ CHRIST./ By

T. H./ . . .LONDON,/ Printed by *J. H.* for *Andrew Crooke,* at the/ signe of the Beare in *Pauls* Church-yard./ 1637./ Pp. 33–668. 4°. Ct, CtHS, MBCong, NNUT. Sabin 32849, STC 13739, Microfilm 1276.

This work deals with the stage of vocation, which follows humiliation in the process of regeneration. Hooker deals in detail with the affections and God's ways of dealing with man's will. Biblical text: Jn. 6:45.

There is considerable overlapping of subject matter and organization between parts of this work (especially pp. 112–124, 188–190, 202–282, and 519–668) and parts of both *The Poor Doubting Christian* and *The Souls Implantation: A Treatise.* In the latter work, pp. 155–219 are strikingly similar in content to pp. 202–282 in *The Souls Effectual Calling.* The relationship between this work and *The Poor Doubting Christian* is much more complicated; see the discussions in Shuffelton, 70–71, and Bush, "The Growth of Thomas Hooker's *The Poor Doubting Christian,*" 8–12. In each case, major stylistic variations are present.

Page numbering of this work reflects the printer's intention to bind it with *The Souls Ingrafting,* which was sometimes done, though most extant copies are bound singly and begin with p. 33.

7a. THE/ SOVLES/ VOCATION/ OR/ EFFECTVAL/ Calling to CHRIST./ By *T.H./* . . . .LONDON,/ Printed by *Iohn Haviland,* for *Andrew Crooke,/* and are to be sold at the Black Beare in S. *Pauls/* Church-yard. 1638. Table of Contents (21 pp.), advertisement (1 page), pp. 33–668. 4°. C, Ct (2), CtHC, CtHS (2), CtY, DFo, DLC, MB, MBCong, MWA, NjPT (2), NN, NNUT. Sabin 32859.

This is a re-issue of the 1637 edition with a new title page and Table of Contents. Where bound with *The Souls Ingrafting,* the 1638 title page typically appears at the beginning of the volume followed by *The Souls Ingrafting* with its own title page, which is in turn followed by the 1637 title page of *The Souls Effectual Calling* and the text of this work.

8. THE SOULES/ IMPLANTATION./ A TREATISE/ CONTAIN-ING,/ The broken Heart, on/ Esay 57.15./ The Preparation of the Heart,/ on Luk. I. 17./ The Soules ingraffing into Christ,/ on Mal. 3. 1. Spirituall Love and Joy,/ on Gal. 5.22:/ . . . .LONDON,/ Printed by *R. Young,* and are sold by *Fulke Clifton/* on New Fish-street-hill./ 1637. Pp. 1–266. 4°. Ct, CtHS, CtY, DFo. DLC, L (2: one 4° and one 8°), MBCong, MH, NjPT. Sabin 32854, STC 13731, Microfilm 1144.

This work contains four sermons on different aspects of the process of regeneration. They are arranged in a chronological sequence, though do not cover all of the stages of redemption in the works listed above. The content is essentially the same as that of *The Souls Implantation into the Natural Olive* (1640) except that the latter is more carefully edited and adds a fifth treatise entitled "Spirituall Joy." The four sermons are as follows:

"The Broken Heart," pp. 1–24. Biblical text: Is. 57:15. This sermon is the basis for the brief 14-page Book IX of *The Application of Redemp-*

tion, which follows the same outline and includes many of the same details but is fully rewritten and considerably shortened.

"The Preparing of the Heart for to Receive Christ," pp. 25–79. Biblical text: Lk. 1:17. This sermon deals with the need for a powerful ministry. It was revised and somewhat expanded in the version appearing in Book III of *The Application of Redemption* (1656), pp. 141–220.

"The Soules Ingrafting into Christ," pp. 81–153. Biblical text: Mal.3:1. This is an expanded version of the much shorter sermon on the same text in *The Souls Ingrafting into Christ* (1637), with pp. 104–135 and 145–153 representing entirely new additions. This sermon is reprinted in facsimile form in Everett H. Emerson, *Redemption: Three Sermons (1637–1656) by Thomas Hooker* (Gainesville, Florida: Scholars' Facsimiles and Reprints, 1956).

"Spiritual Love and Joy," pp. 155–266. Biblical text: Gal. 5:22. This is the same sermon as appears in *The Souls Effectual Calling*, pp. 202–282, where it follows the same outline but is different throughout in its phrasing. The text in *The Souls Effectual Calling*, however, breaks off before the end, omitting pp. 220–266 of this work.

8a. THE SOULES/ IMPLANTATION/ INTO/ THE NATURALL/ OLIVE./ By T.H./ Carefully corrected, and much enlarged, with/ a Table of the Contents prefixed./ . . . .LONDON,/ Printed by *R. Young*, and are to be sold by *Fulke/ Clifton* on New-Fish street hill. 1640. "The Contents" (4), 1–320. 4°. CSmH, Ct (2), CtHC, CtHS, CtY, DFo, LCL, MH, NjPT, NN, NNUT. Sabin 32855, STC 13732, Microfilm 1311.

This is, as the title page indicates, a "corrected, and much enlarged" edition of *The Souls Implantation* (1637). Besides adding a four-page Table of Contents, the new edition frequently divides long paragraphs into shorter ones and eliminates occasional passages, the most notable being five paragraphs at the beginning of "Spirituall Love and Joy" which are present in *The Souls Implantation* (1637). The most important change, however, is the addition of an entire sermon, "Spirituall Joy." The more truncated outline of this new sermon, the presence of Greek and Latin quotations in both the margins and the text proper, and references to "the Virgin" and "Saint *Austine*" may make one suspicious of its authorship. In its style, doctrines, structure, and special emphasis on the uses, however, it is consistent with Hooker's manner and thought.

See item 8 above for full information on scriptual texts and cross-references to other works. Contents:

"The Broken Heart," pp. 1–28.
"Preparing of the Heart for to Receive Christ," pp. 29–92.
"The Soules Ingrafting into Christ," pp. 93–178.
"Spiritvall Love and Ioy," pp. 179–294.
"Spirituall Joy," pp. 295–320. Biblical text: Hab.3:17,18.

9. FOVRE/ LEARNED/ AND GODLY/ TREATISES;/ VIZ./ *The Carnall Hypocrite./ The Churches Deliverances./ The Deceitfulnesse*

of Sinne./ The Benefit of Afflictions./ By *T.H./* . . .Printed at *London* by *Tho. Cotes,/* for *Andrew Crooke*, and are to be sold/ at the signe of the Beare in/ *Pauls* Churchyard, 1638. Pp. (2), 1–293. 12°. C. MB, MH, NjPT, NNUT, O. Sabin 32838, STC 13725, Microfilm 1107.

These four sermons are on miscellaneous subjects but emphasize sin and often stress contemporary applications in England (internal evidence suggests a pre-1630 date).

The title listed in the *Stationers Register* entry for September 1, 1638, reads *ffoure godly and learned treatices.* This wording, which disagrees with the book's title page, is repeated in Sabin, Trumbull, and Woolley.

On the verso of the title page appears the following: *"Imprimatur,/* Tho. Wykes/ 1638." Then follows a 2-page list of "Severall Treatises of this *Authour.*" The four sermons all have individual title pages and appear as follows:

"The Carnall Hypocrite," pp. 1–93. Biblical text: 2 Tim. 3:5. This work appears in *Thomas Hooker: Writings in England and Holland, 1626–1633,* ed., George H. Williams, Norman Pettit, et al. (Cambridge, 1975), pp. 91–123.

"The Churches Deliverances," pp. 95–176. Biblical text: Jg. 10:13. This work appears in *Thomas Hooker: Writings in England and Holland, 1626–1633,* ed., George H. Williams, Norman Pettit, et al. (Cambridge, 1975), pp. 60–90.

"The Deceitfvlnesse of sinne," pp. 177–252. Biblical text: Ps.119:29.

"Heavie afflictions breeds earnest prayers from the wicked," pp. 255–293. Biblical text: Pr.1:28,29. The title printed with this sermon in the body of the work and quoted here is a more accurate reflection of content than the fourth title on the book's title page.

10. THE/ PROPERTIES/ OF/ An honest Heart:/ *Laid out in a Sermon/* upon *Psalme* 51.16./ . . . .*LONDON,/* Printed for *Robert Dawlman,/* at the Signe of the *Brazen/ Serpent* in *Pauls* Church-/ yard. 1638. Pp. 1–53. 12°. LSC. STC 23240. Bound with *The Stay of the Faithfull* (1638).

This is not a "sermon," as the title claims, but a handbook to aid individuals in self-examination, through which the believer could determine the spiritual condition of his soul. The author offers several "motives," "means," and "marks" of "uprightness" of heart. Biblical text: *"Psalm* 51:16" (i.e., Ps.51:6).

11. THE/ SINNERS/ SALVATION:/ Resolving/ This weighty case of/ Conscience; *viz. What/* course a poore soule should/ take that hee may/ bee saved./ . . . .*LONDON,/* Printed for *Robert Dawlman,/* at the Signe of the *Brazen/ Serpent* in *Pauls* Church-/ yard. 1638./ Pp. 1–73. 12°. LSC. STC 22578, Microfilm 1188.

This sermon clearly emphasizes Hooker's preparationist theology by enumerating four "antecedents" to faith, explaining both the reasons why such antecedents are necessary and what their effect on the heart is. Biblical text: Acts 16:31.

12. THE/ SOVLES/ EXALTATION./ A/ TREATISE/ containing/ *The Soules Vnion with Christ,/ on* I Cor. 6. 17./ *The Soules Benefit from Vnion/ with Christ,* on I Cor. 1. 30./ *The Soules Justification, on/* 2 Cor. 5. 21./ By T.H./ . . . .LONDON,/ Printed by *Iohn Haviland,* for *Andrew Crooke,* and/ are to bee sold at the black Beare in S. *Pauls/* Church-yard, 1638. Pp. "A Table" of Contents (12), (1), "Severall Treatises of this AUTHOUR" (1), 1–311. 4°. Ct (3), CtHC, CtHS (3), CtHWatk, CtY, DFo (2), DLC, L, MB, MBCong, MH (2), NjPT, NNUT, O. Sabin 32850, STC 13727, Microfilm 1072.

As the titles of the individual sermons suggest, this work describes the movement of the saint's soul into grace. It follows *The Souls Effectual Calling* in the chronology of redemption. The work contains three separate sections, each having its own biblical text:

"The Sovles Union with Christ," pp. 1–53. Biblical text: 1 Cor.6:17.

"The Sovles Benefit from Vnion with Christ," pp. 55–130. Biblical text: 1 Cor.1:30. This work has a separate title page.

"The Sovles Iustification," pp. 131–311. Biblical text: 2 Cor.5:22.

This book was bound singly and in various combinations with the following: *The Souls Ingrafting* (1637), *The Souls Vocation* (1638), *The Unbelievers Preparing for Christ* (1638), *The Souls Preparation* (1638), *The Souls Implantation into the Natural Olive* (1640), *The Christians Two Chief Lessons* (1640), and *The Danger of Desertion* (1641).

13. THE/ SOVLES/ POSSESSION/ OF CHRIST:/ Shewing how a Christian/ should put on Christ, and/ bee able to doe all things/ through his strength./ *Whereunto is annexed/* A SERMON/ Preached at the Funerall/ of that worthy Divine *M*ʳ./ *Wilmott,* late Minister/ of *Clare,* in Suffolke./ By *T. H./ LONDON,/* Printed by *M. F.* for *Francis Egles-/ field,* at the sign of the *Marigold* in *Pauls/* Church-yard. 1638. Pp. 1–170. 12°. C, Ct, O. STC 13734.

This work follows *The Souls Exaltation* in the series on regeneration. It deals with sanctification and the continuing struggle of both the regenerate and the reprobate with sin. Biblical text. Rom.13:4.

On the verso of the title page appears: "*Imprimatur./* THO. WYKES./ Novemb. 11./ 1637.

This book is bound with *Spiritual Munition,* but the latter has a separate title page and separate pagination.

14. *Spirituall/* MUNITION:/ A/ *FUNERALL/* SERMON./ . . . . *LONDON./* Printed for *Robert Dawlman,/* at the Signe of the *Brazen/ Serpent* in *Pauls* Church-/ yard. 1638. Pp. 1–47. 12°. C, Ct.

This is a brief funeral sermon preached at the funeral of the Rev. Robert Wilmot (c. 1595–1626) who was buried at Springfield near Chelmsford on June 22, 1626. It deals primarily with the need for greater respect for ministers, alluding to the special difficulties faced by them at the time in England. Biblical text: 2 Kg.2:12. Bound with *The Souls Possession of Christ.*

14a. *Thomas Hooker: Writings in England and Holland, 1626–1633*, ed., George H. Williams, Norman Pettit, et al. (Cambridge, 1975), pp. 41–52.

15. *Spiritual Thirst:*/A/ SERMON/ PREACHED/ upon Iohn 7.37./ . . . .LONDON,/ Printed for *Robert Dawlman*,/ at the Signe of the *Brazen*/ *Serpent* in *Pauls* Church-/ yard. 1638. Pp. 1–77. 12°. LSC. STC 23953.
   This is a single sermon on the all-sufficiency of Christ to satisfy the spiritual "thirst" for grace which the true believer has. In its insistence on the necessity of this prior thirst before faith can be acquired, Hooker again stresses his preparationist position. Biblical text: Jn. 7:37.

16. THE/ STAY/ OF THE/ *FAITHFULL:*/ *Together with*/ THE PROPERTIES/ of an honest Heart./ *In two Sermons.*/. . . .LONDON,/ by *M.F.* for *R. Dawl-*/*man*, and are to be sold by/ *Thomas Nichols* in *Popes-*/ *head Alley* at the sign/ of the Bible. 1638. Pp. 1–100. 12°. LSC. STC 23240. Microfilm 1188.
   This work makes direct allusion to the present "times of publike danger" in England in the late 1620's, presumably, warning that God is apt to desert the sinful church or nation but ending with the reassurance that God has given his conditional promise to save his people, and a half-promise from God is far better than a promise of man. Biblical text: Zeph.2:3. Bound with *The Properties of an Honest Heart* but separate pagination.

17. Three Godly/ SERMONS./ I. The Wrath of GOD/ against Sinners./ II. GODS Eternitie, and/ Mans Humanitie./ III. The Plantation of/ the Righteous./ By *T.H.*/ . . . .LONDON,/ Printed by *M.P.* for *Iohn Staf-*/*ford*,/ dwelling in Black-Horse-Alley/ neere Fleetstreet, 1638. Pp. 1–139. 12°. C. STC 12579.
   The title page offers the rare exception to the usual practice of quoting a biblical passage which is not one of the author's texts. Here the reason probably is that the passage quoted is the text for the first sermon, which does not have a separate title page as the other two do. The three sermons are:
   "The Wrath of God against Sinners," pp. 1–60. Biblical text: Rom. 1:18. This sermon is not so much on God's wrath as it is on the nature of spiritual "Truth" and the ways in which carnal men oppose this truth.
   The second sermon's separate title page is dated 1639 and has a more elaborate title than the book's title page offers: A/ GODLY AND/ PROFITABLE/ SERMON:/ Of Gods Eternitie and/ Mans Human-itie./ OR, *The Striving of the Lord*/ with Sinners./, pp. 63–109. This sermon deals with God's spiritual accompaniment of ministers and the Word and his patience with the reprobate. Biblical text: Gen. 6:3.
   The separate title page of the third sermon reads: A/ GODLY AND/ FRVITFVULL/ SERMON:/ THE/ PLANTATION/ of the/ RIGHTEOVS./ This is also dated 1639. Pp. 111–139. This work deals

with the "duties" of Christians—how and when to do them, with emphasis on the importance of doing them "in season." Biblical text: Ps.1:3.

17a. *Three Sermons:/* I. The Wrath of GOD/ against Sinners./ II. GODS Eternitie, and/ Mans Humanitie./ III. The Plantation of/ the Righteous./ By *T.H./*. . . .*LONDON,/* Printed by *M.P.* for *Iohn Stafford,/* dwelling in Black-horse-Alley/ neere Fleetstreet, 1638. Pp. 1–139. 12°. LSC, NjPT.

A reissue of *Three Godly Sermons,* with which it is identical in all details except that the top half of the title page has been reset.

17b. THE/ SAINTS/ GUIDE,/ IN THREE/ TREATISES;/ I. *The Mirror of Mercie,/* on Gen. 6.13./ II. *The Carnall Mans/ Condition,* on Rom. I. 18/ III. *The Plantation of/ the Righteous,* on Psa. I. 3/ By THOMAS HOO-/ KER *Minister in/ New-England./* Printed at London for/ *John Stafford* over a-/ gainst *Brids Church./* 1645. "The Contents" (6 pp.), pp. 1–172. 12°. CtY, L, MH, O. Wing H 2655. Mifrofilm 149.

This work contains the same three sermons as *Three Godly Sermons,* but here a Table of Contents is added and the sermons themselves are revised, expanded, and generally more effective. The order of the first two sermons has been reversed and the titles changed. The second and third sermons have separate title pages.

"The Merror of Mercy," pp. 1–83. This is a revised version of the second sermon in *Three Godly Sermons.*

"The Carnall Mans Condition," pp. 85–140. This is a revised version of the first sermon in *Three Godly Sermons.* The separate title page just preceding the text identifies the author as follows: "By THOMAS HOOKER, late of CHELMSFORD in Essex, now *Minister* of the Gospell in New-*ENGLAND.*" See also item #32 for still another version of this sermon, which is extant in more variant forms (three) than any other Hooker sermon.

"The Plantation of the Righteous," pp. 141–172. This is a revised version of the third sermon in *Three Godly Sermons.* Its separate title page carries the same description of Hooker as that of the preceding sermon. Both of these separate title pages carry the date 1645.

18. THE/ VNBELEEVERS/ PREPARING FOR/ CHRIST./ . . . . By *T. H./* . . . .*LONDON,/* Printed by *Tho Cotes* for *Andrew Crooke,* and are to be/ sold at the Black Beare in Saint *Pauls* Church-/ yard. 1638. Pp. "Severall Treatises of this Authovr" (2), 1–204, "The First Table" (4), 1–119, "The Table" (4). CtHS (2), CtY, DFo, DLC, L, LCL, LSC, MBCong, MWA, NjPT, NN, NNUT. Sabin 32862, STC 13740. Microfilm 1072.

In the series of works on the stages of regeneration, this group of sermons follows the second sermon in *The Souls Implantation,* "The Preparing of the Heart for to Receive Christ," and directly precedes *The Souls Preparation.* The material in this volume formed the basis for the revised versions in Books Four, Five, Seven, and Eight in *The Application of Redemption* (1656).

The book is divided into two sections with separate pagination. The first part, pp. 1–204, contains untitled sermons on the following biblical texts: Rev.22:17, pp. 1–80 (note the striking echoes of this sermon's pp. 46–50 in *The Faithful Covenanter*, pp. 30–31); 1 Cor.2:14, pp. 81–125 (Emerson's *Redemption* reprints this entire sermon); Ezek.11:19, pp. 126–153; Lk.19:42, pp. 154–187; Mt.20:3–6, pp. 188–204. These first five sermons deal with what Hooker calls five "generall Circumstances" which must be recognized before grace can be received: that God's grace is free, that man must will to receive grace before he shall have it, that whoever "truly wills" Christ shall have him, that a man cannot "by nature" receive Christ and grace, and that God's Chosen will meet these qualifications and receive grace.

Between part one and part two of the volume is a four-page "First Table" of contents for the preceding section. The final section, pp. 1–119, is a single long sermon on the biblical text Jn.6:44. This work explains that the "naturall man" is securely settled in the state of sin but that in salvation God draws the sinner out of corruption to himself. The work ends with a four-page "Table" of contents for the second section of the book. Pp. 1–110 were revised as Book VIII of *The Application of Redemption* (1656).

Bound singly and in various combinations with *The Souls Ingrafting* (1637), *The Souls Preparation* (1638), *The Souls Exaltation* (1638), *The Saints Dignity and Duty* (1651), *The Souls Humiliation* (1640), and *The Souls Implantation into the Natural Olive* (1640).

— 1640 —

19. THE/ CHRISTIANS/ Tvvo Chiefe/ LESSONS,/ Viz.{Selfe-Deniall,/ And/ Selfe-Tryall/ AS ALSO/ THE PRIVILEDGE OF ADOPTION/ And TRIALL thereof./ In three TREATISES on the TEXTS/ following:/ Viz.{MATT.16. 24/2 COR. 13.5./ IOHN I.12,13./ By *T.H./* LONDON,/ Printed by *T.B.* for *P. Stephens* and *C. Meredith,* at the/ Golden Lion in S. *Pauls* Churchyard./ 1640. Pp. "Epistle Dedicatory" (6), "A Table of the Contents" and list of errata (14), 1–99, 200–303 (printers error in pagination). 4°. Ct, CtHS, CtY, DFo, MBCong, MH. O. Sabin 32831, STC 13724. Microfilm 1072.

This volume contains three separate sermons, the last much shorter than the first two. They are:

"The Christians First Chiefe Lesson, *Viz.* Self-deniall," pp. 1–"200" (i.e. 100). Biblical text: Mt. 16:24. In a careful use of the term "self," which he identifies with man's essential corruption, Hooker explains the need for men to recognize the evil of "self," to purge themselves of it, and to take up their crosses and follow Christ selflessly. This sermon is thus closely related in subject matter to *The Souls Preparation* and *The Application of Redemption*.

"The Christians Second Chiefe Lesson, *Viz.* Selfe-tryall," pp. 201–284.

Biblical text: 2 Cor.13:5. Here Hooker explains how self-examination is an important and necessary part of the Christian's approach to grace. He gives examples of false signs of grace as well as true "markes" of it.

"The Priviledge of Adoption, and Tryall thereof by Regeneration," pp. 285–303. Biblical text: Jn.1:12,13. Hooker briefly and rather generally explains Christ's adoption of all the faithful and its occurrence at the latter stages of the redemptive process. The compression of the contents of this work was apparently the result of the conditions under which it was actually delivered; Hooker says, near the end, "I am forced to cut off many things."

A six-page "Epistle dedicatory" is addressed "to The Honvrable and truly Religious Lady, the Lady Anne VVake" and is signed by "Z.S.," who was probably Zachariah Symmes, then the minister at Charlestown in Massachusetts Bay. This dedication contains valuable information about the roles of editor, printer, and "scribe" in the publication of this work.

19a. THE/ CHRISTIANS/ Two Chiefe/ LESSONS,/ Viz. . . . ./ 1640.
A facsimile reprint of item 19 published by Arno Press, A New York Times Company: New York, 1972.

20. THE/ PATERNE/ OF/ PERFECTION:/ Exhibited in Gods Image/ on ADAM:/ And Gods Covenant made/ with him./ Where-unto is added an Exhortation, to re-/ deem the time for recovering our losses in the premisses./ And also some *Miscellanies,*/ viz. I. The Prayer of Faith./ II. A Preparative to the Lords/ Supper./ III. The Character of a sound Chri-/stian, in 17. markes./ By *T.H.*/ . . . .London, Printed for *R. Y.* and *F. Clifton*, and are sold/ at his Shop on new Fish-street hill. 1640. Pp. "The Contents" (2), 1–392. Ct, CtHS, LSC, NjPT, NN, O. STC 13726. Microfilm 1276.

The main part of this book (pp. 1–312) is a treatise on the nature of man and his relationship to God, with primary focus on the meaning of the phrase, "God's image." Hooker considers the special roles of Adam and Christ in making the meaning of this phrase known to man, dis-cussing such basic theological subjects as the nature of "the soul," "holiness," "righteousness," "free will," and the covenants of God with man. The focus remains on Adam's role as exemplifying the ideal man-God relationship.

The second part of the book (pp. 313–392) is comprised of three "MISCELLANIES" which are described on the title page. Briefly, they are: 1) a sermon on Jas.1:6 explaining the need for sound faith before prayer can be efficacious, 2) a description of how one knows one has a "title" to the sacrament of the Lord's Supper and how one prepares for it, and 3) a list of seventeen "markes" or trials by which one can tell whether or not one is a "sound Christian."

20a. GODS/ IMAGE on MAN,/ AND/ His Covenant made/ with him in his state of/ Innocency./ *Whereunto is added,*/ AN EXHORTA-

TION/ To Redeem the Time./ Also some Miscellanies, viz.{ 1. The prayer of Faith./ 2. A Preparative to the Lords Supper./ 3. The Character of a sound Chri-/ stian in 17 Marks./ By the Reverend Divine Mr. THOMAS/ HOOKER late Pastor of the Church/ at *Hartford* in *N.E.*/ . . . .*LONDON,*/ Printed by *A.M.* for *John Browne*, at the/ guilded Acorn in *Pauls* Church-yard, 1653. Pp. "The Contents" (2), 1–392. CtHS.

Despite the change in title, printer, and bookseller, this is simply a reissue of the text of *The Pattern of Perfection*, which has not been reset.

THE SOULES/ IMPLANTATION/ INTO/ THE NATURALL/ *OLIVE.*/ . . . .*LONDON,*/ . . . .1640.

See above, item 8a.

— 1641 —

21. THE DANGER/ OF/ DESERTION:/ *OR*/ A FARVVELL SERMON/ of Mr. *Thomas Hooker,*/ Somtimes Minister of Gods Word at *Chains-/ ford* in Essex; but now of *New* ENGLAND./ Preached immediately before his departure/ *out of old* ENGLAND./ TOGETH-ER,/ WITH TEN PARTICVLAR/ rules to be practised every day by/ converted *Christians.*/ . . .*LONDON,*/ Printed by *G. M.* for *George Edwards* in the/ Old Baily in Greene-Arbour, at the Signe/ of the *Angell.* 1641. Pp. "The Epistle to the Reader" (2), 1–29. 4°. Ct, CtHS, CtWatk, DFo (2), DLC, L, MBCong, MH, NNUT, RPJCB. Sabin 32834, Wing H 2645.

"The Danger of Desertion", pp. 1–20, is a single sermon, commonly assumed to have been the last which Hooker preached before his departure from England to Holland in 1631. See Edwin Mead's discussion: "Thomas Hooker's Farewell Sermon in England," Massachusetts Historical Society *Proceedings*, XLVI (1913), 253–274. The "Epistle to the Reader," a brief admiring comment on Hooker, is unsigned. This is the earliest work containing Hooker's full name on the title page. It is a strongly prophetic sermon warning the Church of England that God will desert it and England if they are not worthy of him. Biblical text: Jer.14:9.

Some scholars have assumed the "Ten Particular Rules", pp. 21–29, which has the title "The Rule of the New Creature" in the text proper, to be Hooker's also. Mead settled the matter long ago, however, by quoting the Rev. Edward Reyner to the effect that he was the author of the Ten Rules.

This, the first edition, can be identified by the title's being printed in fourteen lines, as opposed to the fifteen of the second edition, and the text's 29 pages rather than the 28 of the second.

21a. THE DANGER/ OF/ DESERTION:/ *OR*/ A FAREWELL SERMON/ of Mr. *Thomas Hooker,*/ SOMETIMES/ Minister of Gods Word at *Chainsford* in Essex; but now of *New ENGLAND.*/ Preached immediately before his Departure out/ of *Old ENGLAND.*/ *TO-GETHER*/ VVITH TEN PARTICV-/ lar Rules to be practised

every/ day by converted *Christians*./ The second Edition./ . . .LON-
DON, Printed by *G. M.* for *George Edwards* in the Old/ Baily in
Green-Arbour, at the Signe of/ the *Angell*. 1641. Pp. "The Epistle to the
Reader" (2), 1-28. 4°. L, MH, Ct. Sabin 32835, Wing H 2646.

Some copies of this new edition print the phrase "The second Edition"
on the title page, but some do not. All copies of this edition, however,
print the title of the book in fifteen lines rather than the fourteen of the
first edition.

21b. THE/ SIGNES/ OF/ GODS forsaking a People./ Preached/ By
that laborious and faithful Messenger of/ CHRIST, WILLIAM FEN-
NER [sic],/ Sometimes Fellow of *Pembroke/ Hall* in *Cambridge*, and
late *Mi-/ nister* of *Rochford* in *Essex*/ . . . .London, Printed by *E. T.* for
John Stafford. [n.d.]/

This version of Hooker's sermon, incorrectly ascribed to Fenner
some seventeen years after the latter's death, was first printed in:
XXIX CHOICE/ SERMONS/ On severall/ Texts of Scripture./
Preached/ By that Reverend and Faithfull/ Minister of Gods Word,/
WILLIAM FENNER, B. D. sometimes/ Fellow of *Pembroke Hall* in
Cambridge, and/ late Minister of *Rochford* in *Essex*./ . . . .LONDON,/
Printed by *E.T.* for *John Stafford*, at the/Signe of the *George* at *Fleet-
Bridge*. 1657. Pp. 251-262. 4°. NNUT.

21c. THE/ SIGNES/ OF/ GODS forsaking a People./ . . . . in XXIX
CHOICE/ SERMONS/ . . . . By . . . WILLIAM FENNER . . . . 1657.
A reissue of item #21b now bound with numerous other Fenner vol-
umes as a part of a folio volume called: THE/ WORKS/ OF/ *W.
FENNER/* B. of/ DIVINITY./ . . . . Printed for *W. Gilbertson* at the/
Bible in Gilt-spur/ street without/ New-gate./ 1657. Pp. 251-262. Folio.
NcU. Wing F 679.

It was apparently this edition or the one of the following year (see
item #21d) to which Cotton Mather was referring in his brief biography
of Hooker, *Piscator Evangelicus* (Boston, 1695), later reprinted in the
Magnalia Christi Americana (1702), when he wrote: "Amongst Mr.
Fenners Works, I find some Imperfect, and Shattered, and I believe
Injurious Notes, of a *Farewel Sermon* upon Jer. 14. 9. *We are Called by
thy Name, Leave us not.* Which *Farewel Sermon* was indeed, Mr.
Hookers, at his Leaving of *England*." For a brief explanation of how
this Hooker sermon may have come to be included in Fenner's works,
see Winfried Herget, "Preaching and Publication—Chronology and the
Style of Thomas Hooker's Sermons," *Harvard Theological Review*, 65
(April, 1972), 235-236.

21d. THE/ SIGNES/ OF/ GODS forsaking a People./ . . . . in XXIX
CHOICE SERMONS/ . . . .By . . . WILLIAM FENNER . . . . 1657.
Like item #21c this is a reissue of item #21b, identical in all respects
except for the covering title page of the entire volume: THE/ WORKS/
OF/ *W. FENNER/* B. of/ DIVINITY. . . . . Printed by *E. Tyler* for

I. Stafford/ at the *George* neer/ Fleet-Bridge./ 1658. Pp. 251–262. Folio, NjPT. Wing F 681.

21e. *Thomas Hooker: Writings in England and Holland, 1626–1633,* ed., George H. Williams, Norman Pettit, et al. (Cambridge, 1975), pp. 228–252.

— 1644 —

22. THE/ FAITHFUL/ COVENANTER./ A SERMON/ PREACHED AT/ THE LECTVRE IN/ *DEDHAM* IN *ESSEX./* By that excellent servant of Iesus Christ,/ in the work of the Gospel, Mr. *Tho. Hooker,/* late of *Chelmsford;* now in New *England./* Very usefull in these times of Covenanting with God./ . . . .LONDON,/ Printed for CHRISTOPHER MEREDITH at/the Crans in *Pauls* Church-yard. 1644. Pp. 1–43. 4°. Ct, CtHS, CtY, MBCong, MH, O (2). Sabin 32837, Wing H 2648. Microfilm 242.

In the same spirit as *The Danger of Desertion, Spiritual Munition,* and *The Stay of the Faithful,* this work warns Englishmen of the threat of damnation to entire nations as well as to individuals who rebel against God and exhorts them to fidelity in both their personal lives and their forms of worship. Biblical text: Dt. 29:24,25. On p. 43, after "FINIS," appears: "Imprimatur: *Ja. Crawford.*"

22a. *Thomas Hooker: Writings in England and Holland, 1626–1633,* ed., George H. Williams, Norman Pettit, et al. (Cambridge, 1975), pp. 190–220.

— 1645 —

23. A briefe/ EXPOSITION/ OF THE/ Lords Prayer:/ Wherein the meaning of the words is/ laid open to the understanding of weake/ Christians, and what the carriage of their/ hearts ought to be in prefer-/ ring/ each Petition./ By Mr. THO. HOOKER/ Preacher of Gods Word./ . . .LONDON,/ Printed by *Moses Bell* for *Benjamine Allen,/* and are to be sold at his shop in Popes head Alley/ at the signe of the Crown. 1645. Pp. 1–90. 4°. CLU–C, CSmH, Ct, CtHCen, CtHS, DFo, NjPT, NNUT, O, RPJCB. Sabin 32830, Wing H 2642.

A phrase-by-phrase explication of the Lord's Prayer. This edition is a longer version than that published in the same year as *Heavens Treas-ury Opened* (see next item below). See Bush, "Thomas Hooker and the Westminster Assembly," *William and Mary Quarterly,* XXIX (April, 1972), 291–300.

23a. HEAVENS/ TREASVRY/ Opened/ In a Fruitful Exposition/ of the/ Lords Prayer./ *Together with/* The principall Grounds/ OF/ *Christian Religion/* briefly unfolded./ *By* THO. HOOKER./ . . . . LONDON./ Printed for *R. Dawlman./* 1645. Pp. 1–195. 12°. O. Sabin 32839, Wing H 2650.

Despite the claim on the title page, this volume contains only one work. This is the same basic work as that entitled *A briefe Exposition of the Lords Prayer*. This text has been revised, however, to its stylistic advantage, though entire sentences have been excised in the process, making it some 3500 words shorter than the 1638 version. See Bush, "Thomas Hooker and the Westminster Assembly" for fuller discussion of these differences.

24. AN/ EXPOSITION/ OF/ THE PRINCIPLES/ OF/ *RELIGION*./ BY/ *THO: HOOKER*./ . . .LONDON,/ Printed for R. DAWLMAN./ 1645. Pp. 1–58. 8°. L, O. Wing H 2647. Microfilm 384.

A catechism, this is apparently the work mentioned on the title page of *Heavens Treasury Opened*, where it is called *The Principall Grounds of the Christian Religion Briefly Unfolded*. See Bush, "Thomas Hooker and the Westminster Assembly."

THE/ SAINTS/ GUIDE/ . . . .LONDON. . . . ./ 1645. See above, item 17b.

— 1648 —

25. A/ SURVEY/ of the Summe of/ Church-Discipline./ *WHEREIN*,/ The Way of the CHURCHES of/ *NEW-ENGLAND*/ is warranted out of the Word, / and all Exceptions of weight, which/ are made against it, answered: Whereby/ also it will appear to the Judicious Reader,/ that something more must be said, then/ yet hath been, before their Prin-/ ciples can be shaken, or they/ should be unsetled in/ their practice./ By THO. HOOKER, late Pastor of the Church at/ *Hartford* upon *Connecticott* in *N.E.*/ . . . . *LONDON*,/ Printed by *A.M.* for *John Bellamy* at the three Golden Lions/ in *Cornhill*, near the Royall Exchange. M.DC.XLVIII. Pp. (34) 1–139, 184–296, 1–90, 1–46, 1–59. 4°. C, Ct, CtHWatk, CtY, DFo, DLC (2), MiU–C, MWA, NcD, NjPT (3), NN, NNUT, O (3), PU, RPJCB, ViU (2), WU, others. Sabin 32860, Wing H2658.

Hooker's famous explanation and defense of New England church polity, written for an English audience at the request and with the approval of his fellow New England elders. Hooker's death on July 7, 1647, occurred when he was in the last stages of a rewriting of the book to replace a completed version lost at sea when the ship carrying the manuscript sank on the way to England. This is the first posthumous publication in Hooker's canon, therefore, and contains several prefatory items related to his death. Pagination of the body of the text is divided into four sequences but, within these parts, is faulty. The following is a list in order of binding of the parts found in most copies:

"A Preface of the Authour, By way of Introduction to this following Discourse. . . ." (18 pp.).

"To the Reader, especially the Congregation and Church of Iesus Christ in *Hartford* upon *Connecticutt*," signed by Edward Hopkins and William Goodwin and dated at Hartford October 28, 1647 (4 pp).

"In obitum viri Doctissimi THOMAE HOOKERI Pastoris Ecclesiae Hertfordiensis, Novangliæ, Collegæsui," an elegy in English by Samuel Stone (2 pp.).

"*On my Reverend and dear Brother, M^r* THOMAS HOOKER, *late Pastor of the Church at* Hartford *on* Coonectiquot," an elegy by John Cotton (1 1/4 pp.).

"In sepulchrum Reverendissimi viri, fratris charissimi M. THO. HOOKERI," a poem in English by Ezekiel Rogers (1/2 p.).

An untitled editorial note by Thomas Goodwin dated April 17, 1648 (4 pp.).

"The Contents" (3 pp.).

"An Analyticall Table" in the Ramesian dichotomous fashion, showing the organization and various functions of the church (1 p.).

Part I, pp. 1–296, omitting pp. 140–184 in the numbering. On "Ecclesiasticall Policy."

Part II, pp. 1–90. "Of the Church considered as *Corpus Organicum.*"

Part III, pp. 1–46. On church government, the sacraments, and censures.

Part IV, pp. 1–42. "Concerning Synods."

"An Appendix to the former Treatise concerning Synods," pp. 43–59, consisting of "An Epistle of them that sent the Booke over to be Printed," p. 43, and "a few questions" and answers which were "found in his study," pp. 45–59.

Not all extant copies contain all of the prefatory material. Several copies are bound with John Cotton's *The Way of the Congregational Churches Cleared* (London, 1648) and in one case (Ct) also with Thomas Shepard's *A Treatise of Liturgies* (London, 1653).

The "Preface of the Authour" has often been separately printed both singly and in anthologies, especially since its appearance as a pamphlet: "The Way of the Churches of New England," Old South Leaflet, 12th Series, no. 8 [Boston, 1894]. An 1896 reprinting of this pamphlet is owned by many libraries.

25a. A/ SURVEY/ of the Summe of/ Church-Discipline./ . . . . 1648.

A facsimile reprint of item 25 published by Arno Press, A New York Times Company: New York, 1971.

— 1649 —

26. THE/ COVENANT/ OF/ GRACE/ OPENED:/ WHEREIN/ These particulars are handled;/ viz.{ 1. What the Covenant of GRACE is,/ 2. What the Seales of the Covenant are,/ 3. Who are the Parties and Subjects fit to/ receive these Seales./ From all which Particulars Infants Baptisme is/ fully proved and vindicated./ Being severall Sermons preached at *Hartford*/ in New-England./ By that Reverend and faithfull Minister of the/ Gospel, Mr. THOMAS HOOKER./ *LONDON,*/ Printed by *G. Dawson,* and are to be sold at the Crown/ in *Popes-head Alley.* 1649. Pp. 1–85. 4°. C, Ct, CtHS, CtY, DLC, MBCong, NjPT, O, RPJCB. Sabin 32833, Wing H 2644. Microfilm 149.

This work is organized in sermon fashion but it is clearly polemical debate, mainly refuting Anabaptist doctrine on baptism, with a particular concern being to answer the "false" arguments of "Mr. Spilsbery" (John

Spilsbery, who published *A Treatise Concerning the Lawful Subject of Baptism* in London in 1643). Biblical text: Gen.17:23.

— 1651 —

27. THE/ SAINTS/ DIGNITIE,/ AND/ DUTIE./ TOGETHER WITH/ The Danger of IGNORANCE/ and HARDNESSE./ Delivered in Severall SERMONS:/ *By that Reverend Divine,*/ THOMAS HOOKER,/ *Late Preacher in* New-England./ . . . .*LONDON*, Printed by *G.D.* for *Francis Eglesfield*, and are/ to be sold at the Sign of the Marigold in *Pauls*/ Church-yard, 1651. Pp. (4), (4), 1–245, (1). 4°. CtHC, CtHS (2), CtY (2), DFo, L, LCL, LSC, MBCong, MH NNUT, O. Sabin 32848, Wing H2654.

This book is a collection of seven sermons edited by "T.S.," whom most scholars take to be Hooker's son-in-law, Thomas Shepard, of Cambridge, Massachusetts. This is probably correct, though it should be noted that Shepard died in 1649, two years before the appearance of this book. T. S. says in his prefatory essay that there is "no great dependence of these Sermons each upon other," but despite this claim the sermons do follow a logical sequence and, though not as tightly interrelated as some Hooker collections, they are all on the general topic of the relationship between God and the Elect. The contents are as follows:

"To the Reader" by T.S. (4 pp.).

"The Contents of the severall Sermons in the ensuing Work" (4 pp.). In some copies, this appears at the back of the volume.

Title page of the first sermon. On the verso appears a list of "The Particular Titles, and Texts, of each Sermon."

The seven sermons, pp. 1–245. Each sermon has its own full title page, but pagination is continuous. Titles and biblical texts are as follows:

"The Gift of Gifts: or, The End why Christ Gave Himself," pp. 1–43. Tit.2:14.

"The Blessed Inhabitant: or, The Benefit of Christs Being in Beleevers," pp. 45–76. Rom.8:10.

"Grace Magnified: or The Priviledges of those That are under Grace," pp. 77–119. Rom.6:14.

"Wisdomes Attendants: or the Voice of Christ To be obeyed," pp. 121–151. Pr. 8:32.

"The Activitie of Faith; or, Abraham's Imitators," pp. 153–187. Rom. 4:12. This sermon was published in Henry Clay Fish, ed., *History and Repository of Pulpit Eloquence* in two volumes (New York, 1857), II, and in Grenville Kleiser, ed., *The World's Great Sermons* in ten volumes (1908), II, 1–28.

"Culpable Ignorance, or the Danger of Ignorance under Meanes," pp. 189–216. Is.27:11.

"Wilfull Hardness: or the Means of Grace Abused," pp. 217–245. Pr. 29:1.

The verso of p. 245 contains an advertisement of "*Books Printed for Francis Eglesfield.*"

Most copies are bound singly, but it has also been bound with *The Souls Ingrafting* (1637), *The Souls Preparation* (1638), *The Unbelievers Preparing for Christ* (1638), and *The Souls Exaltation* (1638).

— 1653 —

GODS/ IMAGE on MAN,/ . . . .*LONDON*,/ . . . .1653. See above, item 20a.

— 1656 —

28. THE/ APPLICATION/ OF/ REDEMPTION,/ By the effectual Work of the Word, and/ Spirit of Christ, for the bringing/ home of lost Sinners to God./ The first eight Books: In which (besides many other seasonable,/ and Soul-searching Truths) there is also largely shewed,/ I. *Christ hath purchased all spiritual good for HIS./ 2. Christ puts all HIS into possession of all that Good that he hath/ purchased. 3. The Soul must be fitted for Christ before it can receive him:/ And a powerful Ministry is the ordinary means to prepare the/ heart for Christ./ 4. The work of God is free: And the day of Salvation, is while/ this Life last, and the Gospel continue./ 5. God calls his Elect at any Age, but the most before old Age./ 6. The Soul is naturally setled in a sinful security./ 7. The heart of a Natural man is wholly unwilling to submit to the/ word that would sever him from his sins./ 8. God the Father by a holy kind of violence, plucks His out of their/ corruptions, and draws them to beleeve in Christ./* By that Faithful, and known Servant of Christ, Mr./ THOMAS HOOKER, late Pastor of the Church at *Hartford*/ in *New-England*; somtimes Preacher of the Word at *Chelms-*/ *ford* in *Essex*, and Fellow of *Emmanuel* Colledg in *Cambridg./ Printed from the Authors Papers, written with his own Hand./* And attested to be such, in an Epistle,/ By{*Thomas Goodwin*,/ And/ *Philip Nye*./ *London:* Printed by *Peter Cole* at the sign of the Pringtingpress [sic]/in Cornhil, neer the Royal Exchange. 1656. 451 pp. 8°. Ct, CtHC, LW.

This work presents the theoretical underpinning of Hooker's preparationist theology, outlining such basic doctrines as man's corruption, the need for grace, Christ's ability to "apply" grace to the sinner, the need for both preparation for grace and a positive frame of mind, election, and the possibility of hope. The book is a reworking into a larger context of the sermons from some of the earlier works. The major sections of the book and their essential contents, biblical texts, and correspondences with earlier books are as follows:

On the recto opposite the title page appears the following, printed vertically on the page: MR Hooker's { *First, Second, Third, Fourth, Fift, Sixt, Seventh, and Eighth Books made in* New-England.

Title page, blank verso.

"To the Reader." by Thomas Goodwin and Philip Nye (21 pp.).

Advertisement: "*Eleven Books made in* New-England, *by Mr* Thomas Hooker, *and printed from his Papers, written with his own Hand; are now published in three volums, two in Quarto, one in Octavo.*" The ad then lists the contents of each of the eleven "Books" in *The Application of Redemption: The First Eight Books, The Application. . .The Ninth and Tenth Books,* and *A Comment upon Christs Last Prayer,* adding the final statement: "There are Six more Books of Mr. *Hookers,* now printing in two Volumns." [These six books were apparently never published, if indeed Peter Cole ever had them in his possession.] (1 p.)

"The Contents" (20 pp.)

Advertisement: "*Books printed by* Peter Cole *in Leaden-Hall*" (4 pp.).

Pp. 1–451. The individual "Books" are as follows:

Book I on 1 Pet.1:18,19, pp. 1–70. Explains the "Doctrine of Application" and argues against quick and easy (and false) conversion.

Book II on Mt.1:21, pp. 71–139. Insists on doctrine of Election; "Christ died not for all." The initiative in redemption is Christ's, not the sinner's. Stresses the centrality of Christ's death and resurrection and the subsequent importance of using "the means."

Book III on Lk.1.17, pp. 141–221. Defines "preparation" and insists on its necessity in the work of grace. The importance of a "plain and powerful ministry." A revision of *The Souls Implantation,* pp. 25–79, and *The Souls Implantation into the Natural Olive,* pp. 29–92.

Book IV on 2 Cor. 6:2, pp. 221–260. On the freeness of God's entering into the covenant of grace and on the need for man to act energetically to "redeem the time." The first part of this Book is a revision and expansion of *The Unbelievers Preparing for Christ,* pp. 6–26.

Book V on Mt.20:5,6,7, pp. 261–282. Stresses God's usual tendency to "call" his elect before old age; youth and "middle age" are thus the best times for preparation for grace. A revision of *The Unbelievers Preparing,* pp. 188–204.

Book VI on Rev.3:17, pp. 283–301. On the danger of the soul's becoming secure in its sinful condition.

Book VII on Rom.8:7, pp. 302–347. On the "natural" opposition of the soul to God's law and grace. Though on a different biblical text, this is related to the sermon in *The Unbelievers Preparing,* Part I, pp. 81–125.

Book VIII on Jn.6:44, pp. 348–451. The climax to the unit comprised of Books VI, VII, and VIII, this Book describes God's use of a holy violence to drive men out of their comfortably sinful conditions and his "drawing" then home to himself. A revision of *The Unbelievers Preparing,* Part II, pp. 1–110.

28a. THE/ APPLICATION/ OF/ REDEMPTION,/ By the effectual Work of the Word, and/ Spirit of Christ, for the bringing/ home of lost Sinners to God./ The first eight Books: . . . . [see entry for 1656 printing: title pages are identical except for date.] *London:* Printed by *Peter Cole* at the sign of the Printingpress/ in Cornhil, neer the Royal Exchange. 1657./ Pp. (21), (1), (20), (4), 1–451. Ct, CtHS, DLC, NN.

A reissue of the 1656 edition with a new date on the title page.

28b. THE/ APPLICATION/ OF/ REDEMPTION,/ . . . . The first eight Books. . . ./ 1657.

A facsimile reprint of item 28a published by Arno Press, A New York Times Company: New York, 1972.

29. THE/ Application OF Redemption/ By the Effectual Work of the Word, and Spirt [sic] of/ Christ, for the bringing home of lost Sinners/ to God. *The Ninth and Tenth Books.*/ Besides many other seasonable, and Soul-searching Truths, there is also largely shewed,/ [The following 18 points are printed in two parallel columns, the first comprised of points 1–10 and the second points 11–18.] 1. *The heart must be humble and contrite/ before the Lord will dwell in it./ 2. Stubborn, and bloody sinners may be/ made broken-hearted./ 3. There must be true sight of sin, before/ the heart can be broken for it./ 4. Application of special sins by the Mini-/ stry, is a means to bring men to sight of,/ and sorrow for them./ 5. Meditation of sin, a special means to/ break the heart./ 6. The same word is profitable to some,/ not to others./ 7. The Lord sometimes makes the Word/ prevail most, when its most opposed./ 8. Sins unrepented of, makes way for/ piercing Terrors./ 9. The Truth is terrible to a guilty consci-/ ence./ 10. Gross and scandalous sinners, God usu-/ ally exerciseth with heavy breakings of/ heart, before they be brought to Christ./ 11. Sorrow for sin rightly set on, pierceth/ the heart of the sinner throughly./ 12. They whose hearts are pierced by the/ Word, are carried with love and respect/ to the Ministers of it: and are busie to/ enquire, and ready to submit to the/ mind of God./ 13. Sinners in distress of conscience, are ignorant what they should do./ 14. A contrite sinner sees a necessity of co-/ ming out of his sinful condition./ 15. There is a secret hope wherewith the/ Lord supports the hearts of contrite/ sinners./ 16. They who are truly pierced for their/ sins, do prize and covet deliverance/ from their sins./ 17. True contrition is accompanied with/ canfession [sic] of sin, when God calls there-/ unto./ 18. The Soul that is pierced for sin, is/ carried with a restless dislike against it./* By that Faithful, and known Servant of Christ, Mr. THOMAS/ HOOKER, late Pastor of the Church at *Hartford* in *New-/ England;* sometimes Preacher of the Word at *Chelmsford* in *Essex,*/ and Fellow of *Emmanuel* Colledg in *Cambridg/ Printed from the Authors Papers, written with his own Hand./* And attested to be such, in an Epistle,/

By ⎰ *Thomas Goodwin,*
⎱ And
Philip Nye./ London: Printed by *Peter Cole,* at the sign of the Printing-Press in Cornhil,/ neer the Royal Exchange. 1656./ Pp. (22), 1–455, 556–702, (24). 4°. CtHS, DFo, L. Wing H 2639, Microfilm 188.

As the title indicates, this is a sequel to the first eight Books of *The Application of Redemption* and is chiefly an extensive revision and enlargement of *The Souls Preparation,* though particular portions are often very similar. This work describes the stage of contrition in preparation for grace.

The contents are as follows:

On the recto opposite the title page appears the following, printed vertically on the page:

MR HOOKER'S $\begin{cases} \textit{Ninth and Tenth Books,} \\ \textit{made in New-England.} \end{cases}$

Title page, blank verso.

"To the Reader." by Thomas Goodwin and Philip Nye (21 pp.).

On the verso of the last page of "To the Reader" appears a coat of arms with the caption: COLE/ 1216.

Pp. 1–"702" (i.e. 602).

"The Contents" (20 pp.).

Advertisement: "*Books printed by* Peter Cole *in Leaden-Hall*" (4 pp.).

The individual Books are as follows:

Book IX on Is.57:15, pp. 1–14. This is another version of the sermon called "The Broken Heart" in *The Souls Implantation*, pp. 1–24, and *The Souls Implantation into the Natural Olive*, pp. 1–28. It presents the doctrine that contrition and humiliation must precede the Lord's entry into the heart. Emerson reprints Book IX in his *Redemption*.

Book X on Acts 2:37, pp. 15–455, 556–702 (printer's error in pagination). Dealing at length with the topic of contrition, this work is an amplification of *The Souls Preparation*. In elaborating on some points, Hooker in this version occasionally tends to lose the clear outlines of the sermon form, making this at some points more clearly a written book than the earlier work which was transcribed from oral delivery. At other points this version is almost a verbatim transcription of the earlier book.

29a. THE/ Application OF Redemption/ By the Effectual Work of the Word, and Spirt [sic] of / Christ, for the bringing home of lost Sinners/ to God. *The Ninth and Tenth Books.*/ . . . .[see entry for 1656 issue: title pages are identical except for date.] *London:* Printed by *Peter Cole*, at the sign of the Printing-Press in Cornhil,/ neer the Royal Exchange. 1657. Pp. (20), 1–455, 556–702, (25), (5). 4°. Ct, CtHC, CtHS (2), CtHWatk, CtY, LW, NjPT. Wing H 2640.

A reissue of the 1656 printing.

29b. THE/ Application OF Redemption/ By the Effectual Work of the Word, and Spirit of/ Christ, for the bringing home of lost Sinners/ to God. *The Ninth and Tenth Books.*/ Besides many other seasonable, and Soul-searching Truths, there is also largely shewed,/ [The following 18 points are printed in two parallel columns, the first comprised of points 1–10 and the second points 11–18.] 1. *The heart must be humble and contrite/ before the Lord will dwell in it./ 2. Stubborn, and bloody Sinners may be/ made broken hearted./ 3. There must be true sight of sin, before/ the heart can be broken for it./ 4. Application of special sins by the Mini-/ stry, is a means to bring men to sight of,/ and sorrow for them./ 5. Meditation of sin, a special means to/ break the heart./ 6. The same word is profitable to some,/ not to others./ 7. The Lord some-times makes the Word/ prevail most, when it's most opposed./ 8. Sins unrepented of, makes way for pier-/ cing Terrors./* 9. *The Truth terri-/ ble to a guilty consci-/ ence./* 10. *Gross and scandalous sinners, God usu-/ ally exerciseth with heavy breakings of/ heart, before they be brought to Christ./* 11. *Sorrow for sin rightly set on, pierceth/ the heart of the sinner throughly./* 12. *They whose hearts are pierced by the/ Word, are carried with love and respect/ to the Ministers of it: And are busie to/ enquire, and ready to submit to the/ mind of God./* 13. *Sinners in distress of conscience, are/ ignorant what they should do./* 14. *A contrite sinner sees a necessity of co-/ ming out of his sinful condi-/ tion./* 15. *There is a secret hope wherewith the/ Lord supports the hearts of contrite sin-/ ners./* 16. *They who are truly pierced for their/ sins, do prize and covet deliverance from/ their sins.* 17. *True contrition is accompanied with/ confession of sin, when God calls there-/ unto./* 18. *The Soul that is pierced for sin, is car-/ ried with a restless dislike against it./* By that Faithful, and known Servant of Christ; Mr. THOM-AS/ HOOKER, late Pastor of the Church at *Hartford* in *New-/ England;* somtimes Preacher of the Word at *Chelmsford* in/ *Essex* and Fellow of *Emmanual Colledg* in *Cambridg./ Printed from the Authors Papers, Written with his own Hand./* And attested to be such, in an Epistle,/ By *Thomas Goodwin,* and *Philip Nye./ The Second Edition./ London:* Printed by *Peter Cole,* Printer and Book-seller, at the Sign of the Printing./ press in Cornhil, neer the Royal Exchange. 1659. Pp. (20), 1–455, 556–702, (25), (5). 4°. Ct, CtHS (2), CtY, DLC, MB, MH, NN. Wing H 2641, Sabin 32828.

The title page of this edition has been reset; otherwise, it is a reissue of the previous printing.

30. A/ COMMENT/ UPON/ Christ's last Prayer/ *In the Seventeenth* of JOHN./ Wherein is opened,/ The *Union* Beleevers have with God and/ Christ, and the glorious Priviledges/ thereof./ Besides many other Gospel Truths, there is also shewed,/ [The following 8 points are printed in two parallel columns, the first ending with the first line of print in point 5 and the second continuing through point 8.] 1. *That the end why the Saints re-/ ceive all glorious Grace, is, That/ they may be one, as the Father and/ Christ are one./* 2. *That God the Father loveth the/ Faithful, as he loveth Jesus/ Christ./* 3. *That our Saviour desireth to have/ the Faithful in Heaven with/ himself./* 4. *That the happiness of our being in/ Heaven, is to see Christs Glory./* 5. *That there is much wanting in/ the knowledg of Gods Love, in/ the most able Saints./* 6. *That the Lord Christ lends dayly/ direction, according to the dayly/ need of his Servants./* 7. *That it is the desire, and endea-/ vor of our Savior, that the dea-/ rest of Gods Love, which was be-/ stowed on himself, should be gi-/ ven to his faithful Servants./* 8. *That our Union, and Communion/ with God in Christ, is the top/ of our happiness in Heaven./* By that Faithful, and known Servant of Christ, Mr. THOM-AS/ HOOKER, late Pastor of the Church at *Hartford* in/ *New-England;* somtimes Preacher of the Word at/ *Chelmsford* in *Essex,* and Fellow of *Emmanuel* Colledg in *Cambridg./ Printed from the Authors*

own Papers, written with his own/ Hand. And attested to be such, in
an Epistle,/ By { *Thomas Goodwin,*
                  And
                  Philip Nye./ London: Printed by *Peter Cole* at the sign
of the Printing-Press in/ Cornhil, neer the Royal Exchange. 1656.
Pp. (7), (17), 1–222, 323–532. 4°. Ct (2), CtHC, CtHS, CtY (2), DFo,
LCL, MBCong, MH, MiU-C, NjPT, NN, RPJCB. Sabin 32832, Wing H
2643. Microfilm 357.
This work deals with the final stage in the process of regeneration:
glorification, when the soul joins Christ in heaven. In the chronological
sequence of the soul's journey to grace, this work would follow *The
Souls Exaltation.* The sermons in the volume, according to Goodwin and
Nye, were originally given at communion services. The contents are
more purely theological and abstract than are most of his surviving
sermons, dealing with such major subjects as the meaning of divine love,
the nature of the relationship between the Father and the Son, the roles
of the various members of the Trinity, the meaning of the crucial term
"glory," and the nature of heavenly happiness. Biblical text: Jn.17:20–26.
The contents:
On the verso of the fly leaf, facing the title page, the following is printed vertically:

MR Hooker *On the seven-* John { *Being his Seventeenth*
                teenth of   *Book, made in*
                                   New-England.

Title page, blank verso.
"The Epistle to the Reader" by Thomas Goodwin and Philip Nye,
dated June 14, 1656 (7 pp.).
"*The Name of several Books printed by* Peter Cole *in* Leaden-Hall,
London...." (4½ pp.).
"The Contents of Mr. Hooker's seventeenth Book, made in New-
England." (12½ pp.).
The text, pp. 1–222, 323–532 (printer's error in pagination).

— Other Miscellaneous Works —

31. "Abstracts of Two Sermons by Rev. Thomas Hooker. From the
Shorthand Notes of Mr. Henry Wolcott." *Collections* of the Connecticut Historical Society, I (Hartford, 1860), 19–21.
The first of these two sermons was preached at Hartford May 31, 1638,
on the biblical text Dt.1:13; the second was preached at Hartford April
11, 1639, on the text Ex.18: 17, 18. The arguments by some scholars
for Hooker's relative sympathy for "democratic" tendencies in civil government are partly based on these two sermons. See Clinton Rossiter,
"Thomas Hooker," *The New England Quarterly,* XXV (December,
1952), 476-478.

32. [Untitled sermon preached by Hooker June 20, 1647, at Windsor,
Connecticut.] In George L. Walker, *History of the First Church of
Hartford, 1633–1883* (Hartford: Brown and Gross, 1884), Appendix IV,
pp. 429-434.

This work was transcribed from manuscript notes of Matthew Grant by J. Hammond Trumbull. The sermon as preached was apparently a variation of the sermon on the same biblical text preserved in two earlier forms as "The Wrath of God against Sinners" in *Three Godly Sermons* and *Three Sermons* (see items #17 and #17a) and as "The Carnall Mans Condition" in *The Saints Guide* (see item #17b). Biblical text: Rom.1:18.

33. "Touchinge yͤ Crosse in yͤ Banners." In *Proceedings* of the Massachusetts Historical Society, XLII (April, 1909) (Third Series, II), 272–280.

In November, 1634, John Endecott created a controversy by cutting the cross out of a British flag at Salem. In this work Hooker, claiming he has been urged to break his usual custom of avoiding public controversy, explains why he disagrees with Endecott's argument that to allow the cross in the flag is to continue an idolatrous practice. Hooker makes a distinction between idolatrous and civil uses of the cross as a symbol.

34. "Mr Paget's 20 Propositions to Mr. Hooker with his Answere thereto." In Raymond Phineas Stearns, *Congregationalism in the Dutch Netherlands: The Rise and Fall of the English Classis, 1621–1635* (Chicago: The American Society of Church History, 1940), pp. 105–113. Also in Alice C. Carter, *The English Reformed Church in Amsterdam in the Seventeenth Century* (Amsterdam, 1964), pp. 189–200, and *Thomas Hooker: Writings in England and Holland, 1626–1633*, ed., George H. Williams, Norman Pettit, et al. (Cambridge, 1975), pp. 277–291.

This document results from the dispute between the Rev. John Paget, minister of the English Reformed Church in Amsterdam, and his congregation in 1631 over whether or not Hooker should be called to serve as co-pastor with Paget. Paget's questions were designed to expose irregularities in Hooker's theology. See Keith L. Sprunger, "The Dutch Career of Thomas Hooker," *The New England Quarterly*, XLVI (March, 1973), 17–44.

35. *Redemption: Three Sermons (1637–1656) by Thomas Hooker* (Gainesville, Florida: Scholars' Facsimiles and Reprints, 1956). Introduction by Everett H. Emerson.

This reprints pp. 81–125 of *The Unbelievers Preparing for Christ* (1638), pp. 1–14 (all of Book IX) of *The Application of Redemption: The Ninth and Tenth Books* (1656), and pp. 81–153 of *The Souls Implantation* (1637). See above, items 18, 29, and 8.

36. "A Thomas Hooker Sermon of 1638," ed., Everett Emerson, *Resources for American Literary Study*, II (Spring, 1972), 75–89.

This sermon was preached at Hartford on October 4, 1638. Its essential theme is God's Providence, with special emphasis on the mercy and special blessings which God extends to "His." As Emerson points out in his brief introduction, the sermon has special reference to the comparatively bountiful summer of 1638 after the first two more difficult years of the Hartford congregation's settlement in Connecticut. Biblical text: 1 Sam.7:12.

— Letters —

L1. [Ca. April, 1633] Thomas Hooker to John Cotton. Cotton Mather, *Magnalia Christi Americana, I* (Hartford, 1855), III, 340. Also in *Thomas Hooker: Writings in England and Holland, 1626–1633*, ed., George H. Williams, Norman Pettit, et al. (Cambridge, 1975), pp. 297–298.

Written from Holland to John Cotton in England, this letter describes the decline of religious zeal in the Dutch provinces.

L2. [Ca. July, 1636] Thomas Hooker to John Winthrop, Jr. *Collections* of the Massachusetts Historical Society, Fourth Series, VI (Boston, 1863), 387–388. Also in *The Winthrop Papers* (Boston, 1929–1947), III, 280–281.

Deals with the desirability of cooperation among the colonies.

L3. [Ca. May, 1637] Thomas Hooker to John Winthrop. *Collections* of the Massachusetts Historical Society, Fourth Series, VI (Boston, 1863), 388–389. Also in *The Winthrop Papers*, III, 407–408.

Deals mainly with Connecticut's current dealings with Indian allies and enemies.

L4. July, 1637. The Church at Hartford to John Winthrop. *The Winthrop Papers*, III, 520–521.

Written in Hooker's handwriting but signed for the entire church by Hooker, Samuel Stone, and William Goodwin, this letter announces the Hartford church's decision to send both its ministers, Hooker and Stone, to the forthcoming Synod at which the Antinomian controversy would be debated.

L5. [Ca. October, 1637] Thomas Hooker to John Winthrop. *Proceedings* of the Massachusetts Historical Society, Second Series, VI (May, 1891), 425. Also in *The Winthrop Papers*, III, 498–499.

Hooker thanks Winthrop for his hospitality and kindness during Hooker's recent service at the 1637 Synod where the Antinomians were tried and convicted. Contains brief statements of Hooker's philosophy on the correct approach to matters of judicial and political controversy.

L6. [Ca. December, 1638] Thomas Hooker to John Winthrop. *Collections* of the Connecticut Historical Society, I (Hartford, 1860), 1–18.

This publication includes an introduction (pp. 1–3) and notes (pp. 15–18) by the editor, James Hammond Trumbull. The letter discusses the Connecticut colony's relations with the Indians, confederation with Massachusetts Bay, and the question of governmental jurisdiction at Aggawam. The letter is written in polemical fashion as an answer to the questions and charges in Winthrop's letter to Hooker of August 28, 1638.

Also in *The Winthrop Papers* (Boston, 1929–1947), IV, 75–84, without Trumbull's comments.

L7. November 2, 1640. Thomas Hooker to Thomas Shepard. Lucius R.

Paige, *History of Cambridge, Massachusetts, 1630–1877* (Boston: H. O. Houghton & Co. and New York: Hurd & Houghton, 1877), pp. 46–50.

The main subject is the serious financial difficulties being experienced by Shepard and others in Massachusetts Bay at this time, with particular comment on debts. Hooker urges Shepard to move to Connecticut if he can sell his property.

An incomplete version of this letter appears in John A. Albro, *Life of Thomas Shepard* in *The Works of Thomas Shepard* (Boston: Doctrinal Tract and Book Society, 1853 [repr. New York: AMS Press, Inc., 1967]), pp. cxlii–cxlv.

L8. July 15, 1643. Thomas Hooker to John Winthrop. *Collections* of the Massachusetts Historical Society, Fourth Series, VI (Boston, 1863), 389–390. Also in *The Winthrop Papers* (Boston, 1929–1947), IV, 401–402. Original in Massachusetts Historical Society.

The letter is mainly a glowing tribute to Winthrop for his leadership, motivated by his role in establishing the New England Confederation.

NOTE: A dissertation by Andrew Thomas Denholm ("Thomas Hooker: Puritan Preacher, 1586–1647," Hartford Seminary Foundation, 1961), though unpublished, is available on microfilm and worth noting here for its first two Appendices, which are transcriptions of significant manuscript material not otherwise available in print. The two items, which are both owned by the Connecticut Historical Society, appear in Denholm's dissertation as follows:

"Miscellanea," pp. 356–409.

This is Hooker's only preserved notebook, containing his jottings on a variety of theological subjects and including some references to his reading. Denholm does not transcribe all the Latin and Greek passages, but his version is nevertheless a useful resource, considering the great difficulty which Hooker's handwriting poses to the modern reader. (Includes material from one manuscript page owned by the Yale University Library.)

"The Wolcott Diary," pp. 412–419.

Henry Wolcott, Jr. of Windsor, Connecticut kept a book of outlines of many sermons by several Connecticut ministers, including thirty-nine by Hooker which were delivered in Hartford between May 2, 1638, and March 16, 1641. The manuscript is entirely in cipher. Denholm has relied on a translation of the cipher by Douglas Shepard, printing here nine of the sermon outlines.

Works incorrectly attributed to Hooker in previous bibliographies:

The Equal Wayes of God: for rectifying the unequal wayes of man. . . . London; for John Clarke, 1632. Sabin 32836.

The title page of the first edition of this work indicates that it is "By T.H.," which is apparently why it was included without reservation in Trumbull's list of Hooker's works, later to appear also in the lists by Woolley and the *Literary History of the United States*. The work's enlarged second edition, issued in 1639, however, expands "By T. H." to "By Thomas Hayne". The work is correctly attributed to Hayne in the *Dictionary of National Biography*, STC, the British Museum *Catalogue of Printed Books*, and J. Harvey Bloom, *English Tracts, Pamphlets and Printed Sheets: A Bibliography* (London, 1923), II. Everett Emerson argues against Hooker's authorship from internal evidence in his "Notes on the Thomas Hooker Canon," *American Literature*, XXVII (January, 1956), 554–555.

Heautonaparnumenos: Or a Treatise of Self-Denyall. Intended for the Pulpit; but now committed to the Presse for the Publike Benefit. . . London, Printed by W. Wilson, for Richard Royston, at the Angel in Ivy-Lane, 1646. Sabin 32840, Wing 2649.

This misattribution also originates with Sabin. Trumbull included the work though he had not seen it and was doubtful that the title could be Hooker's. He thought the text might be the sermon on self-denial in *The Christians Two Chief Lessons;* it is not. Woolley included it, saying, "It is generally believed not to be one of (our) Thomas Hooker's." The book was published anonymously, though Sabin, Trumbull, and Woolley all state or imply that Hooker's name was on the title page. Internal evidence conclusively indicates that the book is not by Hooker. There was never, in fact, any good reason for supposing that it was, though the attribution is unfortunately widely accepted.

The Immortality of the Soule: The Excellencie of Christ Jesus, treated on. Wherein the faithfull people of God may finde comfort for their Souls. By T.H. . . . ./ London, Printed in the yeer 1646. Sabin 32841, Wing H 2651.

This work is listed under Hooker's name in virtually all major bibliographies. It was published anonymously, however, and, as with the preceding item, it is difficult to see any good reason for the original attribution of the work to Hooker. It is worth noting, too, that Donald Wing, who included the work with his Hooker listings, was careful to say in the Preface to his *Short Title Catalogue*, "I assume no responsibility for authority of attribution." Everett Emerson says, "It is surely not Hooker's" ("Notes on the Thomas Hooker Canon," 555), basing his claim on the only kind of evidence there is in this case, internal evidence, both theological and stylistic. The evidence is strong, however, and, lacking any substantial evidence to the contrary, the work should be removed from the Hooker bibliography. (Similar opinions are expressed by Denholm and Pelman.)

Scriptural Index

Index